# Comrades in Health

**Critical Issues in Health and Medicine**

Edited by Rima D. Apple, University of Wisconsin–Madison, and
Janet Golden, Rutgers University, Camden

Growing criticism of the U.S. health care system is coming from consumers, politicians, the media, activists, and health care professionals. Critical Issues in Health and Medicine is a collection of books that explores these contemporary dilemmas from a variety of perspectives, among them political, legal, historical, sociological, and comparative, and with attention to crucial dimensions such as race, gender, ethnicity, sexuality, and culture.

For a list of titles in the series, see the last page of the book.

# Comrades in Health

## U.S. Health Internationalists, Abroad and at Home

**Edited by**
**Anne-Emanuelle Birn and Theodore M. Brown**

**Rutgers University Press**
New Brunswick, New Jersey, and London

Library of Congress Cataloging-in-Publication Data

Comrades in health : U.S. health internationalists, abroad and at home / edited [by] Anne-Emanuelle Birn and Theodore M. Brown.
  p. ;  cm. — (Critical issues in health and medicine)
Includes bibliographical references and index.
ISBN 978-0-8135-6121-9 (hardcover : alk. paper) — ISBN 978-0-8135-6120-2 (pbk. : alk. paper) — ISBN 978-0-8135-6122-6 (e-book)
  I.  Birn, Anne-Emanuelle, 1964- II. Brown, Theodore M., 1942- III. Series: Critical issues in health and medicine.
  [DNLM: 1. International Cooperation—history—United States. 2. World Health—trends—United States. 3. History, 20th Century—United States. 4. History, 21st Century—United States. WA 530.1]
  362.1'0425—dc23                                                2012038504

A British Cataloging-in-Publication record for this book is available from the British Library.

**To Walter Lear**

# Contents

# Figures

# Foreword

The promotion of corporate interests by the U.S. government takes place in many different forms. Quite frequently it occurs as a military intervention. Indeed, many people in the United States learn geography by looking up the place where the latest U.S. troop intervention has taken place: Iraq, Afghanistan, Yemen, possibly tomorrow Iran, and so on. While military interventions are known for their costs and ineffectiveness, not to mention brutality, their frequency is likely to continue. Further, the "stick" is usually accompanied by the "carrot," called "humanitarian" aid. And within that aid, health care and medical care take a prominent place. These endeavors tend to attract people with humanitarian and social concerns, which make them vulnerable to being used. Health aid workers typically see their work as altruistic, nonpolitical, and oriented to help those in need. How can one be against feeding hungry children and taking care of sick people whom they aim to help? But the U.S. foreign policy establishment and the big private foundations have logics of their own and determine the objectives and parameters within which those well-intentioned humanitarian workers operate. Regardless of personal motivations, goals, and feelings, reality intrudes and the institutions health professionals work for define what they can do, and these institutions are not always well regarded outside the United States. Many times I have encountered health professionals with the best of intentions who, upon arrival in a country that they personally wanted to help, faced great hostility for their association with institutions that were perceived by the local population as responsible for the poor health conditions those professionals were supposed to alleviate.

Medical care and public health are very political interventions, even though professionals working in these fields may not always be conscious of it. Indeed, the health and well-being of populations depend on political, economic, and social realities, not primarily on medical care or public health interventions. A consequence of this reality is that health improvement should be based on collective efforts aimed at the establishment of healthy (that is, redistributive, equitable, and sustainable) economic, social, and political institutions and policies and not primarily on the delivery of one-on-one care in traditional clinical practice. Thus, a health professional working for a foreign policy branch of the U.S. State Department and posted to a country with an existing dictatorship is not only likely to be ineffective in improving the health of the people but also will in all probability contribute to the perpetuation of a sick and sickening society. The foreign "assistance" of the United States, and much international assistance, including health aid, generally has been part of the problem more than part of the solution. This observation also applies to the work of international agencies, from the World Health Organization (WHO) to the World Bank and the International Monetary Fund (IMF): David Stuckler has edited a series of articles in the *International Journal of Health Services* (vol. 39, no. 4, 2009) that document the *damage* to the health of the people created by the IMF.

The valuable collection of essays in this book narrates the experiences of those professionals from the United States who, unlike many other international health professionals, worked in conjunction with political forces committed to the liberation of peoples and, therefore, found themselves frequently in conflict with the policies of their own government. The volume starts with a moving statement by a nurse who supported the antifascist forces in Spain in the 1930s. Her letter is a splendid example of how to relate the individual to collective struggles for democracy and justice. It may be a surprise to many U.S. readers to know that many American antifascists were persecuted in their own country. Political reprisal has often been the experience of internationalists who joined forces with those struggling for justice abroad because by doing so they have confronted and antagonized the interests of Corporate America, whose influence over the U.S. government is enormous. Their history is little known, and this volume makes a major contribution by narrating some of their experiences.

It is enlightening to see the evolution of these experiences. The 1930s and 1940s were decades when internationalists had a clear link to political parties and social movements. Their history was embedded in the history of those movements. But such close relationships between internationalists, progressive parties, and social movements have been somewhat diluted over time, becoming more the history of outstanding individuals rather than a history of collective actors. This is partially a result of the weakening of progressive parties and movements in the United States, with a growing distance between the base of those movements (i.e., the working class) and the academic community. This reality has also somewhat limited the effectiveness of those internationalists, although their courageous examples and unwavering testimony continue to be relevant now as it was at earlier times.

In addition, the struggle for democracy and justice, whether at home or abroad, responds to a similar cause. Class, race, and gender exploitation is at the root of the underdevelopment of health and well-being internationally and in the United States. There is a global alliance of the dominant classes of developed countries with the dominant classes of developing countries that together govern the world today. To confront this alliance of the *dominant* classes, there is a need to establish an international alliance between the *dominated* classes of the developed countries and the dominated classes of the developing countries. And for this to occur there is a need to change the distribution of power in the United States and to stop the overwhelming control of the U.S. government by Corporate America. This is indeed a major task, to be realized by popular mobilizations, including health workers in solidarity, that ask for the establishment of truly democratic institutions in the United States and across the world. In this regard, the struggles abroad and at home are the same. They are part of a growing movement in the United States that aims to guarantee that the preamble of the U.S. Constitution, "We, the people . . ." decide, becomes a reality. This book is part of that history.

**Vicente Navarro, MD PhD**
Professor of Health and Public Policy
The Johns Hopkins University
Editor in Chief
*International Journal of Health Services*

# Acknowledgments

 We have dedicated the book to Walter Lear, who inspired this project—and all of us. Through this collective dedication, we aim to honor his legacy and infuse the book with Walter's spirit, his boundless energy, and his commitment to health left history and activism.

This book has had a lengthy provenance, both in its genesis and its gestation. Its original spark came from a Socialist Caucus meeting at the American Public Health Association's 1999 annual conference, held in Chicago, and organized by the formidable Walter Lear. Various of the participants in that exploratory meeting ultimately wrote chapters for this volume; others contributed through stimulating questions and reflections on the lives of health internationalists (including their own). Walter deputized the two of us to pursue a health internationalists book project, but life's vicissitudes and competing projects kept us from this task for some years. Walter always kept at us and was as delighted as we were when the book finally began to take shape in the late 2000s. Tragically, he died in May 2010 before the manuscript was completed.

This project would not have come to fruition without the indomitable Stranks sisters as research assistants in Toronto. First, Sarah read through early drafts of most of the chapters, and offered extremely useful feedback to the authors from a health student perspective. Then, her sister Marrison took on the heroic task of chief copy editor, organizer, and astute critic—all with poise, great skill and efficiency (Marrison's magic), and good humor. Both Sarah and Marrison are pursuing graduate training in public health and medicine, and we hope they have been inspired as health internationalists at least in part through their involvement in this book.

The Canada Research Chairs program provided considerable support to Anne-Emanuelle Birn and her research assistants, as well as a publication subvention for the preparation of this book. Provost Peter Lennie and Dean of Arts and Sciences Joanna Olmsted of the University of Rochester also provided a generous publication subvention.

At Rutgers, our editors Doreen Valentine and Peter Mickulas have been superb and sometimes motivatingly stern shepherds; we appreciate their enthusiasm for this project and their tireless support. Janet Golden and Rima Apple have been patient series editors and we thank them, too. We have benefited greatly from the professionalism and grace of Suzanne Kellam and the entire production team. We are most grateful, as well, to the anonymous reviewers, whose comments and suggestions were both useful and enlightening.

We appreciate the commitment and feedback from all of the contributors to this book. Two especially helpful authors—Timothy Holtz and Laura Turiano—gave us courage and insight around the framing of the book. We are also indebted to friends and colleagues Laura Nervi, Yogan Pillay, Corinne Sutter-Brown, Stephen Kunitz, Susan Ladwig, Sofia Gruskin, and Mario Rovere for their key input on particular chapters, to Danielle Schirmer in Halifax and Sarah Ndegwa in Rochester for their research and editing assistance, and to Andrew Leyland in Toronto for his diligent work on the index.

Two comrades stand out for their enormous intellectual and creative generosity, which have made this book—and its title—immeasurably better: Nancy Krieger and Nikolai Krementsov. Thank you so much and spasibo bolshoe!

Finally, we each thank those closest to us, and once again offer apologies to our respective families for all of the delayed dinners and missed weekends this project entailed. It may not always seem like it, but we do it all for you . . .

# Part I

# Health Comrades in Context

# Chapter 1

# Introduction

## Health Comrades, Abroad and at Home

**Anne-Emanuelle Birn and Theodore M. Brown**

In January 1937 Lini De Vries, a widowed nurse and former factory worker from New Jersey, volunteered to be part of the American Medical Bureau's (AMB) mission to Spain. For months she struggled to save the lives of brave young men who had been mortally wounded while fighting the enemies of Spanish democracy: General Francisco Franco's army and his fascist allies. As she later recalled:

> Men coming out of anesthesia cowered . . . [o]thers shuddered when they heard planes overhead. Spain, a recognized, legally elected government with representation in the League of Nations, was being brutally attacked . . . I hated what I saw and the forces responsible for this suffering, anguish and death. . . . Perhaps never again in my life will I be with such idealistic, gentle people from so many lands. This was a crusade for the freedom of man. . . . I had played a small part in the uneven struggle of the Spanish people defending themselves against Hitler's forces, Mussolini's Black Shirts . . . I had received far more than I had given to Spain. I had received daily experience in valor, courage, bravery. I saw idealism expressed by men from many lands. I saw democracy in the making. Spain had given me the chance to work, think and act at the highest level of humanity that I was able to attain. In this action I had a chance to grow.[1]

When people think of those dedicated to international or global health[2] nowadays, the image that comes to mind is a person—at least on the surface—much like Lini De Vries. She or he may be pictured as a young, idealistic health professional who travels to a war-torn or impoverished setting where patients are destitute or displaced, medical supplies are limited, and standards of sanitation and safety are inadequate. In such settings, brave souls put careers on hold and sometimes risk their lives in order to offer compassion and clinical skills to suffering people. For a few months or perhaps many years, these nurses, doctors, and other health workers devote themselves to providing the best possible care they can with minimal resources amid daily frustrations and often threatening political instability.

But De Vries was different from today's more typical global health volunteer or professional: she was a health leftist. By leftist we mean someone who adheres to some version of anticapitalist (including socialist, Communist, or possibly anarchist) belief, and who subscribes to the view that "people come before profits." Leftists hold that it is possible for societies to build economic and political democracy premised on respect for human rights. Hence, by definition, leftists oppose economic exploitation, oppression, and discrimination at home and abroad, the latter particularly in relation to colonization, imperialism, and usurpation of indigenous sovereignty and territory. It is also important to note that leftists are willing to expose publicly those who engage in, tolerate, or benefit from exploitation and oppression; leftists correspondingly work collectively to challenge the privileges and priorities of those seeking to maintain and increase private wealth and power at the expense of others, thus denying needed economic resources and rights to large swaths of the population. Although most leftists are linked by their political economy analysis,[3] they have been more variable, past and present, in their grasp of politics pertaining to racism, gender, sexuality, and religion.

It was as a health leftist that De Vries went to Spain, possessing a well-developed political sensibility. This sensibility derived from her teenage years, when she labored in silk, ribbon, and cotton mills, from her years of experience as a social worker and public health nurse in New York, and from her membership in the Communist Party. With strong views about the injustice of the fascist-supported assault on a democratically elected government that was deeply committed to improving the lives of long-oppressed and largely illiterate rural and urban populations, De Vries wanted to offer medical assistance not only for its own sake, but to support a political cause. Experiencing the enormous brutality of Franco's fascist forces firsthand,[4] she developed a clear sense of how health, politics, and struggles for social justice were closely connected.

Thus, there was more than narrowly defined medical aid in what De Vries contributed in international health. Like various of her comrades (a term, borrowed from French, popularized by German socialists in the nineteenth century as a more egalitarian form of address), she returned to North America on a speaking tour to raise awareness and money for the voluntary medical efforts that supported the Republican (antifascist) side in Spain's civil war. She subsequently worked in New Mexico, Puerto Rico, and Los Angeles, providing public health services and training for low-income, working-class communities and serving under the federal Works Progress Administration.[5] Until her death in 1982, DeVries continued to translate the lessons she learned in Spain into a lifetime of community health work, writing, and political engagement, first in the United States and then for two decades in Mexico, where she was exiled during the red-baiting witch hunts of the early Cold War.

This book traces the international involvement of U.S. health profession-als of Lini De Vries's genre—here we refer to them as both "health leftists" and "health internationalists"—and the impact of these experiences on their subsequent work and activism. Those covered in this book represent a range of fields—medicine, nursing, social work, law, policy, advocacy, and public health—and have witnessed and worked in a variety of international settings from the 1930s to the present: these settings have all demanded a mix of urgent medical need and political struggle for equity and justice, with relevance in situ and back home alike. Indeed, a hallmark of the health internationalists included in this volume is that they have transposed their overseas engagement and learning to the U.S. context, where it has shaped and informed their health work and political activities.

The health internationalists who are the authors and subjects of this vol-ume have taken part in endeavors abroad that were and are, at one and the same time, practical, political, and educational—to the health professional herself or himself and to alternatively admiring, critical, or menacing domestic audi-ences. Some were longtime activists whose international commitments were consistent with decades of militancy. Others experienced a political awakening while working overseas, returning to the United States with new sensibilities and novel approaches to fighting for health and social justice. Like De Vries, our protagonists can be characterized by their high ideals, strong convictions, and self-reflectiveness, as well as their dedication to continuing political engage-ment and struggle.

## An American Internationalist Focus

This book focuses on the activities of American health internationalists, although health leftists from other countries who influenced or worked with U.S. activists abroad will also be discussed. Our attention to the American angle of health internationalism derives from the particular political part played by

U.S. health leftists both abroad—where, since the 1920s they have worked to counteract their country's role in military, political, and economic domains—and at home, where left-wing politics, including the forging of a working-class (labor) party and the universal, public provision of health care services remain an elusive goal, exceptionally so for industrialized countries.[6]

U.S. health internationalists have thus served as a small but crucial left-wing counterpart to official foreign policy before, during, and after the Cold War, as well as playing an internationally informed oppositional role on the domestic political front. As such, U.S. health activist efforts may be understood as a form of resistance. Perhaps because biomedicine's professional and scientific ascendancy unfolded simultaneously to the rise of American political power and capitalist ideology, progressive health workers, particularly doctors, have had greater reach and resonance than many other leftists.

Yet the story of American health internationalists remains little known. Little known is, of course, a relative term. American health workers have been inspired by, and subsequently inspired, fellow activists in domestic movements and in international circles. Paradoxically in an immigrant society like the United States, transnational and overseas learning came naturally[7] yet was increasingly rejected as the country became a world power. The pushing aside of internationalists and their ideas, past and present, compounded by repeated Red Scares and prolonged periods of repression before, during, and subsequent to the McCarthy era, means that American health internationalists are not as renowned as they should be.

Our emphasis on Americans, while it helps map the contours of this book, is not a matter of chauvinism (noting that both coeditors are U.S. citizens). To the contrary: we believe that the part played by U.S. health internationalists—almost inevitably countering their own government's foreign policy—has historically marginalized their work, even as it has magnified its importance. Moreover, we depict the often-humbling learning experiences of health leftists who have seen what collective activism in other countries has achieved under often extremely challenging circumstances. As we shall see, at times health leftist groups—and leftists generally—engaged in destructive infighting that weakened their cause; at other moments, political alliances that seemed to offer hopeful prospects for progressive social transformation at one juncture proved catastrophic or repressive at another. We also explore the sacrifices made by countless activists, as well as the difficulties of transnational "knowledge transfer," as these experiences were directed back to the United States in an often-Sisyphean attempt to influence domestic political, social, and health movements.

Our focus on health leftists from the United States means that we will not discuss in detail the lives of two of the most famed health internationalists of the twentieth century, both of whom died fighting for their political beliefs: Canadian Norman Bethune,[8] a surgeon and Communist who campaigned for a system of state-run medical care in Canada, innovated mobile blood transfusions in the Spanish Civil War, then participated (and perished from septicemia in 1939) in the Chinese revolutionary struggle; and the iconic Ernesto "Che" Guevara,[9] the asthmatic Argentine physician turned revolutionary, Cuban diplomat, and minister of industry, who later left Cuba to support guerrilla efforts in Congo and then Bolivia, where he was captured and executed in 1967. Yet Bethune and Guevara are nonetheless present in this book. Virtually all of the contributors to this book are familiar with and inspired by one or both of these figures, and they serve as stirring symbols of health internationalists to wide audiences.

To date the medico-political trajectories of U.S. health internationalists have been covered in a handful of mostly individual autobiographical accounts or as parts of larger stories of international political activism that generally overlook the health and medical aspects of this involvement.[10] This book aims to draw systematic attention to the international activities of U.S. health leftists by presenting a combination of historical analysis and firsthand reflections by several generations of health activists whose work spanned the twentieth century and continues into the twenty-first. We seek to lift these narratives from obscurity and to understand the motivations, experiential learning, contextual influences, courage, commitment "against the grain," and sometimes complex contradictions of a heretofore little known kind of activist. While this recognition of health leftists includes various accounts of bona fide heroism, our aim is not to celebrate these lives uncritically, but rather to subject them to scrutiny, analyzing the often searingly difficult decisions related to, and consequences of, their efforts.

It is important from the outset to distinguish the health internationalists who are the focus of this book from those individuals who serve and have served under the auspices of major international health organizations as advocates, bureaucrats, or field operatives. To be sure, many idealistic and "liberal" (in the North American sense of "left-leaning") individuals, including some of the subjects and contributors to this book, have been involved at all levels of these institutions and have sought to push them—from within and from without—to take more progressive stances and pursue policies and activities based on social justice principles. Yet leading international health agencies, most notably the World Health Organization (WHO) and other UN agencies; international financial and development institutions like the World Bank;

philanthropies, particularly the Rockefeller and Bill and Melinda Gates Foundations; public-private partnerships; religious missions; bilateral aid agencies such as the United States Agency for International Development (USAID); large and small nongovernmental organizations (NGOs) from CARE to Unite for Sight; and the many other organizations that now make up the international/ global health "establishment" did not and do not challenge the tenets of capitalist political economy (even as they may try to meliorate its excesses). These organizations have generally relegated politically progressive efforts to the margins, ignored them, or even consciously worked against them. We will mention earlier varieties of mainstream international health in chapter 2 and later varieties elsewhere in the book; here we emphasize that the majority of people who have worked and now work for the better-known international health agencies are *not* the "health internationalists" highlighted in this book, at least not for the bulk of their careers.

Just as the health internationalists covered in this volume are not equivalent to international organization functionaries, they also cannot be considered public civil servants, even though many (have) served local and national governments in the United States and abroad—welcomed by countries as distinct as Nicaragua and Mozambique. Indeed, no single occupational or professional profile adequately captures their roles. They include nurses, doctors, teachers, public health administrators, physician assistants, activist-scholars, social workers, students, and lawyers: many have worked at universities, some at academic medical centers or small clinics, others for NGOs or activist groups, and still others don multiple hats.

Our protagonists are closer to being part of what political scientists, borrowing from sociology, term "transnational advocacy networks"; that is, networks that build ties "among actors in civil societies, states, and international organizations,"[11] often around particular problems or policies. This term is typically invoked to characterize the participants, structures, activities, and strategies of those engaged in policy and advocacy alliances that traverse borders and influence both domestic and international arenas.

Fascinating as such questions can be, this volume does not strive to uncover general patterns of progressive international health solidarity. Our purpose is somewhat different: we concentrate on revealing the multifarious pathways, varied motivations, and diverse backgrounds, contexts, and conditions that led several generations of Americans to commit themselves to left-wing health activism overseas and in the United States. As we shall see, the factors comprise a mix of academic, familial, cultural-religious, cohort-specific, and serendipitous influences exercised by classmates, neighbors, relatives, mentors, and the imperative of the times. Each trajectory is unique and illuminating; together, these narratives trace political and ideological awakenings, the formation of professional and political identity, the challenges of transnational commitment through crisis and change, the rewards and costs of lifelong activism, and the satisfaction—and disillusionment—of left-wing solidarity in a U.S. context that marginalizes or suppresses it. This combination of particular moments and ongoing movements, we hope, brings historical perspectives into vivid contemporary relief for current (health) activists of all ages contemplating their own trajectories.

## The Book Unfolds . . .

In following U.S. health internationalism over the past century, we have chosen to intertwine broadly defined generational cohorts with historical eras. This allows us to track the role and influence of formative political, social, and cultural contexts both "at home" and abroad. In this way, the long struggles and perseverance of our protagonists, who have often stood contrary to U.S. government policies and actions through multiple decades, can be seen as a commitment of continuity rather than solely of contingency. In addition, this structure highlights cross-generational interchange, for the U.S. health Left has offered a form of education of, for, and by health workers themselves, a tradition we seek to continue with this book.

In chapter 2, Theodore M. Brown and Anne-Emanuelle Birn ponder the diverse provenance of health internationalism: social medicine, the socialist and Communist movements, class and political solidarity across borders, and other forces, particularly in Europe and the Americas. The mix of these ideas, activities, and aspirations in the nineteenth and early twentieth centuries, together with the rising authority of the health professions, made for explosive health politics. By the 1930s, left-wing health internationalism was a twentieth-century force to be reckoned with.

We then move to the first of four generations of U.S. health leftists, this one born, roughly speaking, around the turn of the twentieth century, during the Progressive Era of social reform. Members of this generation reached their stride during the troubled and activist years of the Depression. Due to the time frame covered—the actors from this period have long passed away—the chapters in this section are analytical and biographical rather than autobiographical. We begin with Susan Solomon's account of John Kingsbury's doomed attempt to use his institutional berth at the Milbank Memorial Fund to introduce Soviet "Red Medicine" as a bona fide reform option during the 1930s battles over establishing a national health care system in the United States. Also examining the turbulent decade of the 1930s is Walter Lear's synthesis of the experience of scores of U.S. health workers, many of them members of the Communist Party, who participated in what was arguably the biggest international left-wing effort ever—the antifascist, Republican cause in the Spanish Civil War. Lear concentrates on the American Medical Bureau to Aid Spanish Democracy, exploring its origins and organization and showing the meaning, commitment, influence, and legacy of this extraordinary solidarity calling. As Jane Pacht Brickman discusses in her chapter, those involved with the AMB, together with other outspoken health-Left activists of the 1930s and 1940s, paid a heavy penalty for their international solidarity—accused by U.S. authorities of subversive activity and personally and professionally punished by the witch hunts of the Cold War.

For the generation born in the 1920s and 1930s, who were raised during the Depression and reached adulthood at the same time that oppressive and vindictive attacks were mounted against the American Left, health activism was necessarily "under the covers." The impact of McCarthyism and the Cold War also meant that this generation channeled much of their political energy beyond U.S. borders, subsumed under the promotion of other bold and worthy causes. As a medical student and civil rights activist, Jack Geiger found himself working in the 1950s with Sidney and Emily Kark's antiracist community-oriented primary health care experiments in South Africa, whose principles and approaches Geiger later transported to Mississippi during the civil rights struggle in the United States. Victor and Ruth Sidel, respectively physician and at that time social worker, also recognized the possibilities of "revolutionary" learning from abroad—transforming their openness to China into an embrace of the barefoot doctor concept and its adaptation to a community health participation program in the blighted New York City borough of the Bronx. Cardiologist Bernard Lown, meanwhile, under a cloud during the McCarthy era, later parlayed his substantial scientific reputation and longtime contacts with Soviet professional counterparts into a Nobel Prize–winning struggle to overcome Cold War tensions and end nuclear proliferation, hoping to prevent a nuclear holocaust.

For the subsequent baby boomer generation, the 1960s' wide-ranging domestic struggles for civil rights, women's rights, sexual and reproductive rights, along with economic and labor rights—combined with organizing against the United States' ruthless war in Vietnam—naturally morphed into a forceful health internationalism. Challenging U.S. hegemony was understood by this generation as a quintessentially transnational activity, and the activists sometimes moved from grassroots efforts to national and international agencies, tying together their experiences in several parts of the world. As Howard

Waitzkin recounts, it was in Latin America—the region of the world most bat-tered by U.S. military intervention and economic domination—where the most determined radical medical activism unfolded. Centered in Allende's Chile, this movement challenged U.S. ideological dominance while awakening a generation of American health leftists to the possibilities of social medicine. In the 1980s, as Paula Braveman relays, Nicaragua's revolutionary Sandinista government—which radically transformed the country through redistribu-tive social policies but was under continuous assault by U.S.-backed rebels—became a new generation's Spanish Civil War. After years of solidarity activities in and with Nicaragua, Braveman later worked to bring the health and social justice lessons she learned there first to the WHO and then back to the United States in ongoing struggles for equity in health. Stephen Gloyd, James Pfeiffer, and Wendy Johnson show us how in Africa, too, multiple cohorts of U.S. health leftists have devoted decades of their lives to building community-oriented pri-mary care through their NGO, Health Alliance International (HAI), throughout all the vagaries of revolution and instability in Mozambique. In her reflections on a life of health transnationalism, Mary Travis Bassett describes moving back and forth from North America to Zimbabwe, from her early activism with the Black Panthers to her work within and outside government agencies, striving to make social policy responsive to agendas of social redistribution and health equity.

If the generation born circa 1900 inspired the next one, at a distance, those born in the 1920s and 1930s have worked directly with and influenced the gen-erations that came of political age in the 1960s and after. Generational mixing has produced a variety of activist approaches among a fourth generation born in the 1960s and 1970s, from working with local political opposition groups, to bringing a transnational voice to the voiceless, to institutionalizing health-Left movements and activities in the United States and elsewhere, all with an eye to sustaining these efforts over the long term. Michael Terry and Laura Turiano relate an often-harrowing story of serving El Salvador's revolutionary struggle as a paramedic and a community health organizer and describe the sobering, if hopeful, reality of the slow peacetime political process. As a human rights lawyer, Alicia Ely Yamin has toiled in Mexico and Peru to bring horrific vio-lations of economic, social, and health rights to light. She has also faced the challenges of trying to incorporate health rights into human rights activism in the United States and to get Americans to examine their own society as well as stand in solidarity with those overseas. Working to publicize the debilitat-ing legacy and health effects of nuclear weapons testing and American mili-tary presence in the Marshall Islands, Seiji Yamada confronts his own Japanese heritage and the history of Japanese militarism and imperialism. Lanny Smith,

Jennifer Kasper, and Timothy Holtz trace the origins of their social justice NGO, Doctors for Global Health, and its role in promoting liberation medicine in Central America and beyond and in organizing health solidarity efforts in the United States. Rounding out the autobiographical chapters, Razel Remen and Brea Bondi-Boyd recount how they came to be U.S. medical students at Cuba's Latin American School of Medicine (ELAM) and what they learned about solidarity by studying side-by-side with students from throughout the Americas. They also explain how their Cuban experiences have influenced their work and social justice aspirations as young doctors in the United States.

By no means do the health internationalists presented in this volume constitute an exhaustive survey: our selection seeks to cover distinct time periods, regions, and professions of American health leftists (that is, U.S. citizens, including immigrants who spent their formative years in the United States). Dozens, if not hundreds, of others are not included in the chapters ahead. To name but a few, Vicente Navarro, a Catalan physician (and naturalized American) and longtime Johns Hopkins University professor, has since the 1970s been the world's leading health Marxist, training generations of health internationalists through his courses, writings, journal, and activism in the Americas and Europe. Seminal health internationalists also include the late Dr. Helen Rodriguez-Trias, champion of women's health rights, including the right to abortion and prevention of sterilization abuse in Puerto Rico, the United States, and internationally, and Charlie Clements—U.S. Air Force pilot in the Vietnam War turned pacifist, doctor to Salvadoran villagers amid the country's brutal civil war, and human rights activist. Many others also omitted are remarkable and admirable individuals who have worked transnationally, striving to make the impossible possible, committing their time, reputations, and careers, sometimes at great personal cost, to bring their aspirations of health and social justice to fruition. We simply do not have room for their stories in this book, but their work is alluded to by several of our protagonists and we will highlight some of their contributions in our concluding chapter.

Our final chapter contemplates the themes that cut across the lives of courage, militancy, resistance, and passion portrayed in the book. We also consider how these themes inform and bring meaning to contemporary struggles, even as they reveal moments of contradiction, dissent, pessimism, and regret. Like the famed historian of medicine and health activist Henry Sigerist,[12] we believe that historical understanding and the placing of current challenges into historical context is the first step toward activism. Now we invite you to read on, hoping that these important stories of international engagement and resistance both inspire and provoke reflection and critique among present and future generations.

## Notes

1. Lini De Vries, *Up from the Cellar* (Minneapolis: Vanilla Press, 1979), 207–233 passim.

2. This book will mostly use the term *international health* rather than *global health* because the latter was not employed during most of the historical periods covered here. The term international health was likely coined in the early twentieth century, emerging along with permanent bodies addressing health concerns internationally. It was employed prominently by the Rockefeller Foundation's International Health Commission (later Board and Division) launched in 1913. By the end of World War II, *international health* was in widespread use in its original sense, but during the Cold War the field of international health began to focus on the problems of health in underdeveloped countries and the efforts by industrialized countries and international agencies to address these problems. *Global health*—adopted broadly over the past decade—is meant to transcend past ideological uses of *international health* (as a "handmaiden" of colonialism or a pawn of Cold War political rivalries) to imply a shared global susceptibility to, experience of, and responsibility for health. However, as Ilona Kickbusch has argued, this "new" global health has also been used to assert U.S. "global unilateralism"; that is, a tailoring of the world's health agenda to meet hegemonic U.S. national interests and undercut bona fide internationalist endeavors. See Ilona Kickbusch, "Influence and Opportunity: Reflections on the U.S. Role in Global Public Health," *Health Affairs* 21(6) (2002): 131–141. Notwithstanding the invoked distinctions, the "new" definition of global health bears many similarities to early twentieth-century understandings of international health. See Anne-Emanuelle Birn, "Remaking International Health: Refreshing Perspectives from Latin America," *Pan American Journal of Public Health* 30(2) (2011): 106–110.

3. See, for example, Vicente Navarro, *The Political Economy of Social Inequalities: Consequences for Health and Quality of Life Amityville* (New York: Baywood, 2002); Anne-Emanuelle Birn, Yogan Pillay, and Timothy H. Holtz, "The Political Economy of Health and Development," in *Textbook of International Health: Global Health in a Dynamic World,* 3rd ed. (New York: Oxford University Press, 2009), 132–191.

4. Spanish, and particularly Catalan, nurses and doctors experienced this struggle over their homeland at an entirely different level. See Roser Valls i Molins, ed., *Infermeres Catalanes a la Guerra Civil Espanyola* (Barcelona Publicacions i Edicions de la Universitat de Barcelona, 2008).

5. Lini M. De Vries Papers, Abraham Lincoln Brigade Archives Collection # 272, Tamiment Library/Wagner Archives, New York University; and Papers of Lini M. De Vries, 1910–2002, Arthur and Elizabeth Schlesinger Library on the History of Women in America, Radcliffe Institute for Advanced Study, Harvard University.

6. Vicente Navarro, "Why Some Countries Have National Health Insurance, Others Have National Health Services, and the U.S. Has Neither," *Social Science and Medicine* 28 (1989): 887–897; Colin Gordon, *Dead on Arrival: The Politics of Health Care in Twentieth-Century America* (Princeton, NJ: Princeton University Press, 2003); Alan Derickson, *Health Security for All: Dreams of Universal Health Care in America* (Baltimore: Johns Hopkins University Press, 2005); and Jill Quadagno, *One Nation Uninsured: Why the U.S. Has No National Health Insurance* (New York: Oxford University Press, 2005).

7. On Americans' "international learning" during the Progressive period, see Daniel T. Rodgers, *Atlantic Crossings: Social Politics in a Progressive Age* (Cambridge, MA: Harvard University Press, 1998). Eric Foner has been one of the leading historical

critics of American myopia and distorted assertions of "American Exceptionalism." See in particular his 2000 Presidential Address to the American Historical Association, "American Freedom in a Global Age," *http://www.historians.org/info/aha _history/Efoner.htm* (accessed February 19, 2011).

8. Roderick Stewart and Sharon Stewart, *Phoenix: The Life of Norman Bethune* (Montreal: McGill-Queen's University Press, 2011); Wendell MacLeod, Libbie Park, and Stanley Ryerson, *Bethune: The Montreal Years, An Informal Portrait* (Toronto: James Lorimer & Company, 1978); Larry Hannant, *The Politics of Passion: Norman Bethune's Writing and Art* (Toronto: University of Toronto Press, 1998).

9. For a sampling, see Paco Ignacio Taibo II, *Ernesto Guevara: También conocido como el Che* (México, D.F.: Planeta, 2003); Jon Lee Anderson, *Che: A Revolutionary Life* (New York: Grove Press, 1997); Paulo Drinot, ed., *Che's Travels: The Making of a Revolutionary in 1950s Latin America* (Durham, NC: Duke University Press, 2010); *Ernesto Che Guevara: Escritos y discursos* (La Habana: Editorial de Ciencias Sociales, 1977).

10. Charles Shipman, *It Had to Be Revolution: Memoirs of an American Radical* (Ithaca, NY: Cornell University Press, 1993); Peter N. Carroll, *The Odyssey of the Abraham Lincoln Brigade: Americans in the Spanish Civil War* (Stanford: Stanford University Press, 1994).

11. Margaret Keck and Kathryn Sikkink, eds., *Activists Beyond Borders: Advocacy Networks in International Politics* (Ithaca, NY: Cornell University Press, 1998), 1.

12. Henry E. Sigerist, "The Medical Student and the Social Problems Confronting Medicine Today," *Bulletin of the Institute of the History of Medicine* 4 (1936): 411–422. See also Elizabeth Fee and Theodore M. Brown, eds., *Making Medical History: The Life and Times of Henry E. Sigerist* (Baltimore: Johns Hopkins University Press, 1997); Elizabeth Fee and Theodore M. Brown, "Using Medical History to Shape a Profession: The Ideals of William Osler and Henry E. Sigerist," in *Locating Medical History: The Stories and Their Meanings*, ed. Frank Huisman and John Harley Warner (Baltimore: Johns Hopkins University Press, 2004), 139–164.

# Chapter 2

# The Making of Health Internationalists

**Theodore M. Brown and Anne-Emanuelle Birn**

How did health and left-wing internationalist politics come together in the early twentieth century? We approach this question by tracing the provenance of health internationalism, and how it emerged in the United States, against the odds, from two nineteenth-century sources that later converged. The first source was social medicine, which originated in the middle of the nineteenth century and was based on the premise that health is embedded in the political and social order. The second source was proletarian internationalism, taking shape around the same time and expressed in movements for social justice that transcended national boundaries and identities in an asserted universalism. These two strands of progressive politics, focused on the socially and politically oppressed—and their health conditions—became intertwined in the early twentieth century. Health internationalism, the product of this convergence, first surfaced in Europe after the Bolshevik revolution, and then became a reality lived—and died for—in civil war Spain and revolutionary China. Health internationalism was thus distinct from the modern field of international health, which was becoming institutionalized over the same period. Moreover, mainstream international health was not an inspiration for health internationalism but a parallel endeavor that at different times eschewed, harbored, and gave an occasional platform to health internationalists, who for their part variously supported, sought to influence, critiqued, and rejected it.

## Social Medicine

The social medicine tradition emerged during Europe's Industrial Revolution, when systematic data collection began to reveal unmistakable associations of death and illness patterns with income, occupational status, and living and working conditions. In the 1820s and 1830s, French military surgeon turned social researcher Louis-René Villermé painstakingly compiled census data to demonstrate a strong correlation between poverty rates and mortality in Paris.[1] In the 1840s, English lawyer and civil servant Edwin Chadwick (architect of Britain's detested 1834 Poor Law, which forced the rural poor into urban factories and hellish almshouses) also documented clear links between living and working conditions and infant mortality and life expectancy, which varied dramatically by occupational class.[2] Yet Chadwick, especially, failed to see in these statistical patterns justification for anything beyond continued laissez-faire capitalist development or modest melioration. Chadwick, who held that disease resulted in poverty, recommended environmental cleanup and the appointment of medical officers of health but refused to accede to the position of contemporary epidemiologist-statistician William Farr, among others, that poverty itself was a critical determinant of ill health.

Friedrich Engels, a young German living in Chadwick's England while managing his father's factory, saw things differently. Aware of early socio-medical work, Engels was animated by a revolutionary spirit, using the new statistical data as fuel for a sharp exposé of the misery, suffering, and premature death inflicted on the working class by the unrestrained capitalist system.[3] In one of the most powerful invectives ever written against the evils of capitalism, *Condition of the Working Class in England* (1845), Engels presented evidence to show how: overcrowding and poor ventilation led to high tuberculosis mortality; miserable wages and food shortages caused malnutrition and its sequelae; unshielded factory machinery produced horrific industrial accidents; uncontrolled textile, metal, and coal dust created respiratory and lung problems; and inhumane manufacturing processes caused musculoskeletal problems, eye disorders, and neurological disability. This trenchant critique of the exploitative working conditions created by capitalists and the associated crippling medical consequences helped motivate Engels's militant calls for action.

Engels's work and the spirit of the age caught the attention of a young Prussian physician, Rudolf Virchow, founder of cellular pathology, who was on the cusp of a brilliant academic career.[4] In early 1848, as Europe's capitals were about to explode in revolutionary fervor, Virchow was commissioned to investigate a terrible typhus outbreak among peasants, mostly Poles, in rural Silesia—a very poor area under Prussian authority. He penned a now-famous "Report on the Typhus Epidemic in Upper Silesia" (1848), which argued that economic deprivation, inadequate housing, and a complete failure of the

Prussian bureaucracy to provide adequate food supplies during famine caused massive illness and death.

Caught up in the revolutionary atmosphere, Virchow enthusiastically promoted what he proudly labeled "radical" measures. He rushed back from Silesia in March 1848 to participate on the barricades of Berlin in Prussia's abortive "Revolution of 1848." In July, he helped found *Die Medizinische Reform (Medical Reform)*, a weekly newspaper that focused on the societal origins of disease and the politics of medical reform. Under the banners "medicine is a social science and politics is nothing but medicine on a grand scale" and "the physician is the natural attorney of the poor," *Medical Reform* promoted what French physician Jules Guérin soon christened "social medicine" and advocated an agenda of physician activism on behalf of the vulnerable and downtrodden.

Yet in less than a year, increasingly reactionary political pressures forced *Medical Reform* to suspend publication. Virchow himself retreated for a few years to provincial Würzburg, and many of his radical colleagues and followers were forced underground or into exile. Among the subsequently most famous of these exiles, American pediatric pioneer Abraham Jacobi wound up in New York City, where he and other young German émigré physicians introduced social medicine ideas and practices.[5] By the late 1850s and 1860s, Jacobi's agenda, which fused medical reform with social and political activism, was beginning to become a part of the American campaign for child hygiene and public health.

Meanwhile, Virchow moved back to Berlin and gradually returned to social medicine and reformist politics. In the 1870s the field of social medicine began to flourish again, and diversify, in a now-unified Germany. The little-known Eduard Reich, a "peripatetic medical scholar," conceptualized the subject of "social hygiene" as concerned with societal welfare, most fundamentally, wiping out poverty.[6] More prominently, Max von Pettenkofer, professor of hygiene at Munich and champion of laboratory-based hygiene, delivered two lectures in 1873 on "The Value of Health to a City" in which he advocated, in addition to sanitary reform, the improved housing and feeding of the poor through municipal revenues raised by progressive taxation: "All over the world the rich generally enjoy better health and live longer than the poor. Every epidemic . . . takes a larger toll from the poorer classes, sometimes and in many places to such an extent, that particularly cholera was a few years ago still called a disease of the proletariat."[7]

Even Heinrich Struck, the first director of the German Imperial Health Bureau, called in 1878 for the state to collect medical statistics to address the population's health conditions, a position welcomed by the Socialist Workers

Party (SWP) of Germany, founded in 1875. Yet the same year, Chancellor Otto von Bismarck pushed antisocialist laws through the German Reichstag and outlawed the SWP, even as he offered a few carrots to the working class, including the beginnings of worker's compensation and social insurance. Over the next decade, social medicine faltered under Bismarck's repressive regime, but both socialism and social medicine rebounded in the 1890s when the party by now called the SPD (*Sozialdemokratische Partei Deutschlands* [Social Democratic Party of Germany]) was legalized again.[8] The SPD enjoyed even greater success at the turn of the twentieth century, soon emerging as the strongest party in the Reichstag and carrying social medicine along with it. Key figures included SPD members Alfred Grotjahn, professor of social hygiene at the University of Berlin, who in 1906 launched *Zeitschrift fur Soziale Medizin (Journal for Social Medicine),* a sign of the field's increasing visibility and influence, and Ludwig Teleky, who was appointed chair of the Department of Social Medicine at the University of Vienna in 1907 and, upon returning to Germany twelve years later, became a leader in occupational medicine and defender of the needs and rights of workers.[9]

Although in terms of numbers of practitioners and visibility Germany was social medicine's standard-bearer, Virchow's ideas resonated much further. For example, Vasilii Florinsky, professor of gynecology at the Medical-Surgical Academy of St. Petersburg, heard Virchow lecture in 1861 and then built on his arguments regarding inequality: "The more equal the distribution of a nation's wealth, rights, and privileges, and the fewer exploiting parasites that exist in the society, [the people's forces] will develop with greater harmony and greater success and the masses will be defended from infirmity and degeneration."[10] In succeeding decades, social medicine ideas influenced the ideology behind Russia's *zemstvo* medicine, which relied on *feldshers* (community physician assistants).

In France, social medicine had been suppressed, but returned in the late nineteenth century, focusing on tuberculosis as a "social disease." French chemist/microbiologist Emile Duclaux, together with various French colleagues, promoted the area of hygiène sociale, as per his 1902 book title, to encompass emerging problems such as prostitution and alcoholism, as well as the broader purview of public health.[11]

A significant test of social medicine's resilience was the emergence of reformist (and paternalistic) state medicine in the late nineteenth century. In France and in similar fashion in Britain, flourishing state protectionist policies for workers, women, and children loosely reflected Virchow's ideas regarding the link between social and health conditions.[12] But akin to Chadwick's reforms a generation earlier, these efforts were meliorist—improving working and living conditions on the margins—rather than challenging the fundamental inequalities of political and economic power underpinning capitalism.[13] Amid these developments, a core of "true believers" in Europe continued to call for political economy analyses and solutions, arguing that state-run health insurance and other social protections were far from adequate responses.

Social medicine had also disseminated to the United States, where it took on racial discrimination as a key factor driving ill health and early death. As early as the 1850s, African American physicians James McCune Smith and John S. Rock showed that slavery, combined with poverty, produced enormous racial inequalities in health.[14] Subsequently, in the 1910s, prominent New York surgeon James P. Warbasse forcefully advocated a social medicine perspective in a variety of publications.[15] In one article, he attacked social inequities and the brutalization of workers ("Industry kills and wounds more people yearly than were killed and wounded in any year in the Civil War") and offered this insight: "As much as scientific men are prone to ignore it, no discussion of health can avoid the problem of poverty. The public health can be upon a sound basis only in a society in which every man, woman, and child has adequate food, clothing, work, and play."[16] Along with public health nursing founders Lillian Wald and Lavinia Dock, birth control advocates Victor Robinson and Margaret Sanger, national health insurance pioneer Isaac Max Rubinow, and occupational health physician Alice Hamilton, Warbasse was part of a growing health left movement in the United States.[17]

Warbasse's contemporaries in the U.S. health left joined him in creating a child hygiene movement, picking up the baton from Abraham Jacobi and applying social medicine perspectives to the situation of America's children.[18] Josephine Baker, director of New York City's Bureau of Child Hygiene from 1908 to 1923, was one of the most outspoken and influential of these,[19] showing the correlation between income and infant mortality and the futility of narrow medical approaches.[20]

In Latin America social medicine developed dually via Virchow's disciples, including German pathologist Max Westenhofer, who taught at the University of Chile—influencing, among others, the future health minister and president of Chile, Salvador Allende—and through labor activists and physician-socialist allies, who recognized in the inhuman labor and living conditions of miners and industrial workers in South America the ingredients of ill health.[21] As will be discussed in chapter 9, in many ways Latin American social medicine is the most enduring of social medicine traditions, extending both backward—to Ecuadorian physician Eduardo Espejo, who in the early nineteenth-century liberation struggle against Spain identified the connection between epidemics and poverty, portending Virchow's more famous critique[22]—and forward—to Che Guevara, the Cuban revolution, and beyond.

These health activists thus extended the social medicine tradition, which since the 1840s had been grounded in the belief that the factors shaping health are embedded in the social and political order. That order included the neglect and mistreatment of children, worker exploitation, and the impact of poverty, racism, war, political disempowerment, and social inequality. Through activism one could "run the equation backwards," that is, improve health by engaging in political struggle to improve society. But political struggle with, by, and on behalf of which downtrodden people?

For most of its early history, the social medicine tradition had focused on injustices in particular national settings. There were certain moments of broader sensitivity and sparks of international awareness, as when the Prussian Virchow showed great compassion in 1848 for Silesia's ethnic Poles. In the United States, Josephine Baker was motivated by broad international interests, proclaiming a universal "Magna Carta of Childhood"—which asserted that "There shall be no deaths of babies from preventable causes, and the economic and social factors in every community that have made possible the present high baby death rate shall be corrected."[23] Until the early twentieth century, however, social medicine was pursued largely in national contexts; another impetus would be needed to internationalize it.

**Proletarian Internationalism**

The second development leading to health internationalism was proletarian internationalism. It, too, first emerged during Europe's "Age of Revolution," somewhat earlier than social medicine. Already at the end of the eighteenth century, the French Revolution served as a powerful international model to potential revolutionaries who used the often-romanticized memory of its momentous events as a stimulus and guide to their own plans.[24] Revolutionaries also formed fluid international networks whose members moved from country to country, some by deliberate choice, others due to forced exile. For example, Italian advocate of the French Revolution and the Jacobins, Philippe Buonarroti, traveled to Paris in 1793.[25] He was deported in 1797 for supporting Gracchus Babeuf's "Conspiracy of the Equals," which called for a violent uprising of the proletariat en route to the establishment of "egalitarian communism."[26] Buonarroti moved to Geneva in 1806, then Brussels in 1824. Both cities, along with Paris and London, were becoming gathering places for international communities of revolutionary exiles.[27] Activists across Europe were galvanized by Buonarroti's 1828 *History of the Babeuf Conspiracy,* which served as the "starting point for a distinctive and continuous social revolutionary tradition."[28]

One of the revolutionary émigré groups inspired by Buonarroti was the "League of the Just," founded by German workers in Paris in 1836, whose motto was "All men are brothers." Through a complicated and tangled history, it was transformed into the Communist League, which by 1847 had abandoned its former secret tactics for a more open political style. It also acquired the intellectual leadership of two German-educated, international revolutionaries, Karl Marx and Friedrich Engels.[29] In February 1848 Marx and Engels published the *Communist Manifesto,* written in stirring language that gave it extraordinary power as an internationalist revolutionary statement: "In the national struggles of the proletarians of the different countries . . . [the Communists] bring to the front the common interests of the entire proletariat, independently of all nationality. . . . National differences, and antagonisms between people, are daily more and more vanishing. . . . [T]he Communists everywhere support every revolutionary movement against the existing social and political order of things. . . . Working men of all countries, Unite!"[30]

The *Communist Manifesto*'s publication prophetically coincided with a series of revolutionary uprisings across Europe, and it resonated as far as India, where the Sikhs launched a second war against British colonial rule; Senegal, where authorities proclaimed the liberation of slaves in the French empire; and the United States, where movements for women's rights, the abolition of slavery, and anti-imperialism (particularly the United States' expansionist war on Mexico) were emerging.[31] But strong counterrevolutionary repression followed the heady revolutionary spring of 1848. Popular uprisings were cut off by the imposition of martial law, or quashed with brutal violence across Europe's major cities, while revolutionaries were harassed, censored, thrown in jail, deported, forced to go underground, or driven into exile.[32]

A spring of hope turned into a summer, winter, and decade of intimidation and despair, although revolutionary internationalists did not disappear entirely. They survived through the 1850s in industrial and trade unions and engaged in economic struggle that increasingly took on international dimensions. By the 1860s, the politically organized proletariat was returning to the scene.[33] Marx played a prominent role in organizing a campaign for international proletarian solidarity and by 1864 was centrally involved in founding the International Working Men's Association in London as the "first systematic attempt to invite the proletariat of all countries [to work together] under a single banner."[34] From 1864 to 1866 over a hundred organizations joined what became known as the "First International," which, at its peak, claimed the allegiance of several hundred thousand workers from many countries. In the still-industrializing United States, several thousand reformers, trade unionists, and radicals affiliated with the "International," and competition developed between English-speaking "Yankee" internationalists and recent émigré internationalists, like the German Friedrich Adolph Sorge, who were closely affiliated with Marx and Engels.[35]

Although Marx soon emerged as the dominant figure of the First International, his views on certain key issues were challenged by others. His principal rift was with the "anarchists," first led by Frenchman Pierre-Joseph Proudhon and later by Russian émigré Mikhail Bakunin, who resisted all forms of political authority. Marx insisted that the major goal of the International was to achieve effective, internationally connected working-class political solidarity as an instrument for eventual but not immediate social revolution, and he pushed for direct legislative action on such issues as making the eight-hour day the worldwide legal standard and strictly limiting night work.[36] Yet the "chaos of mutually conflicting ideas" kept resurfacing and pushed toward the eventual dissolution of the First International.

The major split between Marx and the anarchists was intensified by differences over strategy regarding the Paris Commune, the revolutionary working-class government that ruled Paris from March 18 to May 28, 1871 and was hailed by many in Europe and America as the harbinger of the future. The ardent American abolitionist Theodore Tilton claimed that "the same logic and sympathy—the same conviction and ardor—which made us an Abolitionist twenty years ago, make us a Communist now. . . . Having been an Emancipationist, why should we not be an Internationalist?"[37] The Commune drew inspiration from the First International and Marx considered it a possible prototype for revolutionary government in the future. But the Commune was violently suppressed (20,000 communards were killed and another 13,000 were imprisoned or exiled), and by 1872 the First International was, for all practical purposes, defunct.[38]

Marx made a calculated effort to keep the International alive and out of the hands of the anarchists by transferring the secretariat to the United States and placing its leadership in Sorge's loyal hands. The U.S.-based International persevered for another few years but ultimately split apart because of similar internal dissension. Yet after a difficult decade following the suppression of the Commune and the collapse of the First International, clear signs of internationalist proletarian political revival began to appear again in the 1880s. The trade union movement grew rapidly in Europe, the United States, and later Latin America, its increasing power demonstrated by widespread work stoppages.[39]

Self-proclaimed socialist and workers' parties also grew rapidly, for the first time on a mass basis, and these parties forged alliances with the trade union movement. The strongest and most dramatically growing socialist party of all, the revived German SPD, was explicitly committed to Marxist ideology and proletarian internationalism. In 1889, leaders of the labor and socialist movements from twenty countries met to celebrate the centenary of the French Revolution and to launch the Second International.[40] As an expression of international working-class solidarity, they declared May 1 "May Day" to mark the day when workers in every nation would demonstrate in favor of the eight-hour day and other labor demands.[41] May Day also specifically commemorated the 1886 Chicago general strike, the brutal repression against demonstrators, and the hanging of four strike leaders (known as the "Haymarket martyrs").[42] This powerful symbolic gesture of the Second International "stirred profound emotions as an early manifestation of a worldwide proletarian community in the making,"[43] and subsequently annual May Day demonstrations became "what is probably the most visceral and moving institution asserting working-class internationalism."[44]

Over the next quarter of a century, the Second International added other notable expressions of international solidarity. Its congresses grew and by 1907, 884 delegates from twenty-five countries and four continents attended the Stuttgart Congress. Most of the delegates were Europeans, but American socialists were also present,[45] supporting a resolution that decried militarism and international conflict as a ruling-class attempt to distract "the proletarian masses from their own class tasks as well as from their duties of international solidarity."[46] In 1910 delegates to the Copenhagen Congress established an International Women's Day to focus on women's social, political, and economic rights in all countries and circumstances.

But rifts developed in the Second International that grew deeper over its twenty-five-year history. Their roots lay in the very success of the socialist (also often self-labeled "Social Democratic") and labor parties, which, circa 1900, could claim up to 40 percent of voters in certain European countries and were thus significant factors in national politics. They engaged in parliamentary strategy and sometimes entered into alliances with other political parties to achieve what they regarded as key legislative objectives. The "soft embrace" of the Left by centrist parties was often cynically based on the desire to lessen their reach. It also split the proletarian movement. Moderate socialist, social democratic, and labor parties still tried to mobilize under the banner of Marxism, but they tended to concentrate on "the immediate improvements and reforms which the working class might win from governments and employers,"[47] eschewing outright revolt. Radical leftists, antiauthoritarian anarchists, and some trade unionists saw these developments as "reformist and bureaucratized," diverting the movement from revolution and diminishing the collective bargaining power of militant organized labor by opting instead for moderate legislative reform.

Another source of disagreement in the Second International was the strategy of the German SPD, which increasingly tried to impose its political model on the International.[48] This did not sit well with many delegates, any more than did the SPD's strict adherence to an agenda of gradualist parliamentary reform. At early congresses, a vocal group of anarchists agitated before being expelled, and at later congresses a militant group of "syndicalists" (who believed in an anticapitalist and antistatist form of social organization based on trade unions democratically self-managed by workers) continued to insist on the tactics of the "general strike." Famous anarchists like the American Emma Goldman, who had trained as a nurse and midwife, spurned the International and traveled to Europe to attend alternate anarchist congresses instead, and sympathizers of the anarcho-syndicalists published memorials to their heroes like Russian zoologist and revolutionary Peter Kropotkin, who had been banned from the Socialist International.[49] Other radicals who did attend the Second International's congresses continued to believe in direct revolutionary action, such as the attempted 1905 revolution in Russia.[50]

These tensions finally ripped the Second International apart when at the start of World War I the French, Austrian, and German delegations abandoned their proclaimed antiwar positions and exhibited nationalistic sympathies. When, in 1914, parliamentary representatives of the various national socialist parties voted in favor of "war credits"—endorsing fund-raising for war operations—these simmering tensions boiled over and effectively ended the International in Europe.[51]

The American Socialist Party was divided, with many members strongly decrying the "moral failure" of their European colleagues whose abandonment of internationalist principles, they suspected, was fueled by resurgent nationalism. The more militant five-time Socialist Party presidential candidate Eugene V. Debs argued: "When I say I am opposed to war I mean ruling class war, for the ruling class is the only class that makes war. It matters not to me whether this war be offensive or defensive, or what other lying excuse may be invented for it. . . . I would be shot for treason before I would enter such a war."[52] Similar sentiments were expressed in Europe, where the principal internationalist initiative now passed to a group of French syndicalists, German radical intellectuals, and Russian exiles, most notably Vladimir Lenin. In 1915, Lenin argued that "only a revolutionary overthrow of the bourgeois governments . . . opens the road to socialism and to peace among peoples."[53]

In March 1919, following the Bolshevik revolution, the Second International was replaced by the Third (Communist) International, or the Comintern. It was launched at a congress in Moscow called by Lenin and fellow revolutionary Leon Trotsky, and in addition to Russian Bolsheviks and Communists from central and eastern Europe, the Comintern drew heavily from the younger generation and left wing of European socialist, social democratic, and labor parties.[54] Among them were many young socialists "who were for the most part hostile to the official leadership of Social Democratic parties, and who found in the Comintern an outlet for long-suppressed revolutionary ardor and a compensation for the 1914 'betrayal' of the International."[55]

Americans were also drawn to the Comintern, with enthusiasts coming primarily from the left wings of the Socialist Workers Party of America, the American Socialist Party, and the American branch of the Industrial Workers of the World (the "Wobblies").[56] These activists were animated by sympathetic journalists, most notably John Reed, who reported from the battlefields of Pancho Villa's revolutionary forces in Mexico and the front lines of labor strikes across the United States, vividly depicting the struggles of exploited workers and railing against greed, corruption, and U.S. military intervention.[57] In 1918 and 1919 several American journalists—Reed and Lincoln Steffens most famously—visited Russia and on their return wrote and lectured in glowing terms about their admiration for the achievements of the Bolshevik revolution. In late summer 1919, in the year of the Comintern, Reed and about two hundred others founded the American Communist Party in Chicago. Reed was hoping to bring the revolutionary struggle to American workers but was forced by U.S. federal, state, and local government suppression of Left organizations back to Russia, where he died a hero and was buried near the Kremlin wall.[58]

Part of Lenin's motivation in founding the Comintern was to create a worldwide network of Bolshevik supporters and Communist parties because of his fear that the counterrevolutionary powers of world capitalism would crush the Russian Revolution, just as reactionary European powers had crushed the Paris Commune. As a defensive strategy, he organized a new International to create allies and to foment revolution in Europe and elsewhere in the world. But Lenin was also a visionary who saw Russia's Bolshevik revolution as an ecumenical event whose goal was not only to bring socialism to Russia but also to precipitate a worldwide proletarian revolution.[59]

One strategy was to try to gain control over the international trade union movement, and the Comintern even formally established an international body, commonly known as the Profintern, to coordinate Communist activities with unions and promote revolutionary activities.[60] The Comintern was also strongly committed to supporting and exporting revolution to Europe and to decolonized/ing settings in Asia, Africa, and Latin America, especially in the "East" to which Lenin paid great attention.[61] The 1920 statutes of the Third International explicitly stated that the new international "breaks once and for all with the traditions of the Second International, for whom in fact only white-skinned people existed. The task of the Communist International is to liberate the working people of the entire world. In its ranks, the white, the yellow, and the black-skinned peoples—the working people of the entire world—are fraternally united."[62]

By the early 1920s, however, it was apparent that attempts to gain control over the labor movement had failed, with the vast majority of trade union members in Europe and the United States being more interested in "bourgeois" reform, including reform of working conditions, occupational safety regulation, maternal and child protection, and social insurance—all under the oversight of the newly created International Labour Office.[63] Likewise, many of the attempted, Bolshevik-inspired revolutions in Germany, Hungary, Finland, and elsewhere in Europe had failed miserably. To deal with this disappointment and its crucial strategic implications, Lenin, before his death in 1924, turned his attention—both in labor policy and in general revolutionary strategy—fully to the East.[64] China was the focus of particular attention, and even when the stirring 1925–1927 campaign for national liberation led by a Kuomintang (nationalist)-Communist alliance ended brutally with the slaughter of the Communists by Kuomintang general Chiang Kai-shek, internationalist hopes were transferred to Mao Zedong, who in the 1930s became an increasingly important leader of the Chinese rural proletariat.[65] In India, too, many flirted with Bolshevism although Gandhi himself rejected it because it "does not preclude the use of force." Yet Gandhi acknowledged in 1928 that "the Bolshevik ideal has behind it the purest sacrifice of countless men and women who have given up their all for its sake, and an ideal that is sanctified by the sacrifices of such master spirits as Lenin cannot go in vain."[66] As the Comintern saw it, the peasants in the East were ready for world revolution because they had leaders like Mao and Gandhi who shared the internationalist perspective and because their miserable lives meant that they had "nothing to lose but their chains" as they struggled daily with the terrible ravages of oppression, poverty, starvation, and disease.

## The Making of (American) Health Internationalism

In the 1920s and 1930s, proletarian internationalism eventually crossed and fused with social medicine to give the latter an international revolutionary orientation and thus create (militant) health internationalism. But this was not a simple process, for three reasons. First, while social medicine had continued to grow and spread as measured by the expanding number of publications, increasing institutional recognition, and geographic dispersion, many of its practitioners shifted from urging social, political, and economic reform to promoting eugenics. Some, like Alfred Ploetz in late-nineteenth-century Germany, took this in the "negative" direction of "racial hygiene" and foreshadowed the cleansing of "genetic undesirables" from the population.[67] Others, including "scientific socialists" and many public health experts, promoted "positive eugenics" and advocated both birth control methods and programs of social improvement to promote increased reproduction by the most biologically fit. In Uruguay, for example, the first minister of Childhood Protection, a public health pediatrician, backed positive eugenics, calling for "Childhood Social Medicine" to be based on children's social and economic rights.[68] Still others, such as Alfred Grotjahn, abandoned social medicine (which he deemed had become narrowly associated with state medicine and social insurance) for social hygiene. Instead of Virchow's political economy, Grotjahn called for addressing degeneration (hereditarian social pathology) through eugenic improvement, identifying racial hygiene as a subset of social hygiene.[69] Over time, in Germany and elsewhere, the agendas of, and individuals involved in, eugenics, public health, and social medicine overlapped, at times making a distinct social medicine approach difficult to distinguish.[70]

Second, where social medicine did remain faithful to its nineteenth-century roots, it was most often focused on national rather than international concerns. Initially, only a very few of its advocates were able to transcend national boundaries and fuse social medicine with proletarian internationalism to forge a true health internationalism.

Third, social medicine now had to navigate in an expanding world of international health, including the Rockefeller Foundation and the League of Nations Health Organisation (LNHO), in which social medicine principles were partially accepted but proletarian health internationalism was eschewed.

Despite these challenges, variants of social medicine continued to develop in Germany and Austria, spread to other countries in Europe, and extend to the Soviet Union and several countries in Latin America.[71] Among the leading figures of the time were: Alfons Fischer of Germany; Jacques Parisot of France;

J. Alfred Ryle, Richard Titmuss, and Jerry Morris of Great Britain; Gustavo Pit-taluga of Spain; Nikolai Semashko of the Soviet Union; Carlos Paz Soldán of Peru; and Salvador Allende of Chile.

In the United States, there were scattered initiatives but not much that could match work elsewhere. A few U.S. nurses and physician-scientists—most notably W. Horsley Gantt, later of Johns Hopkins—traveled to the Soviet Union in the mid-1920s, and courageously reported positively on social wel-fare and medical gains, yet failed to see the full scope of the broader social and political implications.[72] This relative intellectual barrenness was likely a consequence of the "Red Scare" beginning in early 1917, intensifying after the Russian Revolution, and continuing into the early 1920s, which put a pall over all progressive political activity in the United States. This anti-left pogrom, a disturbing precursor to Cold War McCarthyism, saw the blatant abridgement of free speech, vigilante and government attacks on militant unions and socialist organizations, and the hasty trial and summary jailing of left-wing leaders (most famously, anarchist openly lesbian doctor Marie Equi, "Big Bill" Haywood of the Wobblies, and Socialist leader Eugene V. Debs).[73] Raids against "Bolshevik" aliens led by U.S. attorney general A. Mitchell Palmer resulted in the 1919 deportation to Russia of 249 "dangerous radicals" (including anarchist Emma Goldman).[74] The consequences of the Red Scare were chilling: the disarray of left-wing organizations, the drastic decline in membership of those few that remained, the shift to the right of American labor and the expulsion of hardline union leaders, the exclusion of duly elected socialists from legislative bodies, the rise of xenophobia and violent racism, including lynchings (tolerated by both local authorities and the federal government), and a political climate of intimidation and conformity expressed in newly imposed teacher loyalty oaths and the purging of school textbooks espousing "un-American" points of view.[75] In this environment, would-be American contributors to social medicine of the Virchovian style mostly stayed nervously and quietly under cover.

During the 1920s and 1930s, only a few people might be considered homegrown proponents of social medicine in the United States, and they offered their contributions most discreetly.[76] U.S. Public Health Service statistician-epidemiologist Edgar Sydenstricker spearheaded a series of stud-ies on the severe impact of economic deprivation, poor working conditions, environmental hazards, and limited access to health services upon morbid-ity and mortality of laborers and the poor, continuing this work into the Depression as the Milbank Memorial Fund's research director.[77] Public health leader C.-E.A.Winslow's work focused primarily on communicable diseases, housing, and public health administration, but he also came to share some of Sydenstricker's socioeconomic interests.[78] Michael M. Davis, a pioneering health services researcher, showed sympathy for the health problems of immigrants and contributed to discussions of national health insurance and the public provision of health services.[79] Yet while these researchers all expressed interest in social, environmental, and economic determinants of health and in class-based disparities, none of them explicitly championed "social medicine" or drew attention to its crucial political implications. Ultimately, the resurgence of social medicine in the United States would be tied to the rise of health internationalism.

Enabling this internationalist influence were profound changes in the U.S. political climate from the early 1930s through the mid-1940s. Despite the viciousness of the Red Scare of prior decades, the Great Depression led to a rebirth of radical labor activism and considerable pressure on U.S. president Franklin D. Roosevelt's (FDR) administration to create a "New Deal" for Americans in the form of an incipient welfare state. The unleashing of a "Red Decade" also corresponded to international political affairs and the domestic response to them: Hitler's ascendance to power in 1933 and the rise of European fascism, the U.S. diplomatic recognition of the Soviet Union the same year, FDR's "Good Neighbor" policy toward Latin America, the Spanish Civil War (during which, as we will see in chapter 4, the antifascist cause garnered wide support from the public if not the U.S. government), and the World War II alliance of Britain, the United States, and the Soviet Union.

Building upon these Red Decade factors, it would take three contemporary Europeans—all of them fascinated by the Soviet Union, deeply troubled by the rise of fascism and the brutality of the Spanish Civil War, and linked in some way to the United States—to go beyond dispassionate social analysis, articulate a broad progressive vision, and resurrect the political-economic roots of social medicine, now in an explicitly internationalist context. These pivotal figures were Ludwik Rajchman, Andrija Stampar, and Henry Sigerist; each represented a different type of health internationalism. Rajchman, a Pole, was an institutional internationalist who tried to use his role as head of the LNHO to promote health internationalism under the auspices of the new agency he led from 1921 to 1939. Stampar, a Croatian, was an accidental internationalist who was deeply committed to social medicine in his own national context but was forced to move to the international arena when the ethnic and fascist politics of Yugoslavia pushed him into political exile. Sigerist, a Swiss with strong French and German roots, was a cosmopolitan internationalist who used his worldwide academic fame to win a post at the Johns Hopkins University. There he became a conduit for European social medicine and the charismatic teacher of health internationalism, shaping a generation of American physicians and public health leaders.

Ludwik Rajchman, who became head of the Geneva-based LNHO in late 1921 and tried to use his post as an institutional base for social medicine and health internationalism, would ultimately find himself hemmed in by political opposition. The LNHO began as an Epidemic Commission under Rajchman's leadership (he was a French- and English-trained bacteriologist), to deal with a terrifying typhus epidemic then ravaging Russia and Eastern Europe.[80] When Rajchman transformed the commission into the "permanent" LNHO, he and his staff set an ambitious agenda that included not only infectious disease control but also a broad range of public health issues. Because of the United States' swing to the right and concurrent isolationism, it declined to join the League of Nations. Nonetheless, various Americans took jobs as high-placed administrative staff members in the LNHO, where they became familiar with Rajchman's social medicine inclinations and left-wing political proclivities. Several leading U.S. health experts, including Winslow and Sydenstricker, also worked with Rajchman as advisors or consultants.

Despite the formal absence of the United States in the League, it was a U.S. institution—the Rockefeller Foundation (RF)—that financially sustained much of the LNHO's work. The RF itself was divided between those who focused on top-down campaigns against specific pathogens or vectors, led by aggressive and often arrogant medical personnel, and those who favored a more integrated approach to public health with bidirectional communication and learning.[81] It was the latter group in the RF who supported Rajchman, primarily because he set an agenda for the LNHO that was highly compatible with the foundation's international health priorities—to institutionalize the field, create a transnational network of public health professionals, extend epidemiological surveillance worldwide, and set international standards for drugs, vaccines, and other modern biological products. There were also some in the RF, such as Selskar Gunn and John Grant, who understood and supported Rajchman's social medicine interests.[82] In any case, between 1922 and 1934 the RF contributed a considerable portion of the LNHO operating budget, by 1933 paying for twenty-five of fifty-three full-time staff.[83]

Using Rockefeller resources to build the LNHO in the direction of the RF's overt international public health objectives, Rajchman also carefully and gradually increased the LNHO's attention to social medicine. He appointed well-known Italian socialists to the LNHO's Malaria Commission, created special commissions on maternal welfare and child health, and worked with the

International Labour Office on industrial diseases, workers' compensation, and other progressive issues.[84]

In the 1930s, Rajchman's inclination toward social medicine and health internationalism became more public, influenced by the worldwide economic depression and the social and political disruptions that followed. This shift was signaled by studies on the health effects of inadequate nutrition, poor housing, and the economic depression. He also invested great effort in the study of "rural hygiene," as the overwhelming health needs of the rural poor both in Europe and other parts of the world came into sharp focus. At a 1937 LNHO rural hygiene conference in Bandoeng, Indonesia, participants included representatives from many colonial states in various stages of revolution, anticolonial rebellion, and independent national development. At this meeting there were open references to "rural reconstruction" and "land reform," emphasis on honoring indigenous languages and cultures, and sensitivity to assuring the population's "free will" in adopting plans for "betterment"—all themes central to Comintern-supported independence movements such as those in India and China, where Rajchman worked on special assignment from mid-1933 to mid-1934.[85]

Japanese protests over the League's assistance to China forced Rajchman out of China and back to his position as head of LNHO. But he was outspoken about Japanese military aggression, and this drew sharp criticism not only from the Japanese government but also from nervous French and British diplomats. With the rapid advance of European fascism in the 1930s, Rajchman was labeled by some as "a crypto-Communist," "a friend of the Comintern," and "Jewish-Masonic . . . of the Second and Third Internationals." There was some truth to all of these labels in the sense that Rajchman clearly sympathized with the Marxist Left, although he stopped short of being a Communist Party member.[86] After Italy's annexation of Ethiopia in 1936 and during the Spanish Civil War—when the Italian Fascists and German Nazis lent military aid to Franco's forces—Rajchman's sympathies were unmistakably with the Republican side, while the League sputtered, capitulated to the right, or allowed itself to become captive to foreign policy priorities in support of Munich appeasement.[87] Rajchman was compelled to resign in 1939, his elimination part of a general purge of suspected left-wing elements in the League's secretariat. Yet he continued to inspire many Americans, including the members of the American-Soviet Medical Society, and even traveled in high circles in the United States during the early 1940s, when it was easiest to support publicly the Soviet Union as the U.S.'s military ally.[88] The limitations of health internationalism within official institutional circles were clear, though others would try related efforts again in subsequent decades.

The next figure, Andrija Stampar, we have labeled an accidental internationalist. He grew up in Croatia with strongly socialist inclinations and studied social medicine with ardent SPD member Ludwig Teleky as a medical student in Vienna. At the end of World War I Stampar was appointed head of the Department of Hygiene and Social Medicine in the newly founded Ministry of Public Health in the Kingdom of Serbs, Croats, and Slovenes ("Yugoslavia").[89] Explicitly drawing inspiration from Engels and from the wave of social revolutions taking place after World War I, he strongly advocated "medico-political measures" to redirect resources from "the few [who] profit by this economy" to the "thousands and thousands of human beings [who] are decaying."[90] Already, he argued, "the struggle of the proletariat against capital has brought about great advances in the field of public health . . . But this struggle is far from ended."[91]

Notwithstanding these views, and like Rajchman, Stampar established a good working relationship with the RF, serving as a consultant on public health education and in 1926 receiving a major grant to found a new public health school in Zagreb.[92] Stampar had already been creating a network of epidemiological research centers, antivenereal and antituberculosis dispensaries, maternal and child care centers, and, with the support of the Croatian Peasant Party, rural health stations in the countryside where public health workers engaged in "social pedagogy" and became "teachers of the people" rather than "mere" physicians.[93] He now connected these units with the curriculum of the Zagreb school of public health, using them as field sites for public health education and creating a "Peasants' University" on campus where rural villagers could study health issues in specially designed seminars.[94]

But by 1931 the ethnic politics of Yugoslavia came to a boil and fascism took over. Stampar was forced out of his academic and administrative posts.[95] On Rajchman's invitation, he left for the LNHO in Geneva, where he was put to work investigating public health efforts across Europe. Stampar also visited the United States in late 1931 at the behest of the RF's International Health Division. In part, the RF was attempting to preserve the career of one of its major grantees of the 1920s, but, more importantly, it was very proud of Stampar's educational and service accomplishments and wanted to present them to U.S. public health educators and practitioners as tangible and replicable models.

Later in the 1930s Stampar spent considerable time in China on special missions for the LNHO while also traveling in the company of the RF's John Grant.[96] There, amid China's revolutionary turmoil, Stampar viewed health problems through the dual lenses of social medicine and health internationalism. In 1936, Stampar's detailed official LNHO report[97] stated:

After working nearly three years in China, I am especially impressed by one fact. Successful health work is not possible where the standard of living falls below the level of tolerable existence. . . . It follows that the best health programme is to raise the standard of living of the people and to increase their resources . . . Of perhaps even greater importance is the removal of social grievances, such as the sense of exploitation by the landlord.[98]

In conversation, Stampar was even more candid about where his political allegiances lay: "You must know . . . where my sympathies lie in China, not with the rulers but with the oppressed."[99] Thus Stampar, who had embraced social medicine and proletarian internationalism in the European context as a young man and who had become committed to the plight of Yugoslavia's peasants as a public health professional, now, in a distant international setting, focused on the morally unjust and politically unacceptable health deficits of the downtrodden, exploited, and disempowered peasants of China. He had become an explicit health internationalist by the accidents of his career, an identity strongly reinforced during a visit to the Soviet Union in the summer of 1936 after which he gave the impression of being a "confirmed world revolutionist."[100] Stampar relayed his understanding and experience in social medicine and health internationalism during a second, longer RF-funded visit to the United States in 1938 that took him to such major sites of public health and preventive medicine education as Harvard, Columbia, Johns Hopkins, Vanderbilt, Tulane, University of California, Berkeley, and Stanford.[101] This visit was a carefully orchestrated and widely advertised tour overseen by the RF's influential director of medical sciences Alan Gregg, and included named lectureships, extensive newspaper coverage, articles in leading medical and public health journals, and even a visit with officials of the American Medical Association (AMA). The RF and his local hosts held up Stampar as an exemplary public health leader who was expert in rural hygiene worldwide and especially sensitive to the centrality of socioeconomic improvement for overall public health advancement. Ardent admirer Henry Sigerist, with whom Stampar spent time at Johns Hopkins during his tour, proudly broadcast his Croatian comrade's social medicine insights and heroic achievements in Yugoslavia and China to what had become Sigerist's own large and admiring American following.[102]

We turn, finally, to Sigerist, a cosmopolitan internationalist who in the interwar period was widely regarded as the world's leading medical historian.[103] In 1925, at the precocious age of thirty-four, he became director of the University of Leipzig's pioneering Institute of the History of Medicine, and in

1932, with considerable help from Alan Gregg and the RF, he was recruited as director of the Johns Hopkins Institute of the History of Medicine, recently created on the Leipzig model. From 1932 to 1947, Sigerist turned the Hopkins Institute into the leading center for medical history in North America and into a pioneering outpost for exploring the social aspects of medicine. He transferred his own wide-ranging research (conducted in fourteen languages) and nurtured American medical history efforts already underway.

Sigerist also played an important public role. Welcomed as a learned and urbane scholar, he enjoyed celebrity status at medical society meetings, before civic associations, in colleges and universities, and at intellectual forums and student conventions. He was regularly called upon by philanthropic foundations, public agencies, labor unions, and the media, not only to provide historical perspective but also to interpret contemporary political and medical events. Sigerist thus served as a major spokesperson on such pressing national issues as universal health insurance and was much sought after as a popular lecturer and radio commentator. He published articles in mass circulation magazines (even appearing on the cover of *Time* magazine), as well as in progressive and left-wing reviews such as *Atlantic Monthly, PM, Science and Society,* and *New Masses.*

Most important, Sigerist called Americans' attention to European social medicine and progressive accomplishments in Soviet medicine and public health. In two of his books, *Man and Medicine* (1931) and *The Great Doctors* (1932), he presented the achievements of Virchow, Pettenkofer, and the social hygiene movement. Then, starting in 1933, he began directing his attention to recent developments in the Soviet Union, drawn to this study by intellectual curiosity but also because of worrisome trends in Europe, most disturbingly the rise of fascism and Nazism.

In the summer of 1935, Sigerist made his first visit to the Soviet Union and returned to the United States convinced that he had witnessed a new era in medicine and the beginnings of a new civilization. With generous RF support, he launched new courses on the "sociological aspects" of medicine, training the early cohorts of U.S. health internationalists. With his characteristic conviction that one must not only understand the social dimensions of medicine and their history but work actively to usher in the future, he instructed students on the social distribution of illness, trends in socializing medical costs, and historical tendencies to expand public health services. He also included a unit on developments in Russia, "from Zemstvo to Soviet medicine," which was particularly detailed because Sigerist was actively preparing his next book, *Socialized Medicine in the Soviet Union.*

In these years, Sigerist also threw himself into antifascist campaigns, major organizing and fund-raising efforts for groups defending Spanish democracy and providing direct medical aid to them, and, of course, strong advocacy for the Soviet Union and its medical and public health advances. When *Socialized Medicine in the Soviet Union* was published in 1937, it bore a striking red cover, with a caduceus and hammer-and-sickle printed side-by-side. The book begins with a primer on Marxian socialism, a history of the Bolshevik revolution, and a dedication to "The Young Medical Workers in Whose Hands Lies the Future of Medicine." In the core of the book, Sigerist portrays the radically transformed health system of the Soviet Union as the final stage in the long evolution of health systems. Whereas some Soviet champions had become disillusioned, dozens of enthusiastic local and national groups in the United States invited Sigerist to talk about Soviet medicine. He became the darling of left-wing intellectuals and the idol of medical student and young professional radicals. He was identified as a spokesperson for the Soviet Union, socialized medicine and, of course, for militant health internationalism.

But Sigerist now suffered from both fame and notoriety. As much as he was admired and lionized by some, he was hated by others. He became the target of angry Johns Hopkins alumni, organized medical groups, and red-baiting journalists who linked him to a vast, subversive, pro-Stalinist conspiracy. A former president of the AMA described him as a "foreign communist who [is trying] to impose the Russian system on America." Further, as chapter 5 will discuss, the U.S. Civil Service Commission declared Sigerist unfit for public service. But his influence on the students he taught, the readers he enlightened, and the audiences he enthralled was extraordinary. As one of his former students put it, "[Sigerist] turned on sympathetic students like so many light switches. They speeded up in his presence and came to share the thrill of his ideas and his vision."[104] Many Americans understood for the first time how social medicine and proletarian internationalism were joined in a new health internationalism. But Johns Hopkins officials were far from thrilled and tried to silence him, in part by burdening him with extra administrative work that drained his energy and seriously compromised his physical health. Sigerist dreamed of escape, and in 1947 he emigrated again, this time back to Europe for the last decade of his life. Just as Sigerist was leaving the United States, the rising Cold War in the late 1940s became a monumental obstacle to be overcome by the next generation of internationalists.

But before departing, Sigerist left his legacy, as did Rajchman and Stampar. There was now a new generation of Americans who had been shaped domestically in the 1930s by resurgent labor and left-wing movements, and internationally by antifascist struggles in Spain, and by the U.S.-Soviet wartime alliance, generating an eagerness to promote a positive assessment of Soviet medical and public health achievements. These U.S. health internationalists, whom we will meet in the coming chapters, were ready: to offer their assistance to those political forces demanding social justice, human rights, and the end of oppression; to address health needs and express solidarity with local communities; and to focus intently on the social and economic underpinnings of health. Despite the lingering legacy of the post–World War I Red Scare, Rajchman, Stampar, and particularly Sigerist spurred Americans who came of age in America's Red Decade to be bolder. John Kingsbury, the subject of the next chapter, helped lead the way with his provocative advocacy of "Red Medicine."

## Notes

1. William Coleman, *Death Is a Social Disease: Public Health and Political Economy in Early Industrial France* (Madison: University of Wisconsin Press, 1982); Nancy Krieger, "The Making of Public Health Data: Paradigms, Politics, and Policy," *Journal of Public Health Policy* 13(4) (1992): 412–427.
2. Anne-Emanuelle Birn, "*Historicising, Politicising, and 'Futurising'*—Closing the Gap in a Generation: Health Equity through Action on the Social Determinants of Health," in *Social Determinants of Health: Assessing Theory, Policy and Practice*, ed. Sanjoy Battacharya, Sharon Messenger, and Caroline Overy (Hyderabad: Orient Blackswan, 2010), 85–90; Christopher Hamlin, *Public Health and Social Justice in the Age of Chadwick: Britain, 1800–1854* (Cambridge: Cambridge University Press, 1998).
3. Tristram Hunt, *Marx's General: The Revolutionary Life of Friedrich Engels* (New York: Henry Holt, 2009), 75–112; Howard Waitzkin, *The Second Sickness: Contradictions of Capitalist Health Care* (New York: Free Press, 1982), 66–71.
4. Birn, "*Historicising, Politicising, and 'Futurising,'*" 93–95; Howard Waitzkin, "One and a Half Centuries of Forgetting and Rediscovering: Virchow's Lasting Contributions to Social Medicine," *Social Medicine* 1 (2006): 5–10; Theodore M. Brown and Elizabeth Fee, "Rudolf Carl Virchow: Medical Scientist, Social Reformer, Role Model," *American Journal of Public Health* 96 (2006): 2104–2105.
5. Russell Viner, "Abraham Jacobi and German Medical Radicalism in Antebellum New York," *Bulletin of the History of Medicine* 72 (1998): 434–463.
6. George Rosen, "What Is Social Medicine?" *Bulletin of the History of Medicine* 21 (1947): 702–704.
7. George Rosen, *From Medical Police to Social Medicine* (New York: Science History Publications. 1974), 92; Max von Pettenkofer, "The Value of Health to a City. Two Lectures, Delivered in 1873, by Max von Pettenkofer, Translated from the German, with an Introduction, by Henry E. Sigerist," *Bulletin of the History of Medicine* 10 (1941): 473–503, 593–613.
8. Paul Weindling, *Health, Race and German Politics between National Unification and Nazism, 1870–1945* (Cambridge: Cambridge University Press, 1989), 158, 215–221.
9. Paul Weindling, *Health, Race and German Politics;* Andreas Wulf, *Der Sozialmediziner Ludwig Teleky (1872–1957) und die Entwicklung der Gewerbehygiene zur Arbeitsmedizin* (Frankfurt am Main: Mabuse-Verlag, 2001).

10. V. M. Florinskii, *Usovershenstvovanie i Vyrozhdenie Chelovecheskogo Roda* (St. Petersburg, 1866).

11. David Barnes, *The Making of a Social Disease: Tuberculosis in Nineteenth-Century France* (Berkeley and Los Angeles: University of California Press, 1995); Lion Murard and Patrick Zylberman, *L'Hygiène dans la République: La santé publique en France, ou l'utopie contrariée, 1870–1918* (Paris: Fayard, 1996).

12. Peter Flora and Arnold J. Heidenheimer, eds., *The Development of Welfare States in Europe and America* (New Brunswick, NJ: Transaction Publishers, 1981); Seth Koven and Sonya Michel, eds., *Mothers of a New World: Maternalist Politics and the Origins of Welfare States* (New York: Routledge, 1993).

13. George Rosen, *A History of Public Health* (Baltimore: Johns Hopkins University Press, 1993), 244–247, 396–400; Hamlin, *Public Health and Social Justice.*

14. Nancy Krieger and Anne-Emanuelle Birn, "A Vision of Social Justice as the Foundation of Public Health: Commemorating 150 Years of the Spirit of 1848," *American Journal of Public Health* 88 (1998): 1603–1606.

15. Theodore M. Brown, "James Peter Warbasse," *American Journal of Public Health* 86 (1996): 109–110.

16. James Peter Warbasse, "Conserving Health Versus Exploiting Disease," *Medical Review of Reviews* 23 (1917): 172–178.

17. Walter J. Lear, "Health Left," in *Encyclopedia of the American Left,* ed. Mari Jo Buhle, Paul Buhle, and Dan Georgakas (New York: Garland, 1990), 301–306.

18. Richard Meckel, *Save the Babies: American Public Health Reform and the Prevention of Infant Mortality, 1850–1929* (Baltimore: Johns Hopkins University Press, 1990), 85.

19. Regina Morantz-Sanchez, "Sara Josephine Baker," *American National Biography* 2 (New York: Oxford University Press, 1999), 32–34.

20. Meckel, *Save the Babies,* 144, 176–177, 182–184.

21. Howard Waitzkin et al., "Social Medicine Then and Now: Lessons from Latin America," *American Journal of Public Health* 91(10) (2001): 1592–1601.

22. Jaime Breilh, *Eugenio Espejo: La Otra Memoria (Nueva Lectura de la Historia de las Ideas Científicas)* (Cuenca, Ecuador: Universidad de Cuenca, 2001).

23. S. Josephine Baker, *Child Hygiene* (New York: Harper & Brothers, 1925), 78.

24. For two useful general works, see Eric J. Hobsbawm, *The Age of Revolution: Europe 1789–1848* (London: Weidenfeld & Nicolson, 1962), and Mike Rapport, *1848, Year of Revolution* (New York: Basic Books, 2008).

25. Elizabeth Eisenstein, *The First Professional Revolutionist: Filippo Michele Buonarroti* (Cambridge, MA: Harvard University Press, 1959).

26. R. B. Rose, *Gracchus Babeuf: The First Revolutionary Communist* (Stanford: Stanford University Press, 1978).

27. James H. Billington, *Fire in the Minds of Men: Origins of the Revolutionary Faith* (New York: Basic Books, 1980), 91–93, 173–175.

28. Billington, Fire in the Minds of Men, 173.

29. Billington, *Fire in the Minds of Men,* passim; Hunt, *Marx's General,* passim.

30. Karl Marx and Frederick Engels, *The Communist Manifesto: A Modern Edition with an Introduction by Eric Hobsbawm* (London: Verso, 1998), 51, 58, 77.

31. Krieger and Birn, "A Vision of Social Justice."

32. Eric J. Hobsbawm, *The Age of Capital: 1848–1875* (New York: Charles Scribner's Sons, 1975), 14, 17, 24; Rapport, *1848, Year of Revolution;* Billington, *Fire in the Minds of Men,* 279–282; Hunt, *Marx's General,* 159–162, 164, 172–177.

33. Hobsbawm, *Age of Capital,* 109.
34. Jacques Freymond and Miklos Molnar, "The Rise and Fall of the First International," in *The Revolutionary Internationals, 1864–1943,* ed. Milorad M. Drachkovitch (Stanford: Stanford University Press, 1966), 3–35.
35. The two major books on the International in the United States are Samuel Bernstein, *The First International in America* (New York: Augustus M. Kelley, 1962), and Timothy Messer-Kruse, *The Yankee International: Marxism and the American Reform Tradition, 1848–1876* (Chapel Hill: University of North Carolina Press, 1998). For Sorge, see Philip S. Foner, "Friedrich Adolph Sorge: 'Father of Modern Socialism in America,'" in *Labor Movement in the United States: A History of the American Working Class from Colonial Times to 1890,* ed. Philip S. Foner and Brewster Chamberlin (Westport, CT: Greenwood Press, 1977), 3–41.
36. Julius Braunthal, *History of the International,* vol. 1 (New York: Frederick A. Praeger, 1967), 124; Hobsbawm, *Age of Capital,* 114, 156.
37. Messer-Kruse, The Yankee International, 106.
38. Freymond and Molnar, "The Rise and Fall of the First International," 21–22.
39. James Joll, *The Second International 1889–1914* (London: Weidenfeld and Nicolson, 1955), 6.
40. Braunthal, *History of the International,* vol. 1, 195ff.
41. Joll, *The Second International,* 49.
42. Braunthal, *History of the International,* vol. 1, 245.
43. Gerhart Niemeyer, "The Second International: 1889–1914," in *The Revolutionary Internationals,* ed. Drachkovitch, 117.
44. Eric J. Hobsbawm, *The Age of Empire: 1875–1914* (New York: Pantheon, 1987), 129.
45. Norma Fain Pratt, *Morris Hillquit: A Political History of an American Jewish Socialist* (Westport, CT: Greenwood Press, 1979).
46. Braunthal, *History of the International,* vol. 1, 361.
47. Hobsbawm, *The Age of Empire,* 134.
48. Billington, *Fire in the Minds of Men,* 378–379.
49. Alice Wexler, *Emma Goldman in America* (Boston: Beacon Press, 1984), 135. For an example of the expression of American sympathy for the anarcho-syndicalists, see Victor Robinson's *Comrade Kropotkin* (New York: The Altrurians, 1908).
50. Billington, *Fire in the Minds of Men,* 424; Joll, *The Second International,* 127.
51. Joll, *The Second International,* 181.
52. Eugene V. Debs, "When I Shall Fight," *Appeal to Reason,* September 11, 1915, in Scrapbook X, p. 4, Tamiment Library Scrapbook Collections, Series II, Eugene V. Debs Scrapbooks, TAM.262 Tamiment Library, New York University.
53. Joll, *The Second International,* 183.
54. "Invitation to the First Congress of the Communist International," in *The Communist International, 1919–1943, Documents,* vol. 1, ed. Jane Degras (London: Frank Cass, 1971), 1–5.
55. Milorad M. Drachkovitch and Branko Lazitch, "The Communist International," in *The Revolutionary Internationals,* ed. Drachkovitch, 162.
56. Formed in 1905 by socialists, anarchists, and radical trade unionists opposed to the moderate domestic strategies and international policies of the American Federation of Labor and committed instead to militant strike action and worker solidarity. See Paul Buhle, *Marxism in the USA: From 1870 to the Present Day* (London: Verso, 1987); Theodore Draper, *The Roots of American Communism* (New York: Viking Press, 1957); Bryan D. Palmer, *James Cannon and the Origins of the American*

*Revolutionary Left* (Urbana: University of Illinois Press, 2007); Melvyn Dubofsky, *We Shall Be All: A History of the Industrial Workers of the World* (New York: Quadrangle/New York Times Book Co., 1969).

57. John Reed, *Insurgent Mexico* (New York: D. Appleton and Co., 1914); Granville Hicks, *John Reed, The Making of a Revolutionary* (New York: Macmillan, 1936), ch. 7; Diana K. Christopulos, *"American Radicals and the Mexican Revolution: 1900–1925"* (PhD diss. State University of New York at Binghamton, 1980).

58. Draper, *The Roots of American Communism*, ch. 7, 10, and 11; Granville Hicks, *John Reed*, ch. 14–18, 20, and 21.

59. Eric Hobsbawm, *The Age of Extremes: A History of the World, 1914–1991* (New York: Pantheon, 1994), 56; James W. Hulse, *The Forming of the Communist International* (Stanford: Stanford University Press, 1964).

60. Edward Hallett Carr, *The Bolshevik Revolution, 1917–1923*, vol. 3 (London: Macmillan, 1953); Reiner Tosstorff, *Profintern: Die Rote Gewerkschaftsinternationale 1920–1937* (Paderborn, 2004).

61. Hobsbawn, *The Age of Extremes*, 70; Daniela Spenser, *Stumbling Its Way through Mexico: The Early Years of the Communist International* (Tuscaloosa: The University of Alabama Press, 2011).

62. Braunthal, *History of the International*, vol. 2, 535.

63. Reiner Tosstorff, "The International Trade-Union Movement and the Founding of the International Labour Organization," *International Review of Social History* 50 (2005): 399–433; Alice S. Cheyney, ed., *The International Labor Organization*, vol. 166 of *The Annals of the American Academy of Political and Social Sciences* (Philadelphia, 1933).

64. Drachkovitch and Lazitch, "The Communist International," 174, 180.

65. Li Jui, *The Early Revolutionary Activities of Comrade Mao Tse-tung* (White Plains, NY: M. E. Sharpe, 1977); Michael Lynch, *Mao* (London: Routledge, 2004); Philip Short, *Mao* (New York: Henry Holt and Company, 1999); Ross Terrill, *Mao, A Biography* (New York: Harper & Row, 1980).

66. Gandhi, *The Collected Works of Mahatma Gandhi*, vol. 37 (Ahmedabad: Ministry of Information and Broadcasting, Government of India, 1970), 380.

67. Weindling, *Health, Race and German Politics*, 184–186, 223–226.

68. Roberto Berro, "La Medicina Social de la Infancia," *Boletín del Instituto Internacional Americano de Protección a la Infancia* 9 (1936): 594–609.

69. Dorothy Porter and Roy Porter, "What Was Social Medicine? An Historiographical Essay," *Journal of Historical Sociology* 1 (1988): 90–106.

70. Mark Adams, "Eugenics as Social Medicine in Revolutionary Russia: Prophets, Patrons, and the Dialectics of Discipline-Building," in *Health and Society in Revolutionary Russia*, ed. Susan Solomon and John F. Hutchinson (Bloomington: Indiana University Press, 1990), 200–223; Gunnar Broberg and Nils Roll-Hansen, eds., *Eugenics and the Welfare State: Sterilization Policy in Norway, Sweden, Denmark, and Finland* (Lansing: Michigan State University Press, 1997); Mark B. Adams, ed., *The Wellborn Science: Eugenics in Germany, France, Brazil, and Russia* (New York: Oxford University Press, 1990); Alexandra Minna Stern, *Eugenic Nation: Faults and Frontiers of Better Breeding in Modern America* (Berkeley and Los Angeles: University of California Press, 2005); Alison Bashford and Philippa Levine, eds., *The Oxford Handbook of the History of Eugenics* (Oxford: Oxford University Press, 2010).

71. Weindling, *Health, Race, and German Politics*, 226, 334–335, 337, 347–348, 378, 482; Iris Borowy, "In the Shadow of Grotjahn: German Social Hygienists in the International

Health Scene," in *Of Medicine and Men: Biographies and Ideas in European Social Medicine Between the World Wars,* ed. Iris Borowy and Anne Hardy (Frankfurt am Main: Peter Lang, 2008), 145–172; Esteban Rodríguez-Ocaña and Iris Borowy, "Gustavo Pittaluga: Science as a Weapon for Social Reform in a Time of Crisis," in *Of Medicine and Men,* ed. Borowy and Hardy, 173–196: Lion Murard and Patrick Zylberman, "French Social Medicine on the International Public Health Map in the 1930s," in *The Politics of the Healthy Life: An International Perspective,* ed. Esteban Rodríguez-Ocaña (Sheffield: European Association for the History of Medicine and Health Publications, 2002), 197–218; Etienne Thévenin, *Jacques Parisot (1882–1967): Un createur de l'action sanitaire et social* (Nancy: Presses Universitaires de Nancy, 2002); Lion Murard, "Social Medicine in the Interwar Years: The Case of Jacques Parisot (1882–1967)," *Medicina Nei Secoli* 20 (2008): 871–890; Marcos Cueto, "Social Medicine in the Andes, 1920–1950," in *The Politics of the Healthy Life,* ed. Rodríguez-Ocaña, 181–196; Cueto, "Social Medicine and 'Leprosy' in the Peruvian Amazon," *The Americas* 61 (2004): 55–80; Susan Gross Solomon, "Social Hygiene in Soviet Medical Education, 1922-30," *Journal of the History of Medicine and Allied Sciences* 45 (1990): 607–643; Solomon, "Social Hygiene and Soviet Public Health, 1921–1930," in *Health and Society in Revolutionary Russia,* ed. Solomon and Hutchinson, 175–199; Patrick Zylberman, "Fewer Parallels than Antitheses: René Sand and Andrija Stampar on Social Medicine, 1919-1955," *Social History of Medicine* 17 (2004): 77–92; Waitzkin, *The Second Sickness,* 75–81; Howard Waitzkin, *Medicine and Public Health at the End of Empire* (Boulder: Paradigm Publishers, 2011), 16–24; René Sand, *The Advance to Social Medicine* (London and New York: Staples Press, 1952), passim.

72. See W. Horsley Gantt, "A Medical Review of Soviet Russia. Results of the First Five Year Plan," *Medical Review of Soviet Russia* 2 (1936): 19–22 and ch. 3, n. 11. Michael David-Fox, *Showcasing the Great Experiment: Cultural Diplomacy and Western Visitors to Soviet Union, 1921–1941* (New York: Oxford University Press, 2012).

73. Howard Zinn, *A People's History of the United States, 1492–Present,* rev. and updated ed. (New York: HarperCollins, 1995), 356–373; Nancy Krieger, "Queen of the Bolsheviks, The Hidden History of Dr. Marie Equi," *Radical America* 17(5) (1983): 55–73; James Weinstein, *The Decline of Socialism in America, 1912–1925* (New York: Monthly Review Press, 1967), 230–233.

74. Regin Schmidt, *Red Scare: FBI and the Origins of Anticommunism in the United States* (Copenhagen: University of Copenhagen, 2000); Dubofsky, *We Shall Be All,* ch. 15–18.

75. Draper, *The Roots of American Communism,* 202–208; David Montgomery, *The Fall of the House of Labor: The Workplace, the State, and American Labor Activism, 1865–1925* (Cambridge: Cambridge University Press, 1987), 393–394, 432–433, 437; Robert K. Murray, *Red Scare: A Study of National Hysteria, 1919–1920* (Minneapolis: University of Minnesota Press, 1955), 268, 281; Philip Dray, *At the Hands of Persons Unknown: The Lynching of Black America* (New York: Random House, 2002).

76. Sand, *The Advance to Social Medicine,* 544, 546–547.

77. Dorothy G. Wiehl, "Edgar Sydenstricker: A Memoir," in *The Challenge of Facts: Selected Public Health Papers of Edgar Sydenstricker,* ed. Richard V. Kasius (New York: Prodist, 1974), 3–17; Harry M. Marks, "Epidemiologists Explain Pellagra: Gender, Race, and Political Economy in the Work of Edgar Sydenstricker," *Journal of the History of Medicine and Allied Sciences* 58 (2003): 34–55.

78. Reginald M. Atwater, "C.-E.A. Winslow: An Appreciation of a Great Statesman," *American Journal of Public Health* 47 (1957): 1065–1070; Arthur J. Viseltear, "C.-E.A. Winslow: His Era and His Contribution to Medical Care," in *Healing and History:*

*Essays for George Rosen*, ed. Charles E. Rosenberg (New York: Science History Pub-
lications, 1979), 205–228; Barbara Bridgman Perkins, "Economic Organization of
Medicine and the Committee on the Costs of Medical Care," *American Journal of
Public Health* 88 (1998): 1721–1726.

79. George Rosen, "Michael M. Davis: Pioneer in Medical Care," *American Journal of
Public Health* 62 (1972): 321–323; Jerome Preston, "Michael M. Davis," *New England
Journal of Medicine* 282 (1970): 566–567; Michael M. Davis, *Immigrant Health and
the Community* (New York: Harper, 1921); Michael M. Davis, *Clinics, Hospitals and
Health Centers* (New York: Harper, 1927); Michael M. Davis and C. Rufus Rorem,
*Crisis in Hospital Finance and Other Studies in Hospital Economics* (Chicago: Uni-
versity of Chicago Press, 1932); Michael M. Davis, *Public Medical Services: A Survey
of Tax-Supported Medical Care in the United States* (Chicago: University of Chicago
Press, 1937); Nancy Krieger and Elizabeth Fee, "Measuring Social Inequalities in
Health in the United States: A Historical Review, 1900–1950," *International Journal
of Health Services* 26(3) (1996): 391–418.

80. Borowy, *Coming to Terms with World Health*, 49–67; Marta Balinska, "Assistance
and Not Mere Relief: The Epidemic Commission of the League of Nations, 1920–
1923," in *International Health Organisations and Movements, 1918–1939*, ed. Paul
Weindling (Cambridge: Cambridge University Press, 1995), 81–108; Marta Balinska, *For the Good of Humanity: Ludwik Rajchman Medical Statesman*, trans. from
French by Rebecca Howell and revised by the author (Budapest: Central European
University Press, 1998), 41–61.

81. John Farley, *To Cast Out Disease: A History of the International Health Division of
the Rockefeller Foundation (1913–1951)* (Oxford: Oxford University Press, 2004);
Steven Palmer, *Launching Global Health: The Caribbean Odyssey of the Rockefeller Foundation* (Ann Arbor: University of Michigan Press, 2010); Socrates
Litsios, "Selskar Gunn and China: The Rockefeller Foundation's 'Other' Approach
to Public Health," *Bulletin of the History of Medicine* 79 (2005): 295–318; for a
detailed case study of the Rockefeller Foundation's international health work in
Mexico, see Anne-Emanuelle Birn, *Marriage of Convenience: Rockefeller International Health and Revolutionary Mexico* (Rochester: University of Rochester
Press, 2006).

82. Litsios, "Selskar 'Mike' Gunn and Public Health Reform in Europe," in *Of Medicine
and Men*, 23–43; Socrates Litsios, "On the 'Hitherto Untried Process of Giving Doctors
Adequate Training' in Preventive Medicine and Public Health," *Social Medicine* 5
(2010): 205–217; Litsios, "The Rockefeller Foundation's Struggle to Correlate Its Existing Medical Program with Public Health Work in China," in *Uneasy Encounters: The
Politics of Medicine and Health in China 1900–1937*, ed. Iris Borowy (Frankfurt: Peter
Lang, 2009), 177–203.

83. Borowy, *Coming to Terms with World Health*, 142, notes that "almost fifty Americans" worked with the LNHO in various capacities during its eighteen-year history.

84. Borowy, *Coming to Terms with World Health;* Paul Weindling, "Social Medicine at
the League of Nations Health Organisation and the International Labour Office Compared," in *International Health Organisations and Movements*, 134–153.

85. Borowy, *Coming to Terms with World Health*, 273–360; Theodore M. Brown and
Elizabeth Fee, "The Bandoeng Conference of 1937: A Milestone in Health and Devel-
opment," *American Journal of Public Health* 98 (2008): 42–43; Balinska, For the
Good of Humanity, 81–102.

86. Balinksa, *For the Good of Humanity*, 101–104.

87. Balinska, *For the Good of Humanity*, 113–123; James Barros, *Betrayal from Within: Joseph Avenol, Secretary-General of the League of Nations, 1933–1940* (New Haven, CT: Yale University Press, 1969), 185–188.

88. Balinska, *For the Good of Humanity*, 141ff. For the American political climate newly warm to the Soviet Union, see Walter J. Lear, "Hot War Creation, Cold War Casualty: The American-Soviet Medical Society, 1943–1948," in *Making Medical History: The Life and Times of Henry E. Sigerist*, ed. Elizabeth Fee and Theodore M. Brown (Baltimore: Johns Hopkins University Press, 1997), 259–287.

89. Zylberman, "Fewer Parallels Than Antitheses"; Zeljko Dugac, "Andrija Stampar: Resolute Fighter for Health and Social Justice," in *Of Medicine and Men*, 73–101; Mirko Dražen Grmek, "Life and Achievements of Andrija Stampar, Fighter for the Promotion of Public Health," in *Serving the Cause of Public Health: Selected Papers of Andrija Stampar*, ed. Mirko Dražen Grmek (Zagreb: University of Zagreb, 1966), 13–51.

90. Stampar, "On Health Politics," in Grmek, 58–59.

91. Stampar, "On Social Therapy," in Grmek, 86.

92. Dugac, "Andrija Stampar," 77; Litsios, "Selskar 'Mike' Gunn," 30–31, 38.

93. Zylberman, "Fewer Parallels Than Antitheses," 84–85; Dugac, "Andrija Stampar," 77–78.

94. Ana Borovecki, Biserka Belicza, and Stjepan Oreskovic, "75th Anniversary of Andrija Stampar School of Public Health—What Can We Learn from Our Past for the Future?" *Croatian Medical Journal* 43 (2992): 371–373.

95. Dugac, "Andrija Stampar," 74, 78.

96. Grmek, 37–39; Dugac, 84–87.

97. *Quarterly Bulletin of the Health Organisation of the League of Nations* 5 (1936): 1090–1126. This report is reprinted as "Health and Social Conditions in China" in Grmek, 123–151; quotations are cited in the Grmek edition.

98. Quotation in Grmek, 149–150.

99. Stampar to Julius Tandler written in October 1935; see Dugac, 86–87.

100. Dugac, 87–88; Grmek, 39. See also Memo No. 58, August 28, 1936, Rockefeller Archive Center, Record Group 6 (Paris Field Office), Series 1.1, Box 29, Folder 345. Full quote is: "Spent a very pleasant afternoon with Stampar who has just returned 10 days ago from China via Russia. . . . He has come out of Russia firmly convinced that only such a revolution as that suffered by the Russians will ever obtain for the farmer and laborer in other parts of the world their just dues. Although S. was always inclined towards 'communism' the impression one now gets is that he is a confirmed world revolutionist. I got the feeling that even some of his warmest supporters and former collaborators stand somewhat in awe of the radical turn his enunciations have taken. However his enthusiasm is quite as contagious as ever."

101. Details of this tour come from Rockefeller Archive Center, Record Group 1.1, Series 710A, Folders 16, 17, 18, and 19.

102. Henry E. Sigerist, "Yugoslavia and the Eleventh International Congress of the History of Medicine: Andrija Stampar," in *Henry E. Sigerist on the Sociology of Medicine*, ed. Milton I. Roemer (New York: MD Publications, 1960), 111–117.

103. All biographical details that follow about Sigerist are taken from Fee and Brown, eds., *Making Medical History*.

104. Leslie A. Falk as quoted in Milton I. Roemer, Leslie A. Falk, and Theodore M. Brown, "Sociological Vision and Pedagogic Mission: Henry Sigerist's Medical Sociology," in *Making Medical History*, 325.

# Part II

# Generation Born in the 1870s–1910s

The chapters in this section reflect the experiences of U.S. health internationalists who were born around the turn of the twentieth century, when the world was transformed by the intensification of global capitalism, the imperialist scramble for raw materials, colonies, and markets in Asia, Africa, Latin America, and the Caribbean, and a new glorification of science and confidence in secular solutions for social problems. At the same time, the mobilization of the industrial working class, both nationally and internationally, involved contentious struggles for political power and demands for state protection in the context of a surging international socialist movement. The massive economically and politically driven migration of millions of people to centers of rapid industrialization and growth, especially to the Americas, and the beginning of the great African American migration northward, led to social disruption but also cultural creativity and political activism, inspiring widespread campaigns for urban reform.

The childhoods and early adulthoods of the subjects of these chapters were marked by World War I (the largest and most horrific armed conflict the world had ever seen), the Bolshevik revolution and the formation of the Soviet Union, the frightened reaction by traditional elites to these developments in the form of attempted counterrevolution, suppressive domestic political action, and a reactionary swing to the right. By the interwar period, there was another set of upheavals, including an unequal economic boom, the stirrings of nationalist and independence movements in China, India, and elsewhere, the emergence of fascism and Nazism in Europe, and the immiseration provoked by worldwide economic depression.

This larger environment, whose reality and immediacy were magnified by the proliferation of motion pictures, newsreels, and radio, significantly shaped the perceptions and values of this first generation of U.S. health internationalists. In the 1920s, many among these believed that the Soviet Union represented a new and better world, perhaps most notably through improved health, work, and social conditions, and that leaders like Mao Zedong and Gandhi would guide their people to liberation from the yoke of imperialism. In the 1930s, many saw the Depression as a crisis spelling the death knell of capitalism and thought that socialism would bring a better, fairer, and more rational future. Terrified by the rise of fascism and Nazism, they saw the USSR in a positive light, especially in its lead role supporting antifascist forces in the Spanish Civil War, as the only nation willing to stand up to Fascist aggression. They greeted World War II (even more destructive and horrific than World War I) and the eventual alliance of the United States, Great Britain, and the Soviet Union as just and necessary to defeat Hitler and the Axis powers, and looked to the postwar period with hope and expectations for a better world.

This generation was clearly passionate and idealistic; their experience also raises important questions. Did their zeal sometimes override the evidence before them? Few members of this generation reported on the many forms of brutality in Stalin's regime. Did they choose to deny it, see it but consider it an equivalent phase to the violence of Western industrialization, or view it as a necessary price to be paid for reaching a better future? Or did they project their Utopian wishes with such fervor that their reason and perceptions were clouded? And what about the Spanish Civil War? Many famous participants—British writer George Orwell, for example—witnessed power struggles among the Left in Spain, in which the Communists more than occasionally seemed to use manipulative and amoral tactics. Did American health leftists of this generation return from Spain similarly disillusioned or did their solidarity dwarf these concerns? And why did none seem prepared, based on the repressive politics and punitive tactics mounted domestically in the aftermath of the Bolshevik revolution, for the abuses of the Cold War and McCarthyism, which descended with such fury in the late 1940s and continued well into the 1950s?

# Chapter 3

# The Perils of Unconstrained Enthusiasm

## John Kingsbury, Soviet Public Health, and 1930s America

**Susan Gross Solomon**

In 1933, against the background of intense discussions of the costs, the availability, and the delivery of medical care in the United States[1] and the release of the final report of the Committee on the Costs of Medical Care,[2] Doubleday Doran—the largest publishing house in the English-speaking world—brought out a three-hundred-page book written by Sir Arthur Newsholme and John A. Kingsbury provocatively entitled *Red Medicine: Socialized Health in Soviet Russia*.[3] The book was based on a month-long, nine-thousand-mile fact-finding trip to Russia taken by the authors in 1932 at the behest of the Milbank Memorial Fund[4] to see how "the Soviets handle their public health problem."[5]

*Red Medicine* gave a broad reading of the new Soviet system of public health and medicine. The authors drew attention to the philosophic touchstones of the system: the commitment to universal access to free, high-quality health care paid for by communal funds; the stress on the role of preventive as well as curative medicine; and the assumption that social factors played a seminal role in health and disease. They described in considerable detail a range of institutions for care and after-care (sanatoria, crèches, units for consultation on sex and marriage, rest homes). And they underscored the involvement of government in the education and training of medical workers.[6]

Could the Soviet approach to the provision of health care get a hearing in early 1930s America? The challenge would be formidable. After all, private medicine was strongly entrenched; its defenders were well connected and vocal.[7] No less important, the Red Scare of 1919–1920, which presented Bolshevism as an imminent danger to the United States, was barely a decade old.[8] Yet in the aftermath of the First World War, American politics were particularly open to imported models and ideas, and "no one looking for the cutting edge of change in 1920s Europe could ignore the new Soviet experiment."[9]

### Situating Red Medicine

In the scholarly literature on American portrayals of Soviet health in the 1930s, Newsholme and Kingsbury's book has yet to find its rightful place—for understandable reasons.[10] The trip that produced *Red Medicine* was not the first venture by an American to Russia. In the 1920s, a wave of American "enthusiasts" in medicine and public health—the physiologist Horsley Gantt; the Harvard-based industrial hygienist Alice Hamilton; the leader of the Quaker relief effort in Russia, Anna Haines; the sex researcher-criminologist Alice Withrow Field; and the psychiatrist and later editor of the *Journal of Mental Health,* Frankwood Williams, to name but a few—went to Russia to see for themselves the fruits of the Bolshevik experiment in health care.[11]

Nor was *Red Medicine* the last important report on Soviet medicine published in the years preceding the Second World War. In 1937, Henry Sigerist, then director of the Johns Hopkins University Institute of the History of Medicine, published *Socialized Medicine in the Soviet Union* based on his travels to Russia in the summers of 1935 and 1936. Fueled by his conviction that the future of medical practice lay in state-financed, supervised, and organized medical services, the book became the touchstone for American supporters of national health insurance, socialized medicine, and the Soviet Union itself.[12] In 1944, Sigerist would be accused of belonging to Communist front organizations and would leave America for Switzerland three years later.

Newsholme and Kingsbury's venture to Russia deserves attention on several grounds. First, unlike the American pilgrims to the Soviet Union of the 1920s (who were at the margins of their professions, whether by virtue of their youth or the fledgling specialties in which they worked) or Henry Sigerist (who had only been in the United States since 1932, when he emigrated from Germany), the authors of *Red Medicine* were high-profile members of the public health establishment, accustomed to speaking to policymakers. The senior of the two men, Sir Arthur Newsholme (1857–1943), had been principal medical officer of the Local Government Board from 1908 to 1919, making him effectively the head of the English public health service. After retiring from the British civil service in 1917 and receiving a knighthood, Newsholme was recruited by Dr. William Welch to teach at the newly created Johns Hopkins School of Hygiene and Public Health, a position he held from 1919 until 1921.[13] In the decades that followed, Newsholme wrote and spoke extensively on public health and consulted intermittently for the Milbank Memorial Fund.[14]

It was the younger of the two, John Adams Kingsbury (1876–1956), executive secretary of the Milbank Memorial Fund from 1921 to 1935, who conceived and spearheaded the venture to Russia. Early on, Kingsbury developed a strong commitment to social justice and equity, his quest finding its first home in the Progressive movement of the early twentieth century. Chairman of the New York City Progressive Committee, he attended the Progressive convention in Chicago in 1912 where he discussed the importance of the principles and platform of the Progressive Party with its presidential nominee, Theodore Roosevelt.[15]

Kingsbury, who began his professional life as a primary school teacher and school administrator, brought to his work at the Milbank Fund an impressive track record in charity work and public service. From 1907 to 1918, he was, first, assistant secretary of the New York State Charities Association, then managing director of the New York Association for Improving the Condition of the Poor before becoming commissioner of public charities in New York City. During the First World War, he served with the Red Cross in France. After the armistice, Kingsbury became assistant director of civil affairs of the American Red Cross in France.[16] In 1920, he toured Serbia on behalf of the Serbian Child Welfare Association of America, a project underwritten by the Milbank Memorial Fund.[17]

During his tenure as its executive secretary, Kingsbury encouraged the Milbank Memorial Fund to become an important player in the discussions about the delivery of health care.[18] Kingsbury's work at the Milbank Memorial Fund broadened his contacts, political as well as scientific. During Franklin Delano Roosevelt's (FDR) term as New York senator, Kingsbury got to know well the man who would be president. The acquaintance endured: in letters written from the White House in the early 1930s, FDR addressed him as "Dear John."[19]

Second, in contrast both to the enthusiasts of the 1920s and to Sigerist who went to Russia on their own initiative, Newsholme and Kingsbury were mandated fact-finders, dispatched by the Milbank Memorial Fund to study the Russian health care system as one among a circle of foreign models that might be useful in addressing the problems of the American health care system. Their mandate to "find the facts" meant that Newsholme and Kingsbury had to consider both the advantages and the disadvantages of the Soviet system in relation to other models and approaches. Their approach contrasted with that of the pilgrims of the 1920s who saw the Soviet system as sui generis, and with that of Sigerist, who declared that although he knew the deficiencies of the Soviet system, he had decided against communicating them "because things change so rapidly in the Soviet Union."[20]

The authors of *Red Medicine* had experience exploring the relative merits of a variety of health care systems, both at home and abroad. Among Kingsbury's most important initiatives for the Milbank Memorial Fund were the urban, rural, and metropolitan health "demonstrations" (pilot projects) carried out in the mid-1920s in New York State, which were designed to show how public and private health activities could be coordinated.[21] In the late 1920s, Newsholme undertook for the Milbank Memorial Fund a fact-finding mission on the relation between public and private medicine in eighteen European countries; the results appeared in 1931 as a three-volume work, with a fourth volume devoted to summarizing the findings issued the following year.[22] Newsholme's 1931 study of the balance between public and private medicine in eighteen countries did not include Russia. In 1932, as opposition to compulsory health insurance was mounting within the Committee on the Costs of Medical Care, Kingsbury convinced the Milbank Fund, one of the eight philanthropies that underwrote the committee's work, to broaden the universe of European cases to include Russia on the grounds that the Soviet medical system might provide ideas relevant to the reform of American public health.[23]

*Red Medicine* was not the first exposure of American readers to health care systems that were publicly organized. In the late nineteenth and early twentieth century, Americans discussed the relative merits of both the German system of compulsory sickness insurance and the British system of sickness insurance.[24] But during the First World War, fearing "Prussianization," American physicians turned against health insurance of the German type; a few years later, likely influenced by diatribes against "medical socialism" in the *Journal of the American Medical Association*, American physicians became skeptical of the British scheme.[25]

Threaded through American discussions of publicly funded health care in the first three decades of the twentieth century were references to "socialized medicine," a term whose definition was contested.[26] Advocates referred to government provision of care;[27] critics pointed to government-directed administration of medical care.[28] In *Red Medicine*, Newsholme and Kingsbury described the Soviet public health system as a "fascinating experiment in socialized health," which featured government provision, funding, and administration of health care.[29]

### Presenting Soviet Public Health for American Consumption

How to present the Soviet system to an American audience of policymakers, health care reformers, and practicing physicians? The extensive correspondence between the authors, their patron, and the large community of interested

"Russia watchers," plus three heavily red-penciled drafts of the text of *Red Medicine,* leave no doubt that the authors were grappling with this challenge from the moment their trip was approved.[30] In deciding how to present Soviet health, two issues preoccupied the authors. The first related to the political and social context of Soviet public health. Could one separate the Soviet health care system from its social and political surround? At stake was the broader question of the transportability of public health models across national boundaries.

The second issue related to the interconnectedness of the Soviet public health system—its institutional framework, funding, administration, principles of delivery, and training of health care workers. Could some aspects of that system be disaggregated from the whole? To join the debate on health care costs in America, the authors of *Red Medicine* (and particularly the junior author) narrowed their presentation of the Soviet model. How would this narrowing affect the attractiveness of the Soviet model in the United States?

## The Relevance of Context

The initial plan was to make the Russian study into volume four of Newsholme's three-volume study of the public-private mix in medicine. But even before the authors set off, the opportunity to see Soviet health care up close modified the original plan. At Kingsbury's initiative the authors decided to examine Soviet medicine on its own terms; that is, to compare it against itself.

## Russia Compared Against Itself

Within weeks of its being announced, the projected trip of Kingsbury and Newsholme became something of a public event. Kingsbury received a flurry of suggested questions from knowledgeable "Russia watchers" in America: nongovernmental associations (the New York Association for Improving the Conditions of the Poor,[31] the American Social Hygiene Association[32]), independent bodies of inquiry (the Committee on the Costs of Medical Care[33]) and health administrators (Thomas Parran, commissioner of health for the state of New York).[34]

Without the constraints of having to tailor their inquiry to fit Newsholme's large comparative study, the authors projected an eighteen-chapter book on Russia: a substantial introductory chapter on the country, its population, the central and local government, its vital statistics, and socio-medical background, followed by chapters on the provision of services, measures to combat a variety of diseases, work-related injuries, and types of social deviance (alcoholism and prostitution). A division of labor was worked out: Newsholme would write the nonmedical chapters, Kingsbury the medical ones.

The authors described in detail many facilities they visited.[35] Site visits were interspersed with interviews with medical leaders and officials, including M. F. Vladimirsky, the Russian commissar of public health. Kingsbury's diary shows the authors favorably impressed: some facilities (for example, the tuberculosis hospitals and sanatoria) rivaled those in Britain or America; the absence of modern facilities and some supplies was offset by medical workers' enthusiasm and the commitment to preventive and curative health care.[36]

Treating Russia on its own terms allowed the inclusion of more nonmedical material than Newsholme had included in the profiles of the eighteen countries he surveyed in his previous study. The authors explained, "We have thought it wise to give a somewhat detailed account of social and economic life in Russia in order that its medicine of today may be seen in its natural setting."[37] Newsholme favored including more contextual material,[38] while Kingsbury was inclined to include less.[39]

The real issue was the nature of the nonmedical material. Kingsbury, who was more sympathetic to the Soviet experiment, favored looking at how far Russia had come, rather than at what remained to be done.[40] Newsholme, decidedly more critical, did not hesitate to expose Russia's "warts." Thus, praising the fact that Soviet employers bore the entire cost of social insurance for health, Newsholme listed the "deprived persons" excluded from those benefits: "former landlords, Bourgeoisie, nobles, Tsarist officials, Merchants, kulaks, and Tsarist army officers." He also noted that insurance benefits had not yet been extended to peasants, who "form the vast majority of the population."[41]

Kingsbury wanted fewer blemishes exposed: "The criticism I have . . . is that you lay a good deal of stress on warts which are not on the face at least of our 'subject' . . . we are concerned primarily with the medical problems and . . . cannot give adequate discussion of 'class hatred,' 'class government,' 'preference to the workers,' 'cruelty to the kulaks' unless we really enter into quite a detailed discussion of 'communism,' 'revolution,' and the class struggle generally. On some of these subjects . . . you and I would probably differ. So I wonder if it is necessary to go into the discussion . . . as fully as you do."[42]

Eventually, the authors agreed to delete points of interpretation on which they differed.[43] Before deciding to delete a particular point, the authors often deferred to authorities both Russian and American.[44] But Kingsbury set greatest store by the opinions of the famous British socialist and supporter of the Bolsheviks, Sidney Webb, who made interlinear notations on every chapter of *Red Medicine*.[45] Indeed, one version of the text carried the handwritten note: "Passages by Sidney Webb are underlined thus . . . Typist, do not underline

**Figure 3.1** Caricature of John A. Kingsbury by a Works Progress Administration official in 1936.

Library of Congress, Manuscript Division, John A. Kingsbury Papers, Group II, Box 49.

such passages in typing."[46] The relationship to Webb would turn out to be the authors' Achilles' heel.

### Russia and the United States Compared

In December 1932, the Committee on the Costs of Medical Care filed its final report recommending voluntary rather than compulsory health insurance.[47] When the American Medical Association (AMA) bristled at the prospect of voluntary insurance,[48] the authors of *Red Medicine,* bitterly disappointed, felt compelled to compare the American and Soviet health systems. The binary comparison appears in the book's final chapters, each written by one of the authors. Intriguingly, in the comparative chapters, there was something of a role reversal: it was Newsholme who bracketed out context and Kingsbury who factored it in.

In "The Characteristics of Medical Practice," Newsholme measured the Soviet and American health systems against the list of ten "maladjustments" in American health care cited in the final report of the Committee on the Costs of Medical Care.[49] He concluded that Soviet health care suffered less from the key maladjustments than did the United States! Though medical care was not available to the entire Soviet population, he admitted, "the Soviet service has the great merit that the direct payment of fees has ceased and with it . . . the burning problem of the relation between the private and public practice of medicine, which in capitalist countries is always with us."[50]

In "Concluding Observations," Kingsbury declared, "The position of the U.S.S.R. . . . is very special. In some essential particulars, it has surpassed all other countries in its socialization of medicine."[51] Kingsbury was doubtful that the Soviet model of socialized medicine could be replicated elsewhere. "Other countries," he wrote, "may well envy Soviet Russia's elaborately centralized government in that it has been able to brush aside all complexities and to initiate a nearly universal national medical system on unified lines, untrammelled by such complications as exist in western Europe and America . . . almost certainly progress in western countries toward the goal of a national medical service will not follow the exact procedure."[52]

### Reception

*Red Medicine* caused a stir. Accolades came from a variety of quarters, some expected (from Henry Sigerist),[53] others unexpected (from Nelson Rockefeller).[54] Readers hailed the vivid descriptions and the photographs by Margaret Bourke-White.[55] The positive reviews tended to come from people sympathetic to the Soviet experiment. Ella Winter, the author of *Red Virtue* (1933), reviewed the book for the *New Republic;* the psychiatrist Frankwood Williams, who had recently retired as director of the National Committee for Mental Health, reviewed it for *The Survey.*[56]

The Soviet reaction was also positive. A reviewer for *Na fronte zdravookhraneniia,* the official organ of the Russian Commissariat of Public Health, praised Kingsbury's desire to insert the Soviet approach into American discussions of planning medical services and universal health coverage, though the reviewer noted that in the "most interesting" chapter on the socialization of medicine, the authors stopped short of concluding that the Soviet system could be applied in the United States.[57]

Kingsbury himself registered only one negative review.[58] On January 21, 1934, the *New York Times Book Review* carried a virulent attack by Henry A. Koiransky, a former physician in Tsarist Russia, who accused the authors of undervaluing the accomplishments of Tsarist medicine in their eagerness to claim novelty for Soviet public health.[59] An incensed Kingsbury wrote to Dr. Wolf Bronner, director of the All-Union Bureau for Foreign Sanitary Information in Moscow, requesting ammunition to refute Koiransky; he also wrote to Arthur Hays Sulzberger, editor in chief of the *New York Times* to protest the choice of Koiransky as reviewer.[60] Kingsbury paid no attention to a critical review carried in the *Journal of the American Medical Association;*[61] he clearly expected it.

In early May 1933, even before the published reviews began to come in, the authors ran into trouble with their patron, Albert Milbank, who saw a draft of the text for the first time. To Milbank, the frequent references to medicine and the state sounded like "propaganda." What drew his fire was not what the authors wrote about Soviet public health but what they wrote about the Soviet system. Particularly troubling was their deference to Sidney Webb: "He is recognized generally both in England and in this country as a rather extreme Socialist . . . you are opening yourselves to the criticism that the book is not so much the product of an American and an Englishman interested in the health movement, as the product of men who started from that angle, but who became enamoured of Sidney Webb's interpretation of the whole Russian movement."[62]

Kingsbury responded to Milbank's critique of Webb's role: "I perhaps went too far in calling Webb a collaborator, though he did do extensive work on several chapters, especially the final one and on those dealing with political and economic organization and Party participation."[63] He then defended the book's extensive treatment of the context of Soviet socialized medicine: "A distinguishing thing about the health and welfare service of the Soviet Union is . . . that it is the foundation of the State . . . we could not hope that others would understand the system of socialized medicine in the Soviet Union without . . . the historical background and the social, political and economic setting."[64] Finally, Kingsbury insisted that he was not suggesting that the United States graft Soviet experience onto its health system holus bolus: "I think it is Communism as a method that people most object to. . . . I don't see how anyone can object to some of their ideals, however Utopian and impractical they may seem. . . . I quite understand that the book . . . will show sympathy with the medical organization of the Soviet Union; but I think it shows . . . how impracticable it would be for us to attempt to adopt their system as a whole. I hope it does suggest possibilities of great advance in capitalist countries through a higher degree of socialization of medical services."[65] But Milbank would not be mollified by Kingsbury's defense.

## The Integrated Approach of the Soviet System of Medical Care

After returning from Russia in the autumn of 1932, Newsholme (then over seventy-five years old) retreated to his English country estate to write his memoirs,[66] and Kingsbury "went public," making speeches, granting interviews, and publishing popular articles on Russian public health. Over the next two years, Kingsbury's presentation of the Soviet health care system changed. At first, Kingsbury touted the comprehensiveness of the Soviet system, its integration of prevention and cure, and its network of curative and rehabilitative institutions. By 1934, with the costs of medical care a "hot issue" in the United States, he concentrated on government funding of health care, a topic to which *Red Medicine* devoted only a few pages.[67]

### In Praise of Comprehensiveness

In late October 1932, Kingsbury gave an informal presentation to the Milbank staff. Casting the tuberculosis patient as the "poster boy" for the Soviet system's comprehensive approach to health, Kingsbury detailed the round-the-clock treatment in the clinic and sanatoria and described the social insurance benefits accorded to the patient's family. "When a Russian gets tuberculosis," Kingsbury crowed, "the government does something about it."[68] In an article in *The Survey* two months later, Kingsbury described the tuberculosis prevention, treatment, and after-care institutions as a "benevolent circle."[69] He went on: "What the Russians are doing in the fight against tuberculosis illustrates a unity of purpose that seems to run throughout all their work."[70] Kingsbury was aware that in praising the Soviet system, "one is bound to be classed as a communist or a soviet." He added elliptically, "I have not yet made that decision."[71]

In the months that followed, Kingsbury wrote and spoke widely. In April 1933, while *Red Medicine* was being revised, he published a short article provocatively entitled "Russian Medicine Social Challenge." Here the description of Russian socialized medicine centered on the range of programs designed to deal with tuberculosis, maternity and infancy, venereal disease, social hygiene, and physical culture for children. Although the United States could not graft these programs on to its system, Kingsbury noted, "we would be stupid if we ignored developments in the Soviet Union which really challenge us."[72] In a September 1933 speech entitled "The Soviet Challenge to the World in Human Welfare Work," Kingsbury came out swinging. "While most of the European nations have put us to shame by their systems of social insurance," he said, "the Soviet system shames and challenges the whole capitalist world . . . none except for the Soviets provides a complete and comprehensive system of social insurance and public medical service during the entire period of incapacity or unemployment."[73]

In winter 1934, with positive reviews of *Red Medicine* coming in, Kingsbury grew even bolder. In mid-March, he embarked on a "barnstorming tour of the Pacific Coast," where "I shall make a number of addresses to large and quite important medical and combination medical and lay gatherings on the general topic of socialized medicine."[74] The purpose of the tour was "to make a reply" to the position of Morris Fishbein (editor of the *Journal of the American Medical Association*) and of the AMA against socialized medicine.[75]

In his talk entitled "Is America Headed for State Medicine?" Kingsbury noted that almost all modern countries, except the United States, had some system of medical insurance, whether compulsory, voluntary, or a mix of the two. Only in Russia was there real state medicine, in the sense of the public provision of health care. European insurance systems, he explained, were not instances of state medicine, as the government did not furnish medical services but simply set up machinery to allow people to pool the costs of private medicine. Kingsbury insisted that he was not urging "state medicine or public medicine or the socialization of medicine or anything else that a clever person might call it to confuse the issue" but rather a system of compulsory health insurance to cover the costs of the general practitioner, hospital care, and prescribed medicines. To depoliticize the issue, he noted, "If we increase the scope of our public medicine, it would be about as correct to say that we have sovietized as that Russia has Americanized."[76]

### Retreat

Milbank must have asked to vet the text of the talk. A revised version re-titled "Adequate Health Services for all the People" carries the notation "with Mr. Milbank's changes." In place of the provocative question "Is America heading for state medicine?" the new text asked blandly, "What will be the future place of medicine in society?"[77] Kingsbury underscored that neither he—nor the Milbank Fund—advocated state medicine: "My associates in the Milbank Memorial Fund and I . . . advocate the private practice of medicine and the mutualization of the patients' costs."[78] The scheme he recommended would be supervised publicly; its medical facets supervised professionally; and its grievances supervised by judicial personnel. "There is nothing in our princi-ples or in our proposals," he wrote, "which challenges the fundamentals of our American political or economic system. There is nothing about 'regimenting' either patients or practitioners."[79] The revised talk, delivered at the National Conference of Social Work in Missouri in 1934, cited President Roosevelt sev-eral times. Russia was mentioned once and then only as a model of prevention.

The retreat came too late. By spring 1934, having gotten wind of Kings-bury's "barnstorming tour," the AMA launched a campaign to discredit him for selling "state medicine" and to rein in the Milbank Memorial Fund. The cam-paign intensified in the summer, spurred on by the fact that FDR had appointed his Committee on Economic Security to study social insurance, including health insurance.[80] The Milbank Fund (and Kingsbury) were closely associated with the effort to get compulsory health insurance onto the agenda: Edward Sydenstricker and Isidore Falk, the two men charged with drafting the sickness insurance section of the Committee on Economic Security's report, were on leave from the Milbank Memorial Fund; Kingsbury and Albert Milbank were openly supportive of the Sydenstricker-Falk effort to craft a program for sick-ness insurance. It was known that Kingsbury had gone to Washington to dis-cuss his support of the bill with the president.

As 1934 was coming to an end, the AMA was becoming increasingly res-tive. Aware that the Milbank's largest investments were in the common stock of the Borden Company, certain groups of doctors threatened a boycott of Borden products. The threat hit home: Milbank was not only president of the board of the Milbank Memorial Fund but also chairman of the board of directors of the Borden Company. In January 1935, Albert Milbank warned Kingsbury that the two were going to have "their first fight about the role of the Fund in the health insurance debate."[81] On April 1, 1935, after several months of push-and-pull, Milbank called Kingsbury in and, after what Kingsbury recalled as a two-hour monologue, summarily fired him.[82] That same year, the Health Insurance Bill was deleted from the Social Security Bill.[83]

### Connecting the Dots

In June 1935, with the insult of his dismissal still raw, Kingsbury drew a connec-tion between "THE BOOK" and Milbank's decision to let him go. In a letter to

Alexander Roubakine—the representative of the Russian Commissariat of Public Health in France (1921–1928), whom he had befriended in early 1933 when Roubakine was in the United States as a traveling fellow of the Rockefeller Foundation's International Health Division—Kingsbury wrote, "The Medical profession or rather I should say the 'Merchants of Medicine,' to use your long phrase, succeeded in 'getting my scalp,' to use an Americanism. 'Red Medicine' was partly responsible for it, or at any rate the Merchants of Medicine seized upon that book as an excuse and as a weapon in their fight against me."[84]

In fact, in 1932 Milbank had endorsed Kingsbury's trip to Russia. More to the point, the July 1932 issue of *The Survey* carried an article by Milbank himself entitled "Socialized Capitalism," which read: "It is high time that we explore the possibility of whether the virtues of the two schools may not be combined into a workable scheme that will provide a better foundation than either one of them alone upon which to build an improved economic and social order."[85] And in October 1932, the *Milbank Memorial Fund Quarterly Bulletin* carried excerpts from *Red Medicine,* including passages from Kingsbury's paean to socialized health and the Soviet social system.[86]

But in late 1932, Kingsbury reported to Newsholme that Milbank had expressed concern that Kingsbury might be a Communist.[87] In 1931, Milbank had even felt it necessary to reassure readers of Newsholme's volumes on private and public medicine that, despite his use of the term *state medicine,* Newsholme was no revolutionary.[88] That said, at least until early 1935 when he cut Kingsbury loose, Milbank was able to distinguish the value of ideas from the political allegiances of those who advocated them.

It is impossible to say with certainty whether in and of itself the publication of *Red Medicine* would have so enraged physicians that they demanded Kingsbury's scalp. What is clear is that by 1935 Kingsbury was fighting a losing battle: some (including Milbank) attacked him because of his favorable reading of the social and political context of Soviet public health; others (principally physicians in the AMA or those sympathetic to its position) excoriated him for his suggestions that a version of the Soviet approach to health insurance could be transported to the United States. Despite his (and Milbank's) disclaimers, and Kingsbury's decision to drop references to Russia from his speeches and articles, the battle lines were drawn.

Scholars have differed on who was responsible for the deletion of the Health Insurance Bill from the 1935 Social Security Act. Some lay the responsibility at the door of the AMA opponents of compulsory health insurance who lobbied FDR relentlessly.[89] Others argue that the Committee on Economic Security was divided on health insurance and that FDR, ever the pragmatist, was reluctant to endanger the passage of social security legislation by lending his support to the Health Insurance Bill, which was contentious.[90] Still others go further: they characterize FDR as the angler-in-chief, whose modus operandi was to stir the waters of health insurance (by encouraging all viewpoints until the Social Security Act was passed in August of 1935), but not to set the hook.[91]

## Epilogue

In July 1936, in response to news of Kingsbury's dismissal from the Milbank Memorial Fund, Alexander Roubakine wrote to Kingsbury in a familiar tone that reflected a shared commitment to "internationalism." "Your adventures with Milbank Fund are finished, I hope? . . . You are so active that probably you are fighting something."[92] To some extent, Roubakine got Kingsbury right. Kingsbury did go on after his dismissal to new posts and new battles. In 1935, after his "retirement" from the Milbank Fund, Kingsbury was invited by Harry Hopkins to work as a consultant to the newly created Works Progress Administration.[93] In 1939, Kingsbury published *Health in Handcuffs,* a 200-page, hard-hitting book in which he made the case once again for the importance of health insurance—with no reference to Russia, but with plenty of invective against the AMA.[94]

Two years later, in 1941, moved by the plight of Russia at war, Kingsbury was involved with Russian War Relief. From 1949, with the Cold War gathering force, Kingsbury assumed the chairmanship of the National Council of American-Soviet Friendship. The National Council had been investigated by the House Un-American Activities Committee in 1946 and was indicted the following year for failure to register with the Subversive Activities Control Board.[95] In 1951, the U.S. Supreme Court ruled that the attorney general had acted arbitrarily and illegally by placing the National Council on the List of Subversive Organizations. Three years later, the Subversive Activities Control Board again ruled that, under the McCarran Act of 1950, the National Council was required to register as a Communist front organization. In 1954–1955, Kingsbury, who was still chair of the council (he held the position until his death in 1956), testified before the Subversive Activities Control Board.[96] Insisting that he yielded to no one in his loyalty to his country, Kingsbury argued that the right to free speech included the right to criticize the foreign policy of the government.[97] Moreover, he declared that, "in consistently advocating the restoration of cooperation between the United States and the Soviet Union, cultural interchange and expanded trade, we have performed a patriotic service and have advanced the cause of world peace."[98] Kingsbury died on August 3, 1956, just weeks short of his eightieth birthday. The headline in his *New York Times* obituary listed him as a lecturer and as the chairman of the National

Council of American-Soviet Friendship. His fifteen years of service for the Milbank Memorial Fund were relegated to the second paragraph.[99]

Yet it was his years with the Milbank Fund (and their ignominious end) that stayed longest with Kingsbury. In 1952, in a note to Henry Sigerist, Kingsbury dredged up the dismissal again. Kingsbury's version of his firing changed over time.[100] In 1935 he had pictured Milbank succumbing to the pressure from the "Merchants of Medicine"; in the 1952 letter to Sigerist, Kingsbury blamed Surgeon-General Thomas Parran (then a member of the Committee on Economic Security) and Livingston Farrand (once executive director of the National Tuberculosis Association but from 1921 on, president of Cornell University) for failing to help Milbank ("poor Bert") stand off the critics: "If he had received just a little counter pressure from my friends, especially from 'Tom' Parran, 'Tony' Farrand, and Jim Miller and Homer Folks, I am sure he could have stood up against both the AMA and the Wall St. allies."[101] The cast of villains had broadened, but the portrait of Milbank in 1952 was more benign than it had been when he wrote to his "Dear Friends" in 1935 to announce the dismissal.

What was unchanging was Kingsbury's failure to accept the deep reservations of American ruling circles and the broad public about the Soviet approach to health care. He turned a blind eye to those reservations in 1934 when he undertook his barnstorming tour to sell compulsory health insurance, and again in 1935 when he urged FDR to support the inclusion of the Health Insurance Bill in the Social Security legislation. Acknowledgment of the depth of the political reservations might have suggested a more moderate and tempered approach to advocacy.[102] But Kingsbury was cut from different cloth. Of his 1934 tour he wrote to Newsholme: "there is ample evidence that the time is ripe to get this subject out sharply before the country."[103] Kingsbury not only believed in "telling it as it is," he relished doing so. In 1932, when urging Newsholme to adopt the title *Red Medicine* for their book, Kingsbury wrote, "I am thinking of men like the AMA group, who would pick up the book thinking that they were going to get some red-hot criticism of the Russian medicine and would thus be led into reading something that might give them food for thought."[104]

Kingsbury was not blind to the risks of extolling Soviet approaches to health care. In October 1932, reporting on his trip to Russia to his staff at the Milbank Memorial Fund, he noted "the danger perhaps of talking outside too freely, of saying that you have seen anything favorable at all."[105] Yet Kingsbury's belief in the superiority of the Soviet system and its relevance for the ailing American system of health care made him persist in his advocacy, even into the mid-1950s, when official tolerance of that advocacy was a thing of the past.

## Notes

1. Beatrix Hoffman, *The Wages of Sickness: The Politics of Health Insurance in Progressive America* (Chapel Hill: University of North Carolina Press, 2001); Ronald Numbers, *Almost Persuaded: American Physicians and Compulsory Health Insurance, 1912–1920* (Baltimore: Johns Hopkins University Press, 1978).

2. Committee on the Costs of Medical Care, *Medical Care for the American People: The Final Report of the Committee on the Costs of Medical Care, Adopted October 31, 1932* (Chicago: University of Chicago Press, 1932). The committee was formed in 1927 to study the economic aspects of health delivery in the United States. See Jonathan Engel, *Doctors and Reformers: Discussion and Debate over Health Care, 1925–1950* (Columbia: University of South Carolina Press, 2002), 1–53.

3. Arthur Newsholme and John Adams Kingsbury, *Red Medicine: Socialized Health in Soviet Russia* (New York: Doubleday, 1933).

4. The Milbank Memorial Fund, created in 1905, was dedicated to "the improvement in the general level of public health and public welfare" ("The Milbank Memorial Fund," undated [likely 1928], part II, box 70, John Adams Kingsbury Papers, Manuscript Division, Library of Congress, Washington, D.C.), hereafter JAK Papers.

5. Kingsbury to Newsholme, June 23, 1932, part II, box 76, JAK Papers.

6. For more on Soviet public health, see Susan Gross Solomon, "Social Hygiene and Soviet Public Health, 1921–1930," in *Health and Society in Revolutionary Russia,* ed. Susan Gross Solomon and John F. Hutchinson (Bloomington: Indiana University Press, 1990), 175–199; Tricia Starks, *The Body Soviet: Propaganda, Hygiene and the Revolutionary State* (Madison: University of Wisconsin Press, 2008).

7. Frank Campion, *The AMA and U.S. Health Policy since 1940* (Chicago: Chicago Review Press, 1984); Engel, *Doctors and Reformers.*

8. Robert Murray, *Red Scare: A Study in National Hysteria, 1919–1920* (Westport, CT: Greenwood Press, 1980).

9. Daniel T. Rodgers, *Atlantic Crossings: Social Politics in a Progressive Age* (Cambridge, MA: Harvard University Press, 1998), 380–381.

10. For exceptions, see Arthur J. Viseltear, "Compulsory Health Insurance and the Definition of Public Health," in *Compulsory Health Insurance: The Continuing American Debate,* ed. Ronald L. Numbers (Westport, CT: Greenwood Press, 1982), 25–55; Engel, *Doctors and Reformers,* 90–91.

11. William Horsley Gantt, *A Medical Review of Soviet Russia* (London: British Medical Association, 1928); Alice Hamilton and Rebecca Edith Hilles, "Industrial Hygiene in Moscow," *Journal of Industrial Hygiene* 7 (1925): 47–61; Anna Haines, *Health Work in Soviet Russia* (New York: Vanguard, 1928); Alice Withrow Field, *Protection of Women and Children in Soviet Russia* (London: Gollancz, 1932); Frankwood E. Williams, *Russia, Youth and the Present-Day World* (New York: Farrar and Rhinehart, 1934); David C. Engerman, *Modernization from the Other Shore: American Intellectuals and the Romance of Russian Development* (Cambridge, MA: Harvard University Press, 2003).

12. Elizabeth Fee, "The Pleasures and Perils of Prophetic Advocacy: Socialized Medicine and the Politics of American Medical Reform," in *Making Medical History: The Life and Times of Henry E. Sigerist,* ed. Elizabeth Fee and Theodore M. Brown (Baltimore: Johns Hopkins University Press, 1997), 197–238.

13. William Welch (1850–1934), M.D., was the first dean of the Johns Hopkins School of Medicine, founding director of the Johns Hopkins School of Hygiene and Public

Health, and the first director of the Johns Hopkins University Institute of the History of Medicine). He was succeeded in the latter position by Henry Sigerist.

14. John M. Eyler, *Sir Arthur Newsholme and State Medicine, 1885–1935* (Cambridge: Cambridge University Press, 1997).

15. Arnold S. Rosenberg, "The Rise of John Adams Kingsbury," *Pacific Northwest Quarterly* 63 (1972): 55–62; Allen F. Davis, "The Social Workers and the Progressive Party, 1912–1916," *American Historical Review* 69 (1964): 680ff.

16. For an overview of his life, see the biographical notes in the JAK Papers. Also see Arnold S. Rosenberg, "The War on Poverty: John Kingsbury and the AICP, 1906–1918," *Connecticut Review* 2 (1968): 52–69; Engel, *Doctors and Reformers,* 56–57; Viseltear, "Compulsory Health Insurance and the Definition of Public Health."

17. Engel, *Doctors and Reformers,* 57.

18. Engel, *Doctors and Reformers,* 56–57.

19. FDR to Kingsbury, December 4, 1932, box 32, folder 3, William Welch Papers, Alan Mason Chesney Archives, Johns Hopkins University Library, Baltimore, MD. According to Engel, the connection between the two was less close than it appeared (Engel, *Doctors and Reformers,* 58).

20. Sigerist to C.-E.A. Winslow, November 9, 1937, box 63, folder 18, Henry E. Sigerist Papers, Alan Mason Chesney Archives, Johns Hopkins University Library, Baltimore, MD. For the view that Sigerist did not recognize those deficiencies, see John F. Hutchinson, "Dances with Commissars: Sigerist and Soviet Medicine," in *Making Medical History,* ed. Fee and Brown, 229–258.

21. "New York Health Demonstrations: Report of the Technical Board to Board of Directors of the Milbank Memorial Fund," March 19, 1924, MS group 749, box 49/354, Winslow Papers, Yale University Archives, New Haven, CT; Arthur Newsholme, "The New York State Health Demonstrations in Syracuse and in Cattaraugas County," *Milbank Memorial Fund Quarterly Bulletin* 4 (1926): 49–66.

22. Sir Arthur Newsholme, *International Studies in the Relation between the Private and Official Practice of Medicine, with Special Reference to the Prevention of Disease,* 3 vols. (London: Allen & Unwin, 1931). For the summary volume, see Sir Arthur Newsholme, *Medicine and the State* (London: Allen & Unwin, 1932).

23. Kingsbury to Wilbur, July 8, 1932, part II, box 66, JAK Papers.

24. See Rodgers, *Atlantic Crossings,* 209–266; Hoffman, *The Wages of Sickness;* Numbers, *Almost Persuaded.*

25. Gary Land, "American Images of British Compulsory Health Insurance," in *Compulsory Health Insurance,* ed. Ronald Numbers, 7, 55–76.

26. The term socialized medicine was often used interchangeably with "social medicine" and sometimes with "socialist medicine." See Dorothy Porter and Roy Porter, "What Was Social Medicine? An Historiographical Essay," *Journal of Historical Sociology* 1 (1988): 90–106.

27. Arthur Newsholme, *Public Health and Insurance* (Baltimore: Johns Hopkins University Press, 1920).

28. Ronald L. Numbers, "The Specter of Socialized Medicine: American Physicians and Compulsory Health Insurance," in *Compulsory Health Insurance,* ed. Ronald L. Numbers, 3.

29. Newsholme and Kingsbury, *Red Medicine,* vii.

30. See part II, box 77, 78, JAK Papers.

31. The AICP asked about the degree of choice in the health system, the effectiveness of preventive measures, and the attractiveness of a Soviet medical career (Bailey Burritt to Kingsbury, July 25, 1932, part II, box 66, JAK Papers).

32. The ASHA asked about congenital syphilis and sex education in Russia (William F. Snow to Kingsbury, July 23, 1932, part II, box 66, JAK Papers).

33. Its director asked how physicians compared state-run medical practice to private practice and what the state was doing about tuberculosis and venereal disease (Harry H. Moore to Kingsbury, July 15, 1932, part II, box 66, JAK Papers).

34. Parran asked about the ratio of physicians to the population before and after 1917, the administrative relation between treatment and prevention, and about the control of venereal diseases (Parran to Kingsbury, July 13, 1932, part II, box 66, JAK Papers).

35. Newsholme and Kingsbury, *Red Medicine*, chapter 2.

36. "Itinerary and Summary Diary of a Trip to Soviet Russia made by Mr. Kingsbury Accompanied by Sir Arthur Newsholme," part II, box 66, JAK Papers.

37. Newsholme and Kingsbury, *Red Medicine*, 5.

38. Kingsbury to Newsholme, January 23, 1933, part II, box 76, JAK Papers.

39. Kingsbury to Newsholme, March 1, 1933, part II, box 76, JAK Papers.

40. Kingsbury to Newsholme, March 1, 1933, part II, box 76, JAK Papers.

41. Newsholme and Kingsbury, *Red Medicine*, 189.

42. Kingsbury to Newsholme, January 26, 1933, part II, box 76, JAK Papers.

43. Kingsbury to Newsholme, January 27, 1933, part II, box 76, JAK Papers.

44. Kingsbury to Newsholme, March 1, 1933, part II, box 76, JAK Papers; Freeburg to Kingsbury, March 13, 1933, part II, box 75, JAK Papers.

45. Kingsbury to Newsholme, March 1, 1933, part II, box 76, JAK Papers.

46. "Concluding Observations," part II, box 77, JAK Papers.

47. Viseltear, "Compulsory Health Insurance," 30–34.

48. "The Committee on the Costs of Medical Care," *Journal of the American Medical Association* 99(23) (1932): 1950–1952.

49. For the list of maladjustments, see Committee on the Costs of Medical Care, *Medical Care for the American People*, 1–36.

50. Newsholme and Kingsbury, *Red Medicine*, 276–277.

51. Newsholme and Kingsbury, *Red Medicine*, 309.

52. Newsholme and Kingsbury, *Red Medicine*, 310.

53. Sigerist to Kingsbury, December 13, 1933, part II, box 75, JAK Papers.

54. Nelson Rockefeller to Kingsbury, December 27, 1933, part II, box 75, JAK Papers.

55. The well-known photographer Margaret Bourke-White (1904–1971) had just published a book of photographs taken on one of her trips to Russia (Margaret Bourke-White, *Eyes on Russia*, With a Preface by Maurice Hindus [New York: Simon and Schuster, 1931]).

56. For the review by Ella Winter, see "Two Books on Russia," *New Republic* 78(1005) (March 7, 1934): 108–109. The review by Frankwood Williams appeared as "The Challenge of Red Medicine," *The Survey* 79(3) (1934): 78–80.

57. P.Z., "Sovetskoe zdravookhranenie v anglo-amerikanskoi otsenke," *Na fronte zdravookhraneniia* 10 (1934): 59–62.

58. Kingsbury to Newsholme, March 17, 1934, part II, box 16, JAK Papers.

59. Henry A. Koiransky, "Socialized Medicine in Russia: Messrs Newsholme and Kingsbury Present Their Findings as to Soviet Achievement in the Field of Public Health," *New York Times Book Review,* January 21, 1934, Section 5, 44.

60. Kingsbury to Sulzberger, January 26, 1934, part II, box 75, JAK Papers.

61. "Red Medicine: Socialized Health in Soviet Russia," *Journal of the American Medical Association* 102 (1934): 1254–1255.

62. Milbank to Kingsbury, May 9, 1933, part II, box 75, JAK Papers.

63. Kingsbury to Milbank, May 16, 1933, part II, box 75, JAK Papers.

64. Kingsbury to Milbank, May 16, 1933, part II, box 75, JAK Papers.

65. Kingsbury to Milbank, May 16, 1933, part II, box 75, JAK Papers.

66. Arthur Newsholme, *Fifty Years in Public Health: A Personal Narrative with Comments* (London: Allen and Unwin, 1935).

67. Newsholme and Kingsbury, *Red Medicine*, 267–268.

68. "Mr. Kingsbury's Address to the Staff," October 24, 1932, part II, box 80, JAK Papers.

69. Kingsbury, "When a Russian has TB," draft for *The Survey* article, December 14, 1933, part II, box 70, JAK Papers.

70. "Mr. Kingsbury's Address to the Staff," October 24, 1932, part II, box 80, JAK Papers.

71. "Mr. Kingsbury's Address to the Staff," October 24, 1932, part II, box 80, JAK Papers.

72. John A. Kingsbury, "Russian Medicine Social Challenge," *New Republic* 74 (957) (April 5, 1933), 204–206.

73. Kingsbury, "The Soviet Challenge to the World in Human Welfare Work," Speech to the World Fellowship of Faiths, September 16, 1933, part II, box 80, JAK Papers.

74. Kingsbury to Newsholme, March 17, 1934, part II, box 16, JAK Papers.

75. For Fishbein's position on national health insurance, see Land, "American Images of British Health Insurance," 63.

76. Kingsbury, "Is America Heading for State Medicine?" part II, box 70, JAK Papers.

77. Kingsbury, "Adequate Health Service for All the People," Proceedings of the National Conference of Social Work, Kansas City, 1934, part II, box 16, JAK Papers.

78. Kingsbury, "Adequate Health Service for All the People," Proceedings of the National Conference of Social Work, Kansas City, 1934, part II, box 16, JAK Papers.

79. Kingsbury, "Adequate Health Service for All the People," Proceedings of the National Conference of Social Work, Kansas City, 1934, part II, box 16, JAK Papers.

80. For a description of the committee's work, see Engel, *Doctors and Reformers*, 53–94.

81. Engel, *Doctors and Reformers*, 90.

82. Kingsbury to "Dear Friends," July 19, 1935, part III, box 13, JAK Papers. See also Engel, *Doctors and Reformers*, 89–93.

83. Daniel S. Hirshfield, *The Lost Reform: The Campaign for Compulsory Health Insurance in the United States from 1932–1943* (Cambridge, MA: Harvard University Press, 1970).

84. Kingsbury to Roubakine June 19, 1935, part II, box 18, JAK Papers.

85. Albert Milbank, "Socialized Capitalism," *The Survey* (July 1, 1932), 293; as cited in Newsholme and Kingsbury, *Red Medicine*, 307–308.

86. "Health Activities in Russia to be Surveyed in a Forthcoming Book," *Milbank Memorial Fund Quarterly Bulletin* (October 1933): 271–272.

87. Kingsbury to Newsholme, December 6, 1932, part II, box 76, JAK Papers.

88. Eyler, *Sir Arthur Newsholme*, 364.

89. Engel, *Doctors and Reformers*; Numbers, *Almost Persuaded*.

90. Jaap Kooijman, "Sooner or Later: Franklin D. Roosevelt and National Health Insurance, 1933–1945," *Presidential Studies Quarterly* 29 (1999): 336–350.

91. David Blumenthal and James Morone, *The Heart of Power: Health and Politics in the Oval Office* (Berkeley and Los Angeles: University of California Press, 2009), 21–56.

92. Roubakine to Kingsbury, July 7, 1936, part II, box 18, JAK Papers.

93. Kingsbury helped Hopkins to obtain his first post in the public service. Lewis S. Feuer, "American Travellers to the Soviet Union, 1917–1932: The Formation of a Component of New Deal Ideology," *American Quarterly* 14 (1962): 126–127.

94. John A. Kingsbury, *Health in Handcuffs: The National Health Crisis and What Can Be Done* (New York: Modern Age Books, 1939).

95. For the National Council of American-Soviet Friendship (founded in 1941 as the National Council on Soviet Relations), see "Guide to the National Council of American Soviet Friendship Records TAM 134," dlib.nyu.edu/findingaids/html/tamwag/ncsaf_content.html (accessed November 8, 2009).

96. "1954–1955 National Council of American-Soviet Friendship Inc. Statements Prepared for Presentation Before Subversive Activities Control Board Meeting," September 8, 1955, part II, box 61, JAK Papers. For more on Kingsbury's appearance, see Jane Pacht Brickman, "'Medical McCarthyism': The Physicians Forum and the Cold War," *Journal of the History of Medicine and Allied Sciences* 49 (1994): 398–399.

97. 1954–1955 National Council of American-Soviet Friendship Inc. Statements Prepared for Presentation Before the Subversive Activities Control Board Meeting, September 8, 1955, part II, box 61, JAK Papers.

98. National Council on Soviet-American Friendship News, June 23, 1955, part II, box 61, JAK Papers.

99. See his obituary in the *New York Times,* August 3, 1956, 15.

100. Kingsbury to Sigerist, January 18, 1952, Sigerist group 788, series I, box 15, folder 5, Yale University Archives, New Haven, CT.

101. Dr. James Alexander Miller, president of the National Tuberculosis Association from 1922 to 1929, was a member of the Milbank Memorial Fund's Technical Board; Homer Folks was executive secretary of the New York State Charities Aid Association.

102. Among others, Michael Davis counseled moderation. Engel, *Doctors and Reformers,* 92–93. Michael Davis was an executive of the Julius Rosenwald Fund and a member of the Committee on the Costs of Medical Care.

103. Kingsbury to Newsholme, March 17, 1934, part II, box 16, JAK Papers.

104. Kingsbury to Newsholme, February 20, 1933, part II, box 16, JAK Papers.

105. "Mr. Kingsbury's Address to the Staff," October 24, 1932, part II, box 80, JAK Papers.

# Chapter 4

# American Medical Support for Spanish Democracy, 1936–1938

**Walter J. Lear**

The Spanish Civil War was a seminal moment for U.S. health-Left internationalism. From 1936 to 1938, the Fascist-supported assault on the democratically elected Republican government of Spain intensely engaged the U.S. Left, as it did progressive forces around the world. Approximately 2,800 individuals from the United States joined the Spanish Republican forces in this first major, transnational military action against fascism, which included some 40,000 women and men from over fifty countries.[1] Roughly 800 of the American volunteers lost their lives in Spain, and many more were seriously injured or severely traumatized. This extraordinary enterprise was the American Left's first effort to involve thousands of volunteers as participants in a people's struggle in another country and was mobilized despite official opposition by the administration of U.S. president Franklin D. Roosevelt and the hostility of influential political, business, and media leaders. The American battalion, later called the Abraham Lincoln Brigade, was part of the Fifteenth International Brigade of the Spanish Army. Associated with the brigade but serving other international forces as well as the Spanish Republican Army was a medical corps of doctors, nurses, technicians, and ambulance drivers recruited, equipped, and funded by the American Medical Bureau to Aid Spanish Democracy.[2]

What motivated well over a hundred physicians, nurses, and other health personnel to risk their reputations, careers, and even, for some, their lives for Spain's "Popular Front" government? What did these medical service workers achieve by such unequivocal expressions of their progressive political convictions in solidarity with Spanish Republicans and other internationalist efforts? This chapter addresses these questions and explores, more reflexively, how these volunteers' efforts in Spain subsequently affected their involvement in U.S. (health) politics in both the short term and the long run.

### Origins of the Medical Bureau

Two months after General Francisco Franco's military forces began their attempted July coup, which grew into civil war in the summer of 1936, U.S. unions, liberal and Left political parties, and other organizations launched efforts to aid "Spanish democracy." Although medical assistance was included as an early goal, a group of New York City (NYC) physicians with Communist Party (CP) affiliations became convinced that these efforts were insufficient and that an organization specifically devoted to the medical needs of the Spanish Republican forces needed to be established. These CP connections would mark many of the medical volunteers into the future, subjecting them to anti-leftist punishments and medical McCarthyism's witch hunts (see chapter 5).

At the epicenter of this medical organizing was Edward K. Barsky, a leader of the NYC Communist physicians. In 1936 he was a forty-one-year-old, board-certified surgeon affiliated with Beth Israel Hospital, the primary base of his busy and successful private practice. Like other physicians with left-leaning politics, his response to the Depression included providing clinical services gratis or almost gratis to members of progressive political organizations and their families. For example, he worked in the pioneering medical program of District 65 (Retail, Wholesale & Department Store Workers Union) and served as the personal physician for several leaders of the CP. Barsky recalled how he got involved in Spanish Civil War efforts: "First of all there was an interest in Spain, a country trying, after years of repression, to be a democracy, and in a measure succeeding. So much I had read in newsprint. Then the Spanish government had sent a delegation to beg for American help, American sympathy. I went to a meeting. . . . Two persons [from Spain] . . . spoke movingly . . . The Republicans had almost no medical services. Somebody said 'That sort of thing ought to be our meat.'"[3]

Louis Miller, another NYC physician with CP affiliations, called together a group. It included Barsky and four other male physicians from Beth Israel Hospital—Irving Busch, Milton Feltenstein, Benjamin Segal, and Jesse Tolmac—and one woman, Feltenstein's wife, Evelyn Ahrend, a language specialist. Fredericka Martin, who was to become the medical group's chief nurse, noted: "Several of the founding doctors . . . had the unusual experience of forming and working as a group named Workers' Medical Aid. They covered the waterfront during strikes and cared for other strikers and their families. They were used to working together and serving people in need."[4]

The core group arranged for a public meeting on Sunday, November 5, 1936. The large audience gave enthusiastic approval to the proposal for a separate medical assistance organization. Individuals willing to undertake the job planned an organizing meeting, set up for the following Sunday in the home of Benjamin Miller, a young researcher at the Rockefeller Institute. And so the Medical Bureau for Aid to Spanish Democracy was born. It was often referred to as the American Medical Bureau and known by its abbreviation, AMB.

The AMB affiliated with the North American Committee to Aid Spanish Democracy, a coalition of Spanish aid organizations, and moved into that committee's office in downtown Manhattan. It hired a series of retired military physicians to serve in the executive secretary position and recruited Dr. Walter B. Cannon, one of the country's most famous physicians, to be the bureau's national chairman. He served in that capacity from March 1937 until 1939 when the AMB's work in Spain concluded.[5] Cannon, sixty-five when his chairmanship began, had been a Harvard Medical School professor for over thirty years and was America's premier physiologist. He was internationally respected for both his outstanding research and his outspoken humanitarian concerns. Although he had sympathies for socialism and the Soviet Union, Cannon was not a Communist, belonging to the liberal, "progressive" end of the American political spectrum.[6]

Cannon's deep and well-informed interest in Spain began during a visit there in 1930. He recounted:

> I asked one of [my former] students about Primo de Rivera [then Spain's military dictator]. I never knew a few words to produce such an extraordinary change as these did. Dr. Carrasco turned pale, became visibly agitated, and when he answered, spoke in a voice which quavered with emotion as he told of the tyranny of the dictator. . . . Only one year later, in 1931, the king fled and the Republic was established. During the five years from 1931 to 1936, I watched anxiously the ups and downs of the fate of the Republic. It became obvious that a conflict was brewing between advocates of greater human liberty and the promotion of human welfare on one hand, and reactionary forces intent on continuing feudal dominance on the other hand, and that efforts to better the lives of an impoverished and grossly illiterate people were in danger of being thwarted.[7]

## U.S. Health Personnel, Facilities, and Services in Spain

The U.S. health personnel who went to Spain numbered almost fifty nurses, some thirty physicians, and approximately sixty others, including medical service professionals, administrative assistants, technicians, and ambulance drivers.[8] The physicians ranged in age from twenty-six to fifty-six, and the sole medical student was twenty-four. Of these, a few were fully trained and experienced specialists. Two had prior military medical experience. One was a woman. Several came from NYC, a few from Chicago, Philadelphia, and San Francisco. All but two had Jewish family backgrounds.[9] Three were avowed Communists; several others may also have been. The AMB medical teams also included three physicians from Cuba, two from Canada, and a few refugees from European countries.

Barsky was in the first, seventeen-member, U.S. medical contingent that sailed to Europe in January 1937.[10] Initially, he carried the main organizational responsibility for the medical corps of the American battalions, and in March 1938 he was promoted to head the medical service of the international brigades. Leo Eloesser, professor of thoracic surgery at Stanford University Medical School and a noncommunist leftist, was the most prominent U.S. physician participant and the oldest (fifty-six). He went to Spain in November 1937 with his own surgical team; his skill and energy in the front-line services were formidable. There were also four dentists/oral surgeons, ages thirty to forty-nine, all male, three Jewish and one African American. Two were Communists—the

**Figure 4.1**   Spain: Group [of] AMB nurses.

Credit: Montell/Barsky Collection, Ruth Davidow. Box 1, Folder 3, #3. Frances Patai Photographs Collection, Abraham Lincoln Brigade Archives, Tamiment Library, New York University.

African American, Arnold Donawa, who had been briefly a professor at Howard University Dental School, and John J. Posner, who left his successful practice in NYC to serve as the AMB's chief of dental services.

Forty-six graduate nurses from the United States served with the AMB medical teams—forty-five women and one man. Their ages ranged from twenty-one to forty-nine, and most had had at least five years of work experience, some ten to fifteen.[11] Most were children of working-class immigrants from Eastern Europe and Russia, and more than half were secular Jews. One nurse was African American. Approximately 25 percent of the nurses were members of the CP or the Young Communist League, although the majority consisted of liberals and leftist sympathizers who did not identify with any particular political party. A number were members of the fledgling nurses' union. Two Canadian nurses and a number of Spanish nurses also served on the AMB teams. The AMB's chief nurse Fredericka Martin, aged thirty-two, was from NYC and a Communist.

The AMB medical teams on the front lines worked closely with hundreds of first aid workers, generally called "medics," and stretcher bearers. Although many were Americans, medics were not among the personnel sent directly to Spain by the AMB. Most were Spaniards. The nurses also trained hundreds of Spanish women as nurses' aides, and one dentist trained his driver, a young African American man, to serve as his dental assistant.

The AMB sent approximately sixty others to Spain. About half were drivers for the ambulances and other vehicles. The other half included two anesthetists, three dental assistants, two physiotherapists, four lab technicians, two x-ray technicians, and one pharmacist. There were also three administrators/clerks and interpreters, three engineers and mechanics, two laundry technicians, and one cook. Almost all of the drivers came from working-class backgrounds. Six were Latino, three were from Jewish families, and two were African American. The sole woman driver, Evelyn Hutchins, was a Communist.

The first American woman medical volunteer, Celia Greenspan, was a trained laboratory technician from a working-class New York Jewish background and a CP member. Soon after joining her journalist husband, George Marion, in Spain in October 1936, she helped organize a laboratory for Canadian surgeon and political activist Norman Bethune's innovative blood transfusion service to support the Republican troops.[12] As she noted: "Have assisted at quite a few transfusions . . . They've been so depressing . . . I keep waking up at night thinking about the poor devils."[13] Despite her psychological trauma, in February 1937 Greenspan left Madrid to work in a hospital in Murcia, near one of the fiercest battlegrounds of the war. She became a nurse's aide virtually overnight, never before having done more than put a band-aid on a blood donor. She learned quickly and applied her technical skills to the service of the hundreds of sick and wounded combatants who overwhelmed the meager medical facilities at Murcia. Greenspan stayed until July, amid worsening violence and severe shortages of resources. She set up a laboratory and tended the pharmacy before returning to Madrid, at her husband's insistence, and then to New York City. Greenspan had gone to Spain for love, but, she discovered, "The war has changed me. All the books and all the lectures and all the unit meetings in the world, from now till doomsday couldn't have given me the feeling of personal responsibility to the movement, as being here, working and watching have done."[14]

From 1937 to 1939 the American medical teams organized and staffed eight base hospitals and innumerable temporary field hospitals and provided emergency care immediately behind the fighting lines. In early April 1937 Barsky and Martin set up the main base hospital in the country estate of the Spanish Bourbons in Villa Paz along the Madrid-Valencia road; it was the best equipped and staffed of the American hospitals and served as the headquarters for the AMB in Spain.[15] Two senior dentists provided oral surgery at the main base hospital. Another set up mobile units, traveling to the front and to field hospitals to provide urgent dental services.

The conditions for proper surgical, medical, and dental services, particularly in the field hospitals, were very poor. Not only were there shortages of anesthesia, pain relievers, disinfectants, medications, bandages, x-ray film, and surgical instruments and supplies, but frequently even the basics were lacking. It was often difficult to secure sheets, electricity, lights, water, appropriate room temperatures, or sterile surfaces on which to operate. Faced with such gross inadequacies and large numbers of wounded persons needing major surgery promptly, the surgeons in the field resorted to a variety of shortcuts and makeshifts.

Dr. Sidney Vogel, who arrived from NYC in late May 1937, was posted to Murcia as director of Casa Roja hospital. A few years later he described in vivid terms what he had witnessed in Spain:

> Picture to yourself the scene of war. Fields of dry stubble. Plumes of smoke in the distance and the sporadic clatter of rifle fire. In the foreground the long wavering line of a trench and in the trench, huddled and weary, the vanguard of an army. . . . And then comes an offensive. . . . Thousands of men moving through a barrage of lead and explosion, huddling for shelter, matching the frail mechanism of the human body against the inhumanity of gunpowder and metal. And after the offensive—the

torn and mutilated dead, the even more torn and mutilated living. . . .
When the line of battle shifted, and often during the very heat of battle,
stretcher bearers went out into the field and picked up the wounded. . . .
If there was extensive bleeding the stretcher bearer took care of it on the
field. . . . Otherwise the wounded were not treated until they reached
the classification post. . . . Here, . . . it had to be decided whether or not
a man could stand the transportation to a rear hospital or . . . be treated
at the front hospital. . . . This hospital . . . might be anywhere from eight
to twenty kilometers behind the lines, depending on the shifts of the
battle line. Sometimes the front changed so quickly that the hospital
was actually at the front or just behind it. . . . At this Front Hospital only
operations of great urgency were performed—abdominal surgery; operations to stop major hemorrhages; emergency amputations (often of the
guillotine type); debridements, or the cutting away of dead, jagged and
infected tissue . . .[16]

In addition to the challenges of battlefield medical care, living conditions were
quite rudimentary and food was scarce.

But things could be far worse. Two young U.S. physicians, Seymour
"Rusty" Robbins and Randall Sollenberger, were both killed in July 1937 when
their front-line first-aid stations were bombed. Harold Smith, an ambulance
driver, and Harry Wilkes, a pharmacist, also lost their lives in the conflict. A
number of other health personnel were seriously injured, and all who served
were profoundly stressed emotionally.[17]

### The AMB at Home

Nationally, the AMB had a long list of publicly identified physician sponsors,
mostly respected academics including many of Cannon's friends and cowork-
ers, who helped raise funds and legitimate the AMB's work. Much of the AMB's
initiative and organizational energy, however, came from the CP-USA and its
physician members. They were understandably reticent to acknowledge their
party membership publicly but were enthusiastically responsive to the vigor-
ous support of Spain's Popular Front government by the Third Communist
International known as the Comintern.

The AMB's national office was responsible for evaluating applicants for
service in Spain and for orienting, equipping, and transporting those departing. The Medical Bureau raised money at medical institutions across the country to purchase over one hundred and seventy ambulances, trucks, and other

vehicles and over sixty tons of pharmaceuticals and medical/surgical supplies and equipment.

This required a network of energetic local chapters and extensive fund-raising activity. A staff of AMB field secretaries helped new chapters get started.[18] Of the one hundred or so chapters, the strongest were in Boston, Chicago, Miami, New York City, northern and southern California, and Philadelphia. The backgrounds and motivations of the chapter leaders varied, although those associated with International Labor Defense, International Workers Order, and the CP usually played major roles. Some of the chapters existed only on paper, but many had at least part-time secretaries and the larger ones had staffed offices. At Harvard, Princeton, Swarthmore, the University of Michigan, the Hampton Institute, and more than a dozen other colleges and universities, committees of students, faculty, and staff raised money for ambulances that bore the names of their institutions.[19]

Like the national AMB, chapters typically had numerous local sponsors including both academic and private practice physicians and community leaders such as ministers and rabbis. A number of sponsors were women. Specifics about the personal characteristics of most of the sponsors, particularly their political perspectives, are not known. Undoubtedly, many physician sponsors were attracted by Cannon's leadership and resonated with his pro-democracy and antifacism stance.

Chicago had an exemplary chapter that was organized in the fall of 1936, even before the AMB was established, and quickly raised enough money to purchase medical and surgical supplies and an ambulance.[20] The broadly supported Chicago chapter had subcommittees for four different sections of the city and for nearby Champaign, Peoria, and Springfield, as well as subcommittees for fifteen occupational and ethnic groups, including one for African Americans. The chapter organized fund-raising dinners, dances, film showings, and talks by notables such as Lini (Fuhr) De Vries, the first nurse to return from Spain, Meyer Levin of *Esquire,* and poet Carl Sandburg. Meetings were held in the one-thousand-seat hall of the historic Medical Dental Arts Building.

The AMB's national office in New York provided speakers and produced a wealth of educational materials for hundreds of meetings throughout the country. These included newsletters, brochures, posters, and films, all of which presented compelling photos of the work of the American hospitals and medical teams in Spain. Although some of the speakers were well-known writers, actors, and legislators, many were physicians and nurses who had returned from service in Spain and who described their personal experiences, evoking substantial audience sympathy. Send-off and welcome-home parties were

**Figure 4.2**   Medical Aid for Spain: Ambulance. "From the Negro People of America to the People of Republican Spain."

Credit: Box 1, Folder 20, #1. Frances Patai Photographs Collection, Abraham Lincoln Brigade Archives, Tamiment Library, New York University.

opportunities for education and fund-raising.[21] The physical presence of ambulances to be sent to Spain added an impressive visual focus for events.

In addition to the chapters, the national AMB had active committees of psychologists, social workers, dentists, lawyers, artists and writers, and motion picture workers. Like the chapters, the committees educated and raised funds, frequently with the goal of purchasing an ambulance identifying the sponsor.

## Role of Communist Ideology, the
## Communist Party, and the Comintern

Much recent interest in Spanish Civil War history has been stimulated by new access to the archives in Moscow of the International Brigades, the Comintern, and the Soviet Communist Party. The resulting insights into Stalin's geopolitical considerations and the Comintern's attempted methods of control in the field contribute new understanding to the role of the International Brigades in the Spanish Civil War, although conclusions differ considerably depending upon the political perspectives of the authors.[22] That the International Brigades were dominated by Communists is an essential part of the broader historical context for the AMB story, but controversies about the nature and significance of the Comintern's role are of limited relevance in understanding the actual work of the American Medical Bureau in Spain, the experience of its volunteers, and the significance of that experience for their subsequent health reform engagements in the United States.

Both in the AMB's national leadership and among the American people generally, views about Spain's Republican regime were mixed. Many were sympathetic to it, many others were not, and many were undecided.[23] The labor, civil rights, academic, human service, and political organizations that formally endorsed the AMB were key to its educational and fund-raising work. Although the AMB's educational materials strongly opposed U.S. appeasement of the Fascists and supported the democratically elected Popular Front government of Spain, they were not specifically pro-Communist and were not very different from the educational materials of noncommunist groups, such as the strongly anticommunist American Socialist Party.

Cannon and other prestigious physicians who provided leadership for both the national office and the chapters were overwhelmingly *not* Communists. For example, AMB's early 1937 national "Medical Committee" of thirty-two included only one known Communist and none from the NYC Communist Party group. An early 1939 AMB public letter answering charges of Communist control emphasized that in addition to Cannon, the second national co-chairman was Bishop Francis J. McConnell and that the executive board's chairman was Roger Baldwin, director of the American Civil Liberties Union.[24] In the eyes of many, the mission of the Americans fighting in Spain and of the AMB was simple. As Irving Busch, who took over as head of AMB field operations in Spain when Barsky returned to the United States, put it in February 1938: "We anti-fascist Americans have been sent by [other] anti-fascist Americans to aid the Spanish people on the battlefields of Spain where now is being carried on a world struggle for democracy. We will carry on side by side with the glorious Spanish people."[25]

It must be acknowledged, nonetheless, that Communist physicians did play active, often central roles in the actual work of both the national office and local chapters. Dr. Louis Miller, widely thought to be a Communist, was the first chairman of AMB's Executive Committee.[26] Still, although definitive information is not available, the AMB's executive secretaries were not likely

Communists; in fact, two of the four were retired army colonels. Barsky and Martin were the principal recruiters of the first medical contingent to go to Spain and for this task used their CP roles in unions and hospital staff organizations— but only to provide contacts. Physician Ben Segal, an AMB cofounder, ran the committee selecting personnel to go to Spain. Although a Communist himself, he made clear that CP membership was *not* a requirement but passion about the cause was essential. For those Americans supportive of the Fascist military rebellion—mainly those with isolationist and right-wing ideologies, strong Roman Catholic loyalties, or business interests in Spain—providing medical service for the Spanish Republican Army was itself "proof" that the AMB was atheistic and Communist controlled.

### Motivations and Inspiration of AMB Participants

In letters home and in subsequent writings and interviews, the group of 140 American health professionals who participated in the AMB explained why they went to Spain. The dominant reason was their passionately held prodemocratic and antifascist political convictions. Youth was undoubtedly an enabling factor in that many were not settled in their careers or even employed, and a number of them were looking for experience abroad and excitement. Personal contacts were also important. For instance, Thomas Addis, an active leader of AMB's San Francisco chapter, recruited Eloesser, who in turn recruited a young associate physician, who then recruited several nurses.[27]

Over fifty years after the Spanish Civil War, nurse Hilda Bell Roberts recalled her motivations:

> I grew up in an atmosphere of awareness for working-class concerns. My mother was a member of the ILGWU [International Ladies' Garment Workers' Union]. Both my parents were Socialists—leftist sympathizers and members of the Arbeiter Ring [Workmen's Circle] . . . At their yearly opera performances they always played the International[e]. I thought it was the national anthem of the Jews. My motivation was both political and humanitarian. . . . Even before I was graduated from nursing school [at the Jewish Hospital in Philadelphia], I asked a friend where to go to join up for Spain. [I was] referred to the North American Committee to Aid Spanish Democracy which told me they wanted me, but first I had to graduate. So I did [in 1936], and left for Spain immediately [after]. I was 21. . . . I joined the Communist Party just before I went to Spain because *I thought I had first to be worthy of joining.* I would have gone to Spain anyway because I wanted to—it was necessary and important to do so.

However, *since I was going to Spain, now I was worthy of joining the Communist Party,* and I did so. I was a non-religious Jew, but I was aware of the situation in Europe and concerned about the rise of fascism—fear of fascism was the driving motivation—I feared it as a threat in Spain and to Jews generally.[28]

A second commentary, from physician William Pike, was probably representative of many medical brigadistas with politically amorphous, liberal-Left, perspectives. Pike was trained as an internist but worked reluctantly in a public psychiatric hospital to make a living. He was not directly involved with the NYC physicians who created the AMB but may have known some of them. He was thirty-three years old when he left for Spain in January 1937 with the first group of American volunteers. He explained in a 1975 interview:

My experience of anti-Semitism [during high school, college, medical school, and in jobs] was connected with my identifying with those who were persecuted, and that was the motivating factor, I believe, that was under the surface in going to Spain. I was identifying with those who had been badly treated, pushed around. I had very little involvement politically, hardly any at all. . . . And it's surprising how, emotionally, this business of being Jewish entered in. . . . I felt I was part of something greater than myself, where I did not have to think of myself. For that reason, it was practically the most meaningful experience that I have had in my life.[29]

Perhaps nothing better captures the idealistic motivation and deeply moving experiences of AMB volunteers than this eyewitness account of Sidney Vogel, a Communist or Communist sympathizer at the time of his service:

I had seen many things in Spain, many magnificent examples of the people's heroism and courage that a doctor does not forget. But I had never seen anything to equal the sight in . . . [the blood transfusion room in Barcelona]. It was a big room and bare. Four tall windows flooded it with light. On the floor, arranged in two rows of four, were eight wooden tables draped with hospital sheets. And on each table lay a patient . . . giving blood. . . . From eight human bodies the life blood was flowing, with quiet and orderly precision, into eight glass bottles, guided and controlled by eight white-robed assistants. . . . Bottled blood for transfusions in war time! . . . I looked around me. A new group of donors was being admitted. As each one entered an assistant placed a tourniquet around his arm. He was then turned over to another assistant who placed him on the table, prepared his arm . . . Since the canned blood was good for only eighteen days, the Blood Service had calculated how much blood would be needed during offensives and how much during inactive periods. . . . The day of my visit—the period of the great Fascist offensive—386 blood extractions were made. The citizens of Barcelona, to a man, were blood donor conscious. Each factory, each hotel, each place of work . . . had its "responsable" whose job it was to round up the donors when they were needed. The doctor had merely to telephone the "responsable" in Factory A . . . [and] on the following morning they would be there waiting in line outside the hospital, ready to take their turn in giving blood for the Spanish Republic.[30]

## What Followed

Many of the health personnel who went to Spain engaged in related health activities upon returning to the United States. As the Abraham Lincoln Brigade veterans needed medical care and were frequently unemployed or too poor to pay, a number of AMB physicians provided services for little or no charge. They also supported the efforts to aid Spanish Republican refugees in France and Mexico. In fact, one of the main organizations involved, the Joint Anti-Fascist Refugee Committee, had Barsky as its board chair and Louis Miller as a board member. This later resulted in their notorious 1947–50 battle with the House Un-American Activities Committee, which ended with Barsky serving a six-month prison term and losing his medical license for a time (see chapter 5).[31] Numerous younger health workers eagerly served in the American military forces when the United States entered the Second World War.[32] Sidney Vogel did and later, with the help of the U.S. government's GI Bill (which paid for educational and other benefits for World War II veterans), retrained as a psychiatrist and helped pioneer group therapy for alcoholics. But postwar, many of the other Spanish Civil War medical volunteers had tougher times than Vogel and were subjected to Federal Bureau of Investigation (FBI) scrutiny and harassment, often facing discrimination when they sought employment and professional appointments. Two of the nurses, including chief nurse and administrator Fredericka Martin, decided they had had enough of U.S. red witch hunts and moved to Cuernavaca, Mexico, together with other American ex-pats and Spanish exiles.[33]

Longer term, in the seventy plus years since the Spanish Civil War, many of the American health personnel who supported Spanish democracy have been active in a range of progressive health services and political work. Some of this was done as part of the continuing political efforts of the Veterans of the

Abraham Lincoln Brigade. Another portion of their energy was put to use in the health field, particularly by addressing the crisis in the U.S. health care system or by committing their careers to public service. Yet other energy was devoted to the activities of peace, civil rights, and social justice organizations. Barsky and several other NYC physicians, for example, were among those who in 1939 founded the Physicians Forum, an association of liberal and Left physicians that focused on advocating for a universal national health program. Cannon's next and last progressive political project was providing organizational and editorial leadership to the American-Soviet Medical Society and its journal from their inception in 1943 until his death in 1945.[34]

The post-Spain activities of three nurses, Hilda Bell Roberts, Lini (Fuhr) De Vries, and Ruth Davidow, are impressive examples of lifetime health service and political work. Roberts, now ninety (2010), continues as a frequent activist for peace and social justice causes, including projects organized by the San Francisco veterans. As discussed in the introduction, De Vries later fought for the health and welfare of the disadvantaged mainly in New Mexico and Mexico.[35] In 1960 Davidow journeyed to Cuba (following its revolution), joining a public health organization in Havana where she worked for two years. In 1965 she participated in the civil rights movement in Mississippi working with the Medical Committee for Human Rights. When Native Americans occupied the federal penitentiary at Alcatraz Island in San Francisco Bay, they asked her to run the health care services as one of the very few non-Native Americans allowed on the island. A key subject in several documentaries including *The Good Fight, Their Cause Was Liberty,* and the Academy Award nominee, *Forever Activists,* Davidow became a filmmaker herself, producing twenty-one films on subjects from health care to political activism.[36]

The American health personnel who served in Spain—like their counterparts from across the world—were an integral part of a remarkable moment of progressive solidarity, the mobilization of international support for Spain's Republican Army. They provided crucial medical services and support during a war for democracy and social justice. The physicians, nurses, and others who comprised the AMB, motivated by deep idealism and political commitment, chose to express their commitment in a way that carried obvious and dramatic risks to their careers and even their lives. Yet their experiences were profoundly moving, and most considered their time in Spain the high point of their lives. The memory and resonance of their medical support for Spanish democracy was also a critical bequest to succeeding generations of health activists and contributed greatly to the American health Left's comprehension of world politics and political practice.

## Notes

Anne-Emanuelle Birn and Theodore M. Brown completed the research and writing for this chapter after Walter Lear's death.

1. Among the hundreds of books about American participation in the Spanish Civil War, a subset are notable for their scope, accuracy, and balance: Peter N. Carroll, *The Odyssey of the Abraham Lincoln Brigade: Americans in the Spanish Civil War* (Stanford: Stanford University Press, 1994); Gabriel Jackson, *The Spanish Republic and the Civil War, 1931–1939* (Princeton, NJ: Princeton University Press, 1965); Arthur H. Landis, *The Abraham Lincoln Brigade* (New York: Citadel Press, 1967).

2. There are several books by or about American health personnel who served in Spain: Lini (Fuhr) de Vries, *Up from the Cellar* (Minneapolis: Vanilla Press, 1979); Hank Rubin, *Spain's Cause Was Mine: A Memoir of an American Medic in the Spanish Civil War* (Carbondale: Southern Illinois University Press, 1997); Harris B. Shumacker Jr., *Leo Eloesser, M.D.: Eulogy for a Free Spirit* (New York: Philosophical Library, 1982); and Esther Silverstein Blanc, *Wars I Have Seen: The Play, in Three Acts with Selected Short Stories* (Volcano, CA: Volcano Press, 1996). There are also various journal articles on the subject: Frances Patai, "Heroines of the Good Fight: Testimonies of U.S. Volunteer Nurses in the Spanish Civil War, 1936–1939," *Nursing History Review* 3 (1995): 79–104; Martin F. Shapiro, "Medical Aid to the Spanish Republic during the Civil War (1936–1939)," *Annals of Internal Medicine* 97 (1982): 119–124; Martin F. Shapiro, "Medical Aid Provided by American, Canadian and British Nationals to the Spanish Republic during the Civil War, 1936–1939," *International Journal of Health Services* 13 (1983): 443–458. In addition, there are several reminiscences by physicians and nurses published in anthologies compiled by volunteers who served in Spain, including Edward Barsky, Mildred Rackley, Ray Harris et al., "The American Hospital Unit," in *From Spanish Trenches: Recent Letters from Spain*, ed. Marcel Acier (New York: Modern Age Books, 1937), 9–33; and "Medical Services: Making History and Saving Lives," in *Madrid 1937: Letters of the Abraham Lincoln Brigade from the Spanish Civil War*, ed. Cary Nelson and Jefferson Hendricks (New York: Routledge, 1996), 232–277. An autobiographical extract written by Sidney Vogel in the early 1940s, "War Medicine: Spain, 1936–1939," was recently published by his daughter Lise Vogel in the *American Journal of Public Health* 98 (2008): 2146–2149. Finally, there are at least four unpublished manuscripts that offer autobiographical accounts of medical service during the Spanish Civil War: Edward K. Barsky's book-length manuscript, "The Surgeon Goes to War," Folders 4–21 (undated), Box 5, ALBA #125; Fredericka Martin's "Proud Within Themselves," Folders 7–10 (undated but likely 1970–1984), Box 10, ALBA #1; Frances Patai's "Heroines of the Good Fight: U.S. Women Medical Service Volunteers in the Spanish Civil War (1936–1939)," 1991, Folders 10–11, Box 5, ALBA #131; and Sandor Voros's, "Healing Wounds in Spain: Some Notes on the Functioning of the American Hospitals and the International Sanitary Service in Spain," Unpublished Manuscript on Hospitals and Medical Services in Spain ca. 1937, Folder 15, Box 7, Frances Patai Papers (hereafter FP Papers) (ALBA # 131). All can be found in the Abraham Lincoln Brigade Archives (ALBA), The Tamiment Library and Robert F. Wagner Labor Archives, Elmer Holmes Bobst Library, New York University, New York, New York. Also see http://www.alba-valb.org/index.html/.

3. Edward K. Barsky, "The Surgeon Goes to War," 12–13.

4. Fredericka Martin, "Proud Within Themselves," Part 1, ch. 2, 1–3.

5. Peter J. Kuznick, *Beyond the Laboratory: Scientists as Political Activists in 1930s America* (Chicago: University of Chicago Press, 1987), 165–167, 181–183.

6. For an account of Cannon's political perspective, see Saul Benison, "Walter B. Cannon and the Politics of Medical Science, 1920–1940," *Bulletin of the History of Medicine* 65 (1991): 234–251.

7. Walter B. Cannon, "Natural History of an Anti-Fascist," *American Review of Soviet Medicine* 1 (1944): 380–382.

8. Sandor Voros, "Healing Wounds in Spain," 67.

9. John Gerassi, *Premature Antifascists: North American Volunteers in the Spanish Civil War, 1936–1939: An Oral History* (New York: Praeger Publishers, 1966), 4.

10. "Hospital Group Sails for Spain," *New York Times,* January 17, 1937.

11. Frances Patai, "Heroines of the Good Fight."

12. Mark Zuehlke, *The Gallant Cause: Canadians in the Spanish Civil War* (Missisauga, ON: John Wiley & Sons, 2007), 85.

13. Greenspan to Marion, January[?] 14[?], 1937, Correspondence, Greenspan, Celia. August 1936–July 1937, Box 1, Folder 6, ALBA # 045.

14. Greenspan to Marion, 27/VI/1937, August 1936–July 1937, Box 1, Folder 6, ALBA # 045.

15. Sandor Voros, "Healing Wounds in Spain," 2, 68.

16. Sidney Vogel, "War Medicine: Spain, 1936–1939."

17. Carroll, *The Odyssey of the Abraham Lincoln Brigade,* 178.

18. Medical Bureau, Organizational Letter #2 (April 1937), Fredericka Martin Collection, ALBA # 1, Box 32.

19. For an early account of the chapters, see Francis A. Henson, National Campaign Director, Medical Bureau, American Friends of Spanish Democracy, "Accomplishments and Plans" (report at Eastern Seaboard Conference, February 1937), typescript, 16 pp.; See also Medical Bureau and North American Committee to Aid Spanish Democracy, "Two Years of American Aid to Spain" (November 1938), typescript, 16 pp., Florida International University, Wolfsonian Library, Accession # @ XC2002.05.8.2.

20. "It's Happening in Spain" (pamphlet published by International Labor Defense, 1937), 26–30, Florida International University, Wolfsonian Library, Accession # @ XC2001.02.2.3.

21. Medical Bureau and North American Committee to Aid Spanish Democracy, "Two Years of American Aid to Spain" (November 1938), typescript, 16 (see note 19).

22. Cecil D. Erby, *Comrades and Commissars: The Lincoln Battalion in the Spanish Civil War* (University Park: Pennsylvania State University Press, 2007).

23. Douglas Little, *Malevolent Neutrality: The United States, Great Britain and the Origins of the Spanish Civil War* (Ithaca, NY: Cornell University Press, 1985); Arthur H. Landis, *Death in the Olive Groves: American Volunteers in the Spanish Civil War, 1936–1939* (New York: Paragon House. 1989); Robert A. Rosenstone, *Crusade of the Left: The Lincoln Battalion in the Spanish Civil War* (New York: Pegasus, 1969).

24. Letter from Herman F. Reissig, fourth and last AMB executive secretary, "To Whom It May Concern," February 4, 1939, a two-page response to charges that the AMB and the NAC are "Communistic" or "Communist-controlled." Regarding his own political stance, Reissig states that he "could be called 'Communistic' only by the lunatic fringe which insists that everyone who vigorously espouses liberal ideals is Communistic. [I am] a member of no political party and [have] the confidence of

multitudes of people in every walk of life," Fredericka Martin Collection, ALBA # 1, Box 32.

25. I. Busch, "The American Hospital Centre in Spain," *AMI* #9, February 1, 1938, 3, Daniel McKelvy White Collection, New York Public Library.

26. Hook to Cannon, May 20, 1940, in *Letters of Sidney Hook*, ed. Edward S. Shapiro (Armonk, NY: M. E. Sharpe, 1995), 88. Elsewhere in the letter, Hook writes as follows: "The material which I have seen . . . proves that the Medical Bureau to Aid Spanish Democracy was in reality a Medical Bureau to Aid the Communist Party."

27. Shumacker Jr., *Leo Eloesser, M.D.,* 159.

28. Hilda Bell Roberts, interview by Frances Patai, January 15, 1991, FP Papers, ALBA, 1–2.

29. Wiliam Pike, interview by Paul Margolis, November 7, 1975, from "Dr. Pike's Spanish War," a Bard College senior thesis, ALBA, A18, 16–17.

30. Vogel, "War Medicine: Spain, 1936–1939."

31. Albert Deutsch, "Three Doctors vs. the Inquisition," *PM,* July 8, 1948.

32. Peter N. Carroll, Michael Nash, and Melvin Small, eds., *The Good Fight Continues: World War II Letters from the Abraham Lincoln Brigade* (New York: New York University Press, 2006).

33. Lini (Fuhr) de Vries details her harassment by the FBI in chapters 6 and 7 of her autobiography *Up from the Cellar*, 243–309.

34. Walter J. Lear, "Hot War Creation, Cold War Casualty: The American-Soviet Medical Society, 1943–1948," in *Making Medical History: The Life and Times of Henry E. Sigerist,* ed. Elizabeth Fee and Theodore Brown (Baltimore: Johns Hopkins University Press, 1997), 259–287.

35. De Vries, *Up from the Cellar.*

36. Anonymous, "Ruth Davidow," *The Volunteer* 21(3) (Summer 1999): 20.

# Chapter 5

# Medical McCarthyism and the Punishment of Internationalist Physicians in the United States

**Jane Pacht Brickman**

Studies of the impact of McCarthyism often overlook its effects on medicine. As noted by Manhattan obstetrician and activist Benjamin Segal in the mid-1950s, the "legion of men and women . . . [who were] exiles in their homeland . . . [and faced] economic and social reprisals . . . [by] being labeled subversive" included many physicians.[1] "Medical McCarthyism,"[2] as cardiologist and medical reformer Ernst P. Boas dubbed it, punished physicians who had "internationalist" inclinations with prison sentences, license suspensions, lost income, years of testimony before government review boards, deprivation of hospital privileges, military demotions, tarnished reputations, and psychic wounds. Indeed, the most enduring aspect of medical McCarthyism was its directed attack on a strongly internationalist countervailing medical perspective that had flourished in the 1930s.

This chapter begins with an overview of the political and scientific values that shaped the sensibility of internationalist physicians, their activities in the 1930s and early 1940s, and the swift withering of their activism under the shadow of the Cold War. It also recounts the duels of prominent physicians with loyalty tribunals. Finally, it describes some of the grim realities of life for physicians during the McCarthy period and the significance of this period to U.S. medicine.

Medical McCarthyism arose following two dramatic decades marked by the Great Depression, the advance of fascism in Europe (divisively played out in the Spanish Civil War), the brutality of World War II, and a postwar period that briefly envisioned the building of a lasting peace. Amid these events, the diagnostic and therapeutic advances that bolstered medicine's arsenal, including early achievements (particularly around preventive efforts) of Soviet medicine, emboldened many to imagine that through international collaboration, previously deadly diseases might be controlled, prevented, and perhaps eliminated. It was physicians' involvement in antifascist organizations (especially those supporting Spanish Republicans during and after the civil war), in groups fostering friendship and scientific collaboration with the Soviet Union, and in left-wing efforts to pass national health insurance legislation in the United States that would later make them a focus of political inquisitors.

Guided by the concepts of social medicine, internationalist physicians argued that medical problems had to be addressed politically as well as scientifically.[3] Convinced that medicine was "neutral ground on which . . . [they could] meet in . . . [their] efforts to alleviate the sufferings of humanity, without bias or prejudice," internationalist physicians recognized their political activity as a natural extension of their professional roles.[4]

Nazi aggression and its manipulation of science for state purposes brought internationalist physicians to the forefront of antifascist politics. As the world plunged into chaos, many physicians of considerable heft put aside time from practice and research to harness their professional prestige to resist the siege on democratic and scientific values. Galvanized by "the steady ascendance of autocracy and tyranny in Europe,"[5] internationalist physicians joined organizations that located homes and work for refugee (mostly Jewish) scientists and physicians, defended Republican Spain, sent relief to beleaguered China and Russia, and reinforced the war alliance between the United States and the Soviet Union in 1941.

Internationalist physicians played leading roles in the American Medical Bureau to Aid Spanish Democracy, the American Committee for Democracy and Intellectual Freedom, the Joint Anti-Fascist Refugee Committee, Russian War Relief, the National Council of American-Soviet Friendship, the American Bureau for Medical Aid to China, and the American-Soviet Medical Society— all later targeted as subversive organizations.

To many, Soviet socialism represented a pioneering effort by government to apply scientific principles to secure universal human needs.[6] Especially during the Popular Front period (from 1934 to 1939 Communist parties formed coalitions with liberal and socialist parties in common opposition to the developing fascist threat), many in the scientific community embraced the Soviet Union, crediting it, in contrast to Western democracies, with opposing Hitler in Spain. Most internationalist physicians also believed that the Soviet experiment in socialized medicine offered noteworthy promise (see chapter 3). The Soviet medical model resonated because of its emphasis on preventive services, the social and economic underpinnings of illness, and universal access to care. Admirers attributed dramatically reduced mortality, morbidity, and infant mortality rates to the new Soviet emphasis on preventive interventions.

More than any other account of Soviet medicine, the 1937 publication of Henry E. Sigerist's *Socialized Medicine in the Soviet Union* commanded attention.[7] The quintessential internationalist physician of his generation, Sigerist spent the summers of 1935 and 1936 in the Soviet Union. With near evangelical zeal, he applauded what he saw. Sigerist measured Soviet medical gains against prerevolutionary standards and against the wreckage of famine and epidemic disease left after the Russian Civil War. Sigerist's argument, that Soviet medicine was dynamic and committed to the prevention and elimination of the social etiology of illness, convinced many physicians who were frustrated with the status quo at home that the Soviet Union had much to teach them.

Groups of medical students and interns, emboldened by their elders, also turned their attention to large social and political issues. Excited by Sigerist's description of a social physician trained in both social and medical sciences, student groups urged that medical curricula include courses in medical sociology and social medicine.[8] Public health physician and Sigerist admirer Leonard S. Rosenfeld recalled the shaping of his new awareness: "I studied medicine at New York University . . . in the class of 1937. Moved by the depression and the rise of fascism in Europe, a substantial number of students developed liberal sympathies and interest in social aspects of medicine. There were student organizations and discussions directed at these issues."[9] Progressive medical students established the Association of Medical Students (AMS) in 1937. In 1941 it merged with the Intern Council to become the Association of Interns and Medical Students (AIMS). At its peak in 1945, AIMS had three thousand members.[10] These fledgling physicians joined antifascist campaigns, some taking leave from school to fight in Spain.

For their activism, many of these doctors would later feel the sting of the Red Scare, when the Cold War chill dampened youthful rebellion. In July 1947, physician and health policy analyst Milton Roemer, who worked for the U.S. Public Health Service, lamented the changed atmosphere. Writing to Sigerist, his mentor, Roemer felt the "restrictions on creative work in the federal service . . . getting tighter every day," and decided if he were to continue "to work in the social aspects of medicine," he needed to look for another job.[11] In 1948, another former student, George Silver, wrote to Sigerist that the general climate had "diminished the effective work of most people. Timidity and 'realism' have contributed to a rapid dissipation of advocacy."[12] Five years later, Roemer told Sigerist of the silence that had enveloped the medical world: "[O]ne doesn't talk about politics or political trends and even national health insurance is taboo."[13]

## High-Profile Cases

By the late forties, Cold War tensions trumped discussion of radical reform. President Truman's 1947 executive order establishing a Loyalty Program that armed each federal agency with a loyalty board gave credibility to assertions of pervasive subversive infiltration of the federal government.[14] Although the Democrats held the White House in 1948, red-baiting was unleashed as a potent weapon of partisan politics. The elements of McCarthyism—name calling, anonymous witnesses, dismissals, blacklisting, and intrusive inquiry into political affiliations, as well as the anticommunist assault on medicine— predated Joseph McCarthy's prominent role in this campaign starting in 1950.[15]

Red-baiting had been ubiquitous in the fight around national health insurance legislation from the early decades of the twentieth century. Long before the Cold War whipped the American public into hysteria, relatively modest proposals to change medical care financing were tainted by organized medicine as "un-American." Opponents called health insurance an "entering wedge" for socialism and pitted U.S. freedom against Soviet compulsion.[16] After the establishment of Truman's Loyalty Program in 1947, red-baiting became more lethal, as Americans came to believe "that foreign policy could not be effective unless Communist infiltration of the government was prevented."[17] Internationalist physicians, suspected by some of Communist infiltration, were among the stigmatized. By 1949, membership in the Washington, D.C., chapter of the American-Soviet Medical Society fell from six hundred to thirty.[18]

Henry Sigerist was an early, prominent target. A proponent of socialized medicine, who gave vocal support to the Spanish Republican cause and joined organizations seeking better understanding between the Soviet Union and the United States,[19] Sigerist was called to testify before the Civil Service Commission in 1943. He was grilled about his involvement in groups "looked upon by many persons, as being Communist Front Organizations."[20] Questioned about his work for the Medical Bureau to Aid Spanish Democracy, his trips to Russia, and articles he had published in the *New Masses* and *Soviet Russia Today,* Sigerist failed to mollify the commission. It dropped him as consultant to the Board of Economic Warfare and declared him ineligible for government service. The investigation demoralized him and contributed to his decision to leave Johns Hopkins University in January 1947 and return to Europe.[21]

But it was the House Un-American Activities Committee (HUAC) attack on the board of directors of the Joint Anti-Fascist Refugee Committee (JAFRC) in

1946 that really launched medical McCarthyism. Subpoenas to the board and the subsequent punishment of Dr. Edward K. Barsky initiated the juggernaut. Barsky had graduated from Columbia University's College of Physicians and Surgeons in 1919, and after postgraduate training in Europe, he interned at New York's Beth Israel Hospital, where he remained. When he left for Spain as a volunteer surgeon for the Republican cause in 1937, he was an established surgeon with a substantial patient base, and he had recently joined the Communist Party. In Spain, he headed the American Medical Bureau Hospital and pioneered techniques of battlefront medicine that would save thousands of soldiers' lives in World War II (see chapter 4).[22]

After the Republican forces fell to Franco in 1939, hundreds of thousands of refugees fled the country. Moved to address the needs of the Spanish exiles, Barsky and others established the JAFRC, which maintained a hospital in Mexico City and a scholarship fund for children of refugees. JAFRC contributions also went to Republican refugees in France, North Africa, Portugal, and Switzerland.

In 1946, HUAC subpoenaed the JAFRC books, including lists of contributors and recipients. On First Amendment grounds, the JAFRC board refused to turn over these records. When HUAC called upon JAFRC board members to produce membership lists and the names of refugees to whom JAFRC supplied aid, they refused to take refuge in the Fifth Amendment. Instead, they challenged the legitimacy of the interrogation itself. Board members were cited for contempt of Congress and convicted in June 1947. In 1950, eleven members of the JAFRC board, headed by Barsky, began prison sentences, following three years of appeals and subsequent rejections of pleas for suspended sentences and probation.[23] Barsky got the stiffest sentence, six months and a $500 fine; the others, who included novelist Howard Fast and two physicians, served three months and paid similar fines.

Barsky's travails continued in February 1951, when the New York State Board of Regents suspended his medical license for six months following his contempt of Congress conviction and prison term. As Barsky noted in his appeal, the suspension was punishment for his dissident political beliefs rather than for medical misconduct or "any moral turpitude." He argued: "[I am] not a young man and my family, a wife and young child, are completely dependent upon my earnings. A six months suspension, especially to one of my age, would be catastrophic."[24] Although the Regents' Committee on Discipline voted to rescind the suspension order, the full board overruled the committee. Barsky took his case to the Supreme Court, which in 1954 ruled against him and the suspension became effective on June 25, 1954.[25]

**Figure 5.1** Edward Barsky aboard ship on his way to Spain, ca. 1937.

Credit: Box 1, Folder 6. Edward Barsky Photographs Collection, Abraham Lincoln Brigade Archives, Tamiment Library, New York University.

Other prominent physicians would also exhaust their energies, and sometimes pocketbooks, defending themselves for years before loyalty tribunals. As in academia or the film industry, age and professional accomplishment in the medical field provided no shield. In November 1949, public health luminary C.-E.A. Winslow, then in his early seventies, came under the scrutiny of the Federal Security Agency's Board of Inquiry on Employee Loyalty. Founder of the Yale Department of Public Health in 1915, Winslow had helped to develop international health programs through the International Red Cross, the League of Nations, and the newly founded World Health Organization (WHO). He had visited Russia in 1917 and 1936, first as a member of a Red Cross mission and later with a League group studying Soviet medicine.[26]

Although the assault on Winslow's career was relatively brief, it demonstrated the unbridled character of medical McCarthyism. Based upon Winslow's involvement with the Medical Bureau to Aid Spanish Democracy, his signature on a letter opposing the renewal of HUAC, his association with the National Council of American-Soviet Friendship, and various statements he made praising and defending aspects of Soviet life and foreign policy, the chair of the Board of Inquiry on Employee Loyalty announced an investigation to "determine whether reasonable grounds exist for belief that you [Winslow] are disloyal to the Government of the United States."[27] Winslow had to respond to a lengthy interrogatory, and only a month later was he informed that, subject to a "post-audit" by the Loyalty Review Board, no reasonable grounds for charges of disloyalty had been found. In January 1951, Winslow learned that the Loyalty Review Board had cleared him.[28]

Two years of uncertainty clouded Winslow's life. But Allan Butler and John Peters, who both enjoyed sterling academic positions and reputations, experienced worse treatment. Butler was professor of pediatrics at Harvard Medical School and chief of the Children's Medical Service at Massachusetts General Hospital. He combined roles as clinician, administrator, researcher, teacher, reformer, civil libertarian, and "Cold War critic."[29] Butler traced his political consciousness to his post–World War I work with the American Relief Administration in Poland. There he became an ardent advocate of U.S. membership in the League of Nations and an opponent of foreign intervention in Russia between 1919 and 1923.[30] Joining medical insurgents, he was active in the Committee of Physicians and the Physicians Forum (physician-run groups that lobbied for national health insurance) and instrumental in establishing the White Cross Health Service in 1939, one of the first prepaid medical groups, which cared for twenty thousand people in greater Boston.[31] He also supported medical assistance to Spanish Republicans and, after 1939, to Spanish exiles.[32]

Butler's duel with McCarthyism began in early 1951. He worked nine days a year as consultant to the Children's Bureau, a division of the Federal Security Agency. Its loyalty board claimed that Butler was suspect on the basis of his participation in the JAFRC, the National Council of American-Soviet Friendship, and the China Aid Council. It also cited his support of the Baruch Plan for international control of atomic weapons, a position, the board chair maintained, consonant with the stance of the U.S. Communist Party and the Soviet Union.[33] In response, Butler defended his relief work for Spanish exiles as a reflection of his "profound loyalty to democracy in the best American sense."[34] He insisted that understanding, not ideology, prompted his participation in joint U.S.-Soviet medical and friendship organizations. Butler endured a total of three loyalty hearings, finally resulting in his exoneration in 1953. In the 1960s Butler went on to become a vocal opponent to the war in Vietnam and counseled young men who sought conscientious objector status. In 1968 he testified for famed pediatrician and antiwar activist Benjamin Spock, his friend of thirty years, charged with conspiracy to assist draft resistance.

John Peters, Yale's venerated professor of internal medicine, rode an emotional roller coaster from 1949 to 1955. Like Winslow, Peters, in his first volley with the Federal Security Agency Board of Inquiry on Employee Loyalty, won easy dismissal of the charges. But in December 1951, the board brought sixteen new charges against him. Peters testified for two days in April 1952, denying membership in the Communist Party while vigorously affirming and defending his career as an internationalist physician, his support for a national health program, his opposition to the McCarran Act,[35] and his assistance to Republican Spain.[36] The board dispatched Peters's case within a month, dropping all charges. But the Loyalty Review Board reopened it in April 1953. Again Peters defended himself.[37] Now the review board found sufficient evidence to doubt Peters's loyalty, and in June 1953 the secretary of the Department of Health, Education, and Welfare barred him from government service for three years. Unwilling to allow the stigma of disloyalty to go unchallenged, Peters retained Thurman Arnold, whose Washington law firm took the case without fee. The U.S. Supreme Court agreed to hear the appeal and, in June 1955, decided for Peters. The Court ordered the reinstatement of Peters's government research grants, but he died a few months after the decision.[38]

## The Grip of Medical McCarthyism

Truman's unexpected presidential victory in 1948 revived hopes for passage of the Wagner-Murray-Dingell Bill (which proposed comprehensive national health insurance to be administered by the Social Security Administration), and the American Medical Association (AMA) mobilized for an offensive. With an overflowing treasury, the AMA unleashed vitriolic Cold War rhetoric. Although by 1950 it was clear that Truman's health program would not be enacted, with its new war chest the AMA continued its efforts to nullify medical dissent and reassert professional solidarity.[39] In a guest editorial in the *Journal of the American Medical Association*, FBI director J. Edgar Hoover offered his thoughts for safeguarding Americans' health. He admonished doctors to stay vigilant, lest they fall victim to the "germs of an alien ideology" as insidious as they were contagious.[40] To fight the germs, Hoover urged doctors to report to the FBI "any [suspicious] information" that might fall into their "possession."[41]

Many hospitals and medical schools proved compliant, permitting "the culture of the Cold War"[42] to bully its way into their corridors. Loyalty oaths—that typically went beyond affirmation of allegiance to the state or country, demanding that signatories pledge that in the previous five years they had not belonged to specific organizations—became requirements of hospital employment. In spite of years of devoted service, many doctors lost their hospital appointments for refusing to sign oaths.[43]

Signing a loyalty oath disavowing affiliation with a lengthy list of organizations also became a requirement for military enlistment. Prompted by the military's shortage of physicians during the Korean War, Congress passed the Doctor Draft Act in August 1950, allowing doctors and dentists to be drafted until age fifty, far above the age limit of twenty-six specified under the Selective Service Act of 1948. In return for longer eligibility, doctors would be granted commissions, at least as first lieutenants, and would serve in the Medical Corps. But doctors or dentists who invoked the Fifth Amendment—an option under the act—rather than answer a loyalty questionnaire that inquired about past and present affiliations with two hundred and fifty organizations were denied commissions and instead were drafted as privates, without permission to practice medicine.[44] Various internationalist physicians were demoted and discharged from service due to their refusal to sign loyalty oaths.[45]

These punitive actions had ripple effects. Dr. Hyman Gold, an AIMS veteran, pleaded Fifth Amendment privileges rather than sign a loyalty oath. His commission was revoked and he was drafted into the U.S. Air Force. He served two years. But wanting to avoid charges of coddling Communists, the air force court-marshaled and discharged him. When he left service, he sought membership in a Montefiore Hospital Health Insurance Plan group in New York City. According to Gold, although Montefiore was a liberal institution, letters from the FBI, warning of the loss of government research grants should he be hired, led hospital administrators to reject Gold. Unable to find institutional employment, he was forced to go into private practice.[46]

Even after the Korean War, doctors faced the threat of military draft, followed by demotion if they failed to complete the commissioning application. Dr. Bernard Lown, who had been active in AIMS and international student organizations, found himself blacklisted until 1957. In the U.S. Army Reserve and promoted to captain in 1953, Lown was asked to sign a loyalty oath and indicate in a second part of his application his affiliation, if any, with several hundred organizations. Willing to sign the loyalty oath, he invoked his constitutional rights rather than answer the second part.[47] The army gave Lown an honorable discharge from the Reserve and then drafted him as a private. In the wake of McCarthy's assault on the army, Lown was discharged in 1954. "Once I had the undesirable discharge . . . I was without a job and couldn't get a job any place. . . . wherever I'd go, the FBI was one jump ahead."[48]

In another instance, Dr. Max Pepper adopted an aggressive, albeit risky, strategy. To preempt and prevent the army from drafting him as a private after he refused to sign loyalty oaths in 1955 and 1956, Pepper hired attorney Stanley Faulkner and sued to be commissioned as an officer to practice medicine in the service. At a hearing, the U.S. Army took the position that Pepper was unfit to serve as an officer. The army prevailed. Pepper, however, was never drafted.[49]

At an organizational level, medical reform advocacy groups either dismantled or faced red-baiting. Even before Bella Dodd, the ex-Communist head of the Teachers Union in New York, testified before the Senate Subcommittee on Internal Security in September 1952, claiming that the Physicians Forum and AIMS were arms of the Communist Party, the Forum had been losing members.[50] Between 1948 and 1950 five of its founders resigned. In 1950, at the apex of the Cold War, the Forum reached bottom. Following Dodd's finger pointing, Dr. George Cannon, who served for many years on the Forum's national board, resigned. A Black physician based in New York, Cannon found that "the price I am having to pay to maintain my membership is too great. It is intensified by the fact that I live in a small community [Harlem] within a large city and the pressures exerted have been tremendous."[51] He believed that his resignation would be inconsequential, because "the effective life of the Forum is at an end."[52] While Cannon's pronouncement proved incorrect (the Physicians Forum survives to the present), medical McCarthyism dealt deathblows to other organizations.[53]

## McCarthyism's Long Reach

Measuring the lasting impact of medical McCarthyism involves a degree of speculation. Ellen Schrecker's account of McCarthyism in academia speaks of lost historical possibilities—unexplored ideas, abandoned careers, and paths not taken.[54] Even without counting the shattered careers and precluded research, medical McCarthyism clearly created a "brain drain," both by the expenditure of time it compelled of physicians and through the career detours it imposed.

The life of E. Richard Weinerman provides a good example. Weinerman became visiting professor of medical economics in 1948 at the University of

California's Berkeley School of Public Health, and until the "storm clouds"[55] of McCarthyism altered his course, he was enormously productive, making several important scholarly contributions to the comparative international study of medical education and health systems, among other topics. But when he refused to sign a loyalty oath, Weinerman was not rehired. He departed to work at the Southern California branch of Kaiser Permanente Health Plan. Still hounded by McCarthyism, Weinerman was forced to resign in 1953. To ensure his livelihood, he entered private practice, not returning to teaching and research until 1963, when Yale offered him a faculty appointment after a background check that lasted one year.

Although Dr. Leslie Falk relished his "life in social medicine," friends and colleagues believed that McCarthyism created a permanent roadblock that stymied his career and perhaps limited his contributions. From 1937 to 1940, Falk was a Rhodes scholar and worked in England with Alexander Fleming in the development of penicillin. He returned to the United States and completed his medical degree at Johns Hopkins. After a year's residency, the Rockefeller Foundation awarded Falk a fellowship in social medicine. In 1946, he traveled to Byelorussia on staff with the United Nations Relief and Rehabilitation Administration. On his return to the United States, Falk joined the Public Health Service. But in the dark days of fear, he quietly walked away from a job with the service rather than do battle with a loyalty board. As he wrote, "[f]ar better to have resigned than to have become a cowardly informer when they asked me who else did I know as a Communist."[56]

Similarly, Thomas L. Perry, a Harvard College graduate, who was a Rhodes scholar with Falk and later a graduate of Harvard Medical School, left the United States for Canada after his refusal to cooperate with HUAC and his subsequent dismissal from the Los Angeles Children's Hospital in 1952.[57] Perry had been president of the Harvard AMS chapter, then national president of AIMS. As a practicing physician in California, he joined with others (including three doctors dismissed from Cedars Hospital in Los Angeles) to fight loyalty oaths as a condition of licensure. This group of Southern Californian dissidents pushed for the full racial integration of the medical and allied professions, and "spoke out clearly for peace and for the development of friendly relations between medical men and women and scientists of all nations." For these activities, he, with twenty other California physicians, was subpoenaed by HUAC in October 1952. Perry described the doctors as "thoroughly uncooperative witnesses."[58] Although he continued to collaborate and publish with old colleagues, he never returned to the United States.

Others battled from within public service. In 1949, Milton Roemer reported "the situation in the federal government [is] extremely difficult." In October 1948, he faced an official loyalty hearing. Although other colleagues had chosen to resign, Roemer, "after very careful consideration of all angles," decided "to fight it out. There were correspondence, phone calls, discussions, and decisions to be made almost daily for six months; the FBI investigations go back for ten years."[59] He refused to answer questions about past affiliations, yet in April 1949 he was cleared for continued government work. Although he remained with the Public Health Service, Roemer moved that year to a teaching position at Yale, on loan from the service. When on fieldwork in Europe and enjoying the "liberal spirit" there, an "atmosphere that characterized the large cities in the United States around 1935," he was both invigorated and convinced that however well his work was proceeding at home, "the depressing effect of the general atmosphere is inescapable."[60] He quickly became determined to find work in Europe. He began working for the WHO in December 1950 in Geneva, where he remained until 1953, "when the U.S. government withdrew approval of his appointment under pressure of McCarthyism"[61] due to his refusal to sign a loyalty oath "as a matter of principle."[62]

In spite of his early travails, Roemer went on to an illustrious career. After being forced to resign from the WHO, he served as director of Medical and Hospital Services in Saskatchewan, where "he oversaw the first successful attempt in Canada to introduce universal health insurance."[63] He subsequently held professorships at Cornell and then UCLA, where he remained from 1962 until his death four decades later. Notwithstanding his recognition, Roemer noted that "in the subsequent decades to the present [1993], I have never been asked to serve on a federal government 'review panel' to evaluate health services research applications, although many junior people on my staff have been invited to play this role. In the 1970s, I received a telephone inquiry from the *New York Times,* asking if I had reason to suspect that I was on a 'blacklist' of social science investigators, who were barred from such panels."[64]

Even those who had managed to lay low were affected by McCarthyism's enduring reach. Internationalist George Silver, then chief of social medicine at Montefiore Hospital in the Bronx, faced a year's delay in 1965 in his appointment as undersecretary of the Department of Health, Education, and Welfare because of his membership in the Physicians Forum.[65] Once appointed, Silver promoted child and international health and championed neighborhood health centers, before becoming a well-regarded Yale professor of public health.

Various physicians described the emotional toll of the period. Henry Sigerist spoke of his alienation and depression after his hearing in 1943 and the

**Figure 5.2**    1971 meeting of Milton Roemer (*left*) with Fidel Castro (*right*).
Courtesy of John Roemer.

increasing aloofness of the Johns Hopkins president, Isaiah Bowman. Although
Ernst Boas created firestorms in the New York County Medical Society, he was
never brought before a congressional committee or loyalty review board; nonetheless, he spent the remainder of his life (he died in 1955) wondering when
the ax would fall. FBI agents questioned Mount Sinai physician and medical historian Saul Jarcho and other friends and associates of Boas about his
political connections, and Boas withstood hostile accusations of Communist
affiliation at a membership meeting of the New York County Medical Society.

He also complained of depression.[66] Lingering fear continued to haunt other internationalists.

Even those only indirectly affected by the McCarthyist purges engaged in self-censorship as a protective device. As late as the 1990s, public health policy professor Dr. Milton Terris, also a Sigerist acolyte, strongly urged that I remove an appendix with a list of the names and specialties of Physicians Forum members from an article I was preparing;[67] he worried that the list might endanger the individuals or their families. Such was the imprint of McCarthyism.

Fear of possible repercussions also curbed the enthusiasm of the next generation of medical students. According to George Silver, "[t]he medical students of the thirties, who read Allan Butler's and John Punnet Peters's attacks on the AMA, who devoured Henry Sigerist's social history . . . [who] formed the AMS, later the AIMS to do something about the way students were taught about medicine and what their roles should be," did not at first replicate themselves.[68] The punishment of senior members of the profession resonated among the young. If such figures as Butler, Peters, and Boas faced professional firing squads, what might become of a novice who mixed politics with medicine to challenge conventional wisdom?

AIMS, too, was a fatality of the witch hunt. The Interne, its publication, was an active periodical that discussed many of the problems and controversial issues pertaining to the improvement of the quality and economy of U.S. medicine. However, the AMA pursued AIMS following a report from a drug company representative that AIMS members had attended an international conference with some participants from the Communist bloc. Within two weeks, The Interne lost all of its advertisers. With the "exposure" and subsequent collapse of AIMS, many former members struggled to find internships and encountered tough moments later in their careers.[69]

The perils of medical McCarthyism isolated and silenced some, but in time others found new outlets and expressions for their political commitments. "Second-generation" internationalists became involved in the civil rights movement, in efforts to curb nuclear arms, and in protests over the Vietnam War. Dr. Anna Rand, an OB/Gyn and Physicians Forum activist, blamed the Cold War for what she perceived as a derailing of Leslie Falk's career: "Les Falk came so academically gifted, and yet the only medical school that took him [onto its faculty] was Meharry," a historically Black medical college in Nashville, Tennessee.[70] Yet for Falk, Meharry became a refuge, a safe haven, and a new base for political activism where he transformed his earlier passions into civil rights activism. Like Falk, many who had come of age medically in the late 1930s, 1940s, and early 1950s rechanneled their medical internationalism.

They helped to found the Medical Committee for Human Rights, Physicians for Social Responsibility, and International Physicians for the Prevention of Nuclear War (see chapter 8).[71]

But at least in the short run, medical McCarthyism silenced an articulate opposition.[72] Part of the motivation behind Ernst Boas's stubborn refusal to answer his county society colleagues' questions—about whether he was or ever had been a member of the Communist Party—was his understanding of McCarthyism as nothing less than an effort to eliminate debate and dissent, and in his case "to curtail and destroy the activities of physicians who disagree with the policies pursued by the leadership of the County Medical Society."[73] By de-legitimating minority opinion as subversive, McCarthyism eliminated real discussion of issues and silenced or neutralized colleagues who held internationalist, unconventional, and alternative perspectives. These chilling effects continue to plague the health, medical, and political arenas in the United States today.

### Notes

1. Benjamin Segal, "Freedom of Thought and Expression for Physicians," *Physicians Forum Bulletin* (June 1954): 13. This article focuses on the most prominent (male) internationalist physicians stung by McCarthyism. Most of the female health professionals who bore its brunt were internationalist nurses who participated with the American Medical Bureau and the Abraham Lincoln Brigade during the Spanish Civil War (see chapter 4).
2. Ernst P. Boas, "Letter to the Editor," *New York Medicine* 8 (1952): 13–14.
3. See chapter 2.
4. Henry E. Sigerist to Stuart Mudd, April 30, 1947, Henry E. Sigerist Papers, American Soviet Medical Society 1943–1947 File, Alan Mason Chesney Medical Archives of The Johns Hopkins Medical Institutions. Also see Henry E. Sigerist, "The Johns Hopkins Institute of the History of Medicine during the Academic Year 1942–1943," *Bulletin of the History of Medicine* 14 (1943): 250–270.
5. Ernst P. Boas, "Address," 10th Anniversary Dinner of the Forum, February 20, 1953, Ernst P. Boas Papers, American Philosophical Society Library, Philadelphia (hereafter Boas Papers).
6. See Peter J. Kuznick, *Beyond the Laboratory: Scientists as Political Activists* (Chicago: University of Chicago Press, 1987).
7. Henry E. Sigerist, *Socialized Medicine in the Soviet Union* (New York: W. W. Norton and Co., 1937), 82. John Adams Kingsbury and Sir Arthur Newsholme's 1933 *Red Medicine: Socialized Health in Soviet Russia* is discussed in chapter 3.
8. Sigerist described his conception of the social physician in Henry E. Sigerist, "Remarks on Social Medicine in Medical Education," in *Henry E. Sigerist on the Sociology of Medicine*, ed. Milton I. Roemer (New York: MD Publications, 1962), 362.
9. Leonard S. Rosenfeld to Jane Pacht Brickman, February 2, 1990.
10. Milton I. Roemer to Brickman, June 18, 1993. Roemer estimated that AIMS had chapters in thirty or forty medical schools and attracted between 10 and 15 percent of the medical students and house staff. (The initial spelling was Interne.)

11. Roemer to Sigerist, July 24, 1947, Box 20, File 738, Henry E. Sigerist Papers, Sterling Memorial Library, Yale University, hereafter Sigerist Papers.

12. Silver to Sigerist, December 26, 1949, General Correspondence, Series I, Box 22, File 798, Sigerist Papers.

13. Roemer to Sigerist, November 3, 1954, Box 20, File 742, Sigerist Papers.

14. The executive order mandated that each new federal employee pass a loyalty check, administered by the Civil Service Commission.

15. In 1946, Joseph McCarthy was elected to the Senate from Wisconsin. With a lackluster record, in 1950 McCarthy searched desperately for an issue that would win him a second term. In February 1950, he spoke before a Republican club in Wheeling, West Virginia, claiming to hold in hand a list of 205 Communists working in the State Department. His campaign took off, as he seemed to provide a simple explanation for Communist Cold War gains, and he won reelection in 1952. His tactics held the nation in his grip until the Senate censured him in 1954.

16. See Forrest A. Walker, "Americanism versus Sovietism: A Study of the Reaction to the Committee on the Costs of Medical Care," *Bulletin of the History of Medicine* 53 (1979): 489–504; Ronald L. Numbers, *Almost Persuaded, American Physicians and Compulsory Health Insurance, 1912–1920* (Baltimore: Johns Hopkins University Press, 1978); Beatrix R. Hoffman, *The Wages of Sickness: The Politics of Health Insurance in Progressive America* (Chapel Hill: University of North Carolina Press, 2001).

17. Athan Theoharis, *Seeds of Repression, Harry S. Truman and the Origins of McCarthyism* (Chicago: Quadrangle Books, 1971), 27.

18. See Peter L. Steinberg, *The Great "Red Menace": United States Prosecution of American Communists, 1947–1952* (Westport, CT: Greenwood Press, 1984); Theoharis, *Seeds of Repression;* David Caute, *The Great Fear: The Anti-Communist Purge under Truman and Eisenhower* (New York: Simon and Schuster, 1978).

19. Sigerist was a founder of the American-Soviet Medical Society and edited its journal, *American Review of Soviet Medicine.*

20. "Transcript of the Hearings of 15 November 1943," 2, in the Professional Activities Group, Series II, Box 3, Folder 1, Sigerist Papers.

21. In 1932, William Welch had recruited Sigerist to the United States from Switzerland to direct the Institute of the History of Medicine at John Hopkins University. For more on Sigerist's background, see Elizabeth Fee and Theodore M. Brown, eds., *Making Medical History: The Life and Times of Henry E. Sigerist* (Baltimore: Johns Hopkins University Press, 1997).

22. Edward K. Barsky Papers, Abraham Lincoln Brigade Archives, New York University, Tamiment Library, Robert F. Wagner Labor Archives, hereafter Barsky Papers; Howard Fast, *Being Red: A Memoir* (Boston: Houghton Mifflin Co., 1990).

23. The U.S. Supreme Court refused to hear their appeal, thus upholding the lower court rulings that asking alleged Communists about their politics did not violate the First Amendment. See "Statement Made by Dr. Edward K. Barsky to the House Committee on Un-American Activities," Barsky Papers; Ellen Schrecker, *No Ivory Tower: McCarthyism and the Universities* (New York: Oxford University Press, 1986).

24. Edward K. Barsky, "Appeal to the New York State Board of Regents," undated, Barsky Papers.

25. *Dr. Edward K. Barsky v. The Board of Regents of the University of the State of New York,* 347 U.S. 442 (1954).

26. For biographical information, see C.-E.A. Winslow Papers, MS 749, Sterling Memorial Library, Yale University (hereafter Winslow Papers). For example, "Dr. Winslow, 79, of Yale Is Dead," *New York Times,* 1956.

27. "Interrogatory, November 15, 1949," attached to letter from Joseph E. McElvain to C.-E.A. Winslow, November 15, 1949, Winslow Papers; also, McElvain to Winslow, November 19, 1949; McElvain to Winslow, December 1, 1949; and McElvain to Winslow, January 19, 1951, Winslow Papers.

28. McElvain to Winslow, January 10, 1951, Winslow Papers.

29. See Thomas Paterson, ed., *Cold War Critics: Alternatives to American Foreign Policy in the Truman Years* (Chicago: Quadrangle Books, 1971), 2–4.

30. Allan Butler, "Memorandum on Hearings Before the Board of Employee Loyalty, February 14, 1951," Box New Y-R, PF File, Boas Papers.

31. For more on the Physicians Forum, see Jane Pacht Brickman, "'Medical McCarthyism': The Physicians Forum and the Cold War," *Journal of the History of Medicine and Allied Sciences* 49 (1994): 398–399 and chapter 4.

32. For biographical information, see obituaries: "Allan Macy Butler 1894–1986," *Harvard Medical Alumni Bulletin* (1986–1987): 61–63; "Dr. Allan Butler, Pioneer in Health," *New York Times,* October 9, 1986; Jane Pacht Brickman, "Allan Macy Butler (1894–l986)," *Journal of Public Health Policy* 20 (1999): 356–363.

33. See "Outline of Charges Received from the Board of Inquiry on Employee Loyalty [of the Federal Security Agency], Received February 9, 1951," Box New Y-R, RF File, Boas Papers; "Memorandum, 14 February 1951," Box New Y-R, RF File, Boas Papers.

34. Butler to McElvain, January 27, 1951, Box A, Boas Papers.

35. The McCarran Internal Security Act, also known as the Subversive Activities Control Act, passed Congress in 1950. It required Communist organizations in the United States to register with the attorney general.

36. For a description of the progress of Peters's loyalty investigation, see the ten-page compilation of his statement to the Federal Security Agency Board of Inquiry on Employee Loyalty, summary of charges against him, and correspondence between Fowler V. Harper and Hiram Bingham, chair of the Loyalty Review Board, Box New Y-R, John Peters File, Boas Papers.

37. At Peters's hearing in May 1953, he was supported by such luminaries as Alan Gregg (director of medical sciences at the Rockefeller Foundation), Charles Seymour (former president of Yale), C.-E.A. Winslow, and Eleanor Roosevelt, who submitted an affidavit.

38. See Thurman Arnold to John Peters, February 26, 1954, Professional Papers, Series I, Box 4, File 122, John P. Peters Papers, Sterling Memorial Library, Yale University. See also Fowler V. Harper to Boas, March 5, 1954, Box New Y-R, John Peters File, Boas Papers; Arnold to Peters, January 4, 1955, Peters to Arnold, January 10, 1955, and Arnold to Peters, February 3, 1955, Professional Papers, Series I, Box 4, File 122, Peters Papers; Catherine G. Roraback, "The Public Man Confronts a McCarthy Era Witch-Hunt," *Yale Journal of Biology and Medicine* 75 (2002): 29–32.

39. In 1949, the AMA assessed each member $25 and the next year imposed a $25 membership fee. Oliver Garceau, "Organized Medicine Enforces 'Party Line,'" *Public Opinion Quarterly,* 4 [1950]: 417). See also James G. Burrow, *AMA Voice of American Medicine* (Baltimore: Johns Hopkins University Press, 1963).

40. J. Edgar Hoover, "Let's Keep America Healthy," *Journal of the American Medical Association* 144 (1950): 1094.

41. Hoover, "Let's Keep America Healthy," 1095.

42. Stephen J. Whitfield, *The Culture of the Cold War* (Baltimore: Johns Hopkins University Press, 1992).

43. See Richard W. Lippman to Boas, September 3, 1952, "On the West Coast," *Physicians Forum Bulletin* (December 1951): 4; "Statement on Cedars of Lebanon Injustice," *Physicians Forum Bulletin* (December 1951): 5–6; "Los Angeles Physicians Attack 'Old Guard,'" *Physicians Forum Bulletin* (December 1951): 5; "Cedars' Shame," *Medical Freedom* 1 (1952): 1–4; "Courage is Contagious, The Bill of Rights versus the Un-American Activities Committee," New Y-R, PF File, Boas Papers.

44. In *Orloff v. Willoughby,* 345 U.S. 83 (1953), the U.S. Supreme Court upheld the decision of the air force that stripped Dr. Stanley J. Orloff of his commission as captain in the Air Force Reserves Medical Corps. Orloff was inducted into the army as a private without permission to practice medicine. Box Ch-F, D File, Boas Papers.

45. By 1953, at least twenty doctors and dentists over the age of twenty-six had been stripped of their officer status. See "Doctor Draft Act. Excerpts from County Hearings," *Physicians Forum Bulletin* (May 1953): 21, 25.

46. Dr. Hyman Gold, interview with Jane Pacht Brickman, April 14 and May 21, 1993.

47. See chapter 8.

48. Dr. Bernard Lown, interview with Brickman, February 15 and July 7, 1993.

49. Dr. Max Pepper, interview with Brickman, June 3, 1993.

50. For more on Dodd, see Schrecker, *No Ivory Tower,* 167–169. *New York Medicine,* the mouthpiece of the New York County Medical Society, printed her testimony verbatim in an editorial, without inviting a rejoinder from the Forum. See "Communists and Medicine," *New York Medicine* 8 (1952): 13–14. Bella Dodd, *Subcommittee to Investigate the Administration of the Internal Security Act and Other Internal Security Laws of the Committee on the Judiciary, United States Senate, September 9, 1952, 82d Cong., 2d Sess., on Subversive Influences in the Educational Process* (Washington, D.C.: Government Printing Office, 1952), 36–37.

51. George Cannon to Boas, October 24, 1952, Box New Y-R, PF File, Boas Papers.

52. Cannon to Boas, October 24, 1952, Boas Papers.

53. For information on these groups, see Box B-Cardiotachometer, C File, Boas Papers. For discussion of the capitulation of liberals (those who by purging members thought to be Communists implicitly legitimated the abandonment of civil liberties), see Richard Pells, *The Liberal Mind in a Conservative Age: American Intellectuals in the 1940s and 1950s* (Middleton, CT: Wesleyan University Press, 1985); Robert Griffith, *The Politics of Fear: Joseph R. McCarthy and the Senate* (Rochelle Park, NJ: Hayden Book Co., 1970).

54. Schrecker, *No Ivory Tower;* Nancy Krieger and Elizabeth Fee, "Measuring Social Inequalities in Health in the United States: A Historical Review, 1900–1950," *International Journal of Health Services* 26(3) (1996): 391–418.

55. Leslie A. Falk, "E. Richard Weinerman, M.D., M.P.H.," *Yale Journal of Biology and Medicine* 44 (1971): 3–23.

56. See Leslie A. Falk, "Health Care for All: A Life in Social Medicine," unpublished manuscript (1995), 125. After Falk left the Public Health Service he worked for the United Mineworkers Fund Health Program, organizing group practices in mining communities.

57. Thomas Perry to Boas, February 17, 1953, Boas Scrapbook, 10th Anniversary of the Physicians Forum, Boas Papers.

58. Perry to Boas, February 17, 1953, Boas Papers.

59. Roemer to Sigerist, July 11, 1949, Sigerist Papers.

60. Roemer to Sigerist, October 10, 1950, Sigerist Papers.

61. Ruth Roemer, "Obituary, Milton I. Roemer, 1916–2001," *Bulletin of the World Health Organization* 79 (2001): 481.

62. John Farley, *Brock Chisholm, the World Health Organization, and the Cold War* (Vancouver: UBC Press, 2008), 186.

63. Farley, *Brock Chisholm,* 118.

64. Roemer to Brickman, June 18, 1993.

65. George A. Silver, "The Health Left, 1930s, 1940s, 1950s" (paper delivered at the celebration of Walter Lear's 70th birthday, Philadelphia, May 1, 1993). "In Memoriam: Respected Health Policy Leader, George A. Silver, M.D.," *Health and Medicine,* February 3, 2005.

66. Henry E. Sigerist, *Autobiographical Writings,* ed. Nora Sigerist Beeson (Montreal: McGill University Press, 1966); Boas to Allan Butler, February 4, 1951, Box New Y-R, PF File, Boas Papers; Saul Jarcho to Brickman, September 11, 1994. For Boas's battles with the New York County Medical Society, see Brickman, "'Medical McCarthyism,'" 380–418.

67. Brickman, "'Medical McCarthyism,'" 398–399.

68. Silver, "The Health Left."

69. Butler, "Dear Fitz." See also Walter Lear, "The Pink and Red Physicians of the 1930s and 1940s," unpublished manuscript, supplement to talk presented at the American Association for the History of Medicine annual conference, Halifax, Nova Scotia, May 4, 2006.

70. Dr. Anna Rand, interview with Brickman, January 11, 1993.

71. In a tribute to Richard Weinerman following his death, twenty-one of his colleagues signed a letter published in the *American Journal of Public Health.* They traced the continuity of his activism: "Dick showed a consistent and persistent concern with social justice. Whether it was the travail of the McCarthy era, the events of Selma, the war in Vietnam, the student confrontations . . . Dick had a personal commitment. This was the fabric out of which his designs in health care were cut." *American Journal of Public Health,* 1970, 797–799, in Falk, "E. Richard Weinerman," 3. Medical student activism also revived in the 1960s. See P. Preston Reynolds, "American Medical Student Association: A Success Story," *North Carolina Medical Journal* 50 (February 1986): 95–102.

72. See Richard M. Fried, *Nightmare in Red: The McCarthy Era in Perspective* (New York: Oxford University Press, 1990); Robert Griffith, "American Politics and the Origins of McCarthyism," in *A History of Our Time: Readings on Postwar America, ed.* William H. Chafe and Harvard Sitkoff (New York: Oxford University Press, 1991), 63–73; Griffith, *The Politics of Fear.*

73. Ernst P. Boas, "Letter to the Editor," *New York Medicine* 8 (1952): 13–14.

# Part III

# Generation Born in the 1920s–1930s

The chapters in this section reflect the experiences of a generation born in the 1920s and early 1930s (as immigrants or the children of immigrants) who grew up during the Depression and reached adulthood during World War II, the brief postwar interlude of internationalist optimism, and the Cold War. The pall of McCarthyism led indubitably to caution about overt political expression, especially readily identifiable left-wing perspectives. Members of this generation gravitated, perhaps unconsciously but not by accident, to political causes that could be framed in the less ideologically threatening terms of human rights, international learning and exchange (even with supposed Communist enemies), and global survival.

One major domestic cause to which members of this generation were drawn was the civil rights movement; they eagerly formed alliances with a range of African American organizations. Looking abroad, they joined solidarity groups that supported African liberation struggles and exposed and resisted apartheid and other forms of extreme racist policy in Africa. They also protested the United States' deceitful policy of military aggression and official coverup in Southeast Asia and urged a reversal of policy toward China. Many became deeply concerned about the lethal consequences of atmospheric radioactive fallout resulting from U.S. nuclear testing and the potential nuclear holocaust that increasingly seemed to be inevitable given the weapons race with the Soviet Union. In each of these settings, this generation of health internationalists discovered approaches to improving social justice and community health—and to making human survival itself possible—that could be transported back to the United States.

All of the causes that members of this generation pursued in some way opposed the heavy-handed, manipulative pragmatism of official U.S. foreign policy, whether it was the U.S. government's condoning of apartheid in order to cultivate the South African regime as a bulwark against communism, calling U.S. military engagement in Korea a "police action" and later denying the escalation of military operations in Vietnam, refusing to recognize Communist China as a legitimate nation until the Nixon-Mao thaw of 1972, or demonizing the Soviet Union for its uncontrolled nuclear proliferation while encouraging the United States' own. While this generation managed to pursue—in a new, sophisticated, and indirect way—health-Left solidarity in spite of Cold War repression, they also benefited from the shifting winds of the more activist and politically receptive 1960s.

But the activism of this generation also challenges us to consider the variety of ethical and historical dilemmas of this period. How could health leftists engage in sharing the lessons of solidarity abroad when social and racial realities at home were so problematic? South Africa's community-oriented primary care effort was doomed by an increasingly repressive and racist state—which had echoes in the United States—but was nonetheless hopefully transplanted. China's "blooming of a thousand flowers" was accompanied by the suffering by millions of Chinese people during the Great Leap Forward and then the Cultural Revolution. Did this generation view social development in China the same way the prior generation saw the events in the Soviet Union? Was the Chinese barefoot doctor system an exception or was it perhaps viewed as separable from larger policies, as were many of the earlier advances in the USSR? And was there some truth to the possibility that the Soviet Union cynically manipulated the idealism of U.S. physicians and scientists in the nuclear de-escalation movement in order to achieve their own foreign policy objective of nuclear superiority? Also worthy of reflection is whether the relatively privileged (male, white, physician) status of many prominent health leftists of this generation enabled them to be more outspoken than health internationalists from other backgrounds.

# Chapter 6

# Contesting Racism and Innovating Community Health Centers

## Approaches on Two Continents

**H. Jack Geiger**

This is the story of a pioneering health care innovation—the community health center (CHC)—merging primary medical care with population-targeted public health interventions. It is also the story of another merger—the use of health care as an instrument of social justice and empowerment for those oppressed by racism and poverty. Finally, it is the story of how my early experience with community health centers enabled me to accomplish that merger, that fusion of interests, in my own life and work.

The story begins in the late 1930s and early 1940s, when a group of activist medical students at the University of Witwatersrand in Johannesburg began demanding that attention be paid to the health of South Africa's majority African population, a subject that did not even appear in most medical school curricula at the time. Most of these students, including Sidney Kark and Mervyn Susser, had already been involved in taking over a clinic in Alexandra township outside Johannesburg—a massively congested urban slum—and making it into what was arguably the first attempt at creating a CHC.[1] At the completion of his residency training, Kark was tapped to conduct the first survey of the nutritional state of urban and rural African schoolchildren (with predictably dismal findings of kwashiorkor, stunting, tuberculosis, malaria, pneumonia, and other contributors to appallingly high infant mortality rates).

And then, in 1940, came a window of opportunity. A commission of the "moderate" coalition government (as opposed to the viciously racist and iron-fisted segregationist government that followed) proposed the creation of a National Health Service, built around community health centers, to serve all elements of the South African population. Funding was provided for a first demonstration model center at Pholela, a five-hundred-square-mile so-called native tribal reserve in rural Natal province, and Dr. Sidney Kark was appointed to head it.

Over the next six years, Drs. Sidney and Emily Kark and their colleagues created the first model of what came to be called community-oriented primary care (COPC): assuming responsibility not just for the clinical care of individual patients but also for the health status of the defined community through what today would be called public health interventions in sanitation, nutrition, housing, and the rigorous adoption of epidemiologic surveys and ongoing surveillance to design interventions and evaluate their effectiveness. They recruited and trained local Zulu residents as survey takers, health demographers, data recorders, health educators, and outreach workers, as well as "practical nurses" and other aides of both genders, creating the first corps of what today would be called community health workers. The Karks paid particular and close attention to the social structures and belief systems of the Zulu population, incorporating sociology and social anthropology into their training methods and their interactions with community leaders and patients alike, succeeding in making both groups active participants in the health center's work.[2]

The health situation in Pholela in the 1940s has to be understood as a consequence of South Africa's demonic system of racial segregation. Africans were, in the main, restricted to rural, impoverished "tribal areas," often the worst and least arable land in the country, making subsistence farming and survival marginal—or less, and making malnutrition common. But to provide the labor force for the mines and urban factories that created the nation's wealth, men were forced by economic necessity to leave these rural areas each year on eleven-month contracts, to live in all-male urban hostels. No family members were allowed. (The rest of the urban African and Indian workforce were housed and segregated in residual urban slums and peri-urban townships.) And so, for eleven months of the year, Pholela's thirty thousand residents were mostly women, children, and the elderly. In their twelfth month, the men returned, bringing syphilis, tuberculosis, and a host of other diseases to spread through the reserve, before the men departed to the cities and mining regions again.

Over the next decade, the health center had astonishing success in reversing the existing pattern of morbidity and mortality and lifting the health status of the Pholela community. This record was published in a series of progress reports, articles in South African medical journals, and a book, *A Practice of Social Medicine,* published in Scotland in 1962, but little noticed in the United States.

By the 1950s, the Karks were operating multiple health centers serving African townships, Indian townships, and poor white communities in the Durban area, as part of what was now a national network of nearly forty CHCs.

**Figure 6.1** Providing milk to local children, Durban, early 1940s.
Courtesy of Jeremy D. Kark, MD, PhD.

They had established an Institute of Family and Community Health—a training center—in Durban to meet the unique needs of their health centers. In 1951, when the government finally established a medical school for nonwhites at the University of Natal in Durban, the institute became part of the medical school. A Department of Family and Community Medicine was created with Sidney Kark as its chair, and the first mandatory clerkship in family, community, and social medicine was established. John Grant, the great social epidemiologist who spearheaded a variety of Rockefeller Foundation international health initiatives, provided much of the funding for this move. He had visited Pholela in 1947 (and, since 1921, when he first funded a community-based clerkship at what was then the Peking Union Medical College, Grant had been an advocate of community health centers, as well as social medicine writ large).

I knew none of this, of course.

## Harlem and Beyond—Racial Segregation, Cultural Diversity, and Civil Rights

In 1940, I was at the very beginning of a trajectory that would involve me in civil rights and human rights, social justice, and health care for most of my

adult life. A child of poor Jewish immigrants in New York City who had managed to achieve professional status—my father was a physician, my mother a
microbiologist—I had, at age fourteen, met and been befriended by the great
Black actor of that period, Canada Lee, the star of "Native Son," the Broadway
play based on Richard Wright's novel. I was so moved by that powerful drama
that—with the brashness of youth—I talked my way backstage to his dressing room, where we ended up conversing for an hour. It was the beginning of
a friendship (and mentorship) that would last for years. Lee's apartment on
Harlem's Sugar Hill became my second home, and it afforded me a unique and
unparalleled opportunity for someone of my age and background. In my life
there in Harlem, I got to sit and listen to endless hours of conversation among
Lee and his visitors—some of the great African American artists and activists
of the day, including novelist Richard Wright, legendary baritone and political
radical Paul Robeson, poet and author Langston Hughes, as well as European
and American artistic greats such as playwright William Saroyan, and filmmaker Orson Welles, and liberal politicians like the young Adam Clayton Pow-
ell Jr. and Vito Marcantonio. No less important were the things I learned, and
the friends I made, in my new neighborhood on Harlem's streets. It was a first-
class education in the American caste system, residential segregation, cultural
diversity, and the political and economic struggles of minorities.

I had graduated high school at fourteen, and although I had been awarded a
New York State Regents scholarship, no colleges (in their wisdom) would admit
me. I worked as a copyboy at the *New York Times,* and, at night, hung out in
jazz joints on Fifty-second Street or in Harlem, listening to the likes of jazz and
blues singers Billie Holiday and Mama Yancey and great jazz pianists James P.
Johnson, his protégé Fats Waller, and Art Tatum, or learning to jitterbug (to
the amusement of Black friends much more skilled) at the Savoy Ballroom. In
1941, I finally made it into the University of Wisconsin to begin what I thought
would be a career as a journalist and writer. Almost immediately I became
immersed in running a campaign to end the university's approval of racially
and religiously segregated off-campus housing. A few months later, in early
1942 after Pearl Harbor, I was recruited by Bayard Rustin, civil rights leader
A. Philip Randolph's deputy, into the campaign to block racial discrimination
in defense plant employment by threatening a first "March on Washington," a
tactic that forced President Roosevelt to issue an executive order that opened
all those new jobs up and thus spurred a great migration of African Americans
out of the Jim Crow South to northern cities. In 1943, I met James Farmer, the
founder of CORE (the Congress of Racial Equality) and went on to establish one
of its earliest chapters, in Madison, Wisconsin. It was my introduction to the

Gandhian techniques of nonviolent direct action, passive resistance, and community organizing. CORE was to become the ideological grandparent of the Student Nonviolent Coordinating Committee (SNCC) two decades later, spearheading the civil rights revolution in the South.

In 1943 I enlisted in the U.S. Merchant Marines because it was the only military service that was not racially segregated during World War II. For much of the next three years I sailed as a radio/radar officer on the only ship in the American fleet with a Black captain, Hugh Mulzac, and a multiracial crew of officers. Another learning experience was listening to the emerging politics within the Black community, and dealing with life on the docks and streets in segregated Norfolk, Virginia, to which our integrated ship (named, without apparent irony, the SS *Booker T. Washington*) was frequently sent for refueling. During those layovers, we sometimes put on our dress uniforms, complete with combat ribbons, and—as an integrated group of thirty or more—invaded the "whites only" waiting room at the Norfolk railroad station, daring the authorities (somewhat ahead of our time) to arrest us. Perhaps because of our numbers, they never did.

### Medical (Rude) Awakenings

Somewhere in the North Atlantic during those years, I decided I was interested in medicine, and after discharge I enrolled at the University of Chicago as a premed student. Because merchant seamen didn't benefit from the GI Bill, I worked at night as a journalist; during the daytime, I was a student as well as the campus civil liberties chairman of the American Veterans Committee.

Almost at once, my colleagues and I discovered that the University of Chicago hospitals had both announced and informal rules of racial discrimination. The Lying-In Hospital had a flat-out policy of admitting no Black women. At Billings and the other hospitals, admitting clerks were told to lie to Black patients arriving for outpatient appointments and try to send them to Provident Hospital, the primarily Black hospital on Chicago's South Side. The medical school had not admitted a Black candidate in years, claiming that it just couldn't find any qualified minority applicants, though its admissions committee minutes (which we had obtained from colleagues' wives who were working as secretaries) contained written notations like "this candidate is qualified, but we're just not ready to admit blacks at this time." All of this was perfectly legal in 1947.

That was the start of a three-year campaign that culminated (again, somewhat ahead of our time) in a thousand-member student and faculty protest strike, after the university repeatedly stonewalled negotiations for change.

As part of the effort, I had gone to Howard University Medical School, one of the two historically Black medical schools that then existed, to meet with its activist dean, Dr. Montague Cobb, and arrange for some of the best Howard applicants to apply also to the University of Chicago (where we secretly paired each one, grade point for grade point, with a white applicant, and then challenged the university to explain if it admitted the white member of a pair and not the Black).

In 1949, my premed studies completed, I applied half-heartedly (I was pretty exhausted) to four medical schools in New York. To my astonishment, I got a call from Dr. Cobb—I hadn't applied to Howard—asking me to come to Washington. There, he showed me a letter from a vice president of the American Medical Association (AMA), calling attention to my "extracurricular activities," a kiss of death to any admissions committee. The AMA had sent the letter to all U.S. medical schools, including Howard and Meharry, thus inadvertently alerting them to this attack on my civil rights activism.

I had a good education in science, and I was a competent journalist, so I spent the next five years as science and medicine editor of the old International News Service (now part of United Press International). That provided an even better education in medicine, since I covered all the major meetings, read all the major journals, and interviewed the leading researchers. My interest in medicine did not dwindle, and in 1954 I assigned myself to cover the annual meeting of the Association of American Medical Colleges, following the Willie Sutton principle that if you want to go to medical school, go to where all the deans are. That year, the AMA notwithstanding, I was admitted to the Western Reserve School of Medicine in Cleveland. I was twenty-nine.

It was a fortunate choice. Western Reserve had a pioneering integrated curriculum, a commitment to treating medical students as grown-up graduate students and junior colleagues, and an interest in diversity. I wanted to end up doing nucleic acid research, but it soon became clear to me that I didn't have the patience to work on one enzyme system for five years, and I felt somewhat adrift.

Then came a moment of epiphany and a crucial moment in my trajectory. Standing on the steps of the medical school one day, I could see the university hospital, the contained environment of our health care universe. But beyond that, I could see the sprawl of urban Cleveland. It occurred to me that out there, who got sick and who stayed healthy, why the sick were ill, what happened to them next, and their interactions with us in the health care system were not just biological phenomena: they were social, political, racial, and economic

phenomena as well. It was as if all my earlier life commitments to civil rights
and social justice had merged with medicine, what I had embarked upon now.

## Social Medicine . . . on the Ground in South Africa

I thought I had invented social medicine. I ran to the library and rapidly discovered that the British and the Germans—John Simon, Rudolf Virchow, Will
Pickles, and William Farr—had already figured this out (see chapter 2). But the
American literature of the time was all touchy-feely: social medicine wasn't
anything you actually did, it was just an attitude you had. In some despair, I
wrote to a mentor, Warren Weaver, a vice president of the Rockefeller Foundation with whom I had earlier served on a committee, to explain my "discovery"
and my dilemma. He showed the letter to John Grant, and in return mailed me
a report on Pholela by Grant and a series of papers by the Karks. A crucial connection had been made, in consequence of a crucial insight.

I decided that if social medicine was real anywhere, it was most likely in
this project in South Africa, and I planned ahead. During my clinical clerk-
ships, I scrambled to sequester five months of my senior year—vacation time,
elective time, whatever I could scrounge. I realized it would take three approv-
als to get me there. My medical school had to say I could go; the University of
Natal and the Karks had to say I could come; and some foundation, preferably
Rockefeller, had to say they would pay for it. It was my first exercise in grants-
manship. Fortunately, there was no Internet then, no satellite phones, no fax
lines, no really reliable intercontinental radiotelephone communication. It was
all snail mail. So I wrote to each of them, strongly suggesting that the other two
had already agreed. They all wrote back saying yes.

In June 1957 I arrived at the University of Natal Medical School in Durban.
(I had had to sign an affidavit that I would not register as a student, so that my
white skin would not violate the segregation code.) I spent my first months
working and studying at the Lamontville Health Center, which served a peri-
urban Zulu housing project of about ten thousand residents and an informal
and culturally very different community of impoverished Indians, descendants
of the indentured laborers who had been imported from India a century earlier
to tend the Natal sugarcane fields. (By this time Indians constituted a significant portion of Natal's population and had a thriving commercial center in Durban, but the majority were poor, segregated, and oppressed.)

I had a weekly two-hour tutorial with Sidney Kark himself and the chance
to interact with African medical students. I was taken on an introductory orientation walk through the Lamontville project by Dr. Guy Steuart, the Karks' chief
health educator and community organizer who—years later, as department

head of that field at the University of North Carolina (UNC) School of Public Health—would visit us in Mississippi.

At Lamontville and later for months in Pholela, I learned to practice amid what was a virtual flood of epidemiologic and demographic information on each of those populations. My best guides at each center were the (mostly indigenous) community health workers, each of whom took me through their assigned areas, brought me into thatched huts and cattle kraals (enclosures), showed me the community vegetable gardens, pit latrines, and infant and school-age feeding programs the health center had mounted, including rations of skimmed milk. Nurses and physicians showed me the assessment and evaluation reports, by area, age group, and gender. On the walls of the clinical examination rooms at each health center were posted histograms of the incidence and prevalence of major infectious diseases in each community. I visited *inyangas*—traditional healers—and watched them work; they were the only health care providers other than the health centers themselves. I learned a little Zulu, including the three oral clicks in that language, which always made me drool, to the hilarity of my African teachers.

It was a life-changing experience. Now I knew I wanted a career in international health. I returned to Cleveland, wrote a long thesis (required by Western Reserve) contrasting Pholela and Lamontville with the Western Reserve family medicine clinic, and then moved to Boston for the training I thought was appropriate: a residency in internal medicine on the Harvard medical service at Boston City Hospital—a great public teaching hospital serving the poor—a degree in epidemiology, and a postdoctoral fellowship in the social sciences in medicine, all from 1958 to 1964. In all those years, my only civil rights activity was as one of the minor Boston organizers for the 1963 March on Washington.

But 1964 was the peak of the ongoing civil rights struggles by SNCC, CORE, and the Southern Christian Leadership Conference: Freedom Summer, voter registration, and much more. That spring, I had become one of the twenty or so founding members of the Medical Committee for Human Rights (MCHR), organized to become a medical arm of the civil rights movement and to provide support and care for the civil rights workers in Mississippi.[3] Three of them—Andrew Goodman, James Chaney, and Michael Schwerner—had already been murdered, and many others had been beaten and jailed. In August, just at the end of my clinical training, I went to Mississippi as the MCHR field coordinator. That month-long look at Mississippi almost immediately brought the realization that I didn't have to go to Africa, Southeast Asia, or Latin America to do our work. We had all those problems here, at the same relative, if not absolute, levels in the Black rural South, the northern urban Black and Hispanic ghettos, poor-white Appalachia, and on Native American reservations.

One of the MCHR recruits in Mississippi was Dr. Count Gibson, a native southerner (his Georgia accent was an invaluable resource in Mississippi) who was now chair of the Department of Preventive Medicine at Tufts Medical School, and for whom Freedom Summer was similarly a crucial experience in his own trajectory. In the fall, we kept returning to Mississippi from Boston. I did not think specifically about Pholela, though many of the parallels between Mississippi and apartheid South Africa were striking, but we and other MCHR doctors and nurses talked about intervening. With money from wealthy supporters in Maryland, we started a tiny MCHR clinic, staffed mostly by nurses, in the small hamlet of Mileston, in Mississippi's Holmes County.

### Bringing Learnings Home—The Beginnings of U.S. Community Health Centers

But that was only a beginning, a sort of unsustainable trial run. In December, the Delta Ministry of the National Council of Churches hosted a meeting in Greenville, Mississippi, for many of the indigenous and left-over visiting civil rights activists, including MCHR members still involved, to discuss what to do now. In the afternoon I explicitly recalled Pholela and the University of Natal. I said, "What we really need is a good northern medical school to come down and sponsor a comprehensive community health center to practice community-oriented primary care!" I explained in detail what that was. Everyone chipped in with ideas, particularly Dr. Robert Smith, an African American physician from Jackson who had been the very linchpin of MCHR's work in Mississippi. Another was MCHR's Dr. Desmond Callan. (Both Drs. Smith and Callan went on to become CHC directors.) The idea was met with great enthusiasm, but it seemed to me to be just a pipe dream.

On the way back to Boston, Count Gibson and I were grounded by fog in Atlanta. In our motel room, Count said, "Let's talk about the deal." "What deal?" I asked. "If you can find the money, Tufts Medical School will sponsor it."

It still seemed a pipe dream. But a new window of opportunity was opening, this time from the United States government, which was to have an impact even greater than its South African counterpart in the 1940s. It was the creation, by President Lyndon Johnson and the Congress, of the Office of Economic Opportunity (OEO), part of the so-called War on Poverty, which was designed to be innovative, experimental, nonbureaucratic, and committed to participation with, not just for, poor populations. None of its initially planned programs were focused on health care, though its first pioneering venture, the Headstart program for early childhood intervention, had already started to yield appalling data on mortality and morbidity among poor children.

In January 1965 I went to Washington to meet with another key figure (and largely unsung hero) of the diffusion of the CHC innovation. Sanford Kravitz was the head of OEO's research and demonstrations section. I talked to him for more than two hours, filling a yellow pad with outlines of CHC structures and programs, and emphasizing in particular why CHCs in the United States should be part of OEO's community action programs. This was an opportunity to do something that had been impossible in apartheid South Africa: making the citizens of targeted impoverished communities full participants in the planning and operation of their health services. At the end, Kravitz asked me how much money I wanted. In a classic example of academic faint-heartedness, I asked for $30,000 for a "feasibility study." "You can't have that," he told me. "You have to take $300,000 and do it now." I had no idea what it would really cost. Back in Boston, Count Gibson and I realized that if Tufts Medical School were to sponsor a health center in Mississippi, fifteen hundred miles away, it had better do the same for an impoverished community in Boston, on its own doorstep. We added the Columbia Point Housing Project, a low-rise complex for some eight thousand residents on the edge of the city. When we came back to Dr. Kravitz, the proposed budget totaled $1.2 million.

There ensued a long struggle with OEO, not just over the budget but over the very proposal that the agency should sponsor health care, not only through a new model but in the Deep South. Southern governors, sensing that OEO would bypass all their control mechanisms and gatekeepers, and provide funding directly to poor Black communities to empower them, had fiercely resisted the OEO legislation and insisted on a provision giving governors the right to veto any project headed for their states. But in hopes, perhaps, that their universities might tap into some of that OEO money, they included an exception for grants to institutions of higher education. I realized at once that we would be veto proof. There was nothing in the law to prevent a medical school in Massachusetts from launching a health care program in Mississippi, and only the Massachusetts—not the Mississippi—governor would be involved. We were about to turn carpetbagging on its head. Our veto-proof status was crucial to working in the South.

Sargent Shriver, the OEO director, finally approved the grant in June 1965. On December 11, 1965—exactly one year after the Greenville meeting—the Columbia Point Health Center opened its doors. Mississippi took longer. My grant proposal carefully identified the southern project only as a "southern rural health center," so that the grant would not have to be circulated to any specific state congressional delegation. We actually looked at sites in several southern states, but settled at last on the all-Black town of Mound Bayou as a base to serve a five-hundred-square-mile rural area of northern Bolivar County—the third poorest in the nation—in the Mississippi Delta. Mr. Shriver had insisted on the right to approve the final southern site choice, and he kept waffling and withholding approval in fear of the political consequences. We obtained it only after the Tufts University medical school dean and I staged a sit-in in Shriver's office, "the only time in the 1960s," someone later observed, "that it was a dean and not the students sitting in." Only then did I realize that, however unconsciously, I was replicating Pholela and Lamontville.

But that was only the beginning of what I remember as a long siege of simultaneous struggle, confrontation, and exhilaration. I had to meet and confront the Mississippi white power structure, the state public health department, and the hostile state, county, and local medical societies. One such meeting, I remember, was staged in a courtroom, where I realized I had been placed in the prisoner's dock. I had to buy land and construct a health center building. I had to organize and oversee a census and a health survey of the target population. I had to find and recruit community organizers, physicians, nurses, nurse-midwives, pharmacists, sanitarians, laboratory technicians, and convince them to come to Mississippi. The two small local Black hospitals were on the verge of financial collapse. I had to write a grant establishing them as a merged, OEO-funded community hospital for the poor. I had to find or develop housing for staff.

The first thrill came when key staff members, many of them Blacks of southern origin now working as professionals in the North, recruited themselves as word of the project spread. That began with John W. Hatch, head of community organizing (we called it "community health action"), who spent almost two years patiently building ten local health associations, then merged them into a North Bolivar County Health Council (which began as an advisory committee and now, almost fifty years later, has owned and operated the center for the past thirty years). Another was Sister Mary Stella, an accomplished nurse-midwife and Catholic nun with vast experience. A third was Dr. David Weeks, a superb clinical chief, whom I recruited back to the United States from Saudi Arabia by somehow convincing him that the project in Mound Bayou was the cutting edge of American medicine. Andrew James, a Black sanitarian, arrived from Ohio. Somehow, it all came together, and that was the ultimate exhilaration.

The progress and accomplishments of those first two CHCs have been described in detail elsewhere.[4] Meanwhile, Kravitz had approved funding for four more health centers, all as research and demonstration projects: the

**Figure 6.2**  Dr. H. Jack Geiger (*left*) and Dr. John W. Hatch (*right*) during construction on the Delta Health Center, 1968.

Photo by Dan Bernstein. Courtesy of the author.

Watts area in Los Angeles, the inner-city Mile Square neighborhood in Chicago, the South Bronx in New York City, and a joint project by the Denver Health Department and the University of Colorado. Clearly, there were other American physicians and health planners instantly ready to understand and implement the CHC concept. In the summer of 1966, then Senator Ted Kennedy came to visit Columbia Point. It was the beginning of his lifelong interest in health care issues. At dinner that night, we discussed next steps. On his return to Washington, he drafted and pushed through legislation institutionalizing the health center movement, creating an Office of Health Affairs within OEO, and providing an initial $50 million to fund additional centers. The transplantation of innovation from South Africa to the United States was now firmly under way, and it was to grow steadily over the next half century.

### Comparing Contexts, Comparing Approaches

From the beginning, the COPC concepts elaborated by the Karks, and our prior experience in South Africa, continued to inform the design and programs of those first two health centers. The Delta Health Center, in particular, was Pholela writ large. What had been a two-acre community vegetable garden in Pholela became a five-hundred-acre cooperative farm near Mound Bayou, in which more than a thousand Bolivar County Black families pooled their labor to grow and fully share in thousands of tons of vegetables—not cotton—over the next several years. It was a sort of democratic nutritional sharecropping that effectively ended serious malnutrition in the area. Pholela's program of pit latrines was replaced in the Delta by a massive health center program to build protected wells and construct sanitary privies. As at Pholela, local residents were recruited and trained as health demographers and survey takers, conducting a complete census of the target population and a careful survey of present health status.

Even the political opposition was sometimes eerily similar. When the Karks distributed free skimmed milk to malnourished children, the South African government investigated them for "communism"; when Delta Health Center physicians literally wrote—and arranged to fill—emergency prescriptions for food for impoverished families with seriously malnourished and infected children, and charged the costs to the center's pharmacy budget, the governor of Mississippi made the same accusation. In Lamontville, many of the health problems occurred in young mothers who were, in effect, first-generation immigrants from rural areas, newly arrived in an urban housing project. At Columbia Point, family health teams were increasingly occupied with the problems of single mothers with young children. At both health centers, the stream of visiting health care providers, health policymakers, and legislators arriving to visit and study these new models was so great that special staff positions had to be created to manage their orientations.

The course of events in the two nations was to differ radically. In South Africa, the entire national network of some forty health centers, the Institute of Family and Community Health, and the Kark-led department at the Natal Medical School were abruptly dismantled shortly after the election of the Afrikaner-led, racist, and brutally segregationist government in 1960. Sidney and Emily Kark and many of their colleagues left the country—some to the University of North Carolina at Chapel Hill, where the Karks stopped briefly. The Karks went on to Israel, where they opened two new health centers for service, research, and teaching in a new target population in Jerusalem, and established an academic department at the Hebrew University-Hadassah School of Public Health.

In the United States, by contrast, the health center network grew steadily and rapidly. Many applications and proposals to OEO were initiated by local community groups in poor communities. Others were proposed and supported by local political leaders; some were proposed by existing hospitals, academic medical doctors, or group practices. In the space of a few decades, there were fifty, one hundred, five hundred CHCs. In Congress, the CHC program had broad and unwavering bipartisan support; only once, during the Reagan presidency, was there a serious attempt to cut funding and local independence, and that ended when a presidential veto was over-ridden by a Republican Congress. In 1975, when the responsibility for federal health center programs was transferred from the now-defunct OEO to a new Bureau of Primary Health Care in the Department of Health, Education, and Welfare, a new regulation codified a unique aspect of all federally qualified CHCs. Each had to be a nonprofit corporation, with a locally elected board of directors who were accountable for the federal grant and health center budget, chose the executive or clinical directors, and set their center's policies. And 51 percent of those board members had to be current patients of the center. There is no other component of the American health care system in which patients have that degree of input and control over the delivery of their own essential primary care health services.

In 1982, the Institute of Medicine of the National Academy of Sciences organized a major conference on community-oriented primary care, in effect giving elite medical approval to the concept and the health center network. Key speakers included a senior colleague of the Karks from Jerusalem, some veterans of the growing health center network, and academic leaders. The American Medical Association and other elements of organized medicine, after some initial reservations and concerns, had long since approved the COPC approach. An impressive literature of studies and evaluations by independent researchers had demonstrated that the health centers provided care of high quality at modest cost, not least because they generally combined, under one roof, medical care, dental care, mental health care, pharmacies and clinical laboratories, social work, and other supports in an efficient delivery system.[5] Their growing national staffing needs were met—though only in part—by the parallel growth of a federally funded National Health Service Corps.

As the number of health centers grew, they became more differentiated. Some were large and urban, some smaller and rural. Others were specifically designed and located to serve migrant agricultural labor streams. Some were located in public housing projects; others served student populations in urban high schools. By 2010, they had become the linchpin of a national health safety net. Although they operate in America's competitive health care marketplaces with many other providers of care—private and public hospitals, private practitioners, emergency rooms, large private group practices—most have tried to maintain their focus on roughly defined target populations (communities) and combined one-by-one clinical care with health education and other targeted public health interventions to address major incident and prevalent problems. Now there are more than twelve hundred CHCs in the United States, operating branches at more than eight thousand sites of primary care delivery, and caring for some twenty million patients. The Obama health reform legislation of 2010 provides $12 billion to double the number of CHCs over the next decade and reach a goal of fifty million patients.[6]

The links between South Africans and the first two health centers continued over the ensuing years. In the 1960s, Sidney Kark visited both Columbia Point and the Delta, offering counsel and advice, as did John Cassel, the great UNC social epidemiologist (who earlier in his career had been clinical director at Pholela). In the 1970s, Guy Steuart at UNC supervised the doctoral studies of John Hatch, the Delta's brilliant community organizer, who went on to become the first African American to occupy an endowed chair at the UNC School of Public Health. In 1979, after my colleagues and I had established a new department of Community Health and Social Medicine at the City University of New York's Sophie Davis Medical School, both John Hatch and Sidney Kark arrived as visiting professors, teaching there and at the social medicine residency program of Montefiore Medical Center and the Martin Luther King Jr. CHC in the South Bronx.

This U.S.-South African connection was only a part of the story of the diffusion of innovation. That process became global, mostly because of an initiative of the Karks. In Israel each year for many years, they conducted an international workshop to which physicians, other health care providers, and policymakers from both developed and developing nations came to Jerusalem for a six-week didactic course in COPC, then returned to their home countries to launch a project, then often came back to report and evaluate their success. As one explicit consequence of this sustained effort, an international CHC conference held in Toronto, Canada, in 2011 had health center participants from almost a dozen nations.

Finally, after so many decades, this process returned to its roots in South Africa. In 1992, after the nation's liberation and the election of Nelson Mandela as president, the Karks returned to South Africa, revisiting Pholela and meeting with a new generation of physicians, planners, and political leaders eager to learn what had been created and accomplished more than a half century earlier. (In that same year, John Hatch and I went to South Africa as consultants to its new National Progressive Primary Health Care Network and the nation's emerging schools of public health.) The COPC principles became the platform for South Africa's expanding system of district health centers. It has taken a long time, but it is happening now.

And so this story has not ended. It is ongoing and will have new chapters. Looking back, I can see more clearly how it began and evolved. What happened at the start was a rare convergence of forces and events. The key players were activist medical students and physicians. Windows of opportunity for social change and experimentation in government programs opened at critical points. Great social upheavals—the American civil rights movement and the South African struggle for liberation—provided the pathways to health care innovation. Philanthropic foundations and resources intervened at key points. But all of these had to intersect, at critical junctures, with the lives and evolving political and racial understandings of individuals who became the agents of change. I hope this will keep happening. I am well into my eighties now, and I see my task as doing what I can to nurture the student activists and young professionals who will be the change agents of the future.

## Notes

1. Mervyn Susser, "A South African Odyssey in Community Health: A Memoir of the Impact of the Teachings of Sidney Kark," *American Journal of Public Health* 83 (1993): 1039–1042; Shula Marks, "South Africa's Early Experiment in Social Medicine: Its Pioneers and Politics," *American Journal of Public Health* 87 (1997): 452–459; Derek Yach and Stephen M. Tollman, "Public Health Initiatives in South Africa in the 1930s and 1950s: Lessons for a Post-Apartheid Era," *American Journal of Public Health* 83 (1993): 1043–1049.

2. Sidney Kark and Emily Kark, *Promoting Community Health: From Pholela to Jerusalem* (Johannesburg: Witwatersand University Press, 1999).

3. John Dittmer, *The Good Doctors: The Medical Committee for Human Rights and the Struggle for Social Justice in Health Care* (New York: Bloomsbury Press, 2009).

4. H. Jack Geiger, "The First Community Health Centers: A Model of Enduring Value," *Journal of Ambulatory Care Management* 28 (2005): 313–320; Bonnie Lefkowitz, *Community Health Centers: A Movement and the People Who Made It Happen* (Piscataway, NJ: Rutgers University Press, 2007); Barbara Starfield, "Costs and Quality in Different Types of Primary Care Settings," *Journal of the American Medical Association* 272 (1994): 1903–1908.

5. H. Jack Geiger, "Community-Oriented Primary Care: A Path to Community Development," *American Journal of Public Health* 92 (2003): 1713–1716.

6. Eli Y. Adashi, H. Jack Geiger, and Michael D. Fine, "Health Care Reform and Primary Care—The Growing Importance of the Community Health Center," *New England Journal of Medicine* 362 (2010): 2047–2050.

# Chapter 7

# Barefoot in China, the Bronx, and Beyond

**Victor W. Sidel and Ruth Sidel**

The "barefoot doctor" has come to symbolize the attempts in China, under the leadership of Mao Zedong (Mao Tse-tung)[1] and the Communist Party of China, to improve the provision of medical care for China's vast rural population. The improvements began during the 1930s and 1940s with the work of the People's Liberation Army (the "Red Army") in the "liberated areas" during the Japanese occupation and the revolution. These changes became national policy after what is known in China as "Liberation." On October 1, 1949, Mao announced the establishment of the People's Republic of China (PRC) by declaring in Tiananmen Square in Beijing (Peking) that "the Chinese people have stood up!"

The United States, which had supported Chiang Kai-Shek and his Nationalist forces against Mao and his Red Army during the revolution, maintained diplomatic relations with Chiang's government in Taiwan, where Chiang had moved his forces, and refused to establish diplomatic relations with Mao's government in Beijing. The United States and the United Nations recognized the government in Taiwan as China and referred to the government in Beijing as Mainland China or Communist China. There followed a period of twenty-two years in which there were no diplomatic relations between the United States and the PRC and very few visitors from the United States to the PRC. During the early 1970s the relationship between the PRC and the Soviet Union deteriorated and U.S. president Richard Nixon and Secretary of State Henry Kissinger were interested in exploiting these tensions through diplomatic contacts with the PRC.

## Our Visits to China

In April 1971, table tennis teams representing the United States and the PRC participated in a tournament in Japan. A member of the U.S. team mistakenly boarded the bus transporting the Chinese team and one of the Chinese players established a relationship with him, a contact that violated the instructions the Chinese team had been given but that Mao later called an act of diplomacy. At the completion of the tournament, the U.S. team was invited to the PRC, a visit that became known as the "Ping-Pong breakthrough." On learning of that visit, Professors Arthur Galston of Yale and Ethan Signer of MIT, who had been visiting Vietnam to study the impact of the herbicide Agent Orange that the United States had been using in its war on North Vietnam, applied for and were granted visas at the Chinese embassy in Hanoi, thus becoming the first U.S. scientists to visit the PRC since Liberation.

Vic, who had worked with Galston in analyzing and criticizing the United States' use of chemical weapons in Vietnam, contacted Galston after his return to the United States. Galston wrote a letter to Dr. Kuo Mo-jo, president of the Chinese Academy of Sciences whom he had met in Beijing, suggesting that the two of us (Vic and Ruth) be invited to visit China. Three months later, on September 1, Galston received a reply saying we had been invited. The invitation specified that we come to China "at any time at your convenience within the next two weeks." Since there was no diplomatic recognition between the United States and the PRC at that time, our visas were obtained at the PRC Embassy in Ottawa.

In 1969, two years before the invitation to visit China arrived, our family had moved from Boston to the Bronx when Vic, who had been head of the Community Medicine Unit at the Massachusetts General Hospital (MGH), was named chair of the Department of Social Medicine at Montefiore Medical Center and professor of social medicine at the Albert Einstein College of Medicine. At the MGH, Vic's focus was on strengthening hospital-based medical care and preventive services. In the Bronx the work of the Department of Social Medicine largely concerned relationships between the hospital and the Bronx community, including issues of strengthening community-oriented primary care and improving the ties between public health and medical care programs.

In the early 1970s, Ruth, a social worker at a pediatric health center at Einstein, was especially interested in issues involving women and children and the provision of preschool care, particularly in societies in which most women were members of the labor force. In addition to having long been interested in parent-child issues, she was also involved in providing services in urban communities. In preparation for our visit to China, she studied works by Urie Bronfenbrenner and Melford Spiro to learn about childcare as it was practiced in the then Soviet Union and on Israeli kibbutzim.[2] Both of us hurriedly reviewed what little we knew about the PRC, its medical and social services, and its forms of community organization. Books by reporter Edgar Snow (*Red Star Over China*), by British surgeon Joshua Horn (*Away with All Pests*), and by agricultural expert William Hinton (*Fanshen*), detailing the extraordinary changes in China during and after the revolution, were particularly useful.[3] From these and other sources Ruth developed questions about the care of young children in the PRC that she hoped would be answered during the course of the trip and Vic developed questions about the delivery of community-oriented primary care, particularly in China's poor rural areas, where 80 percent of its vast population lived.

Prior to our visit we had both been politically active in our communities, in the civil rights and anti–Vietnam War movements. We were both raised in politically active families—Vic in Trenton, Ruth in Boston—and had long been concerned about the chilling effects of McCarthyism and the need for greater social and economic justice in the United States and in other parts of the world. In 1961, Vic was one of the founders of Physicians for Social Responsibility and during the 1960s was active in the work of the American Public Health Association and in its local affiliate, the Massachusetts Public Health Association. Ruth had been chair of Brookline PAX, a peace group that stemmed from the third-party candidacy of H. Stuart Hughes, a Harvard professor who ran for a Massachusetts seat in the United States Senate on a peace platform against Edward M. Kennedy in 1962. We both had also been concerned about ways of developing a more humane, caring society that would provide opportunities and first-rate services to those who have least. While we were well versed in our own disciplines, our knowledge of China and its recent changes were rudimentary. We were truly going to be "barefoot in China."

We spent from September 20 to October 14, 1971, in the PRC as members of a group, sponsored by the Chinese Medical Association (CMA), termed the "first U.S. medical delegation to visit the PRC since Liberation." The group, which consisted of renowned cardiologist Paul Dudley White and Ina White, internationally known ear surgeon Samuel Rosen and Helen Rosen, cardiologist E. Grey Dimond and Mary Dimond, and the two of us, traveled extensively in urban and rural areas.

Our Chinese hosts took us to ambulatory care centers, hospitals, and medical schools in urban areas and to primary care and secondary care facilities in rural areas. In addition, Ruth requested that services for women and young children and the structure of urban neighborhoods be added to our primary focus on medical and public health issues. With seemingly no problem or hesitation, our

**Figure 7.1** Ruth (*right*) and Victor Sidel (*second from right*) being greeted by Premier Zhou Enlai (Chou En-Lai; *left*) at the Hall of the People in Beijing (Peking) in September 1971. The photo was taken at a reception hosted by Zhou Enlai (Chou En-lai), premier of the People's Republic of China, for all the North Americans in China on National Day, October 1, 1971.

Courtesy of the Chinese Ministry of Foreign Affairs and the authors.

Chinese hosts arranged visits to nurseries and kindergartens in virtually all of our destinations. We were able to observe preschool facilities on communes, in factories, and in neighborhoods, and even a model facility that housed young children during the entire week, returning home only on weekends. We were also taken to urban neighborhoods where we met with leaders of both residents' and neighborhood committees in an attempt to understand the structure of these groups, their leadership and goals, and their relationship to the broader community. In these meetings we discussed the mobilization of residents around public health issues, the role of women, and the ways birth control was encouraged, as well as the role of the elderly, and, of course, of the Communist Party.

One year later, following considerable study, lecturing, and writing on China, and even some effort to learn to speak and read Chinese, the two of us were invited by the CMA to return. This visit was somewhat longer, from September 4 to October 5, 1972, and we traveled with our two sons, Mark, then age fourteen, and Kevin, thirteen. As in our first visit, we personally paid the expenses of our travel to and from China, but all of our expenses in China were paid by the CMA and we were accompanied by CMA guides and interpreters throughout our visit. We have since made a number of visits to China to observe the changes that have occurred following Mao's death in 1976.

## Innovations in China's Health Care System

During our visits we learned that attempts to correct the crippling problems of poverty, lack of educational opportunity, and inadequate access to medical and social services in China's vast rural areas were a major objective of the Great Proletarian Cultural Revolution initiated by Mao Zedong in the mid-1960s. The policies that were instituted during this time led to profound changes in both urban and rural life. China's revolution in health care services brought medical care to most of the country's immense rural population—some eight hundred million people—a group that previously had largely lacked access to personnel trained in modern medical methods and to facilities equipped with modern medical technology. These innovations included the development of a system of barefoot doctors, a cooperative medical care system, and a three-level health care system.

The barefoot doctor system was grounded in the economic, social, and political units of the countryside known as "communes" and their component production teams and brigades. Barefoot doctors were peasants who were trained for relatively brief periods to perform health and medical care services on a part-time basis. They received income from the production brigade in the same way as did other peasants who did agricultural work.

The cooperative medical care system was a form of medical care insurance supported by the commune economy and by the peasants' regular small payments toward higher-level medical care.

### The Rural Health Care System

The three-level rural health care system consisted of:

1. Basic production-brigade health stations staffed by barefoot doctors, midwives, and health aides;
2. Better-equipped commune facilities supported by the entire commune and staffed by full-time physicians and nurses; and
3. County hospitals, supported by the central government, that were staffed by primary care physicians and some specialists and that provided a higher technical level of care. When necessary, patients would be transferred to higher-level facilities and their care paid for by the cooperative medical care system.

The principles underlying these services and how they were achieved included:

- A fundamental redistribution of health care resources from those who formerly had most to those who had least. This was accomplished, especially after the start of the Cultural Revolution in 1966, through full control over health care resources by the public sector, with little or none remaining in the private sector, and by a shift in emphasis toward narrowing the gap between the urban and rural areas.

- A commitment to encouraging people's self-reliance and mutual help in tackling health problems. This was accomplished through mass education programs, special nationwide campaigns, and intensive local neighborhood organization, using techniques that emphasized the importance of health for the family, the community, and the nation rather than merely for individual well-being.

- The training of a large number of full-time professional health workers. This was accomplished by vastly expanding enrollment in existing schools and establishing many new ones and, especially after the Cultural Revolution, by exploring techniques for shortening training time. But the number of workers who had been trained—though extremely high—was still insufficient to meet the needs of China's population.

- The training of large numbers of part-time health workers—barefoot doctors—who continued at the same time to be peasants, factory workers, or housewives. This was accomplished largely through local initiatives but with the cooperation of professional health workers.

- An emphasis on preventive rather than therapeutic medicine. This was accomplished by formulating nationwide policies for sanitation, immunization, and other preventive measures and then mobilizing for their local implementation.

- Preserving and strengthening that which was most valuable in traditional Chinese medicine, and using it and its practitioners as a vehicle for the wider distribution of modern medicine, by bringing together traditional and modern practitioners in their medical practice and by training each in the other's techniques.

- Fostering a desire to serve others rather than for individual self-aggrandizement. This was accomplished through widespread campaigns using every medium of public communication, emphasizing the importance of "serving the people."

Our learning about the Chinese health care system and the work of barefoot doctors was, as it were, from the ground up. As quintessentially urban Americans, we knew next to nothing about rural life and, of course, still less about rural life in China. On each visit to a commune and, more specifically, to a production team or brigade, we met with one or more barefoot doctors. We learned about their personal stories, particularly how they came to be chosen and then trained as medical workers. Then, most commonly, Vic would discuss in-depth their work including prevention and public health, the kind of illnesses they treated, and their methods of treatment. We were extremely fortunate to have a guide and interpreter, Dr. Xu Jiayu (Hsu Chia-yu), who was a physician from Shanghai. Indefatigable, lively, extremely knowledgeable, with essentially perfect English, Dr. Xu answered every question, explained every political concept and cultural tradition, and never made us feel as uninformed as we really were. He recounted stories of having been sent to poor rural areas during the Cultural Revolution to teach barefoot doctors and to live with them in conditions very different from his life in Shanghai. He described how he had come to admire their dedication to their patients and to their communities.

On these visits to the treatment stations of several barefoot doctors, Dr. Xu and Vic would laboriously and methodically go through every item in the barefoot doctor's medical bag, asking the health worker what the item was and how and when she or he used it. It was through this long process (with Ruth taking copious notes) that Vic came to understand the scope, depth, and limits of the medical worker's training and ability to serve his or her fellow peasants. During these visits neither our hosts, nor the barefoot doctors, nor Dr. Xu ever expressed a moment's impatience even though they could not have anticipated such lengthy, in-depth visits.

The barefoot doctor system in China (and comparable developments in other countries such as Cuba, Tanzania, and India) led to interest by the World Health Organization (WHO) in encouraging the training of similar health workers in other developing nations. Dr. Kenneth Newell, head of the Division of Strengthening of Health Services at the WHO invited us to WHO headquarters in Geneva to consult on a project being conducted by the WHO and the United Nations Children's Fund (UNICEF) called "Alternative Approaches to Meeting Basic Health Needs in Developing Countries." We contributed a case study on China to the study report.[4] This led to an invitation from Dr. Newell to provide a chapter on China's health care delivery system for the book *Health by the People,* which was published by WHO and UNICEF.[5]

## Returning Home and Sharing What We Learned

Upon return from our first visits to China we gave numerous presentations and wrote three books[6] and several articles on our observations.[7] We were careful to emphasize that we were in no way "China scholars." Our publications and lectures, and those of other visitors to China, generated considerable interest and discussion in the United States and in other parts of the world. We found that what fascinated Americans most about the preschool facilities that we visited, for example, was the health and well-being of the children. Many people, raised on the concept of the "starving children in China," were genuinely amazed at their good health, their vitality, and their high spirits; people were equally amazed and fascinated by the values being taught to these young children. Quoting Mao, Chinese teachers would creatively exhort the children to "love and help and take care of each other." To teach these principles they would line the children up one behind the other and have them button the jacket of the child in front of them. Or a child who was more advanced in the subject being taught would help another child who was having trouble learning the material. With the aid of vivid slides of vibrant children taken by Vic, educators and parents across the United States, and in other countries as well, were fascinated and often thrilled to think it might actually be possible to raise more cooperative human beings.

Questions of urban organization were also of considerable interest to our audiences. We described how neighborhoods (the lowest level of city government) were subdivided into residents' committees and then into individual buildings with leaders or representatives chosen from each level. These individuals played many roles such as those of community organizer, mediator of disputes, public health educator, and local police or security official. Often the people most active in these local units were retired workers, particularly women who were expected to retire from their jobs at the age of fifty-five and typically had considerable time, energy, and commitment for community work.[8]

At a personal level, our visits to China had significant impact on our careers. Ruth, who had rarely spoken publicly to large audiences and who had not written for publication prior to this time, felt compelled to speak out about the remarkable advances that had been made in China since Liberation. Her presentations about the innovative policies and egalitarian values in China were enthusiastically received. The many articles and books that we wrote and Ruth's newfound ability to communicate with audiences large and small significantly changed her professional life, leading to a doctorate in sociology and her current position as a professor of sociology at Hunter College.

Vic, who had been lecturing and writing on medicine, public health, and the prevention of war, found new topics and new audiences, and his China presentations were well received professionally. As it turned out, the audiences extended beyond the public health and academic worlds. He later learned through a Freedom of Information request that FBI agents had attended many of his lectures. The agents' written comments ranged from severe criticism of the political content of his lectures to praise for their accuracy and impartiality. Vic experienced no negative professional consequences. Quite the contrary, he was invited to lecture widely and to consult with international organizations such as UNICEF and the WHO.

Closer to home, in the early 1970s, the Department of Social Medicine at Montefiore Medical Center in the Bronx had developed a Community Health Participation Program (CHPP) that recruited, trained, and supervised neighborhood health workers and was in some ways modeled after programs in China, Cuba, and Chile. Dr. Roberto Belmar, who had been in charge of the Chilean National Health Service programs in Santiago and was invited to the United States by Montefiore after the U.S.-financed military coup that resulted in the death of Salvador Allende, was one of the leaders of the CHPP. The community health workers went door-to-door in apartment buildings in the Montefiore neighborhood to determine the central concerns of the residents and to help them organize to deal with some of their health problems. As in China, the focus was on encouraging the residents themselves to serve as leaders and activists within their neighborhoods. And, as in China, Cuba, and Chile, many of these indigenous leaders were women, older people, and retired workers.

The CHPP organized a series of classes, each consisting of sixteen sessions, one evening a week, about three hours each evening, for the people who lived in the surrounding apartment buildings. The participants learned technical skills such as cardiopulmonary resuscitation and how to take blood pressure. Even more important, they learned health education methods for work with their neighbors: how to teach neighbors how to use the health care system more effectively, how to use preventive services, and how to organize the neighborhood for safety and for health. The neighborhood around Montefiore was changing rapidly, with outmigration of Jews and other European immigrants and an influx of Latin American immigrants. Some of the teaching was carried out in Spanish because that was one of the primary languages of the volunteers and one in which they would work with their neighbors.

At the end of each sixteen-week cycle, a graduation was held in English and in Spanish to congratulate those who completed the course, to honor them for the work they did, to present them with a diploma and a badge, and to encourage them to share their skills with their neighbors. About three weeks after one of the graduation ceremonies, one of the graduates died in a terrible accident. She was riding her bicycle in the Bronx and was killed by a truck speeding by. The other people in the program rushed to help with the three young children she left behind. We would have anticipated that. When the family laid her out for her burial, they did so in the dress that she had worn to the graduation ceremony. What was most surprising and moving for us was that the family invited us to the wake and had pinned to her dress the badge she was awarded at the CHPP graduation proclaiming her a member of the program. The family told us she had never before been honored at a graduation ceremony, and because she was so proud of having learned skills that would enable her to help her neighbors, they thought she would like to go to her grave wearing a symbol of what she had accomplished.

### Privatization in China

Dramatic improvements in the health status of the rural Chinese population were reported by us and by others in the 1970s and early 1980s. Although it was difficult to determine to what extent these changes were due to advances in health services or to the remarkable improvements in sanitation, nutrition, housing, education, and other social conditions that occurred, it seemed clear that China's medical and health care system played an important role in rural areas.[9] Indeed, WHO, UNICEF, and other international health agencies found China's rural health care system to be exemplary.

With the death of Mao Zedong and the PRC's longtime premier, Zhou Enlai (Chou En Lai), in 1976, and the ascension of Deng Xiaoping (Teng Xiao Ping) as China's "paramount leader," the principles on which China's economic system and its human services were based began to erode dramatically. To spur private ownership of enterprises and private investments that would speed national economic development, the government dictum "serve the people" was replaced by "to get rich is glorious."[10] This, together with what might in the United States be termed "trickle-down economics," was expected to lead to rapid improvement in the economic status, and therefore in the quality of life and health status, of China's population.[11]

As part of these changes, the communes were dissolved. Because the organization and financing of rural health care were largely dependent on the commune system, rural health care services changed substantially.[12] The health clinic in Chen Village, for example, was sold to the village barefoot doctor "who, true to the prevailing entrepreneurial spirit, alienated patients by raising the fee for any injection."[13] The commune facilities were turned over to the townships (political but not economic entities), and the production-brigade facilities were sold to private owners. Barefoot doctors were largely replaced by "village doctors," who were paid on a fee-for-service, rather than communal, basis. The cooperative medical care system disappeared in all but the wealthiest rural areas. As industrialization, economic reorganization, and urban migration in China proceeded, the commune system that provided the economic basis for the barefoot doctors was disbanded.

Despite China's economic boom in recent years, many people continue to live lives of grinding poverty. The World Bank estimated in 2008 that three hundred million people are abjectly poor, three times as many as the bank's previous estimate.[14] Overall, the gap between the rich and poor and between urban and rural people has widened. Along with these and other problems emerging in China in the wake of the country's new economic policies, reports of corruption among medical suppliers and personnel proliferated. A rural factory was reported to have washed more than one million previously used, disposable hypodermic needles, failed to sterilize them, and then sold them as new.[15] Stories abound of people having to bribe physicians and technicians in order to obtain what should have been routine care. Although informing a pregnant woman of the sex of her fetus (as determined by ultrasonic examination) was illegal in China, numerous physicians and technicians were bribed to perform such examinations and report the outcomes. This apparently resulted in the selective termination of pregnancies of female fetuses and an extraordinary rise in the sex ratio of newborns to 118.5 males for every 100 females.[16] Overuse of parenteral injections, inadequate sterilization of syringes and acupuncture needles, and low levels of immunization against Hepatitis B are further evidence of serious problems in China's current rural health care system.[17] More ominously, the industrialization of the economy, the breakdown in elements of the public health and medical care systems, and the return of prostitution have led to a resurgence of STDs and HIV/AIDS[18] and to a reappearance of schistosomiasis in some parts of China.

In recent years these problems have intensified, in part spurred by the worldwide trend toward globalization, privatization, and the elimination of trade barriers. Reports on changes in China's economic system[19] and in its health care system,[20] as well as on the health of its people[21] indicate continuing shifts away from China's economic and health policies of the 1970s.

Beyond this lies what Perry Link has described as "China's 'core' problem": the absence of a strong civil society and of avenues for dissent in the face of a powerful central government.[22] And even more important is another "core problem," the ideological conflict between a society committed to lessening the gap between rich and poor (as advocated by Mao) and a society willing to tolerate increasing gaps between rich and poor if this contributes to growth in national wealth (as advocated by Deng).

Nonetheless, the emphasis in China on the community rather than on the individual persists, giving hope that some of the developments of the 1960s and 1970s, during the period in which Mao and his principles held sway, will not be entirely lost.

### Lessons to Be Learned

A central lesson that we and so many others learned by having the privilege of observing China's delivery of essential human services during the 1970s is the importance of looking beyond one's own borders—one's cultural, political, and philosophical, as well as geographic borders—at other ways of thinking and other ways of best "serving the people." International observation and comparison inevitably lead to questioning the fundamental premises of one's own society, thereby broadening the scope of what is possible and even desirable.

A comment on the train that brought us from Hong Kong to Canton (Kwangchow) at the start of our first visit to China in 1971 highlights another important lesson that we learned. A British reporter, who was returning to China after writing a well-respected book about the 1962 border clash between India and China, asked us whether we had previously visited India. When we responded no, he said, "You must visit India before you visit China. Otherwise you will not be able to understand what China has accomplished over the past twenty years." Of course we had no intention of turning back and foregoing this unbelievable opportunity. But his advice stayed with us and influenced our later visits to countries in Asia, Africa, Latin America, and Europe.

In China—as indeed in all societies but made more obvious by the dramatic swings of China's policies—a nation's medical and health care system is a reflection of the society's social, political, and economic conditions. Although China's Maoist era certainly entailed major problems—including severe political repression—the period's ideological commitment to community rather than simply to the individual, to improving the quality of life for the most marginalized groups in the population, and to providing equitable services led to an extraordinary and innovative development of rural health services. Conversely, China's current ideology of unrestrained free-market entrepreneurialism, combined at times with political repression, has destroyed the economic and social bases for equitable rural services.

China teaches those concerned with the just delivery of medical and health care a fundamental lesson: unless a society as a whole is concerned with principles of equity and justice in their broadest meanings, that society will have enormous difficulty developing and sustaining equitable provision of health services to all its people. The changes in China since the 1970s, and the failure of the privatization model in other countries, provide lessons for both wealthy and poor nations.

## Notes

We have learned much from reports written by Herbert K. Abrams, a physician who worked for the United Nations Relief and Rehabilitation Administration in China in the 1940s and who continued to report on events in China until his death in 2006. Especially useful were insights on China from our son, Mark Sidel, Doyle-Bascom Professor of Law and Public Affairs at the University of Wisconsin-Madison, who taught in China and worked in China for the Ford Foundation in the 1970s and 1980s and who continues to actively pursue his interest in the changes occurring in China.

1. The Pinyin system now in use in China transliterates Mao's name as Mao Zedong; the names in the Wade-Giles system in common use at the time of our visits in the 1970s follow in parentheses.
2. Urie Bronfenbrenner, *Two Worlds of Childhood: U.S. and U.S.S.R.* (New York: Russell Sage Foundation, 1970); Melford E. Spiro, *Children of the Kibbutz* (New York: Schocken Books, 1963).
3. Edgar Snow, *Red Star Over China* (New York: Random House, 1938); Joshua S. Horn, *Away with All Pests: An English Surgeon in People's China, 1954–1969* (New York: Monthly Review Press, 1969); William Hinton, *Fanshen: A Documentary of Revolution in a Chinese Village* (New York: Monthly Review Press, 1966).
4. Ruth Sidel and Victor W. Sidel, "Case Study: Health Care in the People's Republic of China," in *Alternative Approaches to Meeting Basic Health Needs in Developing Countries*, ed. V. Djukanovic and E. P. Mach (Geneva: World Health Organization, 1975), 35–50.
5. Victor W. Sidel and Ruth Sidel, "The Health Care Delivery System of the People's Republic of China," in *Health By the People*, ed. Kenneth W. Newell (Geneva: World Health Organization, 1975), 1–12.
6. Ruth Sidel, *Women and Child Care in China* (New York: Hill and Wang, 1972); Victor W. Sidel and Ruth Sidel, *Serve the People: Observations on Medicine in the People's Republic of China* (New York: Josiah Macy, Jr. Foundation, 1973); Ruth Sidel, *Families of Fengsheng: Urban Life in China* (Baltimore: Penguin Books, 1974).
7. Ruth Sidel and Victor W. Sidel, "Human Services in the People's Republic of China," *Social Policy* 2 (1972): 25–34 (reprinted in *People's China: Social Experimentation, Politics, Entry onto the World Scene, 1966 through 1972*, ed. David Milton, Nancy Milton, and Franz Schurmann [New York: Vintage Books, 1974], 178–194); Victor W. Sidel, "The Barefoot Doctors of the People's Republic of China," *New England Journal of Medicine* 286 (1972): 1292–1299; Victor W. Sidel, "Serve the People: Medical Education in the People's Republic of China," *New Physician* 21 (1972): 284–291; Victor W. Sidel, "Medical Personnel and Their Training," in *Medicine and Public*

*Health in the People's Republic of China,* ed. Joseph R. Quinn (Washington, D.C.: U.S. Department of Health, Education and Welfare, 1972); Victor W. Sidel, "Some Observations on the Organization of Health Care in the People's Republic of China," *International Journal of Health Services* 2 (1972): 385–395.

8. Ruth Sidel, "Social Services in China," *Social Work* 17 (1972): 5–13; Ruth Sidel, "The Role of Revolutionary Optimism in the Treatment of Mental Illness in the People's Republic of China," *American Journal of Orthopsychiatry* 43 (1973): 732–736; Ruth Sidel, "The Organization of Urban Neighborhood Health and Social Services in China," in *China Medicine As We Saw It,* ed. Joseph R. Quinn (Washington, D.C.: U.S. Department of Health, Education and Welfare, 1974); Ruth Sidel, "People Serving People: Human Services in the People's Republic of China," in *Social Service Delivery Systems: An International Annual,* vol. 2, *Meeting Human Needs,* ed. Daniel Thursz and Joseph L. Vigilante (Beverly Hills: Sage, 1976), 163–196.

9. Ruth Sidel and Victor W. Sidel, *The Health of China: Current Conflicts in Medical and Human Services for One Billion People* (Boston: Beacon Press, 1982); Alan R. Hinman et al., eds., "Health Services in Shanghai County," *American Journal of Public Health* 72 (1982): 7; Myron E. Wegman, "Public Health in China," *American Journal of Public Health* 72 (1982): 978–979; Victor W. Sidel, "Medical Care in China: Equity vs. Modernization," *American Journal of Public Health* 72 (1982): 1224–1225; Matthias Stiefel and W. F. Wertheim, *Production, Equality and Participation in Rural China* (London: Zed Press for the United Nations Research Institute for Social Development, 1983); Vikki Valentine, "Health for the Masses: China's 'Barefoot Doctors,'" www.npr.org (accessed August 30, 2007).

10. Orville Schell, *To Get Rich Is Glorious* (New York: New American Library/Du Hon, 1986).

11. William Hinton, *The Great Reversal: The Privatization of China 1978–1989* (New York: Monthly Review Press, 1990).

12. Victor W. Sidel, "New Lessons from China: Equity and Economics in Rural Health Care," *American Journal of Public Health* 83 (1993): 1665–1666.

13. Anita Chan, Richard Madson, and Jonathan Unger, *Chen Village under Mao and Deng,* 2nd ed. (Berkeley and Los Angeles: University of California Press, 1992), 275.

14. Howard W. French, "Lives of Poverty, Untouched by China's Boom," *New York Times,* January 13, 2008.

15. Stanley Lubman, "In China, Medical System Is Plagued by Corruption," *Boston Globe,* October 6, 1991; Nicholas D. Kristof, "China Is Trying to Stifle Scandal Over Reused Hypodermic Needles," *New York Times,* May 31, 1993.

16. Nicholas D. Kristof, "China Turns to Ultrasound, Scorning Baby Girls for Boys," *New York Times,* July 21, 1993.

17. Serena Clayton et al., "Hepatitis B Control in China: Knowledge and Practices among Village Doctors," *American Journal of Public Health* 83 (1993): 1685–1688.

18. Herbert K. Abrams, "The Resurgence of Sexually Transmitted Diseases in China," *Journal of Public Health Policy* 22 (2001): 429–440.

19. Robert Weil, *Red Cat, White Cat: China and the Contradictions of Market Socialism* (New York: Monthly Review Press, 1996); Wei Zhang, "The Other Side of the Chinese Economic Miracle," *International Journal of Health Services* 42(1) (2012): 9–27.

20. Meei-Shia Chen, "The Great Reversal: Transformation of Health Care in the People's Republic of China," in *Blackwell Companion to Medical Sociology,* ed. William C. Cockerham (Oxford: Blackwell, 2001), 456–482; Sen Gong, Alan Walker, and Guang Shi, "From Chinese Model to U.S. Symptoms: The Paradox of China's Health

System," *International Journal of Health Services* 37(4) (2007): 651–672; David Blumenthal and William Hsiao, "Privatization and Its Discontents—The Evolving Chinese Health Care System," *New England Journal of Medicine* 353(11) (2005): 1165–1170.

21. Tiefu Shen, Jean-Pierre Habicht, and Ying Chang, "Effect of Economic Reforms on Child Growth in Urban and Rural Areas of China," *New England Journal of Medicine* 335 (1996): 400–406.

22. Perry Link, "China's 'Core' Problem," *Daedalus* 122 (1993): 189–207.

# Chapter 8

# Medical Internationalism and the "Last Epidemic"

**Bernard Lown**

I was already middle-aged when I began an emotional and intellectual journey through rugged and uncharted terrain. I risked credibility and even retribution when I joined forces with a perceived enemy to contain the unparalleled terror of nuclear war. The enemy became a friend, and together we launched a global movement.

This is both my story and the story of an organization founded to engage millions of people worldwide in a struggle for human survival. To a large extent my own identity and that of the organization became one. Building the organization became a preoccupation, even an obsession. Although I continued my professional work with fervor, as clinician, cardiologist, teacher, and researcher, the International Physicians for the Prevention of Nuclear War (IPPNW) absorbed even more of my energy.

## Beginnings

In the mid-1930s, when I was a teenager, my family migrated to the United States from Lithuania. The shock of acculturation inflicted pain and at the same time honed sensitivities. Secular parents instilled a conviction that the purpose of being was not self-enrichment but making life better for those who follow. Jewish cultural values imparted deep moral moorings. It led me to principled but sometimes unpopular public stances and to a deep engagement with student activism during my medical school days.

My early life history was a basic training of sorts that prepared me for a plunge into deeper waters. Often, change comes in slow steps. In my case there was a moment of truth after which life was radically different forever. This occurred unexpectedly. The year was 1961. I was an assistant professor at the Harvard School of Public Health preoccupied with research on the baffling and enormous problem of sudden cardiac death. At the same time, I was teaching medical students and house staff at the Peter Bent Brigham Hospital and working with the fabled clinician and pioneer cardiologist Dr. Samuel A. Levine.

I was approached by Dr. Roy Menninger, a postdoctoral trainee in psychiatry readying to return to Topeka, Kansas. Roy was a Quaker. He asked me to accompany him to a lecture by the British peace activist and parliamentarian Philip Noel-Baker, who was speaking in a private home in Cambridge. Two years earlier, in 1959, Noel-Baker had been awarded the Nobel Peace Prize. His topic in Cambridge was the nuclear arms race as a threat to human survival.

I remember little of the content of that evening's lecture except for the essential message: If the stockpiling of weapons of mass destruction continues, they will ultimately be used, and they may extinguish life on planet Earth. I was shaken by an ironic paradox. I was spending every waking moment to contain the problem of sudden cardiac death, a condition that claimed an American life every ninety seconds and far greater numbers throughout the world. It dawned on me that the greatest threat to human survival was not cardiac but nuclear. I had long been a social activist, involved in struggles for universal health care and against racial discrimination. But until the moment I heard Philip Noel-Baker speak, I had shut my mind to the implications of the nuclear age. I had no moral choice but to act.

I called together a small group of medical colleagues from Harvard's hospitals. At forty, I was the oldest among about a dozen physicians in our group. We met biweekly at my suburban home in Newton. Initially the meetings had no set plan. We knew next to nothing about atomic weapons and radiation biology, but we never questioned whether it was legitimate for doctors to enter a controversial political arena far removed from their medical knowledge. Our gatherings had the quality of a book club, except that the book had yet to be written.

Six months after the first meeting in my home, our group had expanded to about twelve consistent attendees, including Victor Sidel and Jack Geiger, two impressive physicians with long records of distinguished political activism on behalf of the poor and disenfranchised. The majority of us were academics, and our forte was to research, analyze, write, and publish. I do not recall who first proposed the idea that we should prepare a series of medical articles dealing with the health consequences of nuclear explosions on specific civilian populations. We aimed high: these articles were intended for the most prestigious journal in the country, *The New England Journal of Medicine*. We intended to present a realistic scenario that had been missing from public discourse about the nuclear threat.

None were better attuned to those tasks than Vic and Jack. Vic was an insistent disciplinarian; like a marine drill sergeant, he kept the small troop hopping and adhering to a taut schedule. Jack, more laid back, was also a workaholic, with the sharp sense of a consummate debater. A former Associated Press correspondent, he assimilated massive reams of diverse information and converted it to highly readable text. Jack chain-smoked while playing the role of a court stenographer, taking down our sage observations—or so we believed. In fact, the endless pages that poured forth were neither summation nor arbitration but much improved renditions, at times only loosely related to what we were arguing about. By December 1961, we had completed five articles in which we described the biological, physical, and psychological effects of a targeted nuclear attack on Boston.

We concluded that the blast, fire, and radiation would claim unprecedented casualties.[1] From a population of 2,875,000 then residing in the metropolitan Boston area, 1,000,000 would be killed instantly, 1,000,000 would be fatally injured, and an additional 500,000 injured victims were likely to survive. Ten percent of Boston's 6,500 physicians would remain alive, uninjured, and able to attend the multitude of victims. In the post-attack period, a single physician would be available for approximately 1,700 acutely injured victims. The implication of this ratio was that if a single physician spent only ten minutes on the diagnosis and treatment of an injured patient, and the workday was twenty hours, eight to fourteen days would be required to see every injured person once. It followed that most fatally injured persons would never see a physician, even to assuage their pain before an agonizing death. We concluded that there could be no meaningful medical response to a catastrophe of such magnitude.

More than one-third of the survivors would perish in epidemics in the twelve months following a nuclear attack due to the combined impacts of malnutrition, crowded shelters, poor sanitation, immunologic deficiency, contaminated water supplies, a proliferation of insect and rodent vectors, inadequate disposal of the dead, a lack of antibiotics, and poor medical care. The rest would be ideal candidates for tuberculosis, overwhelming sepsis, and various fungi, which would constitute the ultimate afflictions for all the survivors.

The series of articles we had drafted emerged as a symposium titled "The Medical Consequences of Thermonuclear War," printed on May 31, 1962.[2] The impact of the symposium was unprecedented. The two leading Boston newspapers covered the findings on the front page. Attention was not limited to our local press; it was worldwide. We expected intense and detailed rebuttal from

Pentagon experts, if not of our data, certainly of our conclusions. Our findings were disquietingly affirmed by the fact that no criticism was ever forthcoming. On the contrary, we were flooded with close to six hundred reprint requests from personnel in various branches of the military services. There were also feelers from the Pentagon and from the Disaster Preparedness Agency to see if we would like to become consultants.

We helped stimulate antinuclear movements around the world and seeded the global terrain for the international organization that emerged some two decades later. Our study served as a template for cities around the world. Much to our surprise, we were anointed instant experts and invited as speakers to diverse groups, and we offered testimony before congressional committees on the medical consequences of nuclear warfare.

## Making the Connection

By the late 1960s I had moved away from the antinuclear struggle. It was psychologically numbing to continue as an apocalyptic evangelist. Yet the undiminished nuclear threat hovered as an inseparable shadow. I read every issue of the *Bulletin of the Atomic Scientists* and kept file cabinets bulging with articles on every aspect of nuclearism. I followed the nuclear arms race with dread and with mounting outrage. It seemed as though in the nuclear arms race the American and Soviet lead runners had lost control of their limbs.

I became increasingly convinced that cultivating trust among Soviet and American medical professionals was an indispensable first step and the key to unlocking powerful forces. Once unleashed, such forces would draw on humanity's deep-seated instinct for survival. But even to suggest a dialogue with the evil empire was to grant them a moral equality that was theretofore taboo. There was no greater American sin than being soft hearted on communism. It occurred to me daily that I was jeopardizing my hard-won career. After all, I had been a victim of the McCarthyite witch hunt in the mid-1950s because of my earlier medical student activism (see chapter 5). It had left my career in shambles and required a decade of intense struggle to pick up the pieces, mend fences, and start afresh. I had no desire to relive that part of my life, and I knew that engaging the Russians carried risk. I visualized myself as a moth with one wing already singed, once again being propelled toward the fire.

At the time my goal was inchoate and fuzzy. My thinking progressed no further than trying to engage Russian doctors in some kind of dialogue on nuclear war; the aim was to find common ground. Even a small beginning with a single human connection, namely a Russian acquaintance, would be a hopeful first step. The candidate who came to mind was academician and cardiologist Eugene Chazov. I had collaborated with him in connection with the National Heart and Lung Institute and Soviet joint study on sudden cardiac death. I liked Chazov, respected his medical ability, and knew he was a leading figure in Soviet medicine.

In spring 1979 I sent Chazov a carefully crafted letter. I described the sheer insanity of the ever-accelerating nuclear arms race as defined by its acronym, MAD (for *mutual assured destruction*). My letter to him went unanswered and I was uncertain how to proceed. Then a visiting Soviet cardiologist showed up in my laboratory at Harvard as a veritable messenger from heaven: Dr. Lidia Niko-laeva indicated that she was the head of cardiac rehabilitation in the clinic of Professor Eugene Chazov at the All Union Institute of Cardiology in the USSR. I immediately invited Dr. Nikolaeva for brunch that Sunday and drafted a letter for her to hand-deliver to Eugene Chazov.[3]

When I asked Dr. Nikolaeva to deliver the letter to Chazov, she became vis-ibly uneasy. I surmised that she feared the letter was a provocative document that could land her in trouble with the FBI—or, worse, the KGB (the Soviet Union's equivalent to a combined FBI–CIA–Homeland Security Agency). To assuage her concerns, I urged her to tear open the envelope and read the con-tents. As she read the letter, she began to cry. Her own fear of the nuclear arms race was quite vivid, and she promised to carry the letter personally and deliver it directly into Chazov's hands as soon as she returned to Moscow. Four months later I received a reply from Chazov. We had lit a small candle.

Chazov's reply foreshadowed a major theme in IPPNW's work. While he agreed with my assessment of the danger of nuclear war and its medical con-sequences, he went even further. The arms race, he said, was already taking a human toll by diverting scarce resources to the military. Continuing the nuclear arms race meant that people were dying right at that moment for a lack of adequate health care and other essential social needs. Though Chazov did not commit to a personal involvement, he did agree that physicians should speak out on the issue. He wrote: "I completely share your point of view that physi-cians have no right to stand aloof and remain silent facing a challenge to com-mon sense and moral principles."

Even in the darkest days of the Cold War, cooperation between doctors of the two rival ideological camps had never ceased. At the very time when mis-siles were multiplied in readiness for presumptive nuclear strikes, American and Soviet physicians struggled shoulder to shoulder in the World Health Orga-nization's (WHO) global campaign to eradicate smallpox. Such acts of camara-derie were persuasive models for the antinuclear struggle.

We needed a Soviet ally with influence, one who would be permitted to engage openly in an international movement, one who could take a message about nuclear war and its consequences to his countrymen, a message that hitherto had been denied to the Soviet people. We needed an ally high in the hierarchy of power, a person of character who would, incrementally, be able to speak truths that others in the Soviet establishment might wish to censor. Chazov met the bill of particulars.

After I gave a series of cardiology lectures in London in March 1980, an opportunity arose for the long-awaited meeting with Eugene Chazov in Moscow. As our meeting began, I immediately launched into the concept of a Soviet-American physicians' organization. He seemed taken aback. While my mind had been racing for months with these ideas, he had not gone beyond some inchoate intellectual interest in the general concept. I needed to slow down and learn why he hesitated. I didn't have to wait long. Chazov stopped me dead in my tracks with words to the effect that there was no way he would become involved in an antinuclear organization.

He expressed surprise at my naïveté. Surely I was aware of the pervasive power of the Pentagon in America. He reminded me of President Eisenhower's warning, some twenty years earlier, about the U.S. military-industrial complex. The success of the doctors' organization depended on media exposure; yet mass channels of communication were controlled by the very corporations who bedded down with the Pentagon. How did I expect to develop a countervailing force against such entrenched power? Chazov warned that with America swinging to the right in the forthcoming election I might jeopardize far more than my career. It could be far worse. He was speaking about me, but I believe he was really addressing his own peril. For Chazov to pursue the agenda I had in mind, he would have to take big risks. After a contentious discussion the meeting broke up as I used intemperate language. Chazov stalked out, and I was certain that was to be the last I would ever see of him.

I was therefore astonished when the next morning he telephoned, as though nothing unusual had transpired, suggesting we get together that very day. When we met at the Myasnikov Institute, Chazov brought along Dimitri Venediktov, a deputy minister of health who had been actively involved in promoting Soviet-American collaboration in WHO's smallpox eradication program and the Alma-Ata Primary Health Care Conference. Although Venediktov was silent throughout, it was apparent that Chazov was the supreme organizational man who had begun seeding allies in key sectors. Chazov insisted that I lay out my ideas about the nuclear threat and the structure, scope, function, and governance of the organization I envisioned. We agreed that, this being a

Soviet-American undertaking, it should have a Soviet-American co-presidency to symbolize the cooperation necessary for human survival in the nuclear age. I emphasized, above all, the apolitical nature of a physicians' movement. I thought we had agreed on essential policy, but to my dismay the document I soon received from Chazov and sixty-two Soviet medical academicians was steeped in Communist political jargon. The nuclear arms race was provoked by U.S. imperialism; the Soviet arsenals were aiming to maintain global peace. Any movement sundered by an ideological divide at the very outset was not seaworthy for the turbulent waters we were intending to sail. Chazov and I decided to convene a meeting in Geneva with three Soviet and three American participants to determine whether the seemingly irreconcilable differences could be resolved.

### Launching the IPPNW

Geneva was a watershed event. It took place in December 1980, one year after the Soviets' Christmas Eve invasion of Afghanistan. Day by day since then, one could note an intensification of the Cold War. Russians were dehumanized as a people; everything Soviet was rejected, belittled, and denigrated. At the same time, a massive campaign portrayed the Russians as technological supermen. We did succeed to bridge our differences by emphasizing our primacy as a physician movement. We agreed to call together a small congress of world medical leaders to set the course for an international antinuclear organization.

That first meeting took place only four months later, in March 1981 at Airlie House, Virginia, in the United States. The Reagan era (the presidency of Ronald Reagan, 1981–1989) had just begun and a chill was congealing intellectual discourse. The new administration was drastically changing the course of thirty years of American foreign policy by abandoning the "peaceful coexistence" that had taken shape under Nixon and Kissinger. Instead of "containment," the new strategic goal was to impose peace through overwhelming military strength, not excluding a nuclear option to roll back the "evil empire." In this political climate some intellectuals, fearing social marginalization, were losing their antinuclear fervor. The prevailing mood was that of a country at war. Any questioning of the Washington consensus was categorized as unpatriotic.

This was the backdrop for the first IPPNW world congress, where a struggle ensued for the soul of the yet-unborn organization. However, the struggle was not between East and West, but among the American physician participants. The key protagonist leading one faction was Helen Caldicott, the militant leader of the resurgent Physicians for Social Responsibility (PSR) movement. Surprisingly, she objected to doctor activism and a grassroots-based international movement. Those of us who had stoked IPPNW were vehemently opposed to having another academic think tank writing learned articles on the evils of nuclearism. The argument was intense but our position ultimately prevailed.

In the USSR, the press widely reported on the Airlie House physicians' antinuclear congress and the key role of the Soviet doctors. *Soviet Life* devoted several pages to sizable excerpts from the main talks. Chazov was able to monopolize Soviet TV for an hour regarding the founding of IPPNW in a broadcast that reached twenty million people. "In keeping with our Hippocratic oath, we have no option but to alert our patients to the threat to their life and limb posed by the uncontrolled arms race," he said.

We were far less successful in cultivating the American media. Journalists, both print and broadcast, were indeed present in Airlie House in substantial numbers. TV cameras were rolling, luminaries were interviewed. The input was at high volume; the output, however, was barely a whisper.[4] The *Boston Globe* was an exception, providing more extensive coverage. No doubt, it was compelled by local pride, since the IPPNW founders were Bostonians.

But the organization was launched. It would be headed by co-presidents, one each from the USSR and the United States, reflecting the core mission of IPPNW—namely, East-West cooperation. Chazov and I had already been designated the IPPNW leaders at the first congress in Airlie House. To foster regional activities, the world was divided into regions, with each headed by a vice president. Affiliates preserved their autonomy and could set the criteria for membership. They were also permitted to define a national agenda that transcended the nuclear issue. For example, the West German affiliate was actively engaged against nuclear energy and Euromissiles, while the Swedish affiliate circumscribed its activities to nuclear weapons.

A rancorous divide was brewing over the issue of Euromissiles. Members from the Communist bloc were concerned about the impending arrival of Pershing II missiles, which threatened to incinerate Europe and leave an irradiated dump. The debate in Europe tilted toward the Soviet view that the United States' deployment of Euromissiles was provocative and would further destabilize a teetering nuclear house of cards. During this period I traveled frequently to the Soviet Union and witnessed the sense of helplessness and mounting agitation. It was especially galling for Russia that a nuclear strike could come from German soil.

I discovered a deeper reason for Russian fear. A launch of U.S.-based intercontinental ballistic missiles (ICBMs) against the USSR would take twenty-five to thirty-five minutes to reach their targets. This interval, brief as it was, would suffice for the Soviets to let go a counterstrike with their own land-based missiles, thereby serving as a powerful deterrent. This asset would be forfeited once Pershing missiles were deployed next door. Euromissiles, within minutes, would decapitate Soviet command-and-control centers, leaving them defenseless against a follow-through ICBM strike. The contentious debate presented IPPNW with unfamiliar terrain. Hitherto, we had focused on nuclear weapons in general. Now we were being pushed to take a position against a specific class of weapons—a U.S. weapons system.

As it turned out, the issue of Pershing missiles in Europe led to one of Chazov's finest hours. At a meeting of the IPPNW council at The Hague in October 1982, the West Germans introduced a motion that IPPNW officially oppose the deployment of Pershing missiles in Europe. Though I was adamantly against deployment, I recognized the likelihood that such a stance would discredit IPPNW. Passing a one-sided motion, especially one directed at a specific U.S. weapon system, would politicize the movement and label us Kremlin apologists. In a deeper sense it would move us away from principled opposition to all nuclear weapons on the tenable medical grounds that they were incompatible with life.

When Chazov's turn came, he was pensive and careful in his choice of words. He pointed out that if IPPNW were to take a position on the Pershings, such a position would serve as a precedent. Sooner rather than later, pressure would mount to single out Soviet weapons for similar criticism. He concluded that the West German motion would take IPPNW beyond its charter as a nonpartisan physicians' movement. Once his remarks sank in, the motion was dead in the water. We then adopted a more evenhanded call for a bilateral freeze on the deployment of all theater missiles in Europe. Chazov, by this time a member of the Communist Party's Central Committee, was like a master magician who could do the unthinkable, if not the impossible. He had never before openly departed from official Soviet policy. I watched with amazement as he grasped that for IPPNW to maintain credibility, it was mandatory to eschew partisan East-West positions. In a sense, we witnessed an unprecedented act of independence: a member of the Central Committee had broken with party discipline at a public forum.

From June 17 to 22, 1983, the third congress assembled in a large amphitheater at the Free University of Amsterdam, with 750 participants from forty-three countries, which was tenfold the attendance of the first IPPNW congress at Airlie House in Virginia. In the two earlier congresses, we called attention to the unimaginable and largely unpredictable consequences of nuclear war, proving the uselessness of medical efforts in the post-attack period, the irrelevance of civil defense planning, and the malfunctioning of technology and the aberration of personality that might trigger an accidental nuclear exchange.

During the third congress we broke new ground. We examined the underlying conceptions dominating the cultural landscape that fueled the nuclear arms race. We dwelled on such illusions as the concept of a limited or prolonged nuclear war, the misbegotten idea of nuclear superiority, the belief in rational planning, the deceptive promotion of security based on burgeoning nuclear arsenals, the cultivation of a spurious faith in defensive systems to protect targeted populations.

The first plenary session of every congress began with greetings from world leaders. We received messages from the UN secretary-general and Pope John Paul II. Chazov brought direct greetings from the general secretary of the Communist Party of the USSR, Yuri Andropov. Word from the White House was personally delivered by the U.S. ambassador to the Netherlands. In the message to IPPNW, President Reagan employed a phrase that would become a mantra of his reelection campaign the following year, "Nuclear war cannot be won and must never be fought."

The new refrain, I believe, was motivated by mounting public concern. The powers that be in Washington chose IPPNW as the centerpiece of their reelection campaign's peace offensive. IPPNW had both domestic and international outreach; the meeting in Amsterdam provided a favorable platform to address a

**Figure 8.1** Bernard Lown (*left*) and Eugene Chazov (*right*) in Amsterdam, 1983. The photograph was used worldwide to promote IPPNW (IPPNW photo archive).
Courtesy of Bernard Lown.

wide public in the United States and in Europe. As a doctors' group we carried credentials of legitimacy. Our achievements made us a credible organization for many constituencies.

The dangerous stalemate in the nuclear standoff was growing more unstable by the day. I came to believe that the absence of results in the numerous negotiations between the Superpowers related to the very process of disarmament negotiations. Controversial at every step, they were held in secret at a snail's pace and conducted by the wrong people—drawing on experts deeply enmeshed with the military-industrial complex. Secret negotiations excluded the critical forces that would compel urgency. Being excluded was the threatened constituency, our patients whose very lives were in jeopardy. I was convinced that without their involvement, nuclear disarmament negotiations could yield no substantive results. Yet the media promoted the illusion that substantive discussions were underway.

I was increasingly convinced that IPPNW needed to promote a new approach, marked by substantial unilateral steps. The first such step should involve a cessation of nuclear testing. The deadlock would be breached by action not by more talk. The role of peace movements was to educate and rouse the public to compel reciprocation. I designated this approach "The Medical Prescription." Whenever I visited the USSR, I focused my agitating on Soviet officials involved with nuclear issues.

## The Strategic Health Initiative

Beginning in the summer of 1984, several events cascaded IPPNW into prominence. A letter from the United Nations Educational, Scientific and Cultural Organization announced that an international jury had chosen IPPNW for the 1984 UNESCO Prize for Peace Education and that Chazov and I were to be the recipients. We received extensive coverage from a hitherto unfriendly quarter, the American Medical Association. Their news publication, which reached two hundred thousand physicians, featured my work with IPPNW. The article was sympathetic in tone and comprehensive in content, providing an in-depth examination of a movement pushing the "profession to a revolutionary leap in its thinking on preventive medicine."[5]

Mikhail Gorbachev's ascent to power with his election as general secretary of the Politburo in March 1985 afforded us a historic opportunity to eliminate nuclear weapons and set the world on a different course. Among Gorbachev's first declarations was support for a bilateral cessation of nuclear testing. Without the courtesy to explore what this new leader had in mind, the United States peremptorily rejected his proposal.[6]

It was time to revisit Russia and learn firsthand about Gorbachev. The fresh breeze wafting from Moscow suggested new possibilities. Fortunately, in April 1985, I was scheduled to chair a cardiology symposium in Montreux, Switzerland, which I could combine with a trip to Moscow. Chazov encouraged such a visit in order to evolve a common agenda for the forthcoming fifth IPPNW congress in Budapest, which would be held in July.

In Moscow I was in for a momentous surprise. The day after my arrival, there was an intimate party for me. The guests included the political savant Georgi Arbatov, the physicist Evgeny Velikhov, representatives of various think tanks involved with nuclear disarmament, and a number of Russian IPPNW stalwarts. The mood was celebratory. A new era was dawning. The atmosphere was crackling with anticipation.

Arbatov took me aside, talking in a low voice as though confiding a state secret. I had no idea what was to follow. He intimated that he was not speaking for himself, without divulging whom he represented. He said that I should feel mightily proud of the campaign for nuclear disarmament. He then whispered to me of a new Soviet initiative that would be launched on Hiroshima Day. He said Gorbachev had decided to announce a unilateral stop to Soviet nuclear testing on August 6. This would be followed by other significant unilateral disarmament steps. I pulled out a handkerchief, embarrassed by my tears.

Over the next few days, I spent much time with Chazov planning the forthcoming congress in Budapest, which was a mere three months away. We strategized to prepare the ground for Gorbachev's important initiative. Utmost in Chazov's mind was how IPPNW should respond to Reagan's Star Wars program. It seemed to me that we needed an affirmative policy projecting a different vision for the uses of space rather than pockmarking the heavens with missiles and antimissiles. What that was to be, I hadn't a clue. But then we hit upon the seed of a novel idea. Why not link the anti-Star Wars program with solving the health problems of the developing world?

The Soviets and the antinuclear community were roiled by President Reagan's so-called Strategic Defense Initiative (SDI). It promised to gum up disarmament negotiations for decades to come.[7] The Russians viewed it as American brinksmanship intended to ratchet up the nuclear threat and accelerate the arms race. We needed to think creatively, to break out of a confining intellectual box. How about reconfiguring Star Wars? Why not use outer space to promote health? Instead of loading satellites with death-dealing weapons, why not fill them with health-affirming information? *Star Health instead of Star Wars.* Instead of SDI, substitute an "H" and you have SHI, Strategic Health Initiative, or SatelLife.

I turned to an imaginative friend, Dr. Kenneth Warren. He was bright, irreverent, contemptuous of conventional thinking, and ready to spring forth with unexpected insights. He directed the Rockefeller Foundation's health sciences division. Ken was preoccupied with health information, its uneven quality, and its lack of circulation to those who needed it most. He was intrigued by the idea of satellites as delivery vehicles for health information. Without much ado, he provided a small grant to assess the feasibility of the Star Health program. We engaged experts, who concluded that it was doable. Low-earth-orbit micro-satellites could be cost effective as conduits for health information around the globe.

During the fifth congress held in Budapest in 1985, the council, the highest governing body of IPPNW, voted unanimously to endorse a nuclear test ban that "would create both psychological momentum and a political climate in which additional disarmament steps will be possible." The policy was in sync with Gorbachev's forthcoming announcement of a unilateral six-month test moratorium. The congress also advanced on another front that mattered deeply to me, the North-South divide. Several speakers indicated that for mere pennies, children could be protected against a number of life-threatening infectious diseases.[8] In my plenary address I urged IPPNW to sponsor a global space-based micro-satellite network to serve the health-information needs of poor countries and to track disease epidemics and hunger. SatelLife, the strategic health initiative, would emphasize the choice now confronting humankind. People should look skyward with hope rather than dread.[9]

### The Nobel Prize and Gorbachev's Moratorium

Friday, October 11, 1985, was a sunny autumn day. Chazov and I met with Halfdan Mahler, director general of the World Health Organization, and scheduled a post-meeting press conference. As described by Geoffrey Lean in the *London Observer,* datelined Geneva, "A few minutes before 11 a.m. on Friday they were holding an ill-attended press conference in a small, airless room. A handful of journalists were going through the motions of taking notes on another set of predictable statements from an obscure group." Standing off to the side was a sandy-haired, bespectacled man, a middle-aged professorial type who asked whether he could make a statement. Usually this meant an attack from an anti-Soviet dissident for the failure of IPPNW to speak out on human rights. From the first words, it was evident that he had come not to fault, but to honor.

He identified himself as the Reverend Gunnar Stalsett, secretary-general of the Lutheran World Federation and a member of the Nobel Peace Prize Committee. Without much ado he began to read from a prepared statement:

The Norwegian Nobel Committee has decided to award the Nobel Peace Prize for 1985 to the organization International Physicians for the Prevention of Nuclear War [which has rendered] . . . a considerable service to mankind by spreading authoritative information and by creating an awareness of the catastrophic consequences of atomic war. . . . Such an awakening of public opinion . . . can give the present arms limitations negotiations new perspectives and a new seriousness. . . . [T]he committee attaches particular importance to the fact that the organization was formed as a result of joint initiatives by Soviet and American physicians.

Chazov and I stood there, overwhelmed and speechless. Within minutes it seemed as though a dam had burst. The tiny room was crowded with world media. Bedlam prevailed with reporters, photographers, radio broadcasters, and TV cameramen jostling one another to gain our attention. For the first time, the media were pursuing us. I realized that miracles sometimes do happen.

The presentation of the Nobel award took place two months later in Oslo. The ceremony was moving, somber, and dignified. Immediately after the ceremony, we sent telegrams to Reagan and Gorbachev requesting an urgent meeting. Within hours, we received a cordial response from the Kremlin. Gorbachev was willing to meet with us anytime. We were ignored by the White House and never received an answer, not even an excuse that the president was too busy.

The visit to Moscow was charged with momentous happenings. For some, a friendly reception in Moscow would have been proof positive that we had aligned with the forces of malevolence. My visit was extensively covered in the Soviet media, with appearances on prime-time television and lengthy interviews in the two mass-circulation daily newspapers, *Pravda* and *Izvestia*. On December 18 at 11 a.m. Chazov and I walked into the Kremlin.

Before the meeting Chazov had indicated that the show was mine. "This is your opportunity to have a private discussion with Gorbachev. I have every chance to see him." As we entered the room, Gorbachev came forward to greet us. His dancing eyes, alive with curiosity, dominated the impression he made. One was immediately caught up in the fine timber of his voice. His words were appropriate, heavily freighted with relevance, and lightened with levity.

With a chuckle he inquired of me, "I hear you are a medical expert. Is your specialty the right or left nostril?" We laughed. The tension was dispelled. I took an instant liking to the man for his sense of humor and his insight into what ails modern medicine. We were seated at one end of a long table covered with a green cloth, with Gorbachev directly opposite me. Gorbachev began by congratulating us on the award of the Nobel Prize to IPPNW. He said, "There

**Figure 8.2**  Bernard Lown (*right*) with Mikhail Gorbachev (*left*) in the Kremlin.
Courtesy of Bernard Lown.

exists in the Soviet Union great respect and sympathy for the activity of this movement, for its socially significant curative mission." He told us emphatically that ending the nuclear arms race and outlawing nuclear weapons were his highest priority.[10]

He complimented us with his familiarity with IPPNW discussions when he said, "We are prepared to pass on from competition in armaments to disarmament, from *confrontation to cooperation*," echoing the slogan of the fifth international congress of the IPPNW in Budapest. "One cannot help but agree with this. Cooperation is nowadays the indispensable condition both for progress of our civilization and of our very survival. . . . The Soviet Union will go as far as needed toward complete elimination of nuclear weapons . . . [thereby] ensuring man's primary right, the right to live." Chazov seemed certain that as a direct result of the meeting the Soviets' unilateral moratorium on testing would continue. It did, for an additional thirteen months. And one month after our meeting, Gorbachev called for the elimination of nuclear weapons by the year 2000.

## Looking Back

As I reflect on these events now, pride wells up considering what we, a small band of doctors, achieved. We contributed to a profound historic transformation, none too soon, and stopped a gallop toward the brink. IPPNW was embraced by a minority of health professionals, rarely exceeding 5 percent of the physicians in any one country. But what IPPNW lacked in numbers was more than compensated for by the commitment of its members.

The aim of IPPNW was to promote citizen diplomacy to cut through the fog of dehumanization that blocked an awareness of our shared plight and threatened to bring about our mutual extinction. We focused on growing arsenals of nuclear weapons as the common enemy of both nations. Our role as health professionals lent credibility to our message.

We opened a wide window for dialogue and cooperation. As a result, IPPNW was held suspect by the ruling establishments of both sides. In the West, we were accused of fraternizing with evil and being KGB dupes. In the East, we were suspected of serving as clever decoys for the CIA. An ancient tradition of professional cooperation among physicians buffered those assaults and allowed us to overcome the ideological nostrums of the day.[11]

Physicians from hostile camps worked together despite stark political and cultural differences. We focused on the single issue of "preventing the final epidemic." We exposed the litany of horrors that would result from a nuclear blast, fire, and radiation. Our message made arrant nonsense of political pontificating about fighting a limited nuclear war and surviving and winning such a conflict. Being awarded the Nobel Peace Prize was a resounding affirmation that our message was heard.

These experiences took place over a brief five-year period over a quarter of a century ago, yet they are full of lessons for today. Foremost is that an advance on any political front does not come as a gift from governing establishments. It needs to be wrested by means of an unrelenting, well-organized struggle. Politicians do not respond to the insistent beckoning of history. They rise to a challenge only when confronted by a public clamoring for change—which, if ignored, threatens the politicians' hold on power.

## Notes

This essay derives from my memoir, Bernard Lown, *Prescription for Survival: A Doctor's Journey to End Nuclear Madness* (San Francisco: Berrett-Koehler Publishers, 2008).

1. Victor W. Sidel, H. Jack Geiger, and Bernard Lown, "The Medical Consequences of Thermonuclear War, Part II: The Physician's Role in the Post-Attack Period," *New England Journal of Medicine* 266 (May 1962): 1137–1145.

2. David G. Nathan, H. Jack Geiger, Victor W. Sidel, and Bernard Lown, "The Medical Consequences of Thermonuclear War: Introduction," *New England Journal of Medicine* 266 (May 1962): 1126–1155; Victor W. Sidel, H. Jack Geiger, and Bernard Lown, "The Medical Consequences of Thermonuclear War, Part II."

3. Letter from Bernard Lown to Eugene Chazov, June 29, 1979. Personal correspondence in possession of the author.

4. Robert Reinhold, "A Prognosis for Doomsday," *New York Times,* March 29, 1981.

5. M. Rust, "MD Continues Battle against Nuclear War," *American Medical News,* July 20, 1984.

6. Phillip G. Schrag, *Global Action: Nuclear Test Ban Diplomacy at the End of the Cold War* (Boulder, CO: Westview Press, 1992).

7. Johan Galtung, "The Real Star Wars Threat," *The Nation,* February 28, 1987, 248–250.

8. Steven Erlanger, "Nuclear War Foes Urge Vaccination Program," *Boston Globe,* June 30, 1985.

9. Bernard Lown, "The Dream Must Not Be Deferred: Final Plenary Address," Fifth IPPNW Congress, Budapest, July 1, 1985.

10. Gorbachev meeting with Lown and Chazov, as reported by TASS, December 19, 1985.

11. Bernard Lown and Eugene Chazov, "Physician Responsibility in the Nuclear Age," *Journal of the American Medical Association* 274 (1995): 416–419.

# Part IV

# Generation Born in the 1940s–1960s

The chapters in this section are written by members of the baby boom generation (born in the postwar decades) who came of age in the 1960s and 1970s amid
the struggles of many new and resurgent political movements and groups—the
civil rights movement and the more militant Black Panther Party and Young
Lords, the anti–Vietnam War movement, the women's movement, the New Left,
the United Farm Workers, the solidarity movements supporting urban welfare
rights groups, the reproductive rights movement, the Gray Panthers, and the
gay rights (later lesbian, gay, bisexual, and transgender) movement. The baby
boomers' focus also shifted outward—primarily to Latin America and Africa—
where they joined inspiring leftist, antiapartheid, and independence struggles.
Investigative reporting had exposed the United States' backing of strong-armed
dictatorships as long as they remained U.S. allies in the Cold War—and the
often murderous activities of the Central Intelligence Agency (CIA) directed
covertly against democratically elected socialist governments. These revelations, together with the uncovering of secret military training of brutal police
forces and antidemocratic insurgent groups, motivated leftists' work with international colleagues in resistance to U.S. foreign policy and hegemony.

This generation's first major internationalist "awakening" was linked to the
1973 toppling of Salvador Allende's legitimately elected socialist government
in Chile and the revelation of the CIA's role in the military coup, just one example of a longstanding pattern of duplicitous heavy-handed U.S. intervention in
Latin America and elsewhere. Members of this generation responded by building a solidarity network to support the victims of the coup in Chile, leading to
similar solidarity movements in Central America and Southern Africa. Health

leftists played a key role in publicizing and directly or indirectly supporting the work of left-wing governments and movements while also providing safe harbor (and work) to health comrades forced into exile. Meanwhile, U.S. opposition to the emerging G-77 movement of nonaligned (developing) countries, calling for economic and political sovereignty as well as fair trade and development, sometimes made U.S. internationalists suspect simply due to nationality. Nor was their credibility helped by the multitudes of U.S. Peace Corps volunteers fanned out across the Third World, whom many believed were serving as agents of the U.S. government.

This generation also had to come to terms with the shifting roles and fortunes of international agencies. The WHO, following decades of Cold War–driven and narrowly technical disease control campaigns, returned to social medicine and universalist principles as embodied in its 1948 constitution. The WHO's stirring 1978 Alma-Ata Declaration (calling for "health for all" by the year 2000) came at a particular historical juncture, when its Scandinavian (socialist) director welcomed decolonized countries and embraced their assertion of collective political power. But the WHO began to suffer from the budgetary and political retribution of the United States, Great Britain, and other Western powers because of its critical stance and efforts to resist the tactics of the global pharmaceutical industry and, more generally, the neoliberal (pro-free market, and anti-redistribution and anti-regulation) agenda. By the late 1980s the WHO was being upstaged by international financial institutions like the World Bank—which displaced the social justice and equity-oriented primary health care approach with privatization and "structural adjustment" programs that "liberalized" economies and forced massive reductions in government spending—thus undercutting many initiatives begun in the spirit of Alma-Ata.

The experience of this generation raises many questions. How were its members to gain trust abroad when the motives of the U.S. government were so widely suspect? How could they sustain internationalist solidarity work at a time when many Americans were becoming increasingly apolitical and disengaged? How could health leftists reconcile their activism with the turn towards identity politics in the United States, which seemed to disavow the class solidarity approaches of the past? How could they challenge international health agencies that were succumbing to neoliberal influences? How could U.S. health internationalists work best to defend elected socialist governments and their health initiatives in such a world?

# Chapter 9

# Social Medicine, at Home and Abroad

Howard Waitzkin

And as a doctor I suffered from two very difficult diseases. I was only beginning to make my way as a surgeon when I came down with a bad case of tuberculosis. . . . My second "sickness" . . . well, that wasn't so simple. . . . I came to understand that tuberculosis was not merely a disease of the body but a social crime. . . . I have learned what must be done to cure this second sickness.

—Norman Bethune, MD, surgeon to the liberation forces of China, 1939

Norman Bethune, a Canadian surgeon, provided an early inspiration for my efforts in social medicine, both internationally and in the United States. In his work with poor and marginalized patients in Detroit, Bethune became infected with tuberculosis, as I myself did while taking care of a family at La Clínica de la Raza, a community health center in Oakland, California. Bethune saw clearly, as do most people who dedicate their work to social medicine, that social conditions often lie behind medical disorders. Without addressing these illness-generating social conditions, health professionals frequently find that the impact of their work remains limited, unfulfilling, and not fully effective. Bethune analyzed tuberculosis first as an infection of the body but secondly as a disease of society. He argued that the cure of tuberculosis in China and many other countries of the world required fundamental changes in the social conditions that generate illness. Bethune's understanding of the "second sickness" became a focus of my subsequent career in social medicine and the title of a book that I wrote to clarify collective action toward change.[1]

I dedicated the book to my grandfather, Abe Waitzkin, who was my main role model as I was growing up. During 1903–1904, facing conscription into the Czar's army, Abe left his farm in Latvia and made his way to the United States. (Reportedly, the name "Waitzkin" came from "wheat" farming, as determined by an immigration agent at Ellis Island.) After his wife, Becky, joined him in the United States, they started a small farm in the tiny village of Wadsworth, Ohio. Abe read and wrote only Yiddish, and Becky was illiterate.

Some highlights of Abe's life illustrate how he came to serve as a role model for me and others. When Eugene V. Debs, the agrarian populist organizer, ran for president during 1900, 1904, 1908, 1912, and 1920 on the Socialist Party ticket, Abe worked on his campaigns. Abe also collaborated with the Industrial Workers of the World (IWW), the labor union that Debs, Big Bill Haywood, Daniel de León, and other leaders organized among workers in the railroad, mining, and farming industries. (My most-prized heirloom inherited from my grandfather is a small bust of Debs.) During the Great Depression of the 1930s, Abe and Becky lost the farm. Later, Abe became a housepainter and union organizer in Akron, Ohio, as well as an active member of the Workman's Circle, a Jewish fraternal organization to which he belonged even though he professed to being an atheist.

Until he died of liver cancer (we thought due to chemicals in the solvents to which he was exposed as a painter) when I was a teenager, Abe's kindness, humor, ability to play poker, critical intellect, and activism provided a continuing source of inspiration. Experiences with him entered my consciousness as values of social justice and the benefits of organizing in communities and in the workplace. That consciousness led me, during high school in Hudson, Ohio, to work with the civil rights movement, when as a crusading high school newspaper editor I led a boycott of local barbershops until their proprietors agreed to cut the hair of Black students. Through that experience, I learned to cope with fear, an emotion that arises from time to time during activism, when I received a handwritten death threat from the Ku Klux Klan.

The same consciousness led me during my undergraduate years at Harvard to become a conscientious objector and resister to the Vietnam War and also to undertake research and activism that focused on housing segregation and the real estate practice of "blockbusting" (a cynical manipulation of racial fears to enhance the sales of homes, resulting in homeowners' financial loss—a process that adversely affected my own parents). During such experiences, I became familiar with the notion that medicine could become a focus of community organizing and empowerment, as advocated by Jack Geiger, Oliver Fein, and other activists who had entered medicine with a vision of its role in social change and whom I met during college. These people and their accomplishments in working with low-income, marginalized communities inspired my eventual decision to enter medicine and to focus my work on the impact of social conditions on health and illness.

In the remainder of this chapter, I discuss two critical phases of my experiences in social medicine. The first, which involved work with the United Farm Workers (UFW) union clinic system, taught me that one did not need to travel outside the United States to find "the Third World." Instead, conditions of underdevelopment and exploitation within the United States created or exacerbated the health conditions of farmworkers and their families. I learned more about clinical medicine by working at these clinics than in any part of my formal medical school and residency training. Most of all, I learned that, in the context of underdevelopment and exploitation, clinical work in medicine is nearly inseparable from activism to change society.

A second important set of experiences emerged during the 1970s and 1980s from my efforts with the international solidarity movement against brutal dictatorships in Latin America. By working in support of colleagues and communities that faced repression and death, I gradually became aware of Latin American social medicine (LASM). This field of scholarship and activism, little appreciated in the United States or elsewhere in the English-speaking or -reading world, also embodied Bethune's vision of the second sickness and profoundly influenced my own vision of purpose in my work. Taken together, the experiences with the UFW clinics and with LASM have shaped my work as a health internationalist and may help inspire others with similar aspirations.

## Third World Conditions in the United States

Several key themes emerged during my work as a primary care practitioner with the UFW clinics. During my residency in internal medicine and fellowship at Stanford (where I was a Robert Wood Johnson Foundation Clinical Scholar), I did what I could to support the international boycott of grapes that the UFW had organized. The boycott supported the efforts of farmworkers to gain recognition by grape-growing corporations as a bargaining agent. Because my fellowship at

Stanford required two to three days per week of clinical work but did not specify where, I explored the possibility of seeing patients at the UFW clinic in Salinas, where my parents had moved from Ohio. (My father was working in the office of a small greenhouse company, and my mother worked as a receptionist and retail clerk.) I also took advantage of time available during the fellowship to learn Spanish at a local community college. Because I then used Spanish in daily clinical work and political organizing, I quickly became fluent.

Between 1973 and 1975, I worked at the UFW clinic in Salinas, as well as UFW clinics in California's Central Valley when I was needed. In addition, I helped the union establish a satellite clinic in the coastal community of Watsonville, where some of the most contentious struggles between farmers and agricultural corporations were occurring. In Salinas, I, together with other health workers, met regularly with union organizers, and we participated in rallies, demonstrations, and marches that the union organized. On several occasions, these events included César Chávez, Dolores Huerta, and other charismatic UFW leaders, whose personal discipline and ethical standards proved inspirational to workers and to us professionals collaborating with the union. Some of these encounters became dangerous, as we received attacks ranging from rocks to bullets (several union activists were injured or killed), involving police officers or "goons" hired by the growers. As Chávez required, our own resistance was always nonviolent. Through these experiences, I saw that working and living conditions for farmworkers in the United States were similar to or worse than those in Mexico and other Latin American countries considered "less developed" economically.

At the UFW clinic, I tried to offer medical services as best I could to each patient. When problems arose in patient care and solutions were not evident, other staff members and I discussed these problems during our regular meetings. Part of these meetings involved "criticism/self-criticism," a method of group evaluation developed in China during and after the Chinese revolution.[2] In criticism/self-criticism sessions, each staff member described work activities or relationship issues in which he or she had participated, together with components of the activities that the staff member believed had gone well and those that needed improvement. Members of the group provided positive feedback to one another on activities that had gone well from their points of view, as well as comments on those that had gone less well; for the latter, group members also provided constructive suggestions for change. The method of criticism/self-criticism encouraged honest and constructive evaluation of oneself and others as a route to improvement on both individual and group levels.

### The Contradiction between Profit and Safety: Farmworkers' Back

Our criticism/self-criticism sessions also helped shed light on the larger political economy context of farmwork. The contradiction between profit and safety arises not only in industry but also in agriculture. Chronic back injury, for example, is one of the most common occupational diseases that farmworkers have endured in the United States and elsewhere. Yet this form of occupational injury has essentially nothing to do with industrialization as it occurs in agricultural work that to this day involves little mechanization and depends almost entirely on manual labor.

*A Disabled Young Farmworker*

As illustrated in the following case history of a patient I cared for at a UFW clinic in California, the contradiction between profit and safety plays out at many levels, including direct effects on the lives of individuals. J. C. was a thirty-two-year-old Chicano father of five. He began working as a farm laborer at age fourteen. He generally worked eight to ten hours a day, in stoop labor with an arched back, on such crops as lettuce. For about ten years he used the "short hoe" required of many farmworkers in the western states. At age twenty-eight, while bending at work, he suddenly felt a sharp pain in his back with radiation down his left leg. His physical exam at that time showed tenderness over the L4-L5 intervertebral space of the back, decreased reflexes and sensation of the left leg, and a positive straight leg-raising test (a test for slipped disk). Imaging studies showed advanced degenerative arthritis of the entire lower spine and a slipped disk at the L4–L5 level. The patient experienced severe pain on bending, which persisted after back surgery. He knew no English, could not find a job outside farm labor, and was applying for permanent disability benefits.

The short hoe has a short wooden handle, about one foot in length. To use the short hoe, a person must work in a stooped posture, bent forward at the waist, so that the hoe can reach the ground. The short hoe has no intrinsic advantage over the long-handled hoe, which a farmworker can use in an erect posture. The only reason for the short hoe is supervision. If the foreman sees that all workers in a crew are bent over, he can be more sure that everybody is working, and fewer supervisors are needed. With long-handled hoes, people can stand with straight backs and supervision becomes somewhat more difficult.

Farmworkers' back is a preventable disease. It occurs in a sector of the economy that is highly profit oriented. The short hoe's human toll is crippling back disease for thousands of farmworkers; the main injuries are slipped disks and degenerative arthritis of the spine. These problems occur in young workers who do stoop labor, and their physical effects are irreversible. Since migrant workers most often lack educational opportunities and frequently know little English, farmworkers' back usually means permanent economic disability.

Since at least the 1950s, physicians have testified about the short hoe's devastating effects. Yet for many years farm owners, especially the agribusiness corporations that have gained control of many agricultural enterprises, refused to stop the short hoe's use. Farm owners usually gave no reason for this policy, except that long-handled hoes would require higher costs. (When analyzed, the costs of longer handles have been shown to be minimal.) The profit motive and the nature of agricultural production has led directly to this illness-generating labor practice.

Until the mid-1960s, farmworkers remained largely unorganized. A "reserve army" of migrant workers was available to replace individuals who were crippled by farmworkers' back or who objected to the conditions of work. Powerlessness resulted from lack of organization; individual farmworkers had no alternative to the crippling effects of the short hoe because resistance meant loss of work.

Starting in the mid-1960s, the UFW organized among farmworkers throughout the West, Southwest, and Southeast regions of the United States. Like other unions, the UFW fought for basic improvements in wages and benefits. Beyond these economic goals, however, the union focused on the conditions of work. The UFW launched organizing and publicity campaigns concerning the short hoe, dangerous insecticides and chemicals, and other occupational health issues.

In response to this pressure, the California legislature ultimately passed a law in 1975 banning the short hoe. Some other state legislatures followed. Agribusiness corporations then obtained a series of court injunctions against the new laws, which accepted the companies' claims that conversion to the long-handled hoe would lead to excessive costs. During the late 1970s and early 1980s, other courts later reversed these injunctions. Despite the passage of legislation, California farmworkers—as well as workers in other states without such laws—were required to continue to use and thus to suffer from the short hoe. Meanwhile, activists have hardly scratched the surface of such occupational health problems as pesticides, herbicides, and toxic chemicals. The contradiction between profit and safety persists in agriculture as it does in other industries.

### The Contradiction between Plentiful Resources and Medical Maldistribution: Children's Preventable Suffering

My work with patients at the UFW clinic also sensitized me to the troubling contradiction between plentiful resources and medical maldistribution. In addition to the contradiction between profit and safety, maldistribution persists as a second widely recognized problem of health systems in capitalist societies. Historically, social barriers limiting recruitment into medicine have created numerical shortages of doctors and other health workers in some settings, even while there is an excess in other settings.

Rural areas like Appalachia and the Great Plains states, as well as urban districts with largely Black or Hispanic populations, experience extreme shortages of health workers. At the same time, more affluent parts of cities and suburbs, especially on the East and West coasts of the United States, have large concentrations of medical personnel. The variation is enormous. For instance, there is a heavy concentration of doctors in such places as Washington, D.C., New York, and Massachusetts, while other states, like Mississippi, Alabama, and South Dakota, have a striking lack of health workers.

Even states with seemingly adequate doctor to population ratios contain severe internal maldistribution. For example, the state of New Mexico (where I now live and practice in a rural area) appears to have an adequate number of health workers when compared to other states. However, when the statewide figure is broken down by county, one finds large discrepancies. Most doctors are concentrated in a single county (Bernalillo), where the state medical school and the largest city (Albuquerque) are located. In more rural areas there are severe shortages of health workers and extremely poor doctor to population ratios; several counties have no doctors at all.

Maldistribution in the face of plentiful resources has effects that are often devastating. General health statistics for a nation or region tend to mask the impact of maldistribution in smaller geographical areas or at different income levels. Many people in the United States and other capitalist countries do not have consistent access to even the simplest form of care. Because of maldistribution, there are still individuals who suffer permanent disability every year. The case presentation ahead involves a patient who used a California UFW clinic, part of a system of clinics set up by the union in response to medical maldistribution and farmworkers' inadequate access to health services.

*A Girl with Preventable Kidney Disease*

O. O. was an eleven-year-old girl. Her family, made up of migrant workers, was living temporarily in a shanty camp without running water. The patient and her family were Spanish-speaking and knew very little English. About a week before she came to the clinic, she scraped both feet on a rock in a fall. She and her parents washed the wounds with water from a well and bandaged them with a makeshift bandage. Four days later, both her feet became painful, hot, red, and swollen. Two days after that, her ankles, fingers, and eyelids became puffy, and she began to feel very sleepy. Her family brought her to a union organizer, who drove them seventy-five miles to the clinic in Salinas—the closest medical facility the family could afford.

At the clinic, a physical exam showed a sleepy girl in no acute distress, with a slight fever and elevated blood pressure. There was no heart murmur. Infected lesions were present on both feet. Her ankles, fingers, and eyelids contained edema fluid. Abnormal lab work confirmed a diagnosis of acute glomerulonephritis (kidney inflammation) that was a complication from a streptococcal skin infection. The patient's wounds were cleaned and dressed with an antibiotic ointment. A course of penicillin, rest, and a nutritive diet was started. After two weeks, the patient felt better. After three weeks, she could resume her usual activities. At six months, her tests of kidney function were still about 60 percent of normal. In a criticism/self-criticism session at the clinic, it was felt there was little the union could have done to prevent the complication of the skin infection, mainly because of the family's physical isolation and the unavailability of health workers in the local area.

This and other cases of preventable suffering compelled me to further my understanding and writings about the roots of medical maldistribution: the structural contradiction of development and underdevelopment. Uneven development is most obvious on an international scale, where the economic disparities between underdeveloped and advanced capitalist nations are evident.[3] National underdevelopment is an important determinant of ill health and early death in Third World countries. However, uneven development also occurs within nations, including those whose aggregate measures of economic and physical well-being indicate high levels of wealth and health.

In the United States, the distribution of health workers and facilities is closely correlated to the distribution of economic resources. Although these correlations are not exact, regions of the country with higher levels of personal income, more concentrated economic enterprises (particularly industrial corporations), and more plentiful nonmedical services (including universities, housing, and cultural facilities) generally command larger numbers of both generalist and specialist physicians, as well as hospitals and other health facilities. Rural-urban differences show these relationships most clearly, but the same pattern emerges even within cities, where maldistribution of health services coincides with income differentials and other measures of economic development at the level of small units like census tracts.

## Advances in Latin American Social
## Medicine Relevant to the "First World"

During my years with the UFW clinic system, I gradually became aware that one does not need to travel outside the United States to find the Third World.

Instead, areas quite close to home manifest problems and challenges that resemble those of countries usually labeled as economically "less developed." At about the same time in my career, from 1973 to 1975, I discovered that advances in LASM—originating in countries considered less developed than the United States—offered illuminating insights into our own "more developed" country. My discovery contradicted the underlying assumptions in my prior education that superior research and intellectual work took place mainly in the United States and similar economically advanced nations.

Specifically, I discovered LASM shortly after the military coup d'état that, on September 11, 1973, ended Chile's three-year democratically elected socialist government (called Unidad Popular, or Popular Unity), led by President Salvador Allende, a physician and leader in social medicine. In the UFW, organizers and members quickly began to talk about the dictatorship that followed and especially the deaths and political repression that the dictatorship perpetrated. Although I had hoped to spend part of the following year in Chile contributing to the advances in medicine and public health that were occurring under the Unidad Popular government, the coup intervened. So instead of going to work in Chile, I became active in the international solidarity movement that tried to assist Chilean health workers and other citizens whom the military dictatorship had tortured, imprisoned, or otherwise threatened. Later, the solidarity movement extended to Argentina, Brazil, Uruguay, and several other countries in South and Central America—all of which were ruled during that period by dictatorships supported by the U.S. government and partly funded by the tax dollars of U.S. citizens.

As part of this solidarity effort, I collaborated with a colleague, Hilary Modell, a U.S. citizen who had worked during the previous two years with the Unidad Popular government in a community-based health program. After the coup, Hilary had escaped in one of the last Red Cross evacuation planes to leave Chile. Because North American health professionals knew little about the efforts of the Unidad Popular or the repression that followed the coup, we decided to write an article to spread knowledge about the situation in Chile. A Chilean colleague also collaborated on the article but chose to remain anonymous, due to reprisals that he feared he would face if his identity were to become known to the dictatorship. Eventually, we were able to publish an influential article in the *New England Journal of Medicine* that received worldwide attention.[4] Although the article mobilized further solidarity work in the United States, Canada, and western Europe, our writing also incensed members of the Chilean dictatorship, which officially condemned Hilary and me. As a result, neither of us could travel to Chile for many years.

While carrying out research for this article in the Stanford University library, I made an astonishing discovery. In the library's card catalogue I found a reference to a book written by Allende in 1939: *La Realidad Médico-Social Chilena* (*The Chilean Medico-Social Reality*).[5] I obtained a copy from the library of the Hoover Institute at Stanford, whose collection the U.S. Central Intelligence Agency funded as a resource for counterinsurgency research. As the Hoover Institute acknowledged, the intended purpose of this collection was to provide information useful in the suppression of revolutionary movements in Latin America, Africa, and Asia.

Reading Allende's book was a transformative experience through which I began to appreciate the importance and relevance of LASM. Allende, who trained as a pathologist, wrote the book as a young minister of health for Chile's newly elected Popular Front government. Supported by his team at the ministry, Allende presented an analysis of the relationships among social structure, disease, and suffering. *La Realidad* conceptualized illness as a disturbance of the individual fostered by deprived social conditions. Breaking new ground in Latin America at the time, Allende described the "living conditions of the working classes" that generated illness. Allende emphasized the social conditions of underdevelopment, international dependency, and the effects of foreign debt and the work process. In *La Realidad,* Allende focused on several specific health problems, including maternal and infant mortality, tuberculosis, sexually transmitted and other communicable diseases, emotional disturbances, and occupational illnesses. Describing issues that had not been studied previously, he analyzed illegal abortion, the responsiveness of tuberculosis to social and economic advances rather than treatment innovations, the role of housing density in the causation of infectious diseases, and differences between generic and brand-name pricing in the pharmaceutical industry.

Seeing the relevance of Allende's book to many issues that we were facing in the United States, I began a long-term effort to study LASM. Eventually, this effort involved visits to several countries in Latin America where social medicine groups were working actively. During 1994–1995, I spent nine months in Latin America, sponsored by fellowships from the U.S. Fulbright Program and the Fogarty International Center of the U.S. National Institutes of Health, to conduct a more in-depth study of LASM. This project allowed lengthy visits with social medicine groups in Chile, Argentina, Uruguay, Brazil, Mexico, Ecuador, and Cuba. In addition to providing me with further reading in LASM, colleagues generously shared their time with me for in-depth interviews. Every two years, with rare exceptions, I have also attended the congresses of the Latin

American Association of Social Medicine (Asociación Latinoamericana de Medicina Social, ALAMES). These meetings have helped me to keep up with current developments in LASM and to maintain long-lasting friendships with Latin American colleagues. ALAMES congresses have facilitated my ongoing efforts to understand the changes in health services and public health policies spearheaded by LASM colleagues who recently, with the advent of progressive governments in various countries (especially Brazil, Ecuador, Argentina, Uruguay, Chile, Venezuela, and Bolivia), have risen to prominent positions in those countries' Ministries of Health.

I have written previously about Allende's work and the field in general.[6] The following paragraphs provide some of the main observations that have proven relevant to my own work and to social medicine practice in the United States. A trilingual (Spanish, Portuguese, and English) Web site that we have developed at the University of New Mexico in collaboration with the University Health Sciences Center at the University of Guadalajara in Mexico provides summaries of major historical and contemporary works on LASM.[7]

**Figure 9.1** The author (*left*) discusses the U.S. economic embargo against Cuba with students at the University of Havana, March 2008. Thumbs-up refer to the hoped-for end of the embargo.

Courtesy of Jean Ellis-Sankari.

Productivity and Danger in Latin American Social Medicine

Many who have worked in Latin American social medicine (such as Allende himself, who committed suicide during the 1973 coup d'état,[8] and hundreds of public health experts, who were tortured under military dictatorships) have experienced dramatic personal histories. These histories show how the very nature of their work—to the extent that it reveals the origins of health problems in the structure of society—can come to be seen as dangerous to sectors of the society who control wealth and wield power.[9]

Among the many interviews I conducted of people who underwent extreme personal hardship for their commitment to LASM, the one I conducted with a public health expert in Chile was perhaps the most jarring because of the banality of the experience it recounted.[10] The public health expert was about to receive torture by electric shock applied to his testicles. His crimes included having taught medical and other health science students in a model community clinic, one of the major teaching sites for the University of Chile. A graduate of the Harvard School of Public Health, he was also accused of conducting research on the relationships between poverty and health outcomes in local communities. He knew that several of his colleagues had already been killed for similar "crimes."

In his interrogation he was asked to provide information about many friends and colleagues, but refused. The torturer, a clean-cut and matter-of-fact person whose military affiliation wasn't quite clear, ordered the public health expert to pull down his pants. He complied, looking at the electrodes in the torturer's right hand. Just then, the torturer glanced at his watch on his wrist.

"Ok," the torturer said, "it's five o'clock—time to go home," and left the room. The public health expert pulled his pants back up and waited for a guard to take him back to his cell.

Recalling this experience in an interview, the public health expert mentioned Max Weber's work on the sociology of bureaucracy[11]—"bureaucratized torture," he called it.

The public health expert eventually escaped, returning to Chile only years later; after the dictatorship ended, he again worked for the Ministry of Health.

Social Policies, Power, Health, and Health Care

Social medicine groups in Latin America have linked their policy research with organizing efforts aimed at changing power relationships. As a result, these groups have provided inspiring examples for me and other activists about the practical value of intellectual work in concrete political struggles. Their actions have sought to expand public debate and to redirect reform initiatives and activism toward meeting the needs of vulnerable populations. Social medicine groups have collaborated with the opposition Party of the Democratic Revolution and the Zapatista Army of National Liberation in Mexico, the coalition of indigenous and labor organizations in Ecuador, the Workers' Party in Brazil, and the Central Organization of Argentine Trade Unions. In their efforts to use research in the service of union organizing, for example, the Ecuadorian group has emphasized the differing health outcomes that women experience in industrial and agricultural work environments. Likewise, microlevel research on the work process in Brazilian health institutions has informed the policy efforts of the national Workers' Party.

Partly reflecting the violent conditions that practitioners of social medicine themselves have confronted, research on violence and trauma has received priority in several countries. In Colombia, the social "tradition" of violence—previously linked to poverty and cycles of rebellion but more recently reflecting narcotics trafficking and paramilitary operations—has led to research on the effects of violence on health outcomes. Chilean investigators have studied families whose members experienced torture, exile, or death during the dictatorship. Influenced by psychological studies of violence in El Salvador by Ignacio Martín-Baró[12]—a U.S.-trained psychologist who himself was assassinated by paramilitary forces—researchers in Argentina have focused on the surviving comrades and family members of the more than thirty thousand individuals who "disappeared" during the Argentine dictatorship.

## Conclusion

Experiences of Third World conditions within the United States through the UFW clinics, as well as the contributions of Latin American colleagues who practice social medicine, have stimulated in my life a sometimes dangerous, but very gratifying, internationalism. A focus on the social origins of illness and early death inherently challenges the relations of economic and political power. As a result, participation in social medicine has led to suffering and even death for some of its most talented and productive adherents.

In my own work, I have faced some life-threatening and financially difficult situations directly related to my activities and teaching in social medicine. For instance, when my colleagues and I tried to deliver health services to UFW members during strikes against agribusiness corporations, we regularly faced violent attacks by security forces and strikebreakers hired by those corporations. During my efforts to support Latin American social medicine projects I also faced physical danger; for instance, by arriving at Nicaragua's airport two hours before it was bombed by U.S.-financed "contras" who opposed the

Sandinista government that came to power after the Nicaraguan revolution deposed the Somoza dictatorship (see chapter 10).

As well, early on in my career I was fired because of my values. When I was at the University of Vermont, I organized a student field project to investigate the class structure of the city's hospital boards, including that of the university hospital. Because the students' findings on unequal class power and the health care system challenged the medical school's own power structure, the dean refused to renew my contract. Even when national professional associations (the American Association of University Professors and the American Sociological Association) censured the university due to infringement of academic freedom in my case, university officials still did not reinstate me.[13]

Practitioners of social medicine use theories and methods that distinguish their efforts from those of traditional public health experts. In particular, a focus on the social and historical contexts of health problems, an emphasis on economic production and social causation, and the linkage of research and education to political practice provide innovative approaches to some of the most important problems of our age. For the United States and other "First World" countries, during an era of globalization and its associated dangers, the courageous work of the UFW clinics and of Latin American social medicine will continue to inspire.

## Notes

I sincerely thank my colleagues in the UFW clinics and in LASM for their inspiration and support. This work was supported in part by grants from the Fulbright Commission (Senior Fellowship for Independent Research, American Republics Program), the Fogarty International Center of the National Institutes of Health (TW 01982), the Pacific Rim Program of the University of California, the American College of Physicians (George C. Griffith Traveling Fellowship), the World Health Organization (Special Programme for Research and Training in Tropical Diseases), the Dedicated Health Research Funds of the University of New Mexico School of Medicine, and the National Library of Medicine (1G08 LM06688).

Epigraph is from Ted Allan and Sydney Gordon, *The Scalpel, the Sword: The Story of Dr. Norman Bethune* (Boston: Little, Brown and Company, 1952), 250.

1. Howard Waitzkin, *The Second Sickness: Contradictions of Capitalist Health Care*, 2nd ed. (Lanham, MD: Rowman & Littlefield, 2000).

2. "Quotations from Mao Tse Tung," www.marxists.org/reference/archive/mao/works/red-book/ch27.htm (accessed October 22, 2008).

3. See David Harvey, *A Brief History of Neoliberalism* (New York: Oxford University Press, 2005).

4. Howard Waitzkin and Hilary Modell, "Medicine, Socialism, and Totalitarianism: Lessons from Chile," *New England Journal of Medicine* 291 (1974): 171–177.

5. Salvador Allende, *La Realidad Médico-Social Chilena* (Santiago, Chile: Ministerio de Salubridad, 1939).

6. Howard Waitzkin et al., "Social Medicine in Latin America: Productivity and Dangers Facing the Major National Groups," *Lancet* 358 (2001): 315–323; Howard Waitzkin et al., "Social Medicine Then and Now: Lessons from Latin America," *American Journal of Public Health* 91 (2001): 1592–1601; Howard Waitzkin, *At the Front Lines of Medicine: How the Health Care System Alienates Doctors and Mistreats Patients . . . And What We Can Do About It* (Lanham, MD: Rowman & Littlefield, 2001); Howard Waitzkin, "Commentary: Salvador Allende and the Birth of Latin American Social Medicine," *International Journal of Epidemiology* 34 (2005): 739–741.

7. This four-year effort to develop the LASM Web site, sponsored by the U.S. National Library of Medicine, emerged from a commitment to bring knowledge about LASM to practitioners and students in the English-reading and -speaking world who could benefit from exposure to the rich and enlightening work accomplished by Latin American colleagues. See http://hsc.unm.edu/lasm/.

8. Although it is widely believed that Allende was assassinated, I learned that he committed suicide in an interview with his personal physician and minister of health, Arturo Jirón, who was the last person to see him alive. See Howard Waitzkin, "Next in Line for NAFTA?: Images from Chile," *Monthly Review* 46 (1995): 17–27.

9. Howard Waitzkin, "Is Our Work Dangerous? Should It Be?" *Journal of Health and Social Behavior* 39 (1998): 7–17.

10. See Hannah Arendt, *Eichmann in Jerusalem: A Report on the Banality of Evil* (New York: Viking Press, 1963).

11. Max Weber, *Max Weber on Capitalism, Bureaucracy, and Religion*, ed. Stanislav Andreski (Boston: Allen & Unwin, 1983).

12. Ignacio Martín-Baró, *Writings for a Liberation Psychology*, ed. Adrianne Aron and Shawn Corne (Cambridge, MA: Harvard University Press, 1994).

13. See Waitzkin, "Is Our Work Dangerous?"

# Chapter 10

# Find the Best People and Support Them

**Paula Braveman**

"Identify the best people and do everything you can to support them." That was the advice of Milton Roemer, for decades a professor of public health at the University of California, Los Angeles and an internationally renowned expert on medical care systems. By "best" he meant the most capable, dedicated to the public good and committed to social justice. Responding to a question from me about the role of an international consultant, his words had a characteristic clarity, depth, and deceptive simplicity. Milton (or Muni, as he was affectionately called by family and friends) had an enormous influence on me, particularly by being an example of commitment both to activism and scholarship. He had helped achieve universal health insurance coverage in Canada and actively advocated for universal coverage in the United States; at the same time he wrote the definitive scholarly works on comparative medical systems (see chapter 5). Muni and his wife, Ruth—a distinguished public health lawyer and leader of international initiatives on tobacco control and reproductive rights, who also became a mentor—were cherished friends and ongoing sources of wise counsel until Muni's death in 2001 and Ruth's in 2005. Both had mentored public health leaders on all continents. Both believed passionately in the importance of mentoring—supporting people they thought would fight effectively for the public good and social justice in the health sphere. This chapter, exploring recollections of my work in international health, is dedicated to their memory.

### Nicaragua, 1980–1991, and How I Got There

I still recall having to fight back the tears. I had been waiting for hours in Managua's relentless, steamy heat to speak with an official at the Foreign

Ministry about obtaining a permit to work in Nicaragua. It was 1981, my family medicine residency would soon end, and my postresidency plan was to work as a physician in Nicaragua for a couple of years. I had done a few brief stints filling in for full-time international volunteer physicians on leave at health posts in Ciudad Sandino, a dusty shantytown on Managua's outskirts, with pigs and roosters roaming the streets. Volunteer physicians were there and throughout Nicaragua, from Cuba, Germany (then both East and West), Switzerland, Italy, Denmark, and elsewhere. Ciudad Sandino had mushroomed out of open space after a 1972 earthquake leveled much of the city. Thousands of poor residents of Managua, left homeless by the earthquake and without help from the Somoza government, put up makeshift shacks on the city's edge. Over time they transformed it into a still dirt-poor but permanent, organized settlement. With the end of the Somoza regime and beginning of the Sandinista government in 1979, Ciudad Sandino began to receive rudimentary services such as water, sanitation, and basic health care. None of these services were adequate by affluent country standards, but they were far more than what had existed before.

**Figure 10.1** Paula Braveman in the center with two workers from the health post in Ciudad Sandino, Nicaragua, 1982. Everyone was thrilled at the prospect of having sewers.
Courtesy of Paula Braveman.

At last, after multiple visits to the Foreign Ministry, slowly working my way up the bureaucratic hierarchy, I was meeting an official with the authority to grant the visa. She said, trying to be tactful: "If you really want to help us, stay in your country and try to change its foreign policy. That is our biggest problem now, not lack of doctors." She said she appreciated my offer of solidarity, but it was the United States' policy toward Nicaragua that was bleeding it dry. The only reply I could think of was a pathetic, selfish restatement of how badly I wanted to work in Nicaragua, so I didn't respond, except to thank her and leave before tears got the better of me.

What was Nicaragua's attraction? Certainly not the climate. The magical, romantic beauty of its land or its penchant for poetry? They probably were part of it. In college I planned to become a university philosophy teacher. I loved school and exploring new concepts. I came to Swarthmore College in Pennsylvania from a large public high school in a working-class suburb of Miami, Florida, unaware of politics, domestic or international. But the year I began college was 1966, and by graduation in 1970 I was, like so many other students during the 1960s, profoundly changed. Support for civil rights struggles and opposition to the Vietnam War were strong on campuses everywhere in the 1960s, but particularly so at Swarthmore, with its Quaker commitment to peace, human rights, and acting on one's conscience even if that meant challenging authority.

Neither of my parents was an activist, and in many ways they were politically conservative, as first-generation immigrants often are, particularly if they have been upwardly mobile. Because of his rebellious spirit, my father never finished the tenth grade; very articulate and persuasive, he sold advertising for newspapers and felt ashamed that he was not doing something of social value. My mother graduated from high school and worked as a secretary until her marriage; when I was growing up, women who worked outside the home were often vilified as bad mothers or wives. My parents raised me with a strong sense of social justice and an abhorrence of racism. This was rooted in their own traumatization by the Nazi Holocaust (which killed all their relatives who had not emigrated to the New World from Lithuania and Russia) and by growing up the only Jews in poor, largely Irish Catholic neighborhoods in Boston. My mother had a teacher who told the students, in my mother's presence, that Jews, like the devil, had tails. Both parents recalled many incidents of anti-Semitic name-calling and physical intimidation. I was brought up with the idea that silence in the face of injustice—the crime of silence, which my parents felt had been committed by so many during the Nazi Holocaust—was unacceptable. The clarion call of the 1960s to speak out against racial injustice and the war in Vietnam resonated with values from my upbringing.

By the time I graduated from college in 1970, I had come to feel that being a college professor was too much of a retreat from what we then called "the real world"; that is, everywhere outside the university. I wanted to be more directly involved in social change than I then believed would be possible on a college campus, although now I see campuses as crucial grounds for effecting social change. For four years after graduation, I sought where it was in the "real world" that I might fit, consonant with my values, strengths, weaknesses, and what I enjoyed. It was a heady time when progressive activism in the health sector was flourishing. For example, feminists were organizing around women's health issues by establishing women's self-help clinics and other initiatives for women to become educated about their bodies and take more control of their own health, particularly their reproductive health;[1] Health/PAC (the Health Policy Advisory Center) was pointing out fundamental flaws in the U.S. medical care system;[2] and community organizers, including members of the Black Panther Party, were establishing neighborhood health centers as part of broader community development efforts. The War on Poverty launched by the administration of U.S. president Lyndon Johnson in the 1960s gave birth to a multitude of community organizing efforts and services, in which medical care played a prominent role.

Eventually, by chance, I found a promising path forward in the health sector, when I was sent by a temp agency to work in a free health clinic. The decision to become a doctor came only after I spent four years as a medical assistant at the clinic, a nursing assistant at the Veterans Administration Hospital, and an emergency room technician at two private hospitals, all in Portland, Oregon, while continuing my involvement in local community organizing. I realized that the contribution I could make in those positions was very limited. I saw firsthand how challenging, uphill, and slow it was to organize workers around workplace issues, and to organize local residents around community issues; I saw that there were others with greater talents than I in those domains. In addition, I realized that I needed more intellectual stimulation from my full-time (vs. volunteer) work, that I had little tolerance for being at the bottom of a chain of command, and that I had other options given my academic credentials and access to student loans.

Unlike most physicians I have known, I had never felt drawn toward medicine as a child. Once I began working at the free clinic in Portland, however, I began to learn—largely through reading and discussion groups with others like me without training in health but involved in organizing around health issues— about progressive work in the health sector, and it was that work that led me to decide to go to medical school. I was motivated by the work of physicians like

Jack Geiger involved in the community health center movement in the United States, who realized that nutritious food, sanitation, and decent shelter were medicine, and who acted on those principles (see chapter 6). I was impressed with the Black Panther Party's efforts to draw people in to community organizing by addressing some of their most pressing material needs, including health care. My decision to go to medical school was also inspired by the examples of U.S. volunteers in the Abraham Lincoln Brigade and by Canadian surgeon Norman Bethune, who helped defend progressive forces against fascism during the Spanish Civil War and who later worked in China supporting efforts to deter Japanese imperialism.

The community health center movement was more than an effort to bring medical care into poor U.S. communities, although that was important. It was part of a long-range strategy for social change focused on strengthening the capacity of disenfranchised communities to advocate for their own interests. Providing medical services was both an end in itself and a means to building a community initiative for broader change. Medical, legal, and other services attracted people to community centers, which were organizing hubs. Physicians and attorneys were needed to staff the community centers. I envisioned how I could contribute as a physician, as part of a larger domestic or international picture, and also escape the boredom and powerlessness of being a blue-collar worker that I had experienced in those four years following college.

After completing premed courses, I enrolled in medical school at the University of California, San Francisco (UCSF) in the fall of 1975. I chose UCSF because I sought an environment that would be supportive of my ideals, fearing being changed by medical training into someone I did not want to become. UCSF's family and community medicine unit, especially its residency program, seemed consonant with my values. Another strategy to prevent my values from being undermined was to engage throughout medical school in social justice organizing efforts, for example, initiatives to protect affirmative action in medical school admissions, defend hospital workers' rights, staff a women's self-help clinic, and support community organizing to prevent cutbacks in vital services. Given medical school demands, I could not take a leadership role in these efforts, but playing a supportive role gave me a lifeline to preserving my identity.

## The Committee for Health Rights in Central America
## and Collaboration with Health Professional Schools
## and the Ministry of Health in Nicaragua

For five decades up until 1979, Nicaragua had been under the rule of the brutal, corrupt Somoza dynasty, installed with U.S. support to keep the region in friendly hands, safe from populist, nationalist, anti-American upstart Augusto Sandino and his ragtag volunteer army. The country, strategically located on the Central American isthmus near the Panama Canal, was often considered a potential alternate site for a transoceanic canal. President Franklin Delano Roosevelt once famously (apocryphally) said of the first Somoza ruler: "He may be a son of a bitch, but he is *our* son of a bitch." Sandino was assassinated by Somoza's troops in 1934 when he responded to their call for a truce. The Sandinista movement, which gathered momentum in the 1970s, decades after his death, drew its inspiration from Sandino's passionately anti-imperialist and populist credo; it called not only for overturning the Somoza dictatorship, but also for a more just social order. Much to the world's (and the Sandinistas') surprise, the uprising was successful, and a new era of Nicaraguan history was inaugurated under Sandinista leadership in 1979. Broad-based popular revulsion for the corruption, brutality, and neglect of the Somoza government, and hope for a more humane and democratic future formed the basis for the Sandinistas' broad support. While an intern at San Francisco's County Hospital I had heard about the Sandinista revolution and the mobilization of many sectors of Nicaraguan society around the democratic and humanitarian ideals that motivated it. I wanted to witness the dramatic changes (for example, a massive literacy campaign and the expansion of health services) and experience the excitement of a country undergoing revolutionary change, in its heady early days.

Yet once they sank in, the words of that Foreign Ministry official denying my work visa rang true, resonating with my own doubts about how to make my efforts useful. So I returned to the United States and intensified work I had begun in the previous years with San Francisco Bay Area colleagues to found the Committee for Health Rights in Central America (CHRICA), which later became the Committee for Health Rights in the Americas. Several health professionals—mostly but not entirely physicians—came together with dual goals. The first was to support the new Sandinista government's efforts to provide medical care to the impoverished majority of Nicaraguans whose only prior medical services had been provided through churches. The Sandinistas made impressive strides in their first few years, establishing health posts across poor urban and rural areas. Most posts had inadequate equipment, supplies, and drugs; some, including a post where I eventually worked, lacked running water. Many were grossly inadequately staffed, but they were a visible symbol of commitment to a better future. At the same time, the Sandinistas made literacy a top priority, attracting legions of youths to an adult literacy campaign in a country with one of the Americas' highest rates of adult illiteracy (and its inevitable partners, poverty, disease, and disenfranchisement). CHRICA's second goal was to inform the U.S. public of what was taking place in Nicaragua—which was not well covered in the mainstream press—of the humanism and the hope, and of how U.S. tax dollars were being used to kill off a flowering plant by poisoning its roots.

The U.S. government, concerned that the Sandinistas were increasingly aligning themselves with Cuba and beholden to the Soviet Union, sought to break off these relationships—just as it had supported military coups and dictatorships in Argentina, Chile, Brazil, Uruguay, and elsewhere in Latin America where progressive political movements were challenging U.S. hegemony and unregulated market forces. The United States bolstered its hostile stance after the Sandinistas nationalized some large landholdings of Nicaragua's few wealthy families, mostly those of Somoza and his top-level cronies. Many relatively well-off (by local standards) Nicaraguans became justifiably fearful when properties were expropriated, sometimes without due process. It seems clear that at times injustices were committed. There was no tradition and no institutions of justice in place, only the legacy of decades of corruption and despotism. Some people lost property because someone better positioned had a personal vendetta against them or just wanted their home or land. Others who had not lost property were afraid they might.

Forces in the U.S. government overtly and covertly allied with disgruntled Nicaraguans against the Sandinista government to organize a military force referred to as "the contras" ("the opposition"). The contras, funded by the U.S. government and wealthy Nicaraguans living abroad (mostly in Miami), waged a war of terrorism against the Sandinistas and their supporters. They systematically attacked and kidnapped medical workers, teachers, and literacy campaign workers and destroyed new health posts and schools, in a calculated attempt to undermine the new government's ability to win over the population. The U.S. public had a distorted notion of the situation, with disinformation preying on anticommunist fears. Ironically, the United States' hostility toward Nicaragua pushed the country into increasing dependence on the Soviet Union and Cuba. I recall guiding a group of U.S. health professionals on an educational tour of Nicaragua in the early 1980s, at which the foreign minister Miguel Descoto explained to them: When you are a small, poor, and non-industrialized country you cannot be independent. The best strategy is to diversify your dependence, so that you do not depend solely on just one or two countries, which could then exert excessive control over you. The United States is pushing us to depend on the Soviet Union. That is not smart nor what we want.

In 1981 and 1982, CHRICA held discussions with representatives from the Health Ministry and the medical school in Nicaragua about how we could be most supportive. The idea that emerged was to hold a large colloquium or conference in Managua, which would create a forum for exchange among U.S. and Nicaraguan health professionals about state-of-the-art medical care. This would address Nicaraguan medical professionals' need to feel less isolated from current advances in their fields; few could afford travel to professional meetings outside Nicaragua and current journals were inaccessible. We hoped the colloquium would draw many U.S. health professionals, including prominent people who might attract press coverage.

The first U.S.-Nicaragua Colloquium on Health, in 1983, convened 212 health professionals from all over the United States and a few from elsewhere. We arranged tours for the visitors to observe local conditions, see what the government was trying to accomplish in health and education, and experience firsthand what the U.S.-funded contras were doing to undermine those efforts. Some participants stayed for only the five days of conference activities, while others stayed for two weeks. Several well-known scientists and public health leaders, including Milton Roemer, participated. There was modest press coverage in the United States, most—but not all—favorable. One particularly galling story portrayed colloquium leaders as well-intentioned but naïve dupes of the Sandinista government.[3]

A colloquium was held annually for over ten years, albeit not on as grand a scale as the first one. These conferences generated myriad other collaborative efforts between U.S. and Nicaraguan health science schools and/or hospitals. Nurse midwives, physical therapists, and medical specialists from the United States came to teach short courses or donate their services for brief periods. Sister hospitals and clinics were established, along with other fund-raising efforts. Journals, books, and equipment were donated to Nicaraguan schools and hospitals—in retrospect, much of dubious utility. Chapters of CHRICA were formed in cities across the United States as offshoots. Material resources— always on a very small scale—were channeled to the medical school, a school of public health newly founded under the Sandinistas, and other health professional training programs. Looking back, the moral support generated by these activities was probably the largest contribution. My colleagues and I were often told by Nicaraguan health personnel that the efforts and presence of U.S. health workers, such as those active in CHRICA and as those like Karen Brudney, MD, and Richard Garfield, RN, who lived and worked as clinicians and public health leaders in Nicaragua for several years, made them feel less alone, and that our belief in the importance of what they were doing helped them to persevere. Although I think we did contribute to educating many U.S. citizens about the situation (with church groups among our most active allies), we clearly did not succeed in reversing U.S. policy. Still, the combined efforts by CHRICA and allies from other countries and sectors may have helped restrain it.

A particularly gratifying experience was working with other CHRICA members and supporters in 1985 and 1986 to win the release of Dr. Gustavo Sequeira, vice director of the medical school in Managua, who had been kidnapped by the contras while he was in a rural area vaccinating children. For months, which felt like years, we pressured the State Department, on the logic that the contras were to a large extent under U.S. control. Dr. Sequeira's ultimate release was one of the most elating moments of my life.

The Sandinistas faced their second elections early in 1990. The Sandinistas were voted out, in an election indisputably influenced by the United States. The opposition emphasized repeatedly that as long as the Sandinistas stayed in power, the United States would keep the country in an economic stranglehold and continue financing the contras, which meant continued death and suffering; voting them out was the only way to peace and economic recovery.

The new president was Violeta Chamorro, the politically inexperienced widow of the revered national hero Pedro Joaquín Chamorro; a journalist and

**Figure 10.2**  This photo, sent to the author by colleagues at the medical school in Managua, shows Dr. Sequeira, surrounded by family and friends, leaving the Managua airport after his rescue, 1986.

Courtesy of Paula Braveman.

outspoken critic of Somoza, he was assassinated by Somoza's forces in 1978, just a year and a half before the Somoza regime was toppled by the Sandinistas. Many observers believed that Chamorro was handpicked by the United States as someone they could easily manage. Her election brought to power the UNO (National Opposition Union), a broad multiparty coalition defining itself primarily in opposition to the Sandinistas. The new president and UNO brought in an agenda far more congenial to policies of the international financial institutions and U.S. foreign policy for Latin America than the progressive agenda of the Sandinistas.

The election results were a shattering disappointment but should not have been a surprise. Although I continued to collaborate with the School of Public Health in Managua for a few years after the election, working with Nicaraguan institutions no longer held the same gravitational pull for me. Nicaragua under Sandinista leadership was a beacon for those who dreamed of the possibility of overthrowing tyranny; it was the mouse that roared. Under the neoliberal Chamorro government, and with the Sandinistas having discredited themselves to a certain extent by corruption in the transition period referred to publicly as "la piñata," I no longer felt that my involvement there was more strategic than involvement in any worthy progressive public health effort anywhere. At the same time, an opportunity to work with the World Health Organization (WHO) on health policy issues for developing countries presented itself, and I also felt a desire to pursue more actively my domestic research agenda, which then focused on access to health care. Throughout my career, I have tried to be strategic about where and how I invest my energies, seeking to contribute to efforts on compelling issues that are timely and have a chance at success within the larger picture.

I cherish the experiences I had working closely with Nicaraguans during the 1980s. I actually never lived in the country for longer than two months at a time, but between 1981 and 1990 I visited several times a year, generally for one to two weeks, and it felt like my second home. Some of my closest friends were there. It was a privilege to work with people who had shown tremendous courage and made great personal sacrifices in the struggle to overthrow Somoza. I will never forget a Nicaraguan friend, who had been a high-level military commander in the insurgency, telling me about the time she and several other insurgent colleagues were hiding in a "safe house"; she became claustrophobic and cranky, and her colleagues told her that she was being so unpleasant that she should go away by herself for a couple of days. During those two days, Somoza's forces killed everyone in the safe house. She felt survivor guilt—but what about the guilt of those of us going on with our comfortable lives and rewarding careers? I often wondered whether I would have withstood the test had I been a Nicaraguan in the 1970s. It was a privilege to feel, if only briefly, part of a wave of hope for a more just, humane world, particularly without having to take the risks that so many Nicaraguans faced. My late friend Rosaura Centeno, with whom I often stayed when in Managua, once said after listening to her daughter Xiomara and me discuss potential mistakes made by the Sandinistas: "All that I know is that before the Sandinistas came in, I felt like I was a beast and in some ways I lived like a beast, pulling a cart of merchandise around town to make a pitiful living. But now I have dignity."

## The World Health Organization, Geneva 1989–2001

In 1989, Muni recommended me for my first assignment at the WHO in Geneva. Health Services Division director Dr. Eleuther Tarimo, another protégé of Muni's, a former national health leader from Tanzania, was seeking a consultant on the topic of health screening. Multiphasic screening tests for healthy persons for early detection of asymptomatic disease or risk factors were increasingly used in the United States, and some developing country leaders were beginning to feel pressure to institute such services. Although I was no expert on the topic, Muni and Tarimo believed that my training in epidemiology and community medicine, my experience in developing countries, and my willingness to work hard would suffice.

I spent two months in Geneva in 1989 initially, and then worked part-time on the project over the next few years, based in the United States with occasional visits to Geneva to meet with WHO staff and other international experts and discuss ideas with Tarimo. After about a month, I concluded that implementing untargeted health screening programs, in settings unable to provide basic medical care to all people, would likely widen disparities between economically better- and worse-off people. I confronted the fact that when basic care, including treatment for serious symptoms, is unavailable, the poor will not seek services for asymptomatic conditions. As a consequence, better-off groups will disproportionately seek screening and effectively demand definitive diagnostic procedures and treatment if the diagnosis is confirmed; the distribution of care will thus become even more inequitable. I feared Tarimo would be displeased because my argument hinged on an explicit concern for equity, which was a value, not a scientific concern.

I was wrong about Tarimo's reaction. He was delighted and, convinced of the usefulness of disseminating the perspective, backed publication of a book[4] (released in English, Spanish, and French), rather than the originally envisioned briefing paper. I learned during my experience at WHO, starting in 1989, that perspectives viewed as radically left in the United States—such as an explicit commitment to social justice—are often mainstream public health views in Europe and many other settings. I realized the extent to which progressives in the United States learn to self-censor to avoid being branded as too far left; this was particularly so before the dissolution of the Soviet Union around 1990, when vestiges of the 1950s McCarthy Communist witch hunt era could still be seen and felt (see chapter 5).

For a while after finishing the book, my teaching and research commitments in the United States prevented me from working with the WHO. In 1994, however, Tarimo made me an offer I could not refuse: to work with him to develop a global initiative on equity in health and health care. At that time, there was increasing activity in Europe focusing on equity—fairness or social justice—in health. Tarimo's vision was to generate global interest while bringing particular attention to issues relevant to developing countries, which had received little consideration by researchers and international organizations up until then.[5] I worked with Tarimo and other WHO staff to shape an initiative focusing on developing capacity in low-income, industrially underdeveloped countries to monitor equity in health and health care and use the information to inform policies.[6]

Working with WHO was thrilling because of the magnitude of the potential impact—and I believe the equity initiative made important contributions.[7] One area was building technical consensus among health sector leaders and researchers about concepts and the measurement of health equity; this was seen as the foundation for promoting ongoing policy-oriented monitoring and study of health inequalities in all countries. The WHO initiative made contributions in that area, particularly for monitoring health equity in low-income countries. Another contribution was framing the issue as not just about equity in health care, but about equity in health itself, with the understanding that equitable social policies as well as the equitable provision of health care are essential to achieving health equity. I wish, however, that we had been able to combine the technical consensus-building with activities focusing more clearly on building consensus about values and policies. Another regret is that in the countries selected for demonstration projects (Zimbabwe, Sri Lanka, Lithuania), we made the mistake of focusing on the WHO initiative's need to demonstrate visible accomplishments early on rather than being more patient and working with local leaders to identify relevant local priorities. This error meant that the efforts of the initiative had limited impact in two of the three countries, reflecting the reality that resource-strapped institutions are often forced to accept funding opportunities even when the proposed projects do not address the most pressing local priorities. This is an old lesson in the field of international health.

## Pursuing Equity and Health for All in the Twenty-first Century

The WHO's rallying cry of "Health For All By the Year 2000," first proclaimed in 1977, inspired many individuals (myself included) and movements globally. For many of us, reaching 2000 with so far to go to achieving health equity was sobering. But what is health equity? When the WHO leadership changed in 1998, new WHO staff in the Evidence for Health Policy Unit advanced the notion that health inequalities referred to differences in health between individuals, not to differences between more and less advantaged social groups or even to differences among any groups.[8] The unit developed and actively promoted a technical approach to defining and measuring health equity and inequalities[9] that essentially removed the social justice content.[10] This approach seemed to be gaining acceptance and a lot was at stake. Adopting it was more than a technical matter; it would mean that countries would not monitor health differences among socioeconomic or racial/ethnic groups, rolling back gains of the 1990s equity initiatives. Documenting these differences between more and less socially advantaged groups and how they change over time is not sufficient, but it is an essential component of strategies to reduce inequalities. I spent considerable time on my own and with colleagues from several countries to unmask the problematic nature of the new approach.[11] Whether a result of our efforts or not, when its leadership changed in 2003, WHO resumed its prior social justice-oriented approach to defining and measuring health equity.

The approach advocated from 1999 to 2003 has not resurfaced internationally—at least not prominently—since then. However, essentially the same issue has reappeared in the United States with regard to the adoption and definition of "health disparities" (a term used only in the United States; elsewhere the concept of social inequalities in health or health inequities is employed). The concept of health disparities is linked with the concept of health equity in that pursuing health equity requires striving to eliminate health disparities. A widely used definition of health disparities among U.S. Department of Health and Human Services agencies (including the National Institutes of Health) refers to health differences between population groups, but without specifying whether the groups to be compared are more or less socially advantaged. This means that the limited resources available to address health disparities by race or social class could be diverted toward public health issues that are not about equity—for instance, if two similarly affluent communities have different rates of a given illness. The latter scenario may be worthy of public health attention, but it is not a health equity issue. An apparently technical and academic matter, such as how to define the concept of health disparities, can have tremendous political implications.

This theme, that what and how we measure things can affect where public attention is directed and how resources get allocated, has recurred repeatedly in my work in many contexts. For example, I continue to see the importance of the reference group selected for social comparisons. Common approaches to selecting the reference group include using the population average, or all non-poor people, which could set the bar too low. Instead, my colleagues and I have felt strongly that the reference group needs to be the most socially/economically advantaged group, because their health indicates what should be possible for everyone, given political will.[12]

In recent years, my international involvement has been sporadic, mainly occasional collaborations with international colleagues through meetings and papers. Meanwhile, I have geared up my involvement in two compelling efforts in the United States. One is an ongoing effort with a state health agency and local program leaders to strengthen California's Black Infant Health Program; another was my role as research director for a national commission on the social determinants of health supported by the Robert Wood Johnson Foundation.[13]

Lessons learned in my work in Nicaragua and with the WHO regarding the importance of building on local leadership have served me well in the efforts to strengthen California's Black Infant Health Program. Lessons learned from working with the Global Equity Gauge Alliance (a network of developing country researchers linked with both top-down and grassroots mobilization efforts working on equitable policies[14]) heightened my awareness, resolve, and ability to be more strategic about considering the range of audiences who need to be reached and what may—and may not—be effective approaches in engaging the diverse actors essential to realizing change. I assume that the balance between international and domestic involvement will continue to shift for me; I cannot imagine retreating from either. The international and domestic experiences inform each other and fulfill my need to feel connected to progressive social change both locally and globally.

The greatest gift that Milton and Ruth Roemer gave me was that their example made me believe that I could not only be a serious scholar but also an activist and advocate. Being an activist means standing up and speaking out for what one believes in; that is a moral obligation of everyone, scientists included. I believe that a scientist's values should shape the research questions she or he prioritizes for study. Once the question is defined, the values must not distort the science, and this requires self-awareness and integrity; activists who are also researchers must be particularly rigorous both to ensure the quality of their work and to withstand the additional scrutiny they will face. I feel very fortunate to have been able to address questions of palpable relevance to social justice in my "day job" and to have been able to integrate my professional and activist efforts. This has been and continues to be profoundly gratifying.

## Notes

1. Barbara Ehrenreich and Deirdre English, *Witches, Midwives, and Nurses: A History of Women Healers, 2nd ed.* (Old Westbury, NY: Feminist Press, 1973); Barbara Ehrenreich and Deirdre English, *Complaints and Disorders: The Sexual Politics of Sickness* (Old Westbury, NY: Feminist Press, 1973).

2. Tom Bodenheimer, Steve Cummings, and Elizabeth Harding, eds., *Billions for Band-Aids: An Analysis of the US Health Care System and of Proposals for Its Reform* (San Francisco: San Francisco Bay Area Chapter, Medical Committee for Human Rights, 1972); Barbara Ehrenreich and John Ehrenreich, *The American Health Empire: Power, Profits, and Politics* (New York: Vintage Books, 1970).

3. "Nicaraguan 'Democracy'—the People Query Their Leaders," *Christian Science Monitor,* November 29, 1983.

4. Paula Braveman and Eleuther Tarimo, *Screening in Primary Health Care* (Geneva: World Health Organization, 1994).

5. Paula Braveman and Eleuther Tarimo, "Social Inequalities in Health within Countries: Not Only an Issue for Affluent Nations," *Social Science and Medicine* 54 (2002): 1621–1635.

6. Paula Braveman, Eleuther Tarimo, and A. Creese, *Equity in Health and Health Care: A WHO Initiative* (Geneva: World Health Organization, 1996); Braveman and Tarimo, "Social Inequalities in Health within Countries"; Paula Braveman, *Monitoring Equity in Health: A Policy-Oriented Approach in Low- and Middle-Income Countries, Equity Initiative Paper,* 3 (Geneva: World Health Organization Department of Health Systems, 1998).

7. Bravemen et al., *Equity in Health and Health Care;* Braveman and Tarimo, "Social Inequalities in Health within Countries."

8. Emmanuela E. Gakidou, Christopher J. L. Murray, and Julio Frenk, "Defining and Measuring Health Inequality: An Approach Based on the Distribution of Health Expectancy," *Bulletin of the World Health Organization* 78 (2000): 42–54; Christopher J. L. Murray, Emmanuela E. Gakidou, and Julio Frenk, "Health Inequalities and Social Group Differences: What Should We Measure?" *Bulletin of the World Health Organization* 77 (1999): 537–543.

9. Braveman, *Monitoring Equity in Health;* Gakidou et al., "Defining and Measuring Health Inequality."

10. Paula Braveman, "Measuring Health Inequalities: The Politics of the *World Health Report 2000,*" in *Health and Social Justice: Politics, Ideology, and Inequity in the Distribution of Disease,* ed. Richard Hofrichter (San Francisco: Jossey-Bass, 2003); Paula Braveman, Barbara Starfield, and H. Jack Geiger, "World Health Report 2000: How It Removes Equity from the Agenda for Public Health Monitoring and Policy," *British Medical Journal* 323 (2001): 678–681.

11. Celia Almeida, Paula Braveman, Marthe R. Gold et al., "Methodological Concerns and Recommendations on Policy Consequences of the World Health Report 2000," *The Lancet* 357 (2001): 1692–1697; Paula Braveman, Nancy Krieger, and John

Lynch, "Health Inequalities and Social Inequalities in Health," *Bulletin of the World Health Organization* 78 (2000): 232–234; Paula Braveman and Sofia Gruskin, "Defining Equity in Health," *Journal of Epidemiology and Community Health* 57 (2003): 254–258; Paula Braveman and Sofia Gruskin, "Poverty, Equity, Human Rights and Health," *Bulletin of the World Health Organization* 81 (2003): 539–545; Paula Braveman et al., "An Approach to Studying Social Disparities in Health and Health Care," *American Journal of Public Health* 94 (2004): 2139–2148; Paula Braveman, "Health Disparities and Health Equity: Concepts and Measurement," *Annual Review of Public Health* 27 (2006): 167–194.

12. See multiple documents at www.commissiononhealth.org.
13. Paula Braveman and Susan Egerter, *Overcoming Obstacles to Health: Report from the Robert Wood Foundation to the Commission to Build a Healthier America* (Princeton, NJ: Robert Wood Johnson Foundation, 2008).
14. Global Equity Gauge Alliance, http://www.gega.org.za/ (accessed May 31, 2012).

# Chapter 11

# Cooperantes, Solidarity, and the Fight for Health in Mozambique

### Stephen Gloyd, James Pfeiffer, and Wendy Johnson

Health Alliance International (HAI) was founded, and continues to be sustained, by individuals strongly motivated by social justice concerns. But those of us participating in international health cooperation through HAI have sometimes found it challenging to maintain our initial idealism and enthusiasm. We have faced not only the overtly threatening opposition of reactionary political and military forces but the more corrosive, subtle, and sometimes principle-testing anxieties of a world increasingly dominated by neoliberal economics, nongovernmental organization competitiveness, and self-promotional entrepreneurialism. How can a solidarity-minded organization like HAI participate in international health cooperation while simultaneously challenging the structures of the larger world order? The answer to this question, and HAI's story, are told here through the personal narratives of the three "generations" of HAI's leadership team.

One of us (Steve Gloyd) began in 1979 as a *cooperante* helping the new socialist government in Mozambique develop its ambitious primary health care project; one (James Pfeiffer) began in 1994 as an antiapartheid solidarity activist and anthropologist committed to working with communities to respond to the concerns they identified; and one (Wendy Johnson) came to Mozambique in 2004 as a family practice doctor and public health practitioner focusing on the devastating AIDS epidemic. Our commitment to support and strengthen public sector health services is the common thread to our work—HAI has expanded from its roots in the 1980s as a solidarity movement with a newly independent Mozambique to include advocacy in the United States and projects in Côte d'Ivoire, East Timor, and Sudan.

**Steve Gloyd**

In the 1970s, I was fresh out of family practice residency and working in Seattle community clinics, trying to understand the political economy of health and health care. My principal job was consulting in a women's clinic and participating in a home-birth midwifery collective. Our aim was to help women take control of their bodies and their health care from our insensitive, patriarchal health care system. I learned a great deal from the expertise and experiences of my female colleagues. I also participated in antiwar and solidarity movements, stemming from the American wars in Vietnam, Central America, and Angola.

Serendipity led me to work in Mozambique. I saw an African Marimba band founded by a Zimbabwean musician, Dumisani Maraire, and quickly fell in love with the music. I started taking lessons, and within a year I was playing in Dumi's band. Our band started a Zimbabwe Medical Drive to support Zimbabweans and their struggle to cast off apartheid Rhodesia (as the region was called under British colonial and white-minority rule—see chapter 12). By 1975, Zimbabwe independence fighters began using Mozambique, newly independent from centuries of Portuguese colonialism, as a base of operations. An armed struggle initiated in the early 1960s by the *Frente de Libertação de Moçambique* (FRELIMO, Mozambican Liberation Front) had finally led to independence, hastened by the fall of Antonio Salazar's decades-long fascist regime (1932–1968) in Portugal. Under the leadership of Samora Machel, FRELIMO began to construct a new socialist nation through nationalization of land and commercial enterprises and the development of health and education systems for its poor majority. In its first years, the FRELIMO government established a model primary health care system that preceded and contributed to the progressive *Declaration of Alma-Ata* of the World Health Organization (see chapter 12). By 1978, most of the population had been vaccinated against smallpox, polio, and measles, and by the early 1980s, twelve hundred rural health posts had been built and staffed. Over eight thousand health workers were trained and employed. During this period about 11 percent of the government budget was committed to health care. The plan aimed to rapidly expand health care to the rural population despite scarce human and financial resources and only about forty physicians for eleven million people.[1]

As the music and political work progressed, a group from FRELIMO came to the United States for a solidarity tour. One of their goals was to recruit young professionals, called *cooperantes,* to help rebuild the country after the flight of the Portuguese professional class. Portuguese colonialism had been especially brutal in its exploitation of African labor (often through a system of forced labor called *chibalo*) and lack of investment in health, education, and other services for the African population.[2] The vast majority of Portuguese settlers (over two hundred thousand) left Mozambique in the late 1970s, leaving behind a deeply impoverished nation. While officially remaining a nonaligned nation, Mozambique quickly established close relations with Cuba and East Bloc socialist countries, sending thousands of its citizens to study and train abroad.[3] Socialist and Communist parties of Europe sent health workers to Mozambique as well. For many progressives, it was an exciting place to go. Only a handful of people came from the United States; I suspect that the openly Marxist orientation of the government scared off most American organizations and individuals.

Inspired by the FRELIMO tour, I wrote to the Mozambican Ministry of Health and offered my services. Months went by and I hadn't heard anything back. Todd Hawkins, a friend and Seattle labor leader who had traveled to Mozambique with labor activists, called his connections in Mozambique on my behalf, and within a few weeks I received an invitation letter and a work contract written in Portuguese. A few months after signing and returning the contract, I got a call from Northwest Airlines saying they had some Seattle-Maputo tickets waiting for me from an obscure African airline. That was it.

In early 1979, I arrived in Maputo. The Mozambique economy was in shambles as the Portuguese colonial power had simply taken or destroyed most of the country's resources when it left. Stores were nearly empty. Within a week I was sent to Beira, a large port city on the Indian Ocean, to learn about the health system. After another month, I was sent to Caia, an isolated rural town along the Zambezi River as the only doctor for a district of seventy-five thousand people. The district had seven health posts, a forty-bed hospital, and a small laboratory. We got electricity for two hours at lunchtime, then again in the evening. With about ten very good nurses, we were responsible for all health care in the district and a community health worker training center. Later in the year, a young Mozambican doctor, Francisco Songane, was assigned to Caia to run the training center and become district director. I was supposed to mentor him, as I was a few years his senior. He impressed me as remarkably smart and seemed to know more than I did about medicine. Songane later became minister of health and remains a close friend.

After a year in Caia, I was transferred to another district of one hundred and fifty thousand people with fifteen health posts, two major hospitals, and no doctors. It was daunting. A typical day would include hospital rounds, seeing thirty to forty patients referred to me by the triage nurses (they each saw one hundred to one hundred and fifty per day), and training the nursing staff. Every Tuesday and Thursday, I traveled to distant health posts, seeing selected patients and making sure the nurses got the medicines, supplies, equipment, and clinical support they needed.

Our staff felt a sense of solidarity that came from a socialized health system. We were encouraged to work together to improve all aspects of the health system. Committees were formed—including orderlies, nurses, lab technicians, and doctors—to decide how to run the hospital and even manage individual patients. Two to three days a week, everybody met at 6:00 a.m. at the hospital for an hour of "collective work," either cleaning the hospital or cultivating the hospital gardens for food. It was a wonderful working environment.

At the same time, we were under attack. Starting before I arrived, the Rhodesian regime tried to snuff out the Zimbabwe rebels in Mozambique. The new Mozambique government supported the Zimbabwean liberation struggle against white rule in then Rhodesia on Mozambique's western border. Zimbabwean fighters set up camps across the border in Mozambique, while Rhodesian secret police began to organize an insurgency in Mozambique to destabilize the country through attacks on infrastructure and government services, sowing terror in the countryside. The Rhodesians helped create a proxy mercenary army, the Mozambique National Resistance, known by their Portuguese acronym RENAMO, made up of disgruntled Mozambicans, many freed from prison. They targeted personnel in the government health and education services, bombed the major cities, and massacred Zimbabweans in refugee camps. With Zimbabwean independence in 1980, the conflict temporarily stopped, but after only eight months of peace, the apartheid South African government began supporting RENAMO. Mozambique took a firm stand against apartheid in neighboring South Africa, and welcomed the African National Congress (ANC), which had its central office in exile in Maputo. Mozambique was also targeted directly by the South African regime and the ANC offices were bombed through air attacks, while the South African special forces and RENAMO attacked infrastructure targets inside Mozambique to undermine the new government. A decade of horribly intense and destructive conflict followed, lasting until peace accords were signed in 1992.[4]

Our work became increasingly difficult as health workers and teachers were targeted. Our vehicles were frequently attacked and many of my colleagues were killed. Landmines were everywhere; about once a week we would treat somebody with a land mine injury. South African forces had blown up a major bridge so I had to take a canoe to get to our health posts. Ultimately, we all became increasingly confined to the safe towns, curtailing much of the outreach and health systems work we had been doing.

By 1990, hundreds of health posts were destroyed and many health workers killed, injured, and terrorized. RENAMO-controlled regions, which constituted nearly 50 percent of the rural areas in some provinces, were devoid of any health services for many years.[5] The conflict quickly became an important front in the Cold War as the Soviet Union lined up behind FRELIMO and provided some military aid, while the United States sided with RENAMO in its early years.[6]

After nearly four years in Mozambique, I returned to the United States to get a degree in public health. I became more deeply involved in the anti-apartheid movement and I helped start anti-RENAMO efforts in the northwest United States. Our Seattle Coalition Against Apartheid struggled against U.S. president Ronald Reagan's administration's support of RENAMO, its misnamed "constructive engagement" policies with South Africa, and its support of structural adjustment programs that forced huge cuts in government spending and social programs in favor of privatization and global corporate investment. In 1984, the United States ended its formal support for RENAMO and began a new policy of rapprochement with FRELIMO in hopes of coaxing it away from socialism and toward a free market economy. The shift was partly influenced by activists and *cooperantes* exposing RENAMO's abuses. However, it is believed by many that the United States continued its support for RENAMO in some form during this period as a means to keep pressure on FRELIMO to reform.

I returned to Mozambique whenever I could. I proudly watched my colleagues rise in the ranks of the Ministry of Health, including my former provincial director, Pascoal Mocumbi, who had become minister of health. During a visit in 1983, he admonished me to organize fellow U.S. *cooperantes* into a support organization similar to those of European solidarity groups. He suggested we adopt a single district to support comprehensive efforts to build primary health care there. His suggestion led to the creation of the Mozambique Health Committee, precursor of HAI.

In 1985, the proceeds from the song "We are the World" (the brainchild of singer and social activist Harry Belafonte, written by pop stars Michael Jackson and Lionel Richie, and sung by a who's who of American entertainers) financed a new foundation, United Support of Artists for Africa (USA for Africa), initially aimed at famine relief. Mozambique was one of their priority countries. A small group, including the handful of Americans who had worked for the Ministry of Health, submitted a proposal to the foundation to do what the minister had asked. We selected Manica district in the mountains on the border with Zimbabwe. The USA for Africa funding we received also supported a national program that trained over thirty nurses to do basic surgery where no doctors were available.

Building on our history, the Mozambique Health Committee operated within a community-based solidarity framework. We sent volunteer doctors, nurses, and midwives, as well as containers of donated equipment. We helped build health posts and water systems. At the University of Washington, we mobilized funds to bring Mozambican doctors to Seattle for master's degrees in public health. And we continued our activism against the devastating effects of U.S. foreign policy in Africa as well as in Latin America.

In 1991, the United States Agency for International Development (USAID) announced funding for Mozambique. Given the consistent support of repressive regimes and proxy wars by the U.S. government, many members of our solidarity group were reluctant to become allied with USAID. The U.S. foreign aid apparatus in Mozambique was viewed as the friendly face of U.S. imperialism, even though the U.S. government had officially turned away from RENAMO and was supporting the FRELIMO government. But several of our Ministry of Health colleagues urged us to apply for USAID funds, saying that they would prefer to work with trusted organizations such as HAI rather than new, unfamiliar organizations. After many months of fractious debates and ambivalent feelings among HAI members, most of us decided to follow the recommendations of the Ministry and register with USAID. However, that decision prompted three of our eight original board members to resign.

Accepting USAID funding allowed us to greatly expand our programs in the field with an opportunity to improve the technical aspects of our work. At the same time, our solidarity mission shifted to a more focused support of the health system, with proportionately less attention to the sociopolitical challenges facing Mozambique as the country became more and more dependent on donors and the neoliberal agenda donors attached to their support. This process accelerated as FRELIMO moved away from its socialist roots. Nevertheless, because many progressive people remain in the Mozambican government to this day, we have taken on the responsibility to support the Ministry of Health's work to preserve primary health care. It has become increasingly important to support the public sector against global efforts to privatize social services and cut government spending. HAI has consistently argued for, and helped implement, the expansion of public sector services and criticized structural adjustment programs.

The evolution of HAI as an organization owes a great deal to our Mozambican partners. Decades of mutual trust and our joint struggle to implement primary health care services helped hone our understanding of global forces that undermine the ability of governments to provide basic services to people. We have learned that the broad and wide reach of the public health system and its

**Figure 11.1**  Stephen Gloyd (*right*) learns about new approaches to AIDS treatment from Dr. Caroline Soi (*left*), a Kenyan physician working with the Ministry of Health in Mozambique. Dr. Soi is part of a new generation of *cooperantes* engaged in South-South technical assistance. Nampula, Mozambique, 2007.

Courtesy of Health Alliance International.

inherent accountability to the Mozambican people make it the most sustainable and logical way to deliver health services equitably.

### James Pfeiffer

My partner, Rachel Chapman, and I were drawn to work in Mozambique through a circuitous route of domestic and international activism. We had both been involved in the U.S. antiapartheid movement during the 1980s where we became aware of the war of destabilization in Mozambique. In college, I was involved with the divestment movement that pressured U.S. colleges and universities to divest from companies conducting business in South Africa. I also participated in antiapartheid groups in New York City after graduation while working as a tenant organizer in Harlem. Through my tenant organizing work I became involved in an antipolice abuse group called the Eleanor Bumpers Justice Committee, which was mobilizing around the killing of an unarmed sixty-eight-year-old African American grandmother by NYC housing police. Eleanor

Bumpers was shot in her apartment by the housing police, who claimed that she had tried to attack them as she was being evicted from her city-owned building. Local communities in northern Manhattan were struggling with a severe housing crisis, ongoing police abuse with a series of high-profile police killings, high unemployment, and racism.

While working as a housing counselor for the Community Law Offices, which supported tenant organizations in abandoned city-owned buildings in northern Manhattan, I helped organize several large antiapartheid marches out of Harlem, East Harlem, and Washington Heights. There was a strong affinity and sense of solidarity with the South African struggle, as it was also a time of great frustration and anger in poor communities in New York, with Ronald Reagan in power, cuts to government services, a crack epidemic, and Reagan's support for the apartheid regime through constructive engagement with the South African government. Many shared the feeling that the progressive gains of the sixties and seventies were unraveling, and it was easy to slip into fatalism and inaction, but some very committed local leaders kept things moving, whether in the Housing Justice Campaign or the Coalition Against Apartheid in NYC.

In the late 1980s, I met Rachel in the medical anthropology graduate program at UCLA. We both joined the local chapter of the South African Students' Congress Organization (SASCO), made up of South African students and U.S. sympathizers supportive of the ANC. Through SASCO, we learned of the nascent Mozambique Support Network (MSN). Several Los Angeles–based activists who had lived and worked in Mozambique as *cooperantes* during the war—Kathy Sheldon (a UCLA historian) and Steve Tarzynski (a doctor)—helped organize MSN and were good friends of Steve Gloyd. Together with them, we created the Los Angeles chapter of MSN, one of twenty-five chapters nationally, modeled on the Central American Solidarity Network. Many people drew the obvious parallels between the two struggles and were drawn to both movements. The Mozambican conflict recalled the contra war in Nicaragua (see chapters 10 and 13); like the contras, RENAMO was an externally funded right-wing insurgency intent on destabilizing a socialist government. We met Prexy Nesbitt, MSN's coordinator, at national meetings in Chicago where MSN was based. Prexy worked for the Mozambican government, organizing support and raising awareness in the United States. It was through MSN that we became aware of the work of HAI in Seattle and Mozambique.

Rachel and I also worked with a group called Friends of the ANC in Los Angeles, an umbrella group of antiapartheid organizations based in the African American community. The organization was led by the legendary African American activist, Michael Zinzun, a former Black Panther and famous activist against police abuse. Friends of the ANC often melded with Zinzun's Coalition Against Police Abuse (CAPA), which led community organizing after the Rodney King beating in Los Angeles in 1991. King, an African American man, had been stopped by police after a high-speed chase and then savagely beaten by a large group of officers. The beating was famously captured on video and shown around the world, sparking a movement to stop racism and abuse by city police departments. The following year, when the policemen were acquitted of charges stemming from the beating, Los Angeles erupted in four days of riots and uprisings that were only suppressed through deployment of five thousand U.S. Marines sent to patrol the streets of the city. We represented the MSN at the Friends of the ANC/CAPA meetings during this turbulent time, and became active in both local and international social justice issues.

The direct connections between these local and international issues were obvious to us at the time, and it was almost a rule of the movement that one could not do the more "glamorous" international antiapartheid work without linking it to antiracism work in the United States. Many of the same activists were also working on single-payer health care reform and efforts to bring affordable health care into south-central Los Angeles. In retrospect, it was an exciting time of activism in Los Angeles, with progressive organizations intersecting with each other in innovative ways. But these were also the years of George Bush Sr.'s conservative presidency, so the sense of running in place was frustrating and challenging. One of the bright spots in the world at the time was the realization that apartheid was crumbling and would soon come to an end. Nelson Mandela was being freed and southern Africa would be transformed.

As graduate students, Rachel and I hoped to do our thesis work in Mozambique. We had always wanted our academic efforts to be applied to political struggle. At that time the war was still raging in Mozambique. In 1990 we traveled there with the San Francisco–based Global Exchange. We visited the HAI project site in Chimoio, a city in the thick of the war. It was a tough time, with widespread famine and an economy completely shut down by RENAMO attacks. Then, in 1992, Steve Gloyd called and offered us jobs in the project, and we jumped at the opportunity.

I began with HAI as the coordinator of the project in Chimoio while Rachel became the health education advisor; we helped set up the project and stayed for over two years during the ceasefire period from 1992 to 1994. The situation in Mozambique changed dramatically in the early 1990s. With the end of the war, there was a huge influx of foreign aid and attendant NGOs. As national liberation movements in Africa waned, U.S. solidarity groups began to disappear or morph into service-providing NGOs. It was the beginning of the neoliberal transformation, and Mozambique began abandoning socialism and embracing market fundamentalism.[7] In this new climate we felt very strongly about supporting the public sector health system in the midst of the new emphasis on privatization and cuts to government services. HAI worked differently from other NGOs that were setting up parallel systems and working independently from the national system: we worked within the public sector, side-by-side with Ministry of Health counterparts.

In 1998, when we went back to Mozambique for another year to work with HAI, NGOs were beginning to dominate the health scene. The country was rebounding from war, but the health system was still drastically underfunded, even while the economy recovered and grew. Health workers' salaries had been cut as a result of structural adjustment programs stemming from World Bank and International Monetary Fund (IMF) loans to the government. Workers were demoralized; salaries dropped in some cases by 70 or 80 percent. Prices were going through the roof, food subsidies were eliminated, and people became more economically vulnerable and scrambled to survive. Equity within the health system and the society as a whole was compromised.[8]

While HAI is committed to working within the national health system, our efforts remain difficult given the system's resource shortages, low wage levels, and poor infrastructure—the lasting effects of structural adjustment. Nevertheless, HAI maintains its focus on health system strengthening in an environment in which privatization is the order of the day. Rachel and I have continued working with HAI in the NGO era because few organizations doing on-the-ground health system support remain committed to the notion of working in solidarity with country counterparts. We are not a charity. Many organizations have unquestioningly jumped on the international aid gravy train that feeds the proliferation of NGOs at the expense of public services. We walk a fine line, trying to maintain financial viability and the confidence of donors while continuing the public system strengthening work that most donors still do not fully understand.

And, of course, HAI has made its share of mistakes—sometimes hiring talented Mozambican workers, thereby removing them from the very system we seek to strengthen, and other times engaging in distracting turf wars with other NGOs vying for work in the same geographical or technical areas within the health system. Both problems result from the conflict that often arises between delivering on short-term goals (often under heavy pressure from donors to show quick results) and staying true to the longer-term goals inherent in our solidarity orientation. So hiring already trained, locally savvy staff out of the health system becomes an attractive alternative to recruiting from abroad or

**Figure 11.2** James Pfeiffer (*center*) and Wendy Johnson (*far right*) at a community meeting in Gondola, Manica Province, Mozambique, in 2005. Community members were voicing opinions and concerns about the activities and programs of international health NGOs in the region.
Courtesy of Health Alliance International.

training new staff when donors want to see rapid evidence of progress, even as this may jeopardize health services delivery.

This trial-and-error learning led us to join with other organizations to draft an NGO *Code of Conduct for Health Systems Strengthening*.[9] The Code enumerates specific principles that solidarity-minded NGOs can follow to limit their harm and help build sustainable public sector systems. These include adhering to hiring and compensation practices that minimize the "brain drain" of personnel away from public health systems, coordinating management and planning with Ministries of Health, and following Ministry priorities over those of NGOs or donors.

We now face major questions about HAI's identity. How do we get bigger without becoming more corporate in our work style and organization? How can we link international and domestic political work and engage in activism more effectively? How do we avoid becoming just another big NGO jumping at every new funding opportunity that comes along simply to guarantee our own continued existence? All the HAI leadership share lengthy personal histories of activism, and we regularly draw on those histories to remain mindful of the pitfalls in the current environment.

**Wendy Johnson**

Like Steve and James, my route to international health work was inspired and fueled by interactions with activists in the United States and Latin America. My first education as an activist and organizer came while working for Ohio Citizen Action in college. The experience started as a way I could earn money for college while engaged in a meaningful job, but it ended up politicizing me and teaching me important organizing skills that I still rely on today. It was the late 1980s, and through the organizers I became aware of the South African divestment and Central American solidarity movements, but I was more focused on domestic activism. Later, through international experiences working in the United Kingdom's House of Commons for a socialist member of Parliament and traveling through India on an American Medical Student Association health care study tour, I became more acutely aware of the importance of connecting local and international activism. But this lesson was most powerfully brought home in Chile.

Through luck and serendipity, I obtained a year-long international health fellowship during medical school. I went to the University of Concepción in Chile and joined fifth-year Chilean medical students on clinical rotations while also working under the mentorship of the chair of the university's Department of Public Health, Dr. Gustavo Molina. It was 1994, a few years after the 1988 plebiscite that ended General Augusto Pinochet's dictatorial regime (he stepped down in 1990). Pinochet had become dictator in 1973 when the United States helped engineer the Chilean military's overthrow of democratically elected socialist president Salvador Allende. Dr. Molina's father, also named Gustavo Molina, had been a friend of Allende's and a well-known exile of the Pinochet regime.

I was exposed to many friends and colleagues who had suffered the consequences of the coup and dictatorship. A fellow medical student in my Chilean class was a fifth-year student in 1994 but had started medical school in 1970. A student activist, Lastra was taken by force from his medical school classroom in 1973, imprisoned and tortured. He was exiled to Panama and spent years working as a medic in Nicaragua. In the late 1980s, he clandestinely returned to Chile and, later, after the plebiscite, camped out for days in front of the medical school dean's office until the administration relented and let him complete his studies. In this very personal way, through the stories of friends, colleagues, and mentors, I learned the history of the human rights movement and the deep U.S. involvement in illegitimate coups, proxy wars, dictatorships, and torture across Latin America. I also learned the importance of solidarity work in the United States (see chapter 9); it was a group of U.S. activists who had saved Dr. Molina's father's life by helping to get him out of Chile.

When I returned to the United States and started residency in New Mexico, I sought out Charlie Clements, who was living in Santa Fe at the time. Charlie served in Vietnam as a pilot and then refused to fly missions after what he had seen. After the war, he quit his family practice residency to serve as a physician in El Salvador behind the front lines with FMLN (Farabundo Martí National Liberation Front) revolutionaries. He recounts his extraordinary experiences in the book, *Witness to War.*[10] I met Charlie in 1996—Bill Clinton was president, and peace accords had been signed in El Salvador and Guatemala. The Nicaraguan Sandinistas had been defeated by the corrupt and conservative Arnoldo Alemán in their attempt to regain the presidency. Neoliberal politicians and forces were consolidating power across Latin America.

But in 1994, a group of indigenous communities in Chiapas, Mexico, launched a "postmodern," largely nonviolent uprising directly aimed at the policies embodied in the North American Free Trade Agreement. Charlie connected me to Doctors for Global Health (DGH), who were working with the Zapatista communities in Chiapas. Through DGH and volunteer work in Chiapas, I met dozens of dedicated, politically motivated health professionals both in the United States and in Central America, from health promoters to social workers, teachers, and doctors, who continue to inspire me today.

The more I learned about health and social justice in Chile and Mexico, the more clearly I saw the situation of disenfranchised groups domestically. During my residency, and later when I returned to Cleveland, Ohio, to work in a community health clinic, I became involved in immigrants' rights issues, the single-payer health care movement, and a local living-wage campaign. I worked on many of these issues side-by-side with patients who were activists as well. I met James and Rachel, who had just moved to Cleveland from Mozambique to begin their academic careers in the anthropology department at Case Western Reserve University.

A few years later, I was appointed medical director for the Cleveland Department of Public Health. I took the job with great enthusiasm to tackle the glaring health disparities in the city. Some predominantly African American and poor Cleveland neighborhoods have infant mortality rates that rival those in the developing world. We had a well-respected home-visiting support program for low-income pregnant women that I hoped to strengthen. I also hoped to improve the city's response to the devastating epidemic of childhood lead poisoning, which disproportionately affects poor, African American children. But this was post-9/11 and soon we were flooded with bioterror money, while funding for other programs to address the city's immediate health problems stemming from socioeconomic and racial inequalities was being cut. We had some successes, but by 2004, I had become disillusioned and accepted a job offer to run HAI's programs in Mozambique.

By that time, HAI was a major PEPFAR (President's Emergency Plan for Aids Relief) partner and had funding from the Bill and Melinda Gates Foundation, the William J. Clinton Foundation, UNICEF, and even the World Bank. Despite my uneasiness with the funding sources, the passion and philosophy of James, Rachel, and Steve convinced me that, unlike the bioterror money at the health department, these funds and donors could be directed to serve the goals of building quality and lasting health systems in collaboration with our local partners—the community and the Mozambican government. Knowing the history of Mozambique and its parallels to Central America, I expected to find other like-minded expatriates working for the same goals. I was naïve.

Instead, I found an aid-industrial complex in full bloom. The streets of Maputo were thick with white logo-bearing SUVs, and upscale restaurants prospered on the patronage of white Europeans and Americans. In my first days in Maputo with Steve, we were invited to a meeting with a representative of one of the "beltway bandits," a term for the private organizations based around Washington, D.C. that thrive opportunistically on government contracts. This particular organization had both nonprofit and for-profit branches, allowing it to take full advantage of the complete panoply of government funding.

The meeting was held in the Hotel Polana, one of the most opulent restored colonial-era hotels in Africa. We sat in the overstuffed chairs in the marble-floored lobby and listened to a well-groomed man in his sixties try to persuade us to join his organization's grant application for USAID funds. He was collecting organizations like baseball cards, and needed us for the appearance of legitimacy. He tried to impress us with some name-dropping and their track record of successful funding. Never did he mention or seem to care about the actual work we were to carry out with these funds. When we asked earnestly what his organization's area of expertise was, he replied, "marketing." We left disgusted.

Up-country, the situation was far different. I was one of only three U.S. citizens living in the midsized town of Chimoio, along the heavily AIDS-afflicted corridor between Zimbabwe and the coast. It was an area of intense need, but few expats wanted to live so far away from the amenities of the capital. The funding we received was largely to expand HIV treatment, and our goal was to use those resources for dual purposes—improve access to HIV care and also strengthen the public primary care health system by building laboratories and pharmacies and investing in preservice training for nurses and other health professionals.

After two years, I returned to Seattle. HAI's experiences in Mozambique now fuel our advocacy work in the United States, largely centered on combating the privatization of health care internationally—whether at the hands of international NGOs or for-profit clinics and hospitals. Specifically, we advocate for increased funding for public sector health and social programs and to remove the restrictions that international financial institutions like the IMF and World Bank put on social spending in the developing world. These efforts take many forms, from participating in national and international coalitions that organize and lobby both U.S. and international institutions, to writing for scholarly and mainstream publications,[11] and holding training sessions for students and representatives of other NGOs to learn more about the effects of macroeconomic policies on health systems. All aim at building a broader and more informed movement.

As HAI has grown larger and received more recognition from U.S.-based donors, maintaining our principles and solidarity-based practices becomes more challenging. The Code of Conduct we spearheaded offers an important road map to ensure that we don't lose our way in the maze of Global Health Inc. In HAI's Seattle base, also home of the Gates Foundation and several other large NGOs, global health is increasingly regarded as an engine for economic growth locally[12] and an opportunity to expand the private sector in poor countries, as opposed to HAI's solidarity and community-oriented efforts.

The struggle between those who care more about free markets than equity and those who believe health and education are human rights continues to play out in Mozambique, in the United States, and far beyond. The lessons we learn about effective activism in one venue are valuable for our work in the other. The arguments and strategies are similar, whether we are advocating with donors like the Gates Foundation and USAID to stop investing in "market" solutions and neglecting the public sector; engaged in the current health reform debates in the United States; or organizing to support a single-payer system or a public health insurance option. Our responsibility is to ensure that the voices of those most affected are heard, unequivocally, by those in power, and to challenge the power structures that remain unmoved and unresponsive.

### Notes

1. Steve Gloyd, "NGOs and the 'SAP'ing of Health Care in Rural Mozambique," *Hesperian Foundation News* (Spring 1996): 1–8.
2. Malyn Newitt, *A History of Mozambique* (London: Hurst, 1995); Barbara Isaacman and Allen Isaacman, *Mozambique: From Colonialism to Revolution, 1900–1982* (Boulder, CO: Westview, 1983).
3. Newitt, *A History of Mozambique.*
4. William Finnegan, *A Complicated War: The Harrowing of Mozambique* (Berkeley and Los Angeles: University of California Press, 1993).
5. Julie Cliff, "The War on Women in Mozambique: Health Consequences of South African Destabilization, Economic Crisis and Structural Adjustment," in *Women and Health in Africa,* ed. Meredeth Turshen (Trenton, NJ: Africa World Press, 1991), 15–33.
6. Newitt, *A History of Mozambique.*

7. Julie Cliff, "Donor Dependence or Donor Control?: The Case of Mozambique," *Community Development Journal* 28 (1993): 237–244; Joseph Hanlon, *Mozambique: Who Calls the Shots?* (Bloomington: Indiana University Press, 1991).

8. Joseph Hanlon, *Peace without Profit: How the IMF Blocks Rebuilding in Mozambique* (Portsmouth, NH: Heinemann, 1996).

9. James Pfeiffer et al., "Strengthening Health Systems in Poor Countries: A Code of Conduct for Nongovernmental Organizations," *American Journal of Public Health* 98 (2008): 2134–2140.

10. Charles Clements, *Witness to War: An American Doctor in El Salvador* (New York: Bantam, 1984). See chapter 13 for details about the revolutionary movement in El Salvador.

11. Wendy Johnson, "G8 Commitments to Africa Unfulfilled," Op-ed, *Seattle Post-Intelligencer,* June 7, 2007; Wendy Johnson and Jennifer Kasper, "Reauthorize Our Pledge to Fight AIDS," Op-ed, *Seattle Post-Intelligencer,* May 30, 2008; Pfeiffer et al., "Strengthening Health Systems."

12. Matthew Sparke, "Global Geographies," in *Seattle Geographies,* ed. Michael Brown and Richard Morrill (Seattle: University of Washington Press, 2011), 48–70.

# Chapter 12

# From Harlem to Harare

## Lessons in How Social Movements and Social Policy Change Health

**Mary Travis Bassett**

### Starting Out

As far back as I can remember, we children were carted along to marches and meetings. I grew up in the multiracial, largely working-class community of Upper Manhattan. My parents are life-long activists, involved in the civil rights movement, the peace movement, and in more local issues, including schools and health care. It was only years later that I realized our family was embedded in a community of leftists, many with ties to the U.S. Communist Party (CP-USA). My great-uncle, Theodore Bassett, was a CP-USA functionary and at one time its Harlem organizer. In our family circle were others who, like me, had one Black and one white parent. When my parents married in 1950, my mother's family, which traced its ancestry to English and Dutch colonial settlers, opposed the marriage, so we had little contact with them in my early childhood years. My father is from Virginia, a state where interracial marriage was against the law until 1968. Our yearly trips to visit his family left an enduring impression on me. My parents always traveled to Virginia separately, and when my mother was present, I was instructed to say one of my aunts was my mother, if anyone asked when we were out in public. Fifty years later, I still remember the anxiety that I might slip up and get the family into trouble if I responded to an innocent question like, "Is your mother here?" by identifying my white mother.

### How I Chose Medicine

In the summer of 1970, between high school and college, I got a job as a census taker in West Harlem. Going door-to-door, visiting people in their homes, I saw many people with obvious health problems. I decided to become a medical doctor, as far as I know the first in my family. During my early years at Radcliffe College, I worked at the Black Panther Party Franklin Lynch Free Health Center in Boston's Black neighborhood of Roxbury. I covered the front desk at the clinic once a week and scheduled doctors' appointments. Many of the doctors were attending physicians at Harvard-affiliated hospitals and, I would later realize, mainly well-regarded specialists practicing in fields usually worlds away from primary medical care. I would badger, bully, and cajole them to fill the physician roster every week.

But my main health project with the Black Panthers was screening for sickle cell anemia in Boston's housing projects. Sickle cell anemia is a genetic disorder that is about as common in African Americans as is cystic fibrosis in Ashkenazi Jews, but in the 1970s there was little public knowledge about it. "Sicklers" get a copy of the gene from each parent and suffer periodic painful crises when their stiff, sickle-shaped red blood cells get stuck in tiny blood vessels, sometimes leading to organ damage and premature death. Treatment was limited (as it is to this day) and parents typically had no idea if they carried the gene.

The Black Panther Party's interest in sickle cell was motivated largely by its neglect compared to other genetic disorders that mainly affected whites. The disease also linked African Americans to their long-ago African past, where the sickle gene offered protection against endemic malaria. We set out to remedy what government had failed to do by screening Blacks for the sickle cell gene. A rapid test made identification of the gene easy—a fingerstick and a couple of minutes was all it took. I recruited other Black premed students from Boston area colleges, and we launched a door-to-door screening program in the housing projects using a screening test made by Ortho Diagnostics. Because this test was expensive, Bill Wallace, one of a handful of Black Harvard graduate students, devised a homemade test. Each Friday evening, I went to his lab to measure out the mixture and test it against controls while Black Panther Party members distributed leaflets to alert residents to the next day's screening program. On Saturday the teams of Black premeds headed out to knock on doors. The program continued until 1972 when, because of various internal crises, the Boston chapter of the Black Panthers was recalled to the San Francisco Bay Area.

By then, our student group had concluded that sickle cell anemia, affecting about one in five hundred Black births (0.2 percent), was not the main health issue faced by the households we visited. True, it was a "Black-related" disease. But it was not tied to poverty and so did not raise all the issues of (lack of) personal responsibility typically invoked as the root of bad health among minorities and the poor. We became alarmed that the federal government was taking up sickle cell as a prototypical Black-related disease, seeming to advance the flawed argument that genetic factors explained ill health among African Americans. To the contrary, much of Black ill health was/is in fact attributable to poverty, including so-called lifestyle choices. For the poor, unhealthful choices too often are easier than healthful ones.

Our group of premed students focused on the health of Black America, but we also read about pioneering doctors who eschewed prestige and income to reach those who most needed care. I read and admired Joshua Horn, British physician, socialist, and author. He wrote *Away with All Pests,* chronicling China's barefoot doctors and the efforts to eliminate schistosomiasis by manually removing its snail vector. I still have my copy of *The Scalpel, the Sword,* a biography of Canadian surgeon Norman Bethune. Both Horn and Bethune committed their working lives, and in the case of Bethune, his life itself, to improving health in China. Perhaps that is why I leapt at the opportunity to travel to China for several months in early 1975, deferring medical school for a year.

## Medical School and Hospital Training

I returned to New York City for medical school, enrolling in Columbia University's College of Physicians and Surgeons. Like most U.S. medical schools and teaching hospitals, it is located in a poor neighborhood, Washington Heights, where the surrounding community provides "clinical material" for student instruction. I did not enjoy my years at Columbia, though my experience improved on the wards, where I encountered people I liked—the patients. I had attended elite, predominantly white, schools all my life, but Columbia was the first setting in which I personally encountered academic racism and a climate laden with the expectation that Black students would perform poorly. Early on, a professor recounted how Black students have trouble with academic subjects but do much better in later clinical years "because they have good people skills."

When I went to my advisor to say that I felt isolated as the sole incoming Black woman in my class and wished to transfer, he responded that "medical school is not for everyone" and offered to facilitate my departure by arranging loan forgiveness. In any case, I stayed. The Washington Heights neighborhood—my neighborhood—was now mostly Black and Latino but, as I recall, there were just three entering Black students in my class of one hundred and forty. Recalling these incidents many years later, I realize they may seem minor. Certainly it was far worse during my father's student years, when he was denied housing and jobs because of his race. But these persistent, arguably petty but demeaning encounters are what plague the Black middle class.

When it came time to select a place for residency training, I chose Harlem Hospital, Columbia's public hospital. Despite its affiliation, no Columbia medical graduate had trained there in some years. My academic advisors thought this choice was unwise, but I was convinced by Department of Medicine chair Gerald E. Thomson, who was the closest I would have to a mentor. Looking back, going to Harlem Hospital was one of my best decisions. Thomson, known among residents as "the jet" for his initials G.E.T., generated high standards around him. He saw to it that we delivered excellent medical care, although our patients' lives and our hospital often made this task difficult. We did not want to fail our community, our patients, or him. As a medical student, I had often heard residents make derisive remarks about poor patients—"dirt balls," "scum bags," or alcoholics who needed "Vitamin V" (valium) against withdrawal. At Harlem, we lacked equipment such as CT scanners, ran out of supplies as basic as penicillin or ventilators, and suspended surgery because there was no air conditioning in operating rooms.[1] I heard anger at our lack of resources and exasperation at negotiating with recalcitrant patients. But I never witnessed the profound disrespect of patients that was routinely expressed elsewhere. I was proud to be there and to this day I am sure all of Thomson's residents would agree that we could not have asked for better training.

The hospital doctors-in-training were unionized under the Committee of Interns and Residents (CIR). I was an officeholder and on its executive board. In 1981, the membership authorized a strike to demand improved patient care. In the end, the union took a beating, though the strike did highlight quality-of-care issues. Other unions were annoyed at the doctors-in-training for failing to consult with them before calling the strike. That was a learning experience on the perils of youthful zeal. New York's Taylor Law prohibits public workers from striking and charges two days' pay for each day on strike. Our salaries were docked and the union was heavily fined. I am pleased to say that the CIR recovered and exists to this day as an affiliate of the Service Employees International Union.

## The (Ill) Health of Harlem

The Harlem I encountered as a resident was not the Harlem of my childhood. That earlier Harlem was crowded, with people sitting at card tables on sidewalks during summer evenings. Yes, it was poor and dangerous, but there was a sense of community. Harlem in the 1980s was beginning a period of rapid population decline, along with loss of housing stock. And this was before AIDS hit. An analysis published in 1990 showed that in 1980, a man in central Harlem was less likely to survive to the age of sixty-five years than a man in Bangladesh.[2]

**Figure 12.1**    Mary Bassett, Harlem Hospital resident, 1981.
Courtesy of Mary Bassett.

And that was what we saw on the wards: people, many young, admitted with advanced disease affecting multiple organ systems. As a first-year intern I made home visits on my own, without hospital supervision. I visited people who lived in abandoned housing with no electricity or water. When I told people about the terrible conditions I saw and about the lives cut short, they usually assumed that the root causes were alcohol, drug abuse, and violence (followed later by AIDS). It was true that these factors took a toll. But the main drivers of Harlem's excess mortality were not "ghetto" behaviors and diseases but the common killers that affect everyone in industrialized countries: cardiovascular disease and cancer. I would later work in Zimbabwe, a poor country, but I never saw people as sick as the patients at Harlem Hospital.

I spent four years at Harlem Hospital, finishing up as the medical chief resident. In that time I got to know patients who were on a revolving door of admission and discharge. Many vignettes still come to mind: A young girl, a heroin addict with hepatitis, asked me if her situation was serious. On her second exam that night her initially enlarged liver was clearly shrinking. I shook my head. She had fulminant hepatitis and by morning was comatose. People with untreated hypertension came in with strokes. A woman in her forties who was in for back pain had metastatic lung cancer. I don't think I ever had a male patient under twenty-five years old who held a steady job.

I liked the practice of medicine, and you could not find a more committed group than the Department of Medicine at Harlem Hospital, but I suspected that if my goal was to make people healthy, I wasn't accomplishing much. I decided to pursue public health training, which took me to Seattle. In my second year at the University of Washington, I met fellow student Nancy Krieger, who has gone on to become a leading social epidemiologist. We had a wonderful time trying to disentangle the impact of race and class on health.[3] When I finished in Seattle, I decided to spend a stint outside of the United States. I wanted to see what it was like to work and live in a country with a government that put human development at the center of its agenda.

## Zimbabwe, 1985–2002

I went to Zimbabwe in 1985 as a junior lecturer in the Faculty of Medicine at the University of Zimbabwe. At the time, I thought I would work there for two years and return to an academic career in the United States. As the plane descended in the early morning into Harare, I looked out to see two nearly full circle rainbows. A good omen, I thought! As it turned out, apart from a two-year return to the United States in the mid-nineties—again to Harlem where I directed the Harlem Prevention Center—I would live in Zimbabwe for the next seventeen years. I was in Zimbabwe during the exhilarating postindependence 1980s and through the 1990s, when AIDS and the adoption of the World Bank's structural adjustment policies contributed to sharp reversals in health.

I have never come up with a simple answer to the question, "Why did you go to Zimbabwe?" Like many Black students in the 1970s, I supported the Zimbabwean struggle and African liberation movements generally. We read the writings of Eduardo Mondlane, Amilcar Cabral, and others.[4] I suppose it is fair to say that the interest of African liberation movements in Marx and Lenin was what prompted us to read these thinkers. And like many in my age group, I wanted to visit Africa.

Of course, I learned much more about Zimbabwe when I lived there. First called Southern Rhodesia—after Cecil Rhodes, the imperialist mining magnate—it became Rhodesia when Northern Rhodesia, now Zambia, gained independence in 1964. A year later, Ian Smith, the Rhodesian prime minister who is famously quoted that he would "never in a thousand years" permit Black rule, issued a "unilateral declaration of independence" (UDI) from Britain and established an "independent," white supremacist government. He used the language of the U.S. Declaration of Independence. Perhaps his party felt an affinity with a document drafted largely by slave owners. The UDI precipitated international sanctions, and Rhodesia had few official diplomatic relations. Despite its isolation and the launch of an armed liberation movement within its borders, Rhodesia held out for over a decade. Following Mozambican independence in 1975, Zimbabwean liberation forces could operate freely across its long shared border with Rhodesia. Mozambique's support would cost it dearly. Not only was it bombed by South Africa for giving shelter to "terrorists," South Africa, with U.S. support, launched an armed opposition to Mozambique's FRELIMO liberation government (see chapter 11). Rhodesia's demise came in 1980, when Zimbabwe held its first all-race elections.[5] The Zimbabwe African National Union (ZANU)—made up of "communist guerrillas" from the liberation movement—received a resounding victory at the polls, and Robert Mugabe became the new prime minister.

The long war had left some twenty thousand people dead and the new government came to power saddled with concessions to the minority white population under the British-brokered Lancaster House Agreement. Also, following ZANU's victory, the North Korean-trained Fifth Brigade of the Zimbabwean army launched a brutal suppression of the minority Ndebele people in Matabeleland, the political base of the Soviet and African National Congress–aligned Zimbabwe African People's Union (ZAPU). (ZANU had allied with China and the Pan-Africanist Congress.) When I arrived in Zimbabwe, the "troubles" in Matabeleland were still ongoing. In a campaign against the civilian population, which ZANU has never fully acknowledged, an estimated twenty thousand people were killed.[6]

When I joined the Department of Community Medicine at the university, it had an interesting assortment of lecturers. Some were progressive white Zimbabweans—Rene Loewenson, David Sanders, and Sue Laver—committed to working closely with the new government. Others staffed the department during UDI years and had stayed on. One of the latter informed me that the

Black students were "just one step out of the stone age" and advised me to revise my teaching standards. None of the faculty was Black Zimbabwean. It seemed those with public health training took positions in the Ministry of Health rather than the university. Although it was already five years postindependence, many colonial trappings persisted at the university. Even the name "Godfrey Huggins School of Medicine" honored a man who described the relationship between Africans and Europeans as that of a "horse and rider." There was ten o'clock tea, served by a "tea boy." Thus it is not surprising that it was the Ministry, not the university, that drove key health policy changes, largely framed on the primary health care principles outlined in the 1978 *Declaration of Alma-Ata.*

I had just completed training in public health at the University of Washington, but it probably should not have been a surprise that I was not especially well prepared for my new job. It seemed that at every meeting I attended people were talking about Alma-Ata. It was obvious that I should know to what they were referring, but I didn't. I was too embarrassed to ask for an explanation so I went to the library to look up this mysterious *Declaration of Alma-Ata.* Issued in 1978 at a seminal WHO-UNICEF conference held in the USSR, it articulated a clear departure from the technical approach to health that characterized the major disease-control initiatives at the time (such as the WHO's smallpox eradication campaign). Alma-Ata situated health advancement in its larger social context, naming national governments as the main guarantors of "Health for All by the Year 2000." As I write now, over thirty years later and nearly a decade after it failed to achieve this ambitious goal, it is worth recalling its words:

> The existing gross inequality in the health status of the people particularly between developed and developing countries as well as within countries is politically, socially and economically unacceptable and is, therefore, of common concern to all countries. . . . Economic and social development, based on a New International Economic Order, is of basic importance to the fullest attainment of health for all and to the reduction of the gap between the health status of the developing and developed countries. The promotion and protection of the health of the people is essential to sustained economic and social development and contributes to a better quality of life and to world peace. . . . The people have the right and duty to participate individually and collectively in the planning and implementation of their health care. . . . Governments have a responsibility for the health of their people which can be fulfilled only

by the provision of adequate health and social measures. A main social target of governments, international organizations and the whole world community in the coming decades should be the attainment by all peoples of the world by the year 2000 of a level of health that will permit them to lead a socially and economically productive life. Primary health care is the key to attaining this target as part of development in the spirit of social justice.[7]

This perspective would drive Zimbabwe's health policy for its first decade. Within my first six months in Zimbabwe, I too could list readily the core elements of primary health care.

## Zimbabwe Health Policy in the 1980s

The new government had immediately announced a socialist agenda, and its most visible outcomes were in health and education. Health care services and primary education became essentially free. There were no fees at health facilities for those who earned under 150 Zimbabwe dollars a month (about U.S. $60), then about 90 percent of the population. The structure of the economy did not change much, a fact that would remain an ongoing challenge for the ruling party. While political control passed to the Black majority, the economy remained in the hands of the local white elite and, more important, multinational corporations that controlled some 70 percent of the pre-independence economy.

The Department of Community Medicine helped to document important gains both in access to health services and in health status during the 1980s. A massive expansion of rural health centers placed roughly 80 percent of the population within eight kilometers of services (about a two-hour walk). Before independence, infant mortality was an estimated 120–150 deaths per 1,000 live births; by 1990, it was down to 60 deaths per 1,000 births. Deaths in children under five years were also halved. Helping to explain these gains was an increase in vaccination rates and better management of childhood diarrhea. Before 1980 about 25 percent of children were fully immunized; by 1990 this proportion stood at 80 percent. Knowledge and use of sugar-salt solution for oral rehydration of children suffering from diarrhea also rose.

Yet Zimbabwe's community-based approach at times provoked conflicts with international authorities. Soon after I arrived, at a meeting in Harare on diarrheal disease control, WHO representatives reprimanded Zimbabwean Ministry officials for not encouraging use of prepackaged sachets containing salt, potassium, and sugar to make oral rehydration solution (ORS). Zimbabwe's provincial medical directors refused to abandon promotion of a simple home-based sugar and salt solution. They argued that the sachets, which were obtained from a clinic, medicalized management thereby potentially delaying treatment. In contrast, sugar, salt, and water could be mixed in empty 250 ml bottles (from Mazowe orange concentrate), items available in virtually every home. The WHO team's critiques were scathing, but the Zimbabwean officials—most just in their thirties—remained firm. Ten years later, a WHO team arrived to study Zimbabwe's management of childhood diarrhea: home-based ORS use in Zimbabwe was among the highest in Africa and inappropriate antibiotic use about the lowest.

The 1980s were a heady time for public health in Harare. The confidence and competence of the Ministry leadership, if occasionally arrogant, succeeded in protecting the government budget allocation for health, even as the country's economic growth stagnated. Yet alongside the successes, there were worrying trends. Childhood undernutrition remained stubbornly prevalent. Over 20 percent of children under five were stunted, a reflection of chronic undernutrition. One interpretation, offered by members of the Department of Community Medicine, was that, unlike vaccine-preventable diseases, improved nutritional status required changes outside the health sector. The root causes of undernutrition lay in the lack of household economic resources, particularly women's lack of access to income. Despite the promise of independence, wages remained stagnant in real terms (adjusted for inflation), equivalent to 1980 levels. By 1990, the government would accede to the World Bank's structural adjustment policies, which, among other things, required sharp reductions in

**Figure 12.2** Mary Bassett at community survey report back, Epworth, an informal settlement outside of Harare, 1987.

Courtesy of Mary Bassett.

social expenditures such as health and education. Together with one of the most severe AIDS epidemics in the world, structural adjustment would become the greatest threat to Zimbabwe's postindependence accomplishments.

## Zimbabwe and AIDS

I had looked after my first patient with AIDS as a resident at Harlem Hospital in early 1981, at the beginning of the U.S. epidemic. Soon after came reports of AIDS patients from Africa, where men and women were equally affected in the absence of "risk factors" of injection drug use or men having sex with men. I wondered about AIDS in Zimbabwe and, shortly after I arrived, I visited the National Blood Transfusion Service. Dr. Jean Emmanuel ran an excellent service; some years later he would take on a similar role for the WHO. He was a very early adopter of screening blood donations for the AIDS virus, which meant that Zimbabwe became perhaps the third country to do so after the United States and France (which had developed the test). In a characteristic effort to scrimp and save, Emmanuel and his staff had developed a strategy of batching the HIV blood screens. When he heard I had training in epidemiology, he asked me to help write up this approach.[8]

And so began my many years of work on AIDS in Zimbabwe, a country that would soon have (and still has) one of the highest adult prevalences in the world, by the 1990s affecting one in three or four adults. Over the years I did epidemiological studies, took care of patients with HIV, launched education programs in rural high schools, helped establish prevention programs in urban factories and programs to reduce mother-to-child-transmission with antiretroviral drugs, and, finally, promoted the introduction of antiretroviral treatment. But none of these activities seemed to slow the epidemic.

What accounted for the rapid spread of HIV in Zimbabwe? We knew how HIV transmission happened but were unsure as to why the spread was so fast and extensive. Even now, this question haunts Africa, the only continent with a generalized population epidemic. At the time, my colleagues and I considered structural causes: male migrant labor, gender inequality, military mobilization, poverty. There is no doubt now that these contributed greatly to Zimbabwe's vulnerability. As we discussed these "social determinants," I must have informed hundreds of people that they were HIV infected. My colleagues joked that they imagined me earnestly telling a patient, "What you need is a social revolution." Instead, I explained how they became infected and how important it was to avoid infecting others. I handed out condoms and treated sexually transmitted diseases.

Looking back, we did not react with sufficient alarm to the unfolding human tragedy that was AIDS. Yes, an AIDS curriculum for high schools did encourage dialogue on such difficult issues as relationships, fidelity, and trust. But it was a little like reacting to a cholera epidemic by teaching first graders about washing hands. Not wrong, but misguided. In any case, the stalled economy meant that young people were mainly preoccupied with how to earn a living. I was at Harare High School one day when new AIDS prevention texts (paid for by UNICEF) were delivered. The headmistress looked them over, noting, "I have four students sharing an English textbook, six sharing a math text. And they send me these—one for each student. How do they think my students will get jobs without English or math? And what difference will these AIDS books make if they can't find work?" She shook her head and waved at the new books, "These are going straight into the storage closet." If Zimbabwe was ill equipped to respond to the AIDS epidemic, the adoption of economic reforms promoted by the World Bank and the International Monetary Fund (IMF) did little to improve the situation.

**Structural Adjustment**

Zimbabwe adopted its Economic Structural Adjustment Programme (ESAP) in late 1990. The government's motivation was clear: access to badly needed capital. Real growth had stagnated in the 1980s and Zimbabwe's manufacturing and industrial sectors, in particular, needed upgrading to become competitive. Textile and steel were said to be well positioned for "take off." The standard loan conditionalities applied, reflecting U.S.-led neoliberal ideology: a reduction of the budget deficit through a combination of cuts in public deficits and public sector employment; trade liberalization with deregulation of prices, foreign trade, investment, and production; phased removal of domestic subsidies; enforcement of cost-recovery measures in health; and the introduction of school fees. Many African nations had already entered into such agreements, and the consequences (such as higher prices for basic goods, lower wages, and social spending cutbacks) made adjustment hugely unpopular. But the Zimbabwean government argued that it had no choice.

Just as Zimbabwe embarked on ESAP, the country experienced its worst drought in a century. I happened to be traveling extensively around the country during this time. Even in Manicaland, which usually has rain, the head-high maize crop had completely withered. We saw dead cattle lying in the fields, an ominous sign in a peasant economy where cattle are crucial assets. Despite growing evidence that the drought would result in total crop failure, Zimbabwe continued to export its stocks of maize. The IMF had argued that maintaining a maize reserve—a practice dating to the colonial period in drought-prone Zimbabwe—was wasteful. Sell it and buy more if needed was the IMF's advice.

In 1992, Zimbabwe was forced to buy maize on the international market. The purchase had a ruinous impact on the country's foreign currency reserves. This misguided advice from the World Bank and IMF—which never deigned to try out their ideas on a small scale but instead experimented on entire continents—still astounds me.

A year or two after ESAP began, a group at the Nordic Institute, led by Peter Gibbon, invited David Sanders, then chair of the Department of Community Medicine, to participate in a network that examined the social impact of structural adjustment in Africa. Leon Bijlmakers and I joined David to design a study and, in 1993, we began prospectively following three hundred rural and three hundred urban households, each with a child under five, for a period of five years. This was advocacy research: we expected to document a decline in both health and use of health services, though it would be hard to untangle the effects of AIDS from those of ESAP. We hoped that the study would help bolster emerging critiques of the shift in economic policy in the country.

The most interesting findings related to household economy. We had hypothesized that rural areas would be better protected from growing economic hardship accompanying ESAP, because peasants at least had recourse to their land and to support from extended family. But that is not what households reported. For rural areas, by the mid-1990s, remittances from migrant household members outstripped agriculture as the main source of income. Moreover, despite the fact that sources of income were diversifying, income levels remained low and a growing proportion of households were classified as poor. Further, both urban and rural communities showed evidence of growing income inequality, with the more affluent (though still generally poor) households experiencing some income gains while the poorest households became even poorer. An alarming 10 to 30 percent of households declared that they had an absolute lack of food, and many economized on food to establish cash savings. Most households also reported that they economized by not seeking health services. For example, in the rural areas the proportion of households reporting women giving birth at home rose from 18 percent to 38 percent.[9]

These data added detail to the bigger picture that was emerging. Together, the ESAP-directed changes, drought-induced crop failures, and AIDS had taken a terrible toll. By 1998, fully 30 percent of government annual expenditure was directed to debt servicing, nearly eight times as much as spent on health care. Despite optimistic predictions in 1991, when ESAP began, the economy was plagued by high inflation, high interest rates, an unstable exchange rate, growing unemployment, and contraction of the traditionally strong textile and steel industries.[10] Everyone, including the World Bank, agreed that adjustment had failed. Of course, there was disagreement as to why, but failed it had.

The unstable economy was also affecting the university, as salaries could not keep up with inflation. A deputy dean of the Faculty of Medicine had bought several commuter minibuses, one of which he drove himself. Having a dean as a bus driver alarmed staff members, but the reality was that many, perhaps most, faculty sought income elsewhere. Even so, it was increasingly difficult to make ends meet. The salaried middle class shared with workers and peasants a growing uncertainty about the future and growing distrust of the ability of the ZANU government to improve the situation.

The roots of the present Zimbabwean crisis, widely attributed to a land grab by Mugabe—described as war hero turned megalomaniac—are not that simple. To my mind, the critical unraveling began with those structural adjustment agreements with the World Bank and the IMF. Certainly lack of control over the postindependence economy, state-building from scratch, and the effects of the ESAP are fundamental. As a U.S. citizen, I often think about a casual remark made by Moeletsi Mbeki, who was then a journalist in Harare (his brother Thabo would become the second president of postapartheid South Africa), to some U.S. visitors: "I would remind you," he said, "that not a single U.S. taxpayer dollar paid for a single bullet for African liberation." The fact is that the United States has little credibility in rendering judgment about African governance, having associated itself with some of the continent's most brutal leaders whose sole virtue was their anticommunism.

### Zimbabwe after 2000

In 2000, Mugabe called a referendum on an amendment to the constitution that would provide him with greater presidential powers. An opposition party was launched, Movement for Democratic Change, comprised of a broad alliance of labor and capital with little in common except their opposition to Mugabe. Even white farmers, who had previously kept to their deal to stay out of politics, were getting involved.

I was sitting in a large meeting of NGOs when we got the word that the vote was in and it was a "no vote." Everyone in the room leapt to their feet and cheered. I am sure that until that moment I had never had a political discussion with anyone there. But now we walked out together, heading back to our offices. Cars were honking their horns. People were shouting out, in soccer parlance, "Mugabe gets a yellow card!" (In soccer, a yellow card is a warning.) Everyone was elated: things would work out. Zimbabwe's electoral process had held sway, and Mugabe was dealt a defeat in the polls. That evening he made a televised speech. He appeared contrite: "The people have spoken," he said. Then, two weeks later, the farm invasions began.

Since 1930, when the final expropriation of African lands occurred, well-off white farmers had occupied the best land in the country. At the time of independence in 1980, these farmers, who numbered fewer than five thousand, controlled two-thirds of the land in a country of eight million people. Theirs remained a closed and privileged world. Staying out of politics and often out of sight, they lived in a cocoon that seemed untouched by Zimbabwe's transition to independence. Some 20 percent of Zimbabwe's African population lived and worked on these commercial farms, where malnutrition rates were among the highest in the country. The farms operated more like feudal estates than modern business enterprises.

Now, twenty years after independence, this was about to end. The government put in place new laws that permitted it to appropriate and redistribute white-owned commercial lands. In a process that cost scores of lives, including the lives of some white farmers, commercial farming would be dismantled. Of some four thousand white farmers when seizures began, fewer than four hundred remain on their farms today. Agricultural output plummeted, and Zimbabwe's political crisis escalated. The West reacted with alarm and rallied to defend the farming community. Yet within living memory these farmlands had been unjustly and violently removed from African hands. It is hard to imagine any process of redress of this historical injustice that would have met the approval of white farmers.

Following 2000, I felt my effectiveness was declining. It was hard to find a way to contribute to an increasingly polarized society. I also felt a growing sense of insecurity. Strict regulations governing foreign currency—amid widespread currency exchange outside the banking system—made it more or less impossible to live without breaking the law. More and more Zimbabwean professionals were leaving the country. I weighed lots of things to make my decision: my contribution, my financial security, and my children's education among them. I left Zimbabwe in August 2002 as Zimbabwe's economy plunged headlong into ruin.

## Back to New York City

I'd left NYC in the 1980s, when the divide between rich and poor areas was growing, making it a city of "gold coast and ghetto." In 2002, I returned to a city where the poor were simply being priced out. Perhaps surprising, much that I had learned in Zimbabwe about public health—sobering lessons in how social policy changes can reverse health gains and perpetuate health inequities—would be relevant to New York.

I came back to a job in the NYC Health Department as a deputy commissioner of health responsible for a portfolio that included noncommunicable diseases and maternal and child health. I felt very lucky to be working on local health issues, as I had in Harare. Colin "Coke" McCord, a surgeon whom I had first met in Mozambique and who also worked at Harlem Hospital, had joined the health department, providing a link to my life in Southern Africa. But returning was quite an adjustment. Two things especially struck me. One was that discussions of race had disappeared, at work and generally. Instead of race, people used new words like "diversity" or "multiculturalism." This gave rise to some strange situations, such as job candidates being referred to as "diverse." Certainly racial inequalities had not been adequately addressed, either in terms of the workplace or population health. When I arrived, the health department senior staff included a handful of Black women, but no Black men. There were even fewer Latinos. Racial differences in health persisted. For example, an analysis of the differences in health by neighborhood showed that relative gaps persisted and were widening for AIDS and diabetes mortality.[11] But these analyses sparked none of the outrage provoked by comparable earlier work.

Additionally, the Left seemed to have vanished, making solid liberals seem positively left-wing. My years away had seen the always-present right-wing tendencies of the United States gain ascendancy, and the reckless years of George W. Bush were just beginning. I found myself advocating for policies and programs within the health department that were scarcely leftist, though I would certainly describe myself as a progressive. Indeed, most of my ideas were ones that any good liberal should support; namely, that instruments of government should be used to protect the public's health.

I brought to my work in New York two key lessons from Zimbabwe: that the policy environment is central to shaping human behavior, and that communities need to be engaged in the pursuit of their own health. To tackle the key "risk factors" for chronic disease—tobacco use, physical inactivity, and unhealthful eating—we relied on the government tools of taxation and regulation. NYC pioneered taxing cigarettes heavily, banning indoor smoking, restricting trans fats in restaurants, and requiring fast-food chains to post calorie counts. Of course, these policies may not influence the larger political and economic environment that makes unhealthful foods more affordable. But by restricting trans fat in restaurants, the NYC Health Department set a precedent in regulating food content to protect against a chronic disease (in this case, heart disease), extending the traditional food safety paradigm beyond bacterial contamination and additives.[12] Building a constituency for community-based prevention was more difficult because there was less political support. We opened new District Public

Health Offices, recalling the rural district offices of the Ministry of Health in Zimbabwe, to serve the sickest neighborhoods in the city: the Bronx, East and Central Harlem, and North and Central Brooklyn.[13]

My international experience also led me to consider the relevance of developing country programs to New York. As the health department representative to the Commission for Economic Opportunity, known as the "Poverty Commission," I, with my staff, looked to a strategy that emerged from Latin America called "conditional cash transfers" (issuing payments to families [equivalent to 20–30 percent of income] provided they sent their children to school and/or visited the doctor regularly) as an innovative approach to poverty reduction.[14] This approach has been promoted by both the Right (who emphasize personal responsibility) and the Left (who emphasize the ability of the poor to resolve many of their own problems if given the means). Making the case that NYC had much to learn from the developing world, I traveled to Mexico with the mayor as part of his delegation to see its *Oportunidades* program firsthand. "Opportunity NYC" drew on this model and was implemented under the auspices of the mayor's Center for Economic Opportunity,[15] the first application of a conditional cash-transfer program in a high-income country.

## Conclusion

My varied experiences have convinced me that to improve the health of a population is fundamentally an exercise in democracy. Many dedicated public health professionals hold that health is something that can be engineered for the poor, who lack capacity and knowledge to seek it themselves. But my time in Zimbabwe convinced me otherwise. I don't mean democracy defined by elections or number of parties. I mean a society in which the citizenry have the possibility and capacity to participate in governance. In the United States, enduring health inequalities by race and income tell a story of a country where social protection has yet to extend to its entire people. Zimbabwe's still short history shows how quickly social advances can be eroded. But I learned there my most important lesson in public health: how much and how fast the health of a population can improve when there is widespread political commitment to achieving this end.

### Notes

1. John C. Brust, P. C. Dickinson, and Edward Healton, "Failure of CT Sharing in a Large Municipal Hospital," *New England Journal of Medicine* 304 (1981): 1388–1393.
2. Colin McCord and Harold P. Freeman, "Excess Mortality in Harlem," *New England Journal of Medicine* 322 (1990): 173–177.
3. Nancy Krieger and Mary T. Bassett, "The Health of Black Folk: Disease, Class and Ideology in Science," *Monthly Review* 38 (1986): 74–85.

4. Eduardo Mondlane, *Struggle for Mozambique* (Harmondsworth: Penguin Books, 1969); Amilcar Cabral, *Unity and Struggle: Speeches and Writing of Amilcar Cabral* (Texts selected by the PAIGC), trans. Michael Wolfers (New York: Monthly Review Press, 1979).

5. Terence O. Ranger, *Peasant Consciousness and the Guerilla War in Zimbabwe: A Comparative Study* (London: Currey, 1985).

6. Catholic Commission for Justice and Peace, *Gukurahundi in Zimbabwe: A Report into the Disturbances in Matabeleland and the Midlands 1980–1988* (New York: Columbia University Press, 2008).

7. "Declaration of Alma-Ata," www.who.int (accessed June 4, 2009); also see Marcos Cueto, "The Origins of Primary Health Care and Selective Primary Health Care," *American Journal of Public Health* 94(11) (2004): 1864–1874.

8. Jean C. Emmanuel, Mary T. Bassett, Health J. Smith, and Jan A. Jacobs, "Pooling of Sera for Human Immunodeficiency Virus (HIV) Testing: An Economical Method for Use in Developing Countries," *Journal of Clinical Pathology* 41 (1988): 582–585.

9. Leon Bijlmakers, "Structural Adjustment: Source of Structural adversity. Socio-economic Stress, Health, and Child Nutritional Status in Zimbabwe. Summary" (PrintPartners Ipskamp B.V.: Enschede, 2003); Mary T. Bassett, Leon Bijlmakers, and David M. Sanders, "Experiencing Structural Adjustment in Urban and Rural Households of Zimbabwe," in *African Women's Health,* ed. Meredeth Turshen (Trenton, NJ: Africa World Press, 2000), 177–187.

10. Lloyd Sachikonye, "ESAP and Industrial Sector Decline," Paper presented at the Synthesis Conference on Structural Adjustment and Socio-Economic Change in Africa. Nordic African Institute, Center for Development Studies. Copenhagen, December 3–5, 1998.

11. Adam M. Karpati, Mary T. Bassett, and Colin McCord, "Neighbourhood Mortality Inequalities in New York City, 1989–1991 and 1999–2001," *Journal of Epidemiology and Community Health* 60 (2006): 1060–1064.

12. Lynn D. Silver and Mary T. Bassett, "Food Safety for the 21st Century," *Journal of the American Medical Association* 300 (2008): 957–959.

13. Andrew Goodman, "President Obama's Health Plan and Community-Based Prevention," *American Journal of Public Health* (August 20, 2009), doi: 10.2105/AJPH.2009.174714.

14. Lia C. H. Fernald, Paul J. Gertler, and Lynette M. Neufeld, "Role of Cash in Conditional Cash Transfer Programmes for Child Health, Growth, and Development: An Analysis of Mexico's *Oportunidades* Program," *Lancet* 371 (2008): 828–837.

15. "Opportunity NYC," www.nyc.gov/html/ceo (accessed August 21, 2009).

# Part V

# Generation Born in the 1960s–1970s

The chapters in this section are written by a fourth generation of health internationalists born in the 1960s and 1970s. They reached adulthood two decades later during the rapid and insidious spread of neoliberalism, the assault on unions and the Left generally, intensified technology–, finance sector– , and corporate-driven economic globalization, and the imposition of free trade agreements that privilege transnational corporations and patent holders over people's lives. The end of the Cold War initially promised a peace dividend, but lingering legacies of the demonization of socialism and persistent U.S. support for antidemocratic regimes friendly to U.S. economic interests, and then the War on Terror, quashed such hopes.

The members of this generation have wide and varying perspectives and priorities, but they share a desire to get beyond old political categories. Self-aware, connected, and deeply concerned about personal values, they struggle to avoid the traps of cultural and professional arrogance. Instead, they are strongly committed to an ethics of solidarity with workers and the most dis-possessed, the principles of human rights and social justice, and the promo-tion of individual and community empowerment. Many in this generation have worked to build new grassroots organizations and solidarity networks in which the formerly disempowered take the lead in agenda-setting, as a counterpoint to existing international/global health agencies and NGOs, many of which are today becoming increasingly business oriented.

Because of the limited leftist activist-political base when this generation was coming of age in the United States, some came to their political positions through self-exploratory journeys that turned into overseas experiences in health solidarity. In other cases, well-trained professionals arrived in an international setting with one agenda but learned on the ground that their initial goals were misconceived, if not wrong-headed. In Central and South America and also in Africa, health activists with strong commitments to social rights and solidarity (including taking up arms) with the most oppressed groups organized around concepts of health and human rights and "liberation medicine," and formed alliances with the broadly based grassroots People's Health Movement, founded in 2000 by health workers in South Asia to revitalize the Alma-Ata agenda. Others have connected past and present struggles to counter imperialism and militarism by identifying with antiracist struggles in the United States and working to stop weapons testing in the Pacific. Finally, some in this generation have risked their U.S. health careers by choosing to learn in the belly of "the socialist beast" in countries like Cuba and Venezuela, and discovered, sometimes to their amazement, better ways of providing medical education, health, and social services than currently exist in the United States.

Current and future generations face a daunting set of challenges. Cuba offers an all but unique example for health leftists of a solidarity-oriented society surviving in spite of the extreme economic challenges created by a longstanding U.S. blockade—yet its flaws merit airing. Should health leftists underplay, for example, its initially repressive forced institutionalization of HIV/AIDS patients in the name of public health, just as earlier generations disseminated only the positive achievements of the Soviet Union or China? How should health leftists respond to funding opportunities channeled through ostensibly philanthropic initiatives that privilege technical over sociopolitical approaches or through the "war on terror," especially as it distorts legitimate public health priorities and focuses energy and resources on a military-like regime of international biological "preparedness?" What are the implications of pursuing transformative social change through human rights approaches as opposed to revolutionary action? How do younger generations, raised in an age of instant telecommunications and rapid technological development, settle in for the long duration of social struggle?

And what is the role of an *American* health Left in a context in which direct cooperation has emerged among countries in the "global South" as a bona fide alternative form of solidarity? Do U.S. health internationalists fit in, or does their presence possibly detract from South-South social-justice-oriented *solidarity?* What role have health leftists taken and what part should they play in the Arab Spring movements, Spain's *indignados* uprising, and the North American "Occupy" movements? What is the best, most resonant, contemporary strategy for internationalist activism with goals of worldwide, national, and local equity and redistributive power and social justice?

# Chapter 13

# Brigadistas and Revolutionaries

## Health and Social Justice in El Salvador

**Michael Terry with Laura Turiano**

In 1981, while I was working in an ice cream shop and getting my GED after being kicked out of high school, the countries of Central America were enduring the worst of their civil wars. People there, especially young men and women my own age, were choosing, or being forced to choose, which side they were on and what they were willing to do for it.

Meanwhile, my government was spending billions of dollars to support the sides it had chosen.[1] In El Salvador and Guatemala, it sided with the governments against armed rebel groups that had coalesced into the Farabundo Martí National Liberation Front (FMLN) and the Guatemalan National Revolutionary Unity (URNG). In Nicaragua, the United States created an opposition rebel group based in Honduras, the contras, to fight the revolutionary Sandinista government, which had overthrown the country's longtime U.S.-backed dictator in 1979. This was not a new foreign policy or a mistake. Since 1800, the United States had invaded and intervened in Central America dozens of times, including sponsoring several coups. These actions were typically organized to rescue U.S. business interests from attempts by nationalist or indigenous forces to reclaim natural resources for domestic benefit.

### Colorado Awakenings

I was a resistant child and a poor student. Raised in a Catholic home, I lost the faith at age six and have since considered religion a cruel hoax. My family relocated six times before I was fourteen as my father moved up the corporate ladder, finally settling in Philadelphia. When I moved to Boulder, Colorado, in the early 1980s, to work as a horse wrangler and attend the University of

Colorado, I was basically apolitical. But the campus and the town itself had very active antiwar and feminist groups, and the campus newspaper regularly covered social justice issues. After attending a talk sponsored by the local sanctuary committee on the history of Central America, I immediately began volunteering for a variety of tasks.[2]

The first Central American I met was a young Salvadoran woman on a speaking tour. Our sanctuary group was protecting and supporting her while she applied for political asylum. She had been kidnapped and tortured by the Salvadoran military after witnessing the abduction of a neighbor, even though she was a teenager who was not involved with the opposition. After several weeks of torture, her father managed to get her released on the condition that she leave the country. After arriving in the United States she had gotten married, only to have her husband deported to El Salvador and disappeared. I was deeply affected by her story. Now I knew someone who was a victim of torture and that person was a woman even younger than me. She was putting her own asylum case at risk by speaking publicly about her experiences.[3] Seeing a face on the problem, I felt a sense of outrage. From that moment on, there was no stopping me. I only worked at paid jobs enough to survive. The beginning of my activism was the end of my student career.

I plunged into political work, getting involved with the Rocky Mountain Peace Center and becoming vice chair of the local chapter of Committee in Solidarity with the People of El Salvador (CISPES). From mass mailings to newsletter production, I would do any needed task. I had always been a joker and storyteller so I joined a political theater group and coproduced a talk show on the local community radio station that featured guests discussing radical politics. I felt successful for the first time. People thought my contributions were valuable, and the radio show won public acclaim. I had an instant group of friends with whom I shared common values and goals.

In the small city of Boulder, the same crowd of activists worked on multiple issues. We organized demonstrations against Central Intelligence Agency (CIA) recruitment on the University of Colorado campus, which led to hundreds of people being arrested for blockading the career services center and ended CIA recruiting there.[4] We protested the Rocky Flats nuclear weapons plant. We threw blood at Colorado senator Bill Armstrong's office for voting for aid to the contras and Salvadoran military. In a campaign resembling a clandestine guerrilla operation, I hiked several times with a few other activists deep into the Nevada Test Site to try to stop a scheduled nuclear test by appearing on top of the blast hole.[5] The first time, I was arrested and spent twenty-one days in jail. The other times I was given fines that I never paid, or I was beaten and released. I was arrested so many times and became so well known to the local police that once, when I pulled up to the site of an antiapartheid demonstration with a friend, all the police radios announced in unison: "Michael Terry and Jimmy Walker have just arrived in Terry's Subaru."

During my solidarity work I learned about some North Americans who had joined the FMLN as combatants. Joe Sanderson was killed fighting in Morazán, El Salvador, in 1982.[6] At the CISPES convention in 1985 I met Lavonne Ishee, the widow of Carroll Ishee, who was killed in the early 1980s, also in Morazán.[7] That same year I heard Charles Clements speak about working unarmed as a doctor in conflictive areas in central El Salvador, as recounted in his book *Witness to War*.[8] It seemed natural to me to want to join the fight, akin to Americans enlisting in the military after Pearl Harbor, or the international volunteers who formed the Abraham Lincoln Brigade during the Spanish Civil War. I traveled to El Salvador and Nicaragua in 1986 hoping to meet a guerrilla unit, but I lacked contacts and people did not admit to knowing this kind of information. I was torn by my desire to become directly involved and the belief, shared by most U.S. activists, that our job was to change U.S. foreign policy.

After several years of intense activism, I became increasingly discouraged by the ineffectiveness of the opposition to U.S. policy in Central America. U.S. aid to El Salvador and Guatemala continued in the face of repeated atrocities committed by their militaries and public opinion against this aid. Funding for the contras in Nicaragua continued even after Congress prohibited it. Working to educate the public, our main strategy, seemed a waste of time since public opinion had almost no effect on policy. The people I worked with were more willing than most to risk arrest and personal discomfort, but our efforts weren't affecting the interests that supported and benefited from the wars. Spending a few days in jail or getting roughed up by cops was nothing compared to the sacrifices of ordinary Central Americans. I began to think that to have an impact, we needed to risk as much as the people who were fighting U.S. imperialism in their own countries.

## Joining the Struggle

Until 1989 health was never a focus of my activism. The only relevant experience I had had was visiting a midwife friend in 1986 who worked in Nicaragua. There I saw how health promoters were trained to work for the community, and I read *Where There Is No Doctor*.[9] The connection between power and health became clearer to me. When I happened to get a job that required completion of an emergency medical technician course, I was surprised by how much I enjoyed it and I began to consider a career as a paramedic. As a chronic underachiever, I hadn't previously thought about having a professional job. It occurred to me that I now had a real skill to offer the FMLN if I could figure out how to enlist.

The opportunity presented itself when friends came on my radio program in the spring of 1990 to talk about their trip to accompany refugees returning to Morazán from a refugee camp in Honduras. Their follow-up plans were to take a caravan of material aid down to their new settlement, Segundo Montes, the following winter. At that moment, I decided I would go with them and try to incorporate into the FMLN.

We spent the next several months acquiring materials and vehicles, and in December thirty people drove thirteen vehicles from Boulder to El Salvador. When the trip was over, most participants went home. A few stayed on in San Salvador as volunteers. I returned to Morazán, snuck past the army checkpoints on the predawn bus to Segundo Montes, and hitchhiked to Perquin, the "guerrilla capital."

With my rudimentary Spanish, I approached every uniformed person I saw and explained that I was trained as a medic and wanted to volunteer with the medical brigade. The guerrillas were relaxed and friendly, cleaning their weapons and waiting for orders. Each person told me to wait for an alternately tall, short, fat, skinny, light-, dark-haired guy who would talk to me. After a few days, during which I was informally interviewed by a few different *compas* (affectionate slang for *compañero*, meaning comrade or companion), a representative of the command structure told me that they had decided I couldn't incorporate. They appreciated my interest, but I should just leave.

Discouraged, I decided to return to San Salvador. As I was walking out of town, a European compa I had met a few days earlier called me over. He asked if I really did want to incorporate. Then he gave me a note, folded up and sealed in several layers of masking tape, and told me to take it to someone in Segundo Montes and follow his instructions. I found the person and he immediately put me to work repairing office equipment, beginning with printing presses. I had no idea how they worked but managed to get a few of them operational.

This overruling of the decision of the commander seemed odd to me at the time, but the FMLN had a much looser hierarchy than a conventional army. The European compa figured there was little risk in keeping an eye on me for a few weeks and then asking the commander to reconsider.

Soon, I was sent back to Perquin, to the press and propaganda unit for Morazán, and assigned to build a darkroom. The process of incorporation was informal. I simply showed up and people told me what to do. I felt I should be treated just like a Salvadoran compa so I began to take my turn on night guard duty, borrowing someone's rifle. After about two weeks, Paco Cutumay, the head of the unit, gave me a nine-millimeter pistol to tuck into my pants. I also kept insisting that I was a medic if they needed me, and I carried around the first aid supplies I had brought.

The Salvadoran army invaded Morazán a few months later, at the beginning of the rainy season. I was given an automatic rifle and our unit headed for the mountains, hiking through downpours all day. We slept on the ground, a few guys wrapped up together in sheets of plastic to keep warm. The plan was to meet up with the mobile guerrilla radio station, *Radio Venceremos* ("We will win"). I didn't have a proper backpack, just an oversized fanny pack over one shoulder, an ammo bag over the other, and an AK rifle. Their straps combined to produce a strangling effect. In addition—trying to make a good impression—I volunteered to carry two sacks of beans. We made the last leg of the trip in total darkness, stumbling and cursing along a muddy rut of trail with no flashlights allowed until we reached the radio unit's hidden location.

As in Boulder, I did whatever I could to be useful. I chopped wood, ground corn, and did guard duty, still insisting I was a medic. I had some fun making oral sound effects, like the sound of explosives, helicopters, trucks, and doors closing, for the comedy segment called *La Guacamaya Subversiva* (the subversive parrot), one of Radio Venceremos's most popular shows. There was a bit about George H. W. Bush entering a room wearing one cowboy boot and one deck shoe, "clump squeek, clump squeek." I even voiced Bush in one episode. Finally, without any explanation, I was reassigned to the medical brigade.

After living with the compas for several months, hearing many individual stories of how the armed struggle developed and why people chose to incorporate, I was more convinced than ever that it was a just and largely unavoidable response to overwhelming state violence. Even with uniforms and more sophisticated weapons, the people I worked with maintained the same beliefs as they did in 1981. Whether their role was to fire mortars, make tortillas, or build a town based upon a new model of development, everyone considered him- or herself a revolutionary.

## My Life as a Brigadista

On my first day with the medical brigade I was assigned to the mobile hospital. The hospital's doctor, Miguel, gave me a book to read on anesthesia and the unit's nurse showed me how to place an IV. Later, Miguel quizzed me on what I had read and told me I would be putting somebody under the next day. Suddenly, I was an anesthetist.

The guerrilla health system in Morazán was organized so that each unit had one or more *brigadistas de salud* ("medics") who would provide initial care of any wounds or illnesses. Ambulatory wounded or sick would be sent to the sole regional clinic, which would treat them until they were well enough to return to duty. The clinic changed location every few days for security reasons. Nonambulatory patients would be taken up to the hospital in the rear guard in the mountains where they could receive a higher level of treatment. The mobile hospital was a subunit of the clinic, comprised of the doctor and an anesthetist, a radio operator, and sometimes another brigadista. When wounded combatants required surgery, the mobile hospital would leave the clinic and hike to wherever the wounded were located. They would set up on a kitchen table and use a lantern and flashlights to operate at night because it was cooler. Eventually, they would either take the patients back to the clinic or send them up to the mountain hospital.

The medical brigade of the FMLN consisted of many foreign doctors and other health care providers working alongside Salvadoran counterparts. The doctor in the mobile hospital where I worked had come to El Salvador from Mexico in 1982 after his year of mandatory social service. The nurse was a former Peace Corps volunteer from the United States who had never participated in political action before joining the guerrillas. The doctor at the mountain

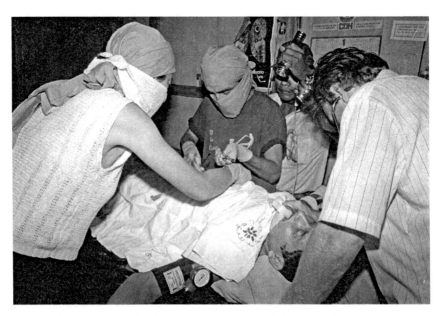

**Figure 13.1**  FMLN medical team operating by flashlight, somewhere in Morazán, El Salvador, 1991. *Left to right:* North American nurse, Dr. Miguel, unidentified brigadista, and Michael Terry.

Photo by Linda Hess Miller. Courtesy of the photographer.

hospital was Uruguayan. Others I met or heard of were from Ecuador, Mexico, Germany, and Spain. Some had been killed. The brigadistas were mostly women with limited education. Many of them had achieved very high skill levels in spite of minimal literacy. Libertad, the lead brigadista, had joined the FMLN in the early days of the war and was assigned to the medical brigade because she was a relatively well-educated high school graduate. She had been good friends with Carroll Ishee and was with him when he died. We began a friendship that continues today.

My first surgery went well—an amputation revision. In addition to amputations, we did hernia repairs, wound and burn debridements, and laparotomies after gunshots to the abdomen. Miguel also taught me how to suture. Because I arrived as the war was winding down—there were only small-scale skirmishes intended to influence the ongoing negotiations—we only did about two surgeries per week and all patients survived. Once, when I complained about the work of washing gauze, the brigadistas scolded me with tales of the 1989 offensive during which they spent each morning doing dressing changes and the whole afternoon and evening washing and sterilizing each patient's gauze.

When we weren't operating, I worked in the clinic doing wound care, consulting on common illnesses, and training new brigadistas on things I knew about or could learn from one of Miguel's books. The more serious problems at the clinic were dengue, psychiatric disorders, fractures, and sexually transmitted infections.

My nature as a person who is not easily embarrassed was put to use giving talks on safer sex and distributing condoms whenever we happened to be near a combat unit camp. The talks became famous because I used drill commands like *"Recargue!"* ("Reload") and *"Atención firmes!"* ("Attention!") to explain how to use a condom. The male compas started to call me *"Capitán Condón."* The talks were one of the few forms of entertainment. Guerrilla life consisted of long stretches of boredom punctuated by terror. Most combatants were young people, often with nothing to do, who might not live to see their next birthday. That resulted in a lot of sex.

Civilians living near the clinic also came for treatment. The only other medical services available north of the Torola River were provided by Médecins Sans Frontières (MSF). MSF had worked in Salvadoran refugee camps in Honduras and continued to provide services in Segundo Montes, the town the refugees founded after their return in 1989, through the postwar period. Notwithstanding their commitment, MSF personnel stood apart from the community because they lived in one of the nicest houses in northern Morazán, employed servants, and ran a generator almost constantly in an area where fuel was scarce.

We never worked with MSF staff, but we were friendly. While we shared similar interests and both groups included educated foreigners, we had to be careful because too much contact with us would tarnish MSF's reputation in the eyes of the Salvadoran government. We never sent them combatants who needed services we couldn't provide, but occasionally we would refer civilians to them for follow-up or for medicines.

Between the time I arrived and the signing of the peace accords, only once did I come close to shooting someone. The army targeted the medical brigade because we weren't trained fighters, and we were loaded with equipment but not heavily armed. We moved around constantly and sometimes had to leave suddenly after a warning, either from civilians or from intelligence, that an attack was imminent. A few times, helicopters firing General Electric Gatling guns shot up one part of a valley while we hid out in another.

But one night, while I was brushing my teeth by candlelight, the sentry reported some suspicious activity at a nearby house. Our position was within range of enemy reconnaissance teams. Compelled to investigate, the sentry and

**Figure 13.2**　Michael Terry receiving his rank of subsargento at an event shortly before the signing of peace accords, December 31, 1991. *From left to right:* Comandante Licho, Comandante Jonas (Jorge Meléndez), and Michael Terry.

Photo by Linda Hess Miller. Courtesy of the photographer.

another compa went to the house while Miguel and I stood guard at two dirt roads nearby. Soon a man came walking up the road toward me in the dark. He was holding a long tubular item on his shoulder. I dropped to one knee, took off the safety, and aimed at his belly button. I waited, trying to decide if I should challenge him or shoot him. After a few more seconds, he took the tube off his shoulder, connected it to the community spigot, and walked back the way he came. I was relieved, to say the least.

## The Postwar Struggle for Health

The functioning of the medical brigade changed after the signing of peace accords between the FMLN and the Salvadoran government on January 16, 1992. The combatants were concentrated into UN supervised camps around the country and lived there for six to nine months while weapons were decommissioned and resettlement arrangements were made. Each camp had access to a clinic, and I worked in two clinics in northern Morazán. The clinics continued to attend to the health needs of the combatants, but their focus shifted to primary care.

Around that time a doctor from Panama, Marianela Landau, arrived and was assigned to supervise the clinic in Perquin. She replaced Miguel, who was chosen to run a peace accords-mandated program to provide specialized medical attention to the demobilized combatants. After twelve years of war, many had significant health problems that the medical brigade had been unable to address. Often the conditions were disabling; many people had more than one problem. A month or so later Miguel sent for me to oversee program logistics and ensure adequate care for combatants from the eastern part of the country.

Recognizing that the government health system on its own did not have the capacity, or, according to some, the willingness to care for the influx of combatants, the Pan American Health Organization (PAHO) financed the program and jointly administered it with the FMLN's January 16th Foundation. Private physicians with privileges at the national hospital were paid a monthly salary to see the program's patients. Previously, these doctors typically favored private patients over public clinic patients, sometimes walking out on a full waiting room at the public hospital to attend to a single patient at their private practice. The program changed this dynamic, demanding that physicians provide quality service to ex-combatants and even firing a few doctors who didn't comply.

At the end of the demobilization process in late 1992, many of the compas from Morazán, taking advantage of terms in the peace accords, settled on land in Usulután along the Pacific coast. Unlike the idyllic but not very agriculturally productive mountains and pine forests of northern Morazán, the Pacific coast is hot and flat with fertile volcanic soil. Before the war led to depopulation of much of the region, it had been the site of large cotton plantations. The specific area offered to the compas, along the eastern side of the lower Lempa River (the *Bajo Lempa*), had reverted almost to jungle, and lacked services of any kind. Marianela, the Panamanian doctor, had the idea that the clinic she was running should move with the ex-combatants so they would have access to health care. The PAHO program was ending, so she asked me and the woman I was seeing, Laura Turiano, a health volunteer from New York State, to come with her.

Laura was initially resistant. She had grown close to the family she was living with and had been thinking that I could work with her in the tiny clinic in Calavera, Morazán, where she had been training local health promoters. The unbearable year-round heat and mosquitoes of the coast also seemed like a bad trade for Calavera's pleasant mountainside environment. The decision to move came when the NGO she worked for, the *Asociación de Mujeres Salvadoreñas* (AMS) was approved to implement a USAID-sponsored maternal and child health project, PROSAMI (*Proyecto de Salud Materno-Infantil*).[10] Although Laura had worked on the application process and prepared a plan for a basic primary care system in the area, PROSAMI had one-size-fits-all requirements that had nothing to do with local reality. For example, all Salvadoran NGOs receiving funds were required to serve a population of ten thousand people with ten health promoters, rather than allowing NGOs to define the appropriate population size for their particular project. PROSAMI disregarded key factors in making this a requirement, including population density, transport problems, topographical barriers, weather, and community size, which could limit how much ground a promoter could reasonably cover. This policy forced some NGOs to poach the clients or health promoters of other NGOs, generating conflict, especially when the NGOs were affiliated with different factions of the FMLN.[11]

Moreover, the doctors hired would not be living in Calavera, thus reproducing the typical rural health ministry clinic situation in which the staff doctor from the city minimized their time at the rural post, never really getting to know the area. Support for meaningful community participation in PROSAMI was minimal. The huge amount of money PROSAMI was offering the small and inexperienced AMS, however, kept its leaders from raising any concerns about the project. In the end, Laura felt that her services would be more needed in the Bajo Lempa, where we would be starting essentially from scratch.

The settlers who gradually filled in the eastern Bajo Lempa included returning refugees and internally displaced communities, demobilized compas, and two groups of demobilized government soldiers. Early on, people squatted on the land, but over several years titles were resolved. In other regions some communities in resistance to the government during the war had developed their own health systems, using mostly community health workers. However, in the Bajo Lempa no system existed because the area was just being resettled. Our first task was to meet the communities and survey their resources. Among the demobilized compas there were highly skilled brigadistas, like Libertad, who came with her partner, an FMLN ex-combatant, and their young son. The returning refugees also included health promoters and birth attendants of varying skill and experience. Many of the communities had established fairly well organized systems of self-governance during their time in refugee or internally displaced settlements.

An NGO called CODECOSTA was formed to coordinate the development activities in the zone. Most eastern Bajo Lempa communities, except the two settlements of ex-government soldiers and their families, affiliated with CODE-COSTA. Our clinic was also affiliated, but we functioned relatively independently.

Marianela put me in charge of the clinic itself, located in a settlement of disabled compas who had returned to El Salvador from Cuba the year before and established the *Cooperativa San Hilario.* In 1986, then president Napoleón Duarte agreed to let the FMLN send people who needed rehabilitation to Cuba, in exchange for his daughter, whom the FMLN had kidnapped. The compas had received excellent care and were busy developing income-generating projects when we arrived. The members of a civilian workers' cooperative lived in the same area, on a former hacienda turned over to them in the 1972 land reform.

Laura and I built a small shack with a zinc roof under an enormous Guanacaste tree. We furnished our first home with the table, chairs, stovetop, and propane tank that I received, like all combatants, as part of the demobilization process. Soon, we had neighbors and their animals living on both sides. On the left was a pair of sisters, the only members of their family to survive the massacres of the early 1980s in Morazán. One had a three-year-old with severe epilepsy. On the right lived a man with his fourteen-year-old daughter, who had been a cook in one of the camps, and her baby. The baby's father, a compa who was living in a different settlement with another woman, had abandoned them. The typical refugee plank and zinc dwellings kept us dry, but everyone knew everyone else's business.

Marianela and Laura worked to coordinate the nascent local health services. They set up the existing health promoters with supplies, established community health committees, and identified needs and goals for the system as a whole. Over the next year, almost every woman received a gynecological exam, composting latrines were installed, and a training program for midwives was funded and implemented. At the clinic, with backup from Laura and

**Figure 13.3**  Map of El Salvador by Thomas Turiano.
Courtesy of Laura Turiano.

Marianela, I treated everything from wounds to malaria to urinary obstruction, using borrowed trucks or even my motorcycle as an ambulance when necessary.

Caring for patients came naturally to me. I realized that medicine was not just for eggheads with long years of schooling. I could read medical books and figure out what patients needed. I also established close relationships with my patients; somehow I almost always knew how to handle persons in emotional distress. I also found, once again, that gentle humor at the right time was a powerful antidote to stress and helped reduce tension among people and build trust. As a demobilized compa, I was readily accepted in the community.

The overall goal of FMLN-linked community organizations was to reform the health system to make it responsive to community needs and subject to community participation. The *Declaration of Alma-Ata* served as our model (see chapter 12). One objective was to ensure that the health ministry legitimized the former brigadistas and other popular health workers so that they would have an income (reinsertion into civilian life was a major concern at the time), and to ensure that community health workers were actually from the community. We wanted to create a functioning alternative health system financed by local sources and external donations and then, once in place, have the government assume its funding, now that the FMLN had been turned into a legitimate political party by the peace accords.

Then MSF got involved. Around early 1993, they received a contract from the European Community to address health issues including water and health system revitalization in the Bajo Lempa and elsewhere in Usulután. We initially hoped that MSF would be an ally; however, its new country director only grudgingly met with the local communities and existing NGOs working in health. MSF hired health promoters away from community-based groups and sent them to work in other areas. It also intervened to prevent the legalization of a health center built on community-owned land that had been financed by the family of Marta Gonzáles, a Spanish physician killed in combat during the war. They spread rumors about our motives. After a while, we suspected that MSF's goal was to replicate the prewar system and then hand it over to the government. Several years later, our suspicions were confirmed when we read "'Popular' Health and the State: The Dialectics of the Peace Process in El Salvador" by Sandy Smith-Nonini.[12] This paper chronicles the unsuccessful attempt by community organizations in Chalatenango to obtain Ministry of Health recognition for their highly developed primary health care systems and health promoters. The process closely paralleled our contemporaneous experience with MSF. As Smith-Nonini describes, "confrontations grew out of a reverberating dialectic between the Ministry's commitment to an extremely centralized, biomedical model dominated by physicians and the popular system's commitment to health care delivery with a strong degree of community control . . . based on local lay health promoters."[13]

Before leaving, about a year later, MSF dug a few wells—in places where the local people thought (correctly) that the water would be brackish—but did not build a desired water system.[14] They also built a clinic on land owned by one community that the Ministry of Health agreed to staff. Subsequently, however, the staffing was minimal compared to other nearby Ministry-owned health units. From 1994 until 2009 Libertad, the former brigadista, now with a bachelor's degree in nursing, was the only consistent staff at the clinic.

The FMLN-affiliated NGOs along the eastern coast, including ours, began to consider PROSAMI funding; it appeared to be the best hope of financing health work and health promoters' salaries. We thought the promoters might have a better chance of being recognized by the government with USAID's seal of approval. As a group, we negotiated with PROSAMI to train our own health promoters, with the idea that our training would be more comprehensive and incorporate the values of women's empowerment and community participation. We used the funding to train all of the promoters, not just those hired by PROSAMI. When the work got underway, the promoters not hired—who continued to do everything not covered by PROSAMI—resented the relatively high salaries of the PROSAMI promoters. When corruption was uncovered at CODECOSTA, the project was taken away.

Ultimately, the Ministry of Health didn't hire any of the health promoters we trained or worked with; almost none of them work in health today. Many public health practitioners and academics have praised PROSAMI for contracting with local NGOs and demonstrating improvements in maternal and child health indicators.[15] From our perspective, however, PROSAMI was a mediocre, vertical health program. Raising health indicators is easy when basic services are applied to areas where they were previously nonexistent. The PROSAMI and MSF projects brought an end to the hopes of a comprehensive community-based primary care system in the Bajo Lempa.

### Bringing the Lessons Home

Despite significant activism in El Salvador around health, only minimal progress was made in the years following the peace accords because the government remained under the control of the right-wing ARENA party. But the March 2009 election of FMLN candidate Mauricio Funes to the presidency has resulted in significant social policy improvements around old-age pensions, school meals, job training, and other poverty alleviation measures, even amid the challenge of enhancing democratic governance. Three of his appointees to the health ministry, including Minister of Health Dr. María Isabel Rodríguez, are connected to the People's Health Movement (PHM), an international network of health activists and organizations working toward the Alma-Ata vision of "health for all."[16] The appointees have a real commitment to health as a human right and to primary health care: user fees have been eliminated in the public system, hundreds of comprehensive primary health care units have been created in remote rural areas, and a 2012 medicines law addresses rampant pharmaceutical profiteering. Dr. Rodríguez has also become a forceful advocate for "health sovereignty" in international cooperation, so that nationally defined agendas for health equity in El Salvador and other developing countries can be realized.[17] Yet the needs remain significant, and many reforms continue to be stymied by the global economic context and the state's fiscal problems, as well as the ARENA-dominated legislature and medical establishment.

We didn't know it back in the 1980s and 1990s, but the struggle for health in El Salvador was a PHM incubator. U.S. citizens who had worked in El Salvador were among the very few North Americans present at PHM's founding assembly in Bangladesh in 2000. Activists with a connection to El Salvador make up the backbone of PHM in the United States—Laura has been involved with PHM since 2005—and are disproportionately represented among its international founders and leaders. Many others have their roots in the liberation struggles of Southern Africa, Bangladesh, and Central America.

In mid-1994, Laura and I returned to the United States and trained as physician assistants. We continue to be in solidarity with the people we lived and worked with in El Salvador through my service on the board of Voices on the Border.[18] Today I work in a public emergency department and teach in a physician assistant program. My initial success as a health worker was related to my relationship with my patients: I was treating my own comrades in arms. Now as a professional integrated into the U.S. health care system, I have resisted becoming just a cog in the bill-generating machine. In my first job at a community health center, I was a shop steward for the staff union. I make a point of connecting with all my patients, especially the agitated and mentally ill. I try to set an example for my colleagues and students by ensuring that my working relationship is with the patient and not the chart. As a committed leftist, I feel most at home in the county hospital (where physician assistants assume greater responsibility) treating patients without insurance.

However, I know that I am pulling people out of the water rather than keeping them from falling in. The emergency department is where people go when they have no other option, and we can often do little to help except give them a sandwich. Choosing to work with the poor and treating each patient with dignity is in its own way a political act, but it is not enough. As in El Salvador, by the time many people reach me, their bodies and psyches are worn down from enduring conditions of great inequity. The Salvadorans had certain advantages—a degree of social connection and a sense of common purpose—that gave them a resilience I seldom see here.

I sometimes think about my work in the U.S. medical system as a form of training for a return to work in a crisis situation. Just as when I left in 1990, political activism in the United States feels like shoveling steam. With my own professionalization and commitments to a family, I had, until recently, become less politically active and less willing to take risks than before. This has been a mistake, but I am not alone in having made it. With few exceptions, the Left in the United States has been even more timid and fragmented than it was in the 1980s, although the crises we face as a nation and a planet are more severe.

Only the Occupy Movement has shown any chance of overturning the status quo, so I have incorporated into Occupy Oakland Medics. We must choose now, or soon be forced to choose, which side we are on and what we are willing to do for it.

## Notes

1. The United States provided more than $1 billion between 1980 and 1991 to the El Salvadoran armed forces and other security forces alone, in addition to approximately $3.2 billion in economic assistance. Seth G. Jones, Olga Oliker, Peter Chalk, C. Christine Fair, Rollie Lal, and James Dobbins, *Securing Tyrants or Fostering Reform? U.S. Internal Security Assistance to Repressive and Transitioning Regimes* (Santa Monica, CA: RAND Corporation, 2006).

2. The sanctuary movement was a network of U.S. congregations that defied the government by providing Central American refugee families with housing, legal representation, food, medical care, and employment. For a concise overview of the sanctuary movement and U.S. immigration policy, see Susan Gzesh, "Central Americans and Asylum Policy in the Reagan Era," www.migrationinformation.org (accessed September 20, 2009).

3. The United States regularly deported Central Americans, who were likely to be tortured and killed upon their return.

4. Tony Vellela, *New Voices: Student Activism in the '80s and '90s* (Boston: South End Press, 1988), 61–62.

5. Frank Clancy, "Showdown at Ground Zero," *Mother Jones Magazine*, November 1986: 38–46.

6. Héctor Tobar, "An American Adventurer's Death in El Salvador," *Los Angeles Times*, August 23, 2008.

7. Michael W. Drudge, "Salvadoran Rebels Report Death of American Fighting for Them," *St. Petersburg Times*, January 25, 1984.

8. Charles Clements, *Witness to War: An American Doctor in El Salvador* (New York: Bantam, 1984).

9. David Werner with Carol Thuman and Jane Maxwell, *Where There Is No Doctor* (Berkeley, CA: Hesperian Foundation, 1992).

10. PROSAMI was a highly praised USAID-funded maternal and child health project implemented in several countries in Central America. In El Salvador it ran from 1993 until 1998 and funded Salvadoran NGOs to provide basic maternal and child health care through community health promoters supervised by physicians. Each NGO received a Jeep Cherokee, essential medicines and other supplies, and two years' funding to pay health promoters and other staff salaries.

11. The FMLN was a coalition of five separate political parties that maintained separate military and grassroots organizing structures.

12. Sandy Smith-Nonini, "'Popular' Health and the State: Dialectics of the Peace Process in El Salvador," *Social Science and Medicine* 44 (1997): 635–645.

13. Smith-Nonini, "'Popular' Health and the State," 638.

14. In 2002, the communities raised money and independently built a system to pipe in potable water from outside of the contaminated former cotton plantation area. Asociación Intercomunal de Comunidades Unidas para el Desarollo Económico y Social del Bajo Lempa, "Proyecto de los Ultimos Dos Años," www.comunidadesunidas-es .org/?page_id=117 (accessed September 20, 2009).

15. Sandy Smith-Nonini, "Health 'Anti-Reform' in El Salvador: Community Health NGOs and the State in the Neoliberal Era," *Political and Legal Anthropology Review (PoLAR)* 21 (1998): 99–113.

16. People's Health Movement, *www.phmovement.org;* Françoise Barten, Mario Rovere, and Eduardo Espinoza, eds., *Salud Para Todos una Meta Posible. Pueblos Movilizados y Gobiernos Comprometidos en un Nuevo Contexto Global* (Buenos Aires: IIED—América Latina Publicaciones, 2009).

17. Equipo Editorial, "Avances y Proyecciones de la Reforma del Sistema de Salud Salvadoreño: Cuatro Entrevistas Acerca de los Escenarios Actuales del Proceso de Reforma de Salud en El Salvador," *Salud: Pensamiento Crítico y Diálogo Nacional en Torno a la Salud* 1(1) (2011): 6–45; Ministerio de Salud, "Capítulo 14: Dimensión Internacional," *Informe de Labores 2010–2011* (junio 2010–mayo 2011) (San Salvador, El Salvador: Ministerio de Salud El Salvador, 2011); María Isabel Rodríguez, *Construyendo la Esperanza: Estrategias y Recomendaciones en Salud 2009–2014* (San Salvador, 2009).

18. Voices on the Border, www.votb.org.

# Chapter 14

# Health and Human Rights in Latin America, and Beyond

## A Lawyer's Experience with Public Health Internationalism

Alicia Ely Yamin

I was in Baborigame to document military atrocities, but the helicopter going to the military base was full that morning. So I stayed behind with the nuns, who were the only source of health care for the impoverished Tepehuac Indians in this remote area of northern Mexico. By the time his mother brought him in, the infant was so dehydrated and weak that he couldn't even cry. Given the nuns' meager supplies, there was nothing to be done but watch as he faded from his tiny little body. His mother held his body and cried softly. The old canard that in other cultures they feel less grief over the loss of a child because it is a common event seems a cynical justification for indifference in a world of gross inequity. If nothing else in doing human rights fieldwork, we become painfully aware of the myriad textures of human suffering.

Yet what this mother did not express was the anger that I felt—that her community lived without adequate water, sanitation, and food or accessible health care—and this was why her son had died. Although she recognized the military's detentions, tortures, and theft of livestock and destruction of property as human rights violations—indeed, denouncing those abuses to my delegation is what had brought her down the mountain to the nuns' infirmary—her outrage did not extend to her living conditions. Human rights lawyers traffic in righteous indignation, and we find endless opportunities to feed this outrage. But what was striking on that cold morning in 1993 was the absence of the mother's sense of the terrible injustice of her son's death.

## Human Rights Beginnings

Many of the defining moments of my life have occurred abroad, which seems perfectly natural given that I grew up in a family where what happened "out there" in the world did not seem so far away. My grandfather, whom I adored, was a housepainter. He was a Wobbly (a member of the Industrial Workers of the World) and an organizer for the Lincoln Brigade in the Spanish Civil War. My father lied about his age to fight against Hitler. My mother, who grew up in Argentina and whose family remained there, dedicated her career to helping Latin American artists in exile in the United States. Friends, godparents, and honorary aunts and uncles came from all over the globe—especially from South America. I always had the feeling that but for certain military coups, my parents would have chosen to raise us in Buenos Aires. From early on, identity and friendships—and, in turn, solidarity—transcended nationality.

It was my connection to Argentina and Latin America that drew me into human rights work, and not the other way around. I was still very young when the activities of the right-wing death squad, the Triple A, and then the full-blown Dirty War converted this land of family stories into a hell on earth, an example of the evil human beings were capable of inflicting on one another.[1] But it was in college that I began really to see the connections between gaping social inequities in the region, on the one hand, and the military dictatorships that were committing rampant abuses while maintaining oligarchic control over resources, on the other. I also began to understand the role of the United States government in propping up those dictatorships and pursuing its own corporate interests in one country after another.

In 1988, I went to Harvard Law School after spending a year in Argentina taking in the silent marches of the *madres* (mothers) of the Plaza de Mayo, the coup attempts by disgruntled military officers, and the profound economic and social convulsions of that country's return to democracy. At law school, I immersed myself in the Human Rights Program and found in human rights a language and a framework through which to channel my convictions, as well as a community of like-minded people who saw in human rights an opportunity to promote social justice. Some of those friends formed the Harvard Study Group on Iraq, which sent the first delegation into Iraq after the first Gulf War in 1991 to assess the effects of the U.S. bombings on nutritional status and water and sanitation. The Center for Economic and Social Rights was formed out of that study group, where I currently serve as chair of the board.

I graduated with a fellowship to do human rights work in Mexico with a local NGO. My husband, who had similarly just graduated from business school, and I were married on a Saturday night and boarded a flight the next morning for Mexico City. By Monday morning, I was working on my first case, searching for a boy who had gone missing—a teenager who had been playing soccer with his friends and was caught urinating in public by the police; he ended up dead in a jail cell and the police tried to make it look like a suicide.

Mexico is notorious for police abuse and corruption, and in the early 1990s when I lived there the most feared and loathed of all police organizations was the Federal Judicial Police (*Policía Judicial Federal*, or PJF)—which was responsible for investigating federal crimes, including drug trafficking. When I started examining records of torture and extrajudicial executions closely—from complaints filed with the NGO and with the National Human Rights Commission (NHRC), as well as newspaper accounts—it struck me that many of the same PJF agents were involved in multiple incidents. I decided to document the pattern of abuses, which suggested not only impunity but complicity from the very top echelons of the Mexican Attorney General's Office.

The NGO that had initially sponsored me was reticent to make the claims public for security reasons. But, out of a combination of naïveté, indignation, and stubbornness, I persisted. I took my evidence to Teresa Jardí, a human rights lawyer who was in the process of forming a new human rights NGO, affiliated with the archdiocese of Mexico City. Jardí, a lawyer and the widow of a renowned attorney who had defended many accused of terrorism in the 1970s, was intrepid, and immediately outraged by what I showed her. We agreed to complete the investigation together, publish it, and send it to the United Nations; I agreed to help her found the human rights group.

The report created an enormous scandal when it came out in 1992.[2] The UN Committee Against Torture issued scathing statements about Mexico's culture of impunity. Ignacio Morales Lechuga, the attorney general, resigned and Jorge Carpizo, then president of the NHRC, was appointed as his successor. Of course, that was not in any way the end of the corruption or the impunity, but the NHRC has subsequently tracked the careers of officers allegedly involved in abuses.

However, there was a price to be paid. Our car was broken into; our home phone was tapped (as was the public phone on our block); our mail was opened; the streetlights on our street were knocked out; I was perpetually followed; and agents even came to our home in the middle of the night to question and harass me. But Teresa Jardí had it far worse; she received death threats and had to have police escorts (from a different police organization) everywhere she went; so did her family.

I was close in age to Jardí's two sons and she treated me more like a daughter than a colleague. I adored her and learned from her a model of womanhood that I had never known growing up. When she went to remote areas where we were told she was in particular jeopardy, I went with her. I slept in a single bed with her as a kind of human shield, in the hope that having to kill a *gringa* would be some deterrent to murdering her. In retrospect, I suppose that showed solidarity; at the time I just couldn't bear to lose her.

Mexico was and is a dangerous place for human rights advocates. Eventually regimes changed in the PJF, power shifted, and the death threats against Jardí stopped; others were not so lucky. Digna Ochoa, a nun and lawyer with whom we worked, was assassinated in 2001 for investigating military abuses. After we moved back to the United States, Mexican friends would stay with us in New York as a respite from the constant, wearing stress of living with the threats and harassment. Just recently, my husband and I were in Mexico with our children and saw Pilar Noriega, a dear friend and one of the bravest human rights lawyers I've ever met who is still living with her police escort over a decade later. All these years later, I felt the familiar oppressiveness wash over me, and the simultaneous relief and guilt of knowing I could leave.

## Applying Human Rights to Health

I came to health through human rights, steeped in the lexicons of justice and social change, and not of healing. I already felt strongly that there was a need to expand on traditional human rights frameworks. Until the 1990s, there was an almost exclusive focus among the mainstream human rights community on civil and political rights—for example, the right to be free from torture, due process, freedoms of association and expression—as opposed to economic and social rights (ESR) such as health, education, shelter, and food. Far too often, human rights advocates and the reports they wrote relegated the conditions of people's lives to background considerations rather than perceiving them as indicative of equally important rights violations. It was in those years of living in Mexico that the death of the infant in Baborigame—and so many other incidents—convinced me at a visceral level of the need to shift the focus of my own human rights work and career. Increasingly, the civil and political rights framework seemed frustratingly inadequate to me if we were really going to "speak truth to power," as the old slogan goes.

In those years I had witnessed up close not only how disproportionately the poor and marginalized suffered from torture, arbitrary detention, and other civil rights violations, but also how violations of ESR illuminated fault lines of discrimination in a society. Working in and with indigenous communities from Chihuahua to Chiapas, it became clear that the lack of healthy living conditions—for example, water, sanitation, nutrition, shelter—as well as access to health care was a principal form in which rural *campesinos* experienced poverty and marginalization in Mexico. After years of fieldwork in countries throughout Latin America, as well as in Africa and India, I have found this lack of access to healthy preconditions as well as health care to be a constant marker of exclusion for many disadvantaged groups in society.[3]

The understanding of health as a matter of rights does not guarantee anything.[4] It is certainly hollow in the absence of social mobilization and accountability mechanisms. Yet, the way in which we think about things changes what we do about them. Without an understanding of health as a question of rights rather than charity—by those affected, as well as by decision makers and people who live comfortable lives in the global North—we will not be able to transform the power relations that underpin the structural inequalities which, in turn, produce the persistent misery and suffering faced by so much of the world.

In the mid-1990s, when I received training in public health, I was fortunate to become part of an international health and human rights movement that was beginning to take shape. Among other things, two extraordinarily important global conferences took place that forged significant bridges between sexual and reproductive health and rights. At the International Conference on Population and Development (ICPD) in Cairo in 1994, a dramatic conceptual shift changed the underlying paradigm of population policies from one driven by demographic imperatives to one that placed reproductive and sexual rights, and women's choices, squarely at the center. A year later at the fourth World Conference on Women held in Beijing, a broad understanding of women's health and the forces determining their health was reaffirmed: "Women's health involves their emotional, social and physical well-being and is determined by the social, political and economic context of their lives, as well as by biology. . . . A major barrier for women to the achievement of the highest attainable standard of health is inequality, both between men and women and among women in different geographical regions, social classes and indigenous and ethnic groups."[5] Echoing earlier formulations of health in the World Health Organization (WHO) Constitution, the conference declarations made it clear that health is a product of social (and power) relations, and of equality and nondiscrimination—that is, of fundamental questions relating to social justice—just as much as of biological processes.[6]

Of course, the language enshrined in the conference declarations was the culmination of years of work by scholars and activists around the world. Moreover, sexual and reproductive health was not the only domain in which the linkages between public health and human rights were being forged. In fact, since the 1970s, strands of work on torture's health effects, disability rights, humanitarian emergencies, and HIV/AIDS, among other things had been coalescing into a distinct field of research and practice calling itself "health and human rights."[7] I was fortunate to study with Jonathan Mann, founder of the Francois-Xavier Bagnoud Center on Health and Human Rights at the Harvard School of Public Health, who was a pivotal force behind the creation of this international movement.[8]

It was an exciting time to be entering the public health field; there were great expectations about the promise of applying human rights analysis and strategies to health. However, we quickly realized that there was an enormous gap between the aspirational language of the conference declarations and the operationalization of reproductive rights and health in practice.[9] Institutional efforts easily tended to become diffuse or to repackage the same programs with different names.

Moreover, it was disappointing to find that the early years of advocacy and research in the United States on health and human rights mirrored the larger human rights movement's focus on civil and political rights, mostly relating to questions of autonomy and consent, and the health effects of torture. With important exceptions—principally from the sexual and reproductive rights field—relatively few people in the United States were devoting attention to the conceptualization and implementation of the right to health per se, or to the other ESR underpinning the social determinants of health.[10] However, I was soon to find a very different reality in Latin America.

### Building a Health Rights Movement in Peru

In 1999, my husband and I moved—with an infant in tow—from New York, where I was staff attorney at the Law and Policy Project and a faculty member of the Mailman School of Public Health at Columbia University, to Lima, Peru. I had been working throughout the region for years and was as much a participant in the Latin American human rights community as I was in the United States. It was a fascinating time to be moving to Peru, and I immediately became involved in a nascent movement to articulate health-related demands as rights and to locate rights on the agenda for democratization under the autocratic regime of Alberto Fujimori.

There is no doubt that the conditions under which we do international work determine the nature of our relationships with local activists and scholars, as well as the work itself. When I moved to Peru, with the immensely generous support of the late dean Allan Rosenfield, my department head and direct supervisor, I was able to retain my position at Columbia while at the same time having no preset, fixed notions for how I was going to contribute to research and advocacy on the right to health. This freedom was essential to allowing me to participate in many aspects of this incipient health rights movement as an equal, rather than as an outsider with a specific project I wanted to achieve and the need to defend some institutional terrain.

If there is any country that is ripe for an approach to health that goes beyond the biomedical arena and links health with basic rights, it is Peru.[11] In the region of the world that has the greatest disparities in income between rich and poor, Peru's record stands out as among the worst.[12] Over half of the population lives below the poverty line and approximately 24 percent lives in extreme poverty. In Peru, just as in Mexico and elsewhere I had worked, poverty means lack of access to education and health care, adequate living conditions, sufficient potable water and basic sanitation, food security, and employment.

By 1999, health was already being defined as a site of the struggle for the country's democratization, in large measure because of revelations relating to the Fujimori administration's campaign of systematic sterilization without informed consent. Giulia Tamayo, a fiery lawyer with whom I instantly became friends, and her colleagues at the regional office of the Latin American and Caribbean Committee for the Defense of Women's Rights (CLADEM), documented that between 1996 and 1998 over 260,000 people—overwhelmingly indigenous women—had been sterilized without appropriate consent.[13] The revelations created enormous scandals on multiple levels, including a U.S. congressional investigation of USAID's role, as the agency had underwritten much of Peru's family planning program.[14]

The response by women's rights groups to the sterilizations would not have been possible without the international conferences in the mid-1990s. Reflecting the frameworks set out in the ICPD and at Beijing, the sterilization campaign was framed by women's rights groups as emblematic not only of Fujimori's autocratic social engineering, but of the lack of full citizenship for rural indigenous women in Peruvian society.[15] Demands for the ability of women to make free and informed decisions about their own bodies and for justice for those who had been subject to abuse became inextricably linked to calls for justice and democratization more broadly.

Women's reproductive rights were the focal point, but not the only health rights that had been trampled by the Fujimori regime. By 1999, it was clear that the proliferation of neoliberal reforms, pushed in large measure by the U.S. government and international financial institutions, had had a serious impact on health and retirement benefits.[16] Other scandals erupted relating to inappropriate treatment regimes for tuberculosis patients and the lack of treatment for HIV/AIDS patients.[17]

The year 2000 was nothing short of surreal in Peru as Fujimori at first appeared committed to engineering his illegitimate third term in office by any means necessary and then, after scandal upon scandal erupted, eventually fled the country and faxed his resignation from Japan. During that tumultuous year of protests and marches, a number of civil society initiatives were beginning to take shape, which took as their premise that transformational change was required in Peruvian health policy in order to create the conditions for true democracy and the enjoyment of all human rights.

Among these initiatives was a program I cofounded with Mario Ríos on human rights and health at the *Asociación Pro Derechos Humanos* (Association for Human Rights or APRODEH), the largest human rights NGO in Peru. Mario and I assumed joint responsibility for almost all tasks—from strategic planning to grassroots education and outreach to fundraising. There were all the inevitable differences in work styles and vision, but we were able to work through those disagreements and APRODEH gave me complete authority to speak on behalf of the organization publicly and in relations with U.S. and other foreign groups. Workshops we organized around the country led to the creation of a national coalition on the right to health composed of local human rights NGOs and community-based organizations, health practitioners, and advocacy groups.

In 2002, two other networks were formed, both of which also aimed at promoting rights-based approaches to health.[18] Although these three networks all had different compositions and outlooks, as collectives, they shared two important features. First, they were created as mechanisms to increase active participation and social monitoring (*vigilancia ciudadana*), which became the centerpieces of the burgeoning rights-based health movement in Peru. The second key feature that these networks shared was their inclusion and vision of health professionals as allies in the struggle for democracy in Peru. There was a common understanding that the underlying causes of violations of the right to health in Peru (as elsewhere) are largely institutional and structural, rather than individual. Indeed, policies in the health sector often violated the labor rights of health workers as well as the rights of patients.

The insight that in order for health professionals to become allies in a struggle for democratization of the country they needed to be educated in human rights led to the formation of another group: EDHUCASalud—translated to Human Rights Education Applied to Health. EDHUCASalud began as a small group of medical and other students who talked passionately about health and human rights over pizza in my apartment, among other venues. In 2000, I was able to help them secure funding from the Ford Foundation, and EDHUCASalud carried out a series of ambitious education and documentation activities. In 2005 EDHUCASalud became a member of the International Federation of Health and Human Rights Organizations—an important network for the young Peruvians and a testament to how far they had come. Almost ten years after EDHUCASalud was founded, the members of this group are no longer kids; they have grown into extraordinarily accomplished physicians, lawyers, and public health professionals.

In his report on his site visit to Peru in June 2004, Paul Hunt, then UN Special Rapporteur on the Right to Health, commented on how impressed he was with "many aspects of the work of civil society, such as NGOs, church groups, patient groups, health professional associations and academics, including their familiarity with and commitment to the right to health."[19] There is no doubt that Peru is far ahead of most countries—including many in the global North—in terms of having a significant number of citizens informed about and active in promoting rights-based approaches to health policymaking and programming. In 2002, an Observatory on the Right to Health was established to monitor and create cutting edge scholarship on the pressing debates with respect to rights-based approaches. Even small NGOs have adopted explicitly rights-based frameworks and discourse for their work.[20] In academia, the Universidad Peruana Cayetano Heredia created a unit on human rights within its public health faculty and, supported by seed funding from the United Kingdom's Department for International Development, has been able to offer a diploma course in health and human rights.

However, it would be misleading to romanticize what has been accomplished in Peru; building and sustaining movements is a long-term proposition. Ten years later, the health rights movement remains small and highly concentrated in Lima. The broad use of a rights-based discourse has been enormously important in social mobilization, but it has also been accompanied by a dilution of its more radical implications. Rights-based approaches have too often been reduced to arguments for tinkering with the social insurance scheme or other health care delivery issues without fundamentally reappraising the structural inequalities built into the Peruvian health system and the social determinants of health. The wider use of references to human rights by many state and non-state actors and the media has too often devolved into sloganeering, divorced from its original challenge to the powers-that-be.

For me, the years I lived in Peru came to define who I was both professionally and personally. Grassroots advocacy work is never a nine-to-five

**Figure 14.1** Alicia Ely Yamin on a fact-finding mission in Puno, Peru, as director of Research and Investigations for Physicians for Human Rights. *From left to right:* Lorenzo Quispe Vargas, Alicia Ely Yamin, and Geronimo (local shaman and partero). Tococori Choquechambi, Puno, Peru, 2007.

Courtesy of Marion Brown on behalf of Physicians for Human Rights.

proposition, and everything during those years of acute political turmoil and movement-building took on a heightened intensity. I grew immensely attached to Peru and to the friends who had become part of the texture of my life. When I became director of research and investigations at Physicians for Human Rights (PHR) in 2005, I sought appropriate projects that would draw me back to Peru, and in 2007 I conducted an investigation on maternal mortality that led to both legal and structural changes, especially in relation to maternal health.[21]

### Working in the United States and Beyond, on Internationalism

Since those years in Mexico in the early 1990s, I have been among a small but growing group of activists in the U.S. human rights movement pushing for increased attention to ESR, and rights-based approaches to health in particular, both at the domestic and international level. With regard to sexual and reproductive health, we have made great strides. We have brought landmark court cases leading to enforcement of entitlements to maternal health care, and, using human rights documentation and fact-finding strategies, we have managed to change governmental laws, policies, and programs relating to gender equality as well as health.[22] At the UN level, the UN Human Rights Council has issued three historic resolutions regarding maternal mortality.[23] In the third resolution in 2012, the Human Rights Council adopted a "Concise Technical Guidance on the application of a human rights-based approach to the implementation of policies and programmes to reduce preventable maternal morbidity and mortality." This Technical Guidance is the first document of its kind on the implications of a human-rights-based approach to any development issue.[24]

Moreover, work on maternal health has brought groups that were long reticent about ESC rights into the fray, including Human Rights Watch and Amnesty International. In addition to advocating for changes relating to countries as poor as Sierra Leone, Amnesty International also applied human rights methods to the enormous disparities in maternal health in the United States.[25] Although 99 percent of maternal mortality occurs in the global South, U.S. statistics show shocking disparities between whites and women of color— reflective of inequalities in the overall society—as well as an appalling lack of oversight and accountability for maternal health. The Amnesty USA campaign was influential in the introduction of legislation related to creating a centralized institution to address maternal health in this country.

These experiences have also transferred to the classroom. At the Harvard School of Public Health, I have co-taught a required ethics course for nine years, which unlike many elective offerings, is filled with students—overwhelmingly physicians—who are not necessarily convinced of the relevance of human rights to U.S. health care policy. In the class students begin to consider certain issues, such as racial inequalities in the U.S. health system as matters of human rights, often for the first time. That the United States is the only industrialized country in the world that does not legislate universal access to health care, even after the passage of the 2010 Patient Protection and Affordable Care Act, comes as a surprise to many students.[26]

Since 2011, with a full-time appointment in the Department of Global Health and Population and directing a program that has a substantial research project in East Africa, I now also teach a course that allows Harvard students to go to Tanzania to study the right to health in resource-poor settings, with a focus on maternal health. Invariably, U.S. students are challenged to reexamine their own assumptions about what is possible and to formulate strategies that go beyond conventional public health approaches.

## Concluding Reflections: What Does a Lawyer
## Have to Do with Progressive Health Work?

One of my favorite "clients" in Mexico was an elderly campesino named Timoteo Lopez. Don Timoteo was a subsistence farmer who had refused the local
drug lord's request to plant poppies for heroin on his land. The police, who
were working for the local drug lord, harassed him and then murdered his
youngest son and tried to murder him. He had survived a bullet wound to the
stomach and was recuperating in Mexico City while we figured out what to do
for him and how to prosecute the police.

As we got to know each other, Don Timoteo told me his life story. He told
me how Mexican president Lázaro Cárdenas, "the Great One," had given his
family the plot of land.[27] He told me how he had promised God he'd never
drink again if only his wife survived her illness and how she died, but he never
drank again. He told me about his older sons, who didn't understand the land
the way he did and had left for the city. And he told me about the day his
youngest son had been murdered and he had been shot, about how uniformed
men came with badges, giving him hope for just a moment, and about how the
officer with the gold tooth stepped with his boot on Timoteo's son's neck after
he shot him and spit on his face.

Every time he came to see me, Don Timoteo would say, "*doctorita,* won't
you make sure I'm doing OK?"—meaning wouldn't I examine his belly. *Doctor*
can refer to a lawyer as well as a medical doctor in Spanish, but Don Timoteo
had blurred the distinction between the two, believing I could help him in
more ways than one. No matter how many times I explained to him I was not
actually a physician he would say, "oh please, doctorita, it would make me feel
better to know you looked at it." And so I would gingerly palpate his wounded
abdomen—with no conclusions—and he would present me with an apple. I
protested that he need not bring me an apple; he would insist that a doctor
should be paid "but only when the patient gets good care." We usually ate the
apple together and he enjoyed that, telling me the story of how he had selected
this particular fruit from a particular vendor.

In the end I could not help Don Timoteo. His abdominal wound healed but,
against all advice, he insisted on going home, and he was eventually murdered
by the same police who had tried once before. If I failed him, it was as a human
rights lawyer, not as a "doctor." On countless other occasions over the years of
doing this work, I have been acutely aware that I do not possess the skills or
capacity to heal people.

I have, however, come to see how lawyers' skills can help alleviate immediate suffering as well as to attack the underlying causes of ill health, which
are almost invariably located in deep cultural, social, and economic structures
and relations. Whether negotiating an arrangement for a hemorrhaging woman
to receive treatment or documenting the foreseeable effects of the World Bank's
privatization of water for the poorest segments of the Ghanaian population, I
have come to see that legal skills have a place in advancing the health of the
most marginalized sectors of society. Garnering the strength of international
and domestic laws, and the procedures to enforce them, has allowed the activist groups I've worked with to ensure that children are not denied vaccinations
and benefits because they are delivered at home instead of in the hospital; to
help remedy discrimination, abuse, and neglect in mental hospitals; and to
bring about significant policy and legislative changes that do, in the end, prevent suffering and save lives. But of course it can never be enough.

For those of us who are outraged by the savage inequities in global health,
appalled by the simultaneous deprivation and obscene gluttony in our increasingly globalized, neoliberal world, and continually amazed by the indifference
of policymakers and the public alike, we need to work together—across borders
and disciplines. Collectively, we need to try to meet the immediate needs of
the people with whom and for whom we struggle. But solidarity also means
addressing the social, political, and economic policies and decisions that systematically create patterns of disease and suffering among poor and marginalized peoples. We—activists, lawyers, epidemiologists, health practitioners, and
others—do not always understand one another even when we are speaking
the same language. Interdisciplinary collaboration poses enormous challenges,
but it is also crucial if we are to effect true change. Doctors can be the attorneys of the poor, as Virchow famously said; but poor people also need legal
advocates—and all kinds of advocates who will stand with them and not just
speak for them.

## Notes

1. The Triple A, or *Alianza Anticomunista Argentina* (Argentine Anticommunist Alliance), was an ultraconservative death-squad active in Argentina during the 1970s
and in particular during Isabel Perón's administration (1974–1976). It later became
linked to the military regime that assumed power in 1976, which unleashed the so-
called Dirty War.

2. Alicia Ely Yamin, *Justice Corrupted, Justice Denied: Unmasking the Untouchables
of the Mexican Federal Judicial Police* (New York: World Policy Institute, 1992).

3. What is perhaps different about Mexico is that lack of healthy conditions and access
to care were recognized—at least by some—as a violation of human rights. During
the years prior to their uprising in 1994, health and health care stood out as priorities

for the *Ejército Zapatista de Liberación Nacional* (EZLN or Zapatistas). In the *First Declaration of the Lacandón Jungle*—in which the EZLN declared war against the Mexican army—the Zapatistas explicitly pointed to hunger and death from curable illnesses as among the principal reasons giving rise to the armed uprising. Indeed, what will perhaps be most striking about the Zapatista movement in the long term is how they managed to inculcate an understanding among local campesinos of health and other social rights issues as claims of entitlement and assets of citizenship—and of their current situation as one of rampant rights violations. "Primera Declaración de la Selva Lacandona," *http://www.nodo50.org/pchiapas/chiapas/documentos/ selva.htm* (accessed June 23, 2009).

4. This is unfortunately illustrated by the stagnation of the Zapatista struggle and the continuing, and even deepening, misery of so many there. When I returned on behalf of Physicians for Human Rights in conjunction with a study carried out by PHR and the Mexican institutions, *El Colegio de la Frontera Sur* (ECOSUR) and the *Defensoría del Derecho a la Salud-Centro de Capacitación en Ecología y Salud* (DDS-CCESC), it was evident that during the first six years of the conflict the politicization of government services, including those related to health on the one hand and the civil resistance by the Zapatistas on the other, had functioned in unfortunate synergy to create ever-greater social polarization within regions, communities, organizations, and even families. Among other things, the use or rejection of specific health services presupposed a specific political sympathy or militancy. On a number of different indicators, the PHR/ECOSUR/DDS-CCESC study found that people in the conflict zone had fared even worse than the overall population of Chiapas, which stands out for its lagging health indicators. Physicians for Human Rights, *Excluded People, Eroded Communities: Realizing the Right to Health in Chiapas, Mexico* (Cambridge, MA: PHR/ECOSUR/DDS-CCESC, 2006).

5. Beijing Declaration and Platform for Action, Fourth World Conference on Women, September 15 1995, A/CONF.177/20 (1995) and A/CONF.177/20/Add.1 (1995).

6. World Health Organization, *Preamble to the Constitution of the World Health Organization* (Geneva, Switzerland: World Health Organization, 1946).

7. Sofia Gruskin, Edward Mills, and Daniel Tarantola, "History, Principles and Practice of Health and Human Rights," *Lancet* 370 (2007): 545–555.

8. Mann held conferences at Harvard in the 1990s to bring together various actors and founded a journal, *Health and Human Rights,* to serve as a forum for the interchange of ideas and experiences among both academics and practitioners. What Mann et al. originally set out as a "provisional framework" for the multivalent relationship between health and human rights is still often cited today. Jonathan Mann et al., "Health and Human Rights," *Health and Human Rights* 1 (1994): 7–24.

9. Alicia Ely Yamin, "Promising but Elusive Engagements: Combining Public Health and Human Rights to Promote Women's Well-being," *Health and Human Rights* 8 (2005): 62–92.

10. In the last decade, significant attention has been devoted at the international level to fleshing out the meaning of the right to health. Among other things, the UN Committee on the Elimination of Discrimination Against Women and the UN Committee on Economic, Social, and Cultural Rights issued important authoritative interpretations of norms relating to "women and health" and the "right to the highest attainable standard of health" in 1999 and 2000, respectively. Further, the United Nations appointed the first Special Rapporteur on the Right to Health, Paul Hunt, who opted to focus on the linkages between poverty and health as one of two major themes

during his mandate. United Nations Commission on Human Rights, *The Right of Everyone to the Highest Attainable Standard of Physical and Mental Health: Report of the Special Rapporteur, Paul Hunt, Submitted in Accordance with Commission Resolution 2002/31*, E/CN.4/2003/58 (2003).

11. These extremes of wealth and access to services have been described by Paul Farmer as "pathologies of power." Paul Farmer, *Pathologies of Power: Health, Human Rights, and the New War on the Poor* (Berkeley and Los Angeles: University of California Press, 2005).

12. Coletta Youngers, *Deconstructing Democracy: Peru Under President Alberto Fujimori* (Washington, D.C.: Washington Office on Latin America, 2000).

13. The CLADEM investigation documented numerical goals for surgical contraception and systematic supervision of the achievement of such goals directly by the central government. The investigation also uncovered a series of other practices violating informed consent, such as sterilization of women in the context of other procedures (for example, post-birth, post-miscarriage), and sterilization of women through intimidation or deceit. CLADEM, *Nada Personal: Reporte de Derechos Humanos sobre la Aplicación de la Anticoncepción Quirúrgica en el Perú 1996–1998* (Lima, Peru: CLADEM, 1999).

14. Jaime Miranda and Alicia Ely Yamin, "Reproductive Health without Rights in Peru," *Lancet* 363 (2004): 68–69.

15. CLADEM, *Nada Personal;* Contrast the quality-of-care framework set out in a report produced by Population Council, *Peru: Providers' Compliance with Quality of Care Norms.* Federico León, *Peru: Providers' Compliance with Quality of Care Norms* (Lima, Peru: Population Council, 1999).

16. Very shortly after arriving in Lima, I began working with a labor rights group, the Peruvian Medical Association (whose then dean was a longtime militant in progressive politics), and unions of health care workers to raise public awareness of the right to health and to challenge the prevailing discourse of health and health care as a commodity. See Alicia Ely Yamin, *Conjurando Inequidades: Vigilancia Social sobre el Derecho a la Salud* (*Conspiring Inequities: Social Monitoring of the Right to Health*), 2nd ed. (Lima, Peru: Centro de Asesoría Legal, 2002).

17. Osvaldo Jave Castillo, *La Tuberculosis Multirresistente en el Perú* (Lima, Peru: Foro-Salud & Consorcio de Investigación Económica y Social, 2003).

18. The first was the *Mesa de Vigilancia Ciudadana en Derechos Sexuales y Reproductivos* (Round Table for Monitoring Reproductive and Sexual Rights), which was established in 2001. The second and larger network was the Civil Society Forum on Health (*Foro de la Sociedad Civil en Salud, Foro Salud*), which was founded in August 2002, with the aim of constructing a national movement through which to set out programmatic proposals aimed at responding to the "social needs of all Peruvians" and promoting health and development policies with more social equity. There are now regional health fora in nineteen out of the twenty-four departments of Peru and fifteen thematic working groups. See "Foro de la Sociedad Civil en Salud," www.forosalud.org.pe/foros.html.

19. United Nations Commission on Human Rights, *Report Submitted by the Special Rapporteur on the Right of Everyone to the Highest Attainable Standard of Physical and Mental Health, Paul Hunt, Mission to Peru*, E/CN.4/2005/51/Add.3 (2005).

20. See, for example, Web sites for *Salud sin Límites* and *MingaPeru* at www.saludsin limitesperu.org.pe/misionvision.html and www.mingaperu.org/quienes.htm, respectively.

21. Physicians for Human Rights, *Deadly Delays: Maternal Mortality in Peru. A Rights-Based Approach to Safe Motherhood* (Cambridge, MA: Physicians for Human Rights, 2007).

22. For example: a national protocol on obstetric emergencies and legislative reform ensued after the PHR/CARE Peru report and campaign based on *Deadly Delays*.

23. UN Human Rights Council (2009) Resolution 11/8. *Preventable maternal mortality and morbity and human rights* (11th Session), U.N.Doc. A/HRC/RES/11/8; UN Human Rights Council (2010) Follow-up on Resolution A/HRC/RES/11/8 on Preventable maternal mortality and morbidity and human rights (15th Session), U.N.Doc. A/HRC/15/L.27; UN Human Rights Council (2010). *Report of the Office of the United Nations High Commissioner for Human Rights on preventable maternal mortality and morbidity and human rights*. A/HRC/14/39; UN Human Rights Council (2011). *Report of the Office of the United Nations High Commissioner for Human Rights on Practices in adopting a human rights-based approach to eliminate preventable maternal mortality and human rights*. A/HRC/18/27.

24. UN Human Rights Council (2012). Technical guidance on the application of a human rights-based approach to the implementation of policies and programmes to reduce preventable maternal morbidity and mortality. A/HRC/21/22.

25. Amnesty International, *Deadly Delivery: The Maternal Health Crisis in the US* (New York: Amnesty International, 2010).

26. When it takes full effect, the PPACA will extend insurance coverage to an estimated 31 million people. PPACA (Patient Protection and Affordable Care Act) 2010. *42 USC 18001* (2010). Available at http://www.healthcare.gov/law/full (accessed November 10, 2012).

27. Lázaro Cárdenas was president of Mexico from 1934 to 1940 and oversaw a massive land redistribution during that time.

# Chapter 15

# History, Theory, and Praxis in Pacific Islands Health

Seiji Yamada

Why don't our leaders tell the people the truth? When they're going to destroy Iraq, say, why don't they announce: "Look, we want to control the international oil system. We want to establish the principle that the world is ruled by force, because that's the only thing that we're good at." . . . Why don't they just say that? It has the advantage of being true. It's much easier to tell the truth than to concoct all sorts of crazy lies. Much less work. Why don't they say that? Because they know that people are basically decent. In fact, that's the only reason for all the fabrication. Our leaders believe that people are decent and that there is hope.

—Noam Chomsky, 1992

## Antecedents

My father is from Hiroshima. Members of his immediate family were scattered far enough from the epicenter on August 6, 1945, to escape the bomb's immediate physical effects. As a thirteen-year-old, together with his brother, he had been evacuated across the mountains. My father admits that witnessing the atomic bomb impressed him with the power of physics, which encouraged him to pursue its study, obtaining his PhD in Japan, then working as a postdoctoral fellow in Europe and the United States. At Cornell, he worked under Robert Rathbun Wilson, a Quaker who during the Manhattan Project (the U.S.-led secret effort to build the first atomic bomb during World War II) objected to plans to use the bomb on Japanese civilians.[1] Wilson recruited my father to work at Fermilab outside of Chicago. Growing up close to Fermilab, I met physicists from the Soviet Union and China—for even during the Cold War, international collaboration on basic science was possible. As a teenager, I imagined a career for myself in physics.

My mother was born in Harbin, in occupied Manchuria. Her father, originally from Hiroshima, was a physician there when Manchuria was under Japan's colonial rule in the 1930s. During the war, he was in the army. I must have been about five years old when, one day, my grandfather showed me the Japanese army-issue lunch pail that he had stored away in the dark storage area at the side of his house. In later years, as I learned some history, I often thought that he must have at least known about the human medical experiments conducted by the military medical units on Chinese people.

After the war, my mother's father brought his family back to live amid the rubble of Hiroshima. He cared for patients with a variety of ailments from the atom bomb. I was born there in 1962. While my father spent a year in Germany, my mother, my infant brother, and I stayed in my grandfather's house (where he had his clinic). In my grandfather's yard, I dug up shards of scorched roof tile. I recall that one day, as my grandfather and I walked through Hiroshima stopping to view shadows of people etched in stone, he told me that Japanese people are for peace, for they know full well the senselessness of war.

## Political Conscientization

When our family left Japan, I was six years old. We moved to Naperville, Illinois, a bastion of the Republican Party. Years later I learned about the town's history. During the late nineteenth century there were worker uprisings for an eight-hour workday. On May 4, 1886, a large rally, organized in Chicago's Haymarket Square in support of striking industrial workers, erupted in brutal police violence after a pipe bomb killed a police officer. A group of anarchists were tried for murder, four of whom were put to death. In the aftermath of the Haymarket Riot, when Illinois governor John Peter Altgeld pardoned the surviving, imprisoned anarchists in 1893, he was hanged in effigy by Naperville residents. Across his breast were painted two hands clasped in friendship, one labeled "Altgeld," the other labeled "Anarchy."[2]

All of our neighbors subscribed to the *Chicago Tribune,* the newspaper of Chicago's Republican establishment. By some accident, my family had a subscription to the *Chicago Daily News.* At one point, my mother wanted to conform to the neighborhood norm and switch to the *Tribune,* but I wouldn't let her because by then I was a fan of columnist Mike Royko, a gadfly of Chicago's Democratic political machine.

Having grown up in Naperville, which was then nearly all white, I found entering college and gathering with other Asians in the Harvard-Radcliffe Asian-American Association (AAA) was a novel experience. Most of my friends in the AAA were Chinese Americans. The AAA was a forum for the discussion of identity and politics. Imagining ourselves to be in solidarity with the Third World, the AAA joined with other minority student organizations in calling on the university administration to create a Third World Center. The administration's response was to create a Race Relations Institute.

While I was in college, a friend took me to see the films of Costa-Gavras, *Z*[3] and *State of Siege,*[4] and suggested that I read Noam Chomsky and Edward Herman's *The Washington Connection and Third World Fascism.*[5] This provided me with a framework for understanding the international scene. I subsequently took every opportunity to hear Chomsky speak. Chomsky's lectures and political writings were my entrée into protest and anarchism. He spoke and wrote about U.S.-supported repression in East Timor and Central America long before the corporate-controlled media made any mention of the United States' contributory role. I participated in marches against U.S. involvement in Central America, apartheid in South Africa, and nuclear weapons. Imagining myself an activist, I tried selling *The Guardian,* a now-defunct revolutionary newspaper from New York, in front of the freshman dining hall.

My political conscientization made me critical of science. Growing up among physicists and studying physics in college gave me a materialist view of the world; that is, I believed that the description of phenomena in terms of subatomic particles was a reflection of reality.[6] But the description of the universe has changed much since I was formally studying physics. Explanatory frameworks come and go. Now that I stand outside of the hard science community, I see how science, too, is a social product, a product of human activity. I now find myself drawing upon my knowledge of physics in my activism against weapons testing and war.

Ronald Reagan was president while I attended college in the early 1980s. Some of my friends looked back on the 1960s with nostalgia and hoped that it was possible to radically change society. As an undergraduate, I spent time on the edges of the League of Revolutionary Struggle, a party that took a position supporting the right of national peoples to self-determination and viewed minorities as the future of revolution in the United States. Friends who were activists in Boston's Chinatown led our study groups of Marxist literature. The materialism of Marxism I could appreciate. But dialectics confused me. It was not until later, by reading Richard Levins and Richard Lewontin, that I came to appreciate aspects of dialectical materialism as consistent with science.[7] I recall being particularly struck by Marx's eleventh thesis on Feuerbach as a way of being in the world: "The philosophers have only interpreted the world, in various ways; the point is to change it."[8] It made me want to be done with studying and be out in the world to try to change it somehow.

Having been born Japanese (becoming a U.S. citizen when I was twenty), I viewed it as my responsibility to learn about Japanese imperialism and militarism. I also learned about Japanese anarchists who had opposed Imperial Japan and had maintained relations of solidarity with other peoples in Asia. For example, Kōtoku Shūsui, a radical journalist and socialist, opposed the Russo-Japanese War (1904–1905)—a war over rival imperial ambitions in Manchuria and Korea. Though he was not involved in a plot to assassinate the Japanese emperor, Kōtoku was executed for treason in 1911. Ōsugi Sakae, a writer and agitator, also sought to cooperate with fellow Asian anarchists. He and his companion were brutally murdered by the police in the aftermath of the Great Kantō Earthquake in 1923.

Taking cues from those who opposed such forces in Japan, I see it as my responsibility to oppose imperialism and militarism in my adopted home country of the United States. My analysis is that underlying imperialism are racism, capitalism, and authoritarianism—leading me to my identification with anarchism.

Having entered college with the intent of becoming a scientist, my plans changed after I spent a summer working in an after-school children's program in Boston's Chinatown and tutoring in the marginalized African American and Latino neighborhood of Roxbury. I began to desire work that would allow me to participate more directly in improving societal conditions. I saw medicine as a means to this end. Biomedical research per se did not (and still does not) interest me in the least. My attitude toward the study of medicine was to gain a practical skill to place in the service of others. Studying Marx taught me that one cannot operate in a capitalist society without participating in exploitation. Reading Vicente Navarro's[9] and Howard Waitzkin's[10] application of Marxism to the health system helped me understand that medicine reproduces class relations and that the world of medicine is particularly hierarchical.

I returned to Chicago to study medicine. While in medical school at the University of Illinois at Chicago (UIC), I encountered little political activism. On the one hundredth anniversary of the Haymarket Riot, I visited the original site in the vain hope of finding some sort of tribute. Throughout the world, this event is commemorated on May 1 (May Day) as International Workers' Day, but in the United States May 1 is Law and Order Day or Loyalty Day.

Preclinical medical education at UIC was singularly uninspired, with courses taught along disciplinary lines—anatomy, biochemistry, pathology, and so on. I could not wait until my third year to start seeing patients. Interested in learning medicine of utility to most patients in any setting, I chose to enter family practice. I hoped that its orientation toward community rather than hospital care would allow me to be socially engaged. In recent years, the term *family practice* has been replaced by *family medicine*—a change that I regret, as I value the etymological connection to the idea of praxis, that theory and practice are interrelated and shape each other.

During my residency at Cook County Hospital in Chicago, I cared for patients suffering from the hopelessness borne of the inner city: alcoholism, endocarditis, and end-stage AIDS from injection drug use. In the late 1980s most of my patients were African American or Mexican, and I saw firsthand how racism, classism, and other forms of oppression played intertwining roles in the production of disease. I joined the International Committee Against Racism, which took the position that nationalism is racism. I marched with friends on May Day and joined their efforts to shut down a racist Ku Klux Klan/neo-Nazi rally. I also got into trouble with the hospital administration for announcing on local television that some doctors would not cross picket lines if Cook County's nurses went on strike. My subsequent bid to become the president of the hospital's House Staff Association—when I ran as the antiracist candidate—was unsuccessful, undoubtedly because of my outspoken activism.

### The Pacific

After completing residency, I took my first job, sight unseen, in Saipan in the Commonwealth of the Northern Mariana Islands (CNMI). Seeking work outside of the United States proper, I found the listing in a newsletter on international medical opportunities. In its heyday of tourism (now over) in the late 1980s and early 1990s, Japanese tourists flocked to Saipan's beaches. I often overheard young Japanese wondering why scenic lookouts bore names such as Suicide Cliff and Banzai Cliff. In June 1944, Saipan had been the site of a major Pacific

War battle between Japan and the United States. Many Japanese civilians who were living in Saipan at the time believed propaganda that they would be savaged by the advancing Americans and jumped to their deaths from cliffs on the northern end of the island.

After three decades as part of the U.S. trusteeship, the Northern Marianas became a U.S. Commonwealth and gained control of its own immigration and minimum wage laws. This allowed garment factories to bring in workers from around the world, pay them meagerly, and label their goods as "Made in the U.S.A.," thereby avoiding tariffs. In Saipan I cared for women garment factory workers, from China, Thailand, Micronesia, and even Guatemala, who came to the hospital with a variety of ailments brought on by the stress of low-wage work and due to being uprooted from their homes.

While I was there, nativist sentiment began to take root among the people of the CNMI: they complained that "alien workers" had taken their jobs. Most of this ire was directed at Filipinos who had come to outnumber the indigenous people. In the early 1990s a number of incidents took place that could only be described as lynchings of Filipino workers. When one victim of a firebombing was under my care, I made calls to the U.S. attorney general for the CNMI to demand justice for this man's civil rights, with little result.

Island societies, because of their size, might seem more amenable to social change than large, complex societies. My experience, however, taught me that it is difficult to make an impact even in the smallest island society, especially as an outsider. I attempted to exert political influence as an individual, but what was needed was a social movement. My own circle, however, was made up of expatriate health workers and I found it difficult to make contacts among local workers. It was also difficult to advocate for change while working for the government. I was told by the head of health services, in no uncertain terms, that if I didn't like it in Saipan, I should leave.

In Saipan the remnants of militarism were never far. At one point, I was sent over to the nearby island of Tinian to work at a small hospital. Flat as the deck of an aircraft carrier, Tinian was the site from which B-29 bombers departed for Japan during World War II. In one corner of the island, hidden among an overgrowth of *tangan tangan* (*Leucaena leucocephala,* seeded from the air in the postwar period to revegetate the defoliated islands), are the pits where Little Boy and Fat Man, the atomic bombs dropped on Hiroshima and Nagasaki respectively, were temporarily housed. From one of the pits grows a coconut tree that bears deformed fruit. From the other pit grows a tree that bears no fruit at all. It is a forlorn sight.

Popular conceptions of the Pacific Islands, among Japanese and Americans alike, are of idyllic tourist destinations. But the historical reality is that they were the scenes of fierce battles. Relics and stories of World War II are scattered throughout the Pacific; in some places the war is memorialized, in others not. For example, some years after working in CNMI, when I was visiting Micronesia collecting data on cancer incidence, a Pohnpeian friend told me that as the Japanese Imperial forces were pulling out, they tried to herd the Pohnpeians into a cave so that they could gas them. For me, such stories serve as reminders that the Japanese imperialists painted other nonwhites as inferior and Westerners as barbarians. My relatives often express disbelief that they could have been so naïve as to believe the pronouncements of the Imperial government—from the divinity of the emperor, to the humanizing mission of the Imperial Army in Asia, to continued claims that the war would be won—while the South Seas Empire fell, island by island.

In turn, World War II–era American propaganda depicted Japanese people as monkeys or rats, deserving of extermination. Sotto voce, Japanese express the belief that the Americans would never have dropped the atomic bomb on Germans, fellow Caucasians. It was not so long ago that Japanese and American soldiers, influenced by such propaganda, ferociously killed each other. Now partners in business as well as in military endeavors, we seem to have forgotten how our views of each other were so subject to propagandistic control. Does it need to be pointed out that in present-day America we see similar racist portrayals of Arabs and Muslims? As during World War II, such xenophobia has been used to justify imperial projects in Iraq and Afghanistan in the name of combating terrorism.

## The Marshall Islands

Since leaving Saipan in 1993, Hawai'i has been my home. After two and a half years at a community health center, I joined the University of Hawai'i's Department of Family Practice and Community Health with the hope of becoming involved again in Pacific Islands health. As a faculty member, I was sent to the Marshall Islands on brief visits, starting in 1999, to oversee resident physicians and provide care, mainly to survivors of the U.S. government's postwar testing of nuclear weapons.

Following World War II, from 1946 to 1957, the United States tested sixty-seven nuclear weapons in the Marshall Islands. In comparison to the Nevada Test Site, where only relatively small kiloton (equivalent to a thousand tons of TNT) shots were conducted for a total of about one thousand kilotons—in the Pacific, a total of 152 megatons (each megaton consisting of one million tons of TNT) of devices were tested.[11] The fifteen-megaton Bravo blast of March 1, 1954, was America's largest. It rendered the island of Bikini uninhabitable and exposed the people of Rongelap and Utrik to nuclear fallout.

Providing primary care and screening for new cancers for the remaining survivors of the 1954 Bravo test, I found that our patients were suspicious of our motives. "Are you really providing medical care?" they would ask, "Or are you conducting medical experiments? Are we your guinea pigs?" My initial reaction was to think and reply, "of course not." But in the Department of Energy clinics (descended from the Atomic Energy Commission medical program) where I worked, I discovered files dating back to the first days after the Bravo test that documented the effects of fallout such as falling serial blood counts. In my historical digging, I learned that the background documents for Bravo, which dated from November 1953, included plans for a study—to be undertaken just after the Bravo test—called Project 4.1, or "Study of Response of Human Beings Exposed to Significant Beta and Gamma Radiation Due to Fall-Out from High-Yield Weapons." On the U.S. Department of Energy's Human Radiation Experiments Web site, just before it was taken down, I saw that under the guise of medical assistance, Project 4.1 subjects were administered radioactive substances without their knowledge or consent. I came to agree with the Marshallese people that they were, indeed, deliberately subjected to Bravo's fallout.

Because I was attached to the U.S. Department of Energy I had permission to stay on Kwajalein Island, the largest in the Kwajalein Atoll in the Marshall Islands, then known as U.S. Army Kwajalein Atoll (since renamed the Ronald Reagan Ballistic Missile Defense Test Site). Kwajalein Island feels like a cross between a tropical army base and a physics laboratory. There are barracks for temporary workers and bungalows for long-term residents, together with a pristine beach, swimming pools, well-provisioned grocery stores, plentiful fresh water, shaded streets, and a golf course. Most of the two to four thousand non-Marshallese residents are employees of the armaments industry. Massive radars housed in geodesic domes are located throughout the island. Intercontinental ballistic missiles, shot from Vandenberg Air Force Base in California, are tested here, using Kwajalein Atoll as the bull's eye. I am still struck by the first time I witnessed Kwajalein Island residents watching the night sky for incoming missiles, talking about the trails as though they were fireworks. "They're talking about MIRVs," I thought—multiple independently targetable reentry vehicles, each capable of carrying a warhead that can annihilate a city.

Marshallese people are not allowed to live on Kwajalein Island, though many commute to work there from the underdeveloped island of Ebeye as cooks, cleaners, groundskeepers, and other laborers. Aside from the Marshall Islands government, the missile range is the largest employer in the country, drawing people from throughout the archipelago. A small number of residents were relocated to Kwajalein Atoll after the nuclear testing, but most people who remain in Ebeye are there because of the jobs. On Ebeye there is little greenery: many of the houses are made of corrugated tin and plywood, and there is no space for the crop plants that used to make up the traditional diet of the Marshallese. The reef around Ebeye is too polluted for the people to gather reef resources. The electricity often goes out, sometimes for extended periods, making refrigeration unreliable. Thus, the people subsist on imported white rice and canned meats, with little access to fresh vegetables or fruits. The result is undernutrition in children and obesity and diabetes in adults.[12] Water is also scarce on the island; people rely on water collected in plastic containers from the docks at Kwajalein Island. When it rains, the sewage backs up. In December 2000 there was a cholera epidemic on Ebeye with over four hundred cases of cholera and six deaths.

The racism evident in the apartheid-like Kwajalein-Ebeye setup is palpable for the Marshallese, though for the most part, the American residents of

**Figure 15.1** Marshallese workers approaching a hand print-reading machine at the dock for entry onto Kwajalein Island, Republic of the Marshall Islands, July 14, 2000.

Courtesy of Seiji Yamada.

Kwajalein seem oblivious to it. Indeed, racism was inherent in the decisions to conduct nuclear and ballistic missile testing in the Marshall Islands. After all, who would willingly volunteer their home to be a target for missiles shot from another continent?

I have tried applying various theories to better understand the Marshall Islands situation: Farmer's historically deep, geographically broad approach as a corrective to the biopsychosocial model,[13] Hardt and Negri's concept of Empire,[14] and Krieger's ecosocial model.[15] A better description should help us decide on courses of action, in other words, determine praxis. The underlying impetus for the present situation remains weapons development—business as usual in terms of the role of the Marshall Islands in American imperialism. Although the Kwajalein-Ebeye military complex serves as a source of employment for many Marshallese, as well as wealth for a few landowners, we must oppose it on moral grounds. Theoretical considerations aside, I feel that the only sane reaction to the Kwajalein-Ebeye complex, similar to what I experienced when I listened to people talking about MIRVs, is horror at the abomination of it and the responsibility to resist it. How else can one respond to an apartheid-like system dedicated to developing weapons of mass destruction? At every opportunity I have, I speak out against it.

**Practice, Teaching, and Activism**

What I have observed in the Marshall Islands has sharpened the lenses through which I now view my adopted home of Oahu, Hawai'i, where 22 percent of the land is controlled by the military.[16] I therefore make it my business to be involved in the struggle to keep more Hawaiian lands from being put to military uses, such as training grounds for the Stryker urban assault vehicle.

My clinical practice in Hawai'i has focused on community health centers serving immigrants and the homeless. For patients who come from the U.S.-associated Pacific Islands, I have an understanding of their backgrounds. While they may denigrate the care they have received at home, I am quick to support the practitioners who work under difficult circumstances.

Before joining the University of Hawai'i, most of my teaching of medical students and family practice residents, in the classroom and in clinical settings, employed conventional methods. I learned about problem-based learning (PBL)—the educational philosophy of using cases as prompts for self-directed, adult learning—at the University of Hawai'i. I have since become a proselytizer for PBL in a way that only a convert can be. I have worked to use PBL as a vehicle for teaching and learning about patient-centered, cross-cultural, and social medicine.[17]

**Figure 15.2** Learning together with Micronesian physicians using PBL methods in Chuuk State, Federated States of Micronesia, on August 23, 2005. Author is on the left. At the easel is Victor Ngaden (deceased) of Yap.

Courtesy of Gregory Maskarinec.

When the opportunity arises, I introduce critical topics in my courses, such as the political economy of health and illness in the Pacific Islands. I have also encouraged examination of events such as 9/11 and the wars waged in the Balkans, Afghanistan, and Iraq. As premedical education and medical schools do not prepare graduates to engage in social, historical, or political economy analysis, I often find the need to review basic history with residents. By doing so, I risk evaluations from students of my teaching such as, "Politics should not be a part of medical education." I remain inspired, however, by the long tradition in social medicine, from Rudolf Virchow to Salvador Allende to Paul Farmer, of viewing political economy as central to health and illness.[18]

While I worked in the Department of Family Practice, I was constantly told to "tone down" my writings and lectures. I assume that my critiques of the use of the Marshall Islands for ballistic missile defense testing threatened the department's U.S. Department of Energy funding, but I contend that racism and militarism cannot be sugar coated. For my political views, I was forced out of the Department of Family Practice in 2002. When I was fired, I was told that the care I delivered to patients and the teaching and research that I did were fine, but that my views ran counter to those of the chair, and therefore, my contract was not going to be renewed. One's right to free speech only goes so far, even in academia.

Afterward, I managed to stay on for some time in the medical school, with funding for bioterrorism and preparedness training research. I traveled with a team to Sri Lanka in the aftermath of the December 2004 tsunami to study the response. In November 2005, I was a civilian volunteer with the U.S. Public Health Service in New Orleans after Hurricane Katrina. In both settings I saw how tragedies of inadequate infrastructure for marginalized local populations were turned into corporate profit-making bonanzas.

In Sri Lanka, I saw few resources directed toward rebuilding the fishing villages most affected by the tsunami. The government declared that private dwellings could not be rebuilt within one hundred meters of the shoreline, on the face of it a reasonable rule; however, as noted by Naomi Klein in her book on disaster capitalism, commercial interests were allowed to take over this coastal land to build tourist resorts.[19] The grassroots organizations we observed assisting survivors of the tsunami did not own the heavy equipment to respond to twenty-five- or thirty-million-dollar requests for proposals put out by aid and disaster relief organizations such as the U.S. Agency for International Development (USAID). Thus, USAID was funding major contractors to build water and sewer facilities for tourist resorts. In the end, the tsunami served as an excuse to give taxpayer dollars and donor funds to multinational corporate interests.

In New Orleans, the U.S. Public Health Service's response to Katrina was to set up daily makeshift clinics in parking lots, made up of pop-up tents and folding tables and chairs. Meanwhile, the U.S. government granted no-bid, cost-plus contracts to the same corporations that had received contracts in postinvasion Iraq: the Shaw Group, Bechtel, Fluor, CH2M Hill, Halliburton.[20] As we witnessed, even with such huge windfalls, these corporations failed to provide proper protective gear to the underpaid Latin American workers who were doing the actual cleanup work.

In recent years I have been working at a community health center in urban Honolulu. Many of our patients are immigrants from Asia and the Pacific. Defending the right of Micronesian patients' access to health services in the face of threats of Medicaid cutbacks by the state has been the focus of my extracurricular activities.[21] Most recently, after nine years of exile, I have made my way back into the Department of Family Medicine and am again allowed to teach residents and students.

## Conclusion

After the Cold War and the threat of nuclear war subsided, much of the concern with weapons testing and its long-term effects also subsided. I have sought to revive attention to these issues through my writings and activism. I see this as a natural outgrowth of being from Hiroshima. But I don't make it to every protest. Sometimes I stay at home to read or write. I tell myself that I can make a contribution by working in the world of ideas. I use what Chomsky tells us about U.S. militarism and imperialism to advocate for those who are directly harmed by it. I apply what Chris Hedges tells us about the state of our nation[22] to my own teaching and practice of social medicine. I also try to educate more widely outside of medicine to keep such issues alive. Above all, I cannot afford to stop reading, writing, and speaking out.

Well over a half century after Hiroshima, the threat of nuclear weapons still looms. Global climate change, social inequalities, militarism, and imperial ventures could mean a future filled with a succession of disasters and conflicts. If we want to avert such a dystopian future, with effort and persistence, we can build local and transnational movements to end these gross violations of humanity. This should give us hope.

## Notes

Epigraph from Charles M. Young, "Noam Chomsky: Anarchy in the U.S.A.," *Rolling Stone,* May 28, 1992, www.chomsky.info/interviews/19920528.htm (accessed September 14, 2008).

1. Kai Bird and Martin J. Sherwin, *American Prometheus: The Triumph and Tragedy of J. Robert Oppenheimer* (New York: Alfred A. Knopf, 2005).
2. "Altgeld Hanged in Effigy," *New York Times,* June 29, 1893.
3. Constantin Costa-Gavras, *Z* (Office national pour le commerce et l'industrie cinématographique, 1969).
4. Constantin Costa-Gavras, *État de siège* (Cinema X [es], 1972).
5. Noam A. Chomsky and Edward S. Herman, *The Washington Connection and Third World Fascism* (Cambridge, MA: South End Press, 1979).
6. Richard Rorty, *Objectivity, Relativism, and Truth* (Cambridge: Cambridge University Press, 1991).
7. Richard Levins and Richard Lewontin, *The Dialectical Biologist* (Cambridge, MA: Harvard University Press, 1985).
8. Karl Marx, "Theses on Feuerbach," *Marx/Engels Selected Works, Volume One* (Moscow, USSR: Progress Publishers, 1969). Available from: http://www.marxists.org/archive/marx/works/1845/theses/theses.htm.
9. Vicente Navarro, *Medicine Under Capitalism* (New York: Prodist, 1976).
10. Howard Waitzkin, "A Marxist Analysis of the Health Care Systems of Technologically Advanced Societies," in *The Relevance of Social Science for Medicine,* ed. Leon Eisenberg and Arthur Kleinman (New York: Reidel, 1981).
11. Steven L. Simon and William L. Robison. "A Compilation of Nuclear Weapons Test Detonation Data for U.S. Pacific Ocean Tests," *Health Physics* 73(1) (1997): 258–264.

Available from: http://tis.eh.doe.gov/health/marshall/marshall.htm (accessed July 25, 2004).

12. Seiji Yamada et al., "Diabetes Mellitus Prevalence in Out-Patient Marshallese Adults on Ebeye Island, Republic of the Marshall Islands," *Hawaii Medical Journal* 63 (2004): 47–53.

13. Seiji Yamada and Neal Palafox, "On the Biopsychosocial Model: Political Economic Perspectives on Diabetes in the Marshall Islands," *Family Medicine* 33 (2001): 348–350.

14. Seiji Yamada, "Cholera in the Marshall Islands: Ecology, Globalization, and Empire," in *Global Public Health in the Pacific,* ed. Deane Neubauer and James Rae, www.hawaii.edu/global/publications_media/GlobalPublicHealthPacific.pdf (accessed September 14, 2008).

15. Seiji Yamada and Wesley Palmer, "An Ecosocial Approach to the Epidemic of Cholera in the Marshall Islands," *Social Medicine* 2 (2007): 79–86.

16. Kyle Kajihiro, "A Brief Overview of Militarization and Resistance in Hawai'i," March 1, 2007, www.dmzhawaii.org/overview_military_in_hawaii.pdf (accessed September 14, 2008).

17. Seiji Yamada and Gregory Maskarinec, "'Authentic' PBL, Instrumental Rationality, and Narrative," *Asia-Pacific Journal of Family Medicine* 2 (2003): 226–228; Seiji Yamada and Gregory Maskarinec, "Strengthening PBL through Discursive Practices," *Education for Health* 17 (2004): 85–92.

18. Matthew Anderson, Lanny Smith, and Victor Sidel, "What Is Social Medicine," *Monthly Review* 8 (2005), http://www.monthlyreview.org/0105anderson.htm (accessed September 5, 2009).

19. Naomi Klein, *The Shock Doctrine: The Rise of Disaster Capitalism* (New York: Metropolitan Books, 2007).

20. Tom Engelhardt and Nick Turse, "The Reconstruction of New Oraq," September 13, 2005, www.tomdispatch.com/index.mhtml?pid=21843 (accessed September 14, 2008).

21. Dina Shek and Seiji Yamada, "Health Care for Micronesians and Constitutional Rights," *Hawaii Medical Journal* 70 (11 supp) (2011): 4–8.

22. Chris Hedges and Joe Sacco, *Days of Destruction, Days of Revolt* (New York: Nation Books, 2012).

# Chapter 16

# Doctors for Global Health

## Applying Liberation Medicine and Accompanying Communities in Their Struggles for Health and Social Justice

**Lanny (Clyde Lanford) Smith, Jennifer Kasper, and Timothy H. Holtz**

Doctors for Global Health (DGH) began in 1995 in rural El Salvador during the years that the country began to rebuild after a devastating twelve-year civil war.[1] Founding members of DGH had been invited three years prior by local community leaders to engage with them in transforming the fundamental causes of ill health plaguing their communities and to create together a new and stable environment for the war-torn region. Since 1995, DGH has grown from a small, informal group working in one area of El Salvador to a more formal international nongovernmental organization whose member-volunteers work with communities in their struggles for social justice and human dignity—in El Salvador, Guatemala, Chiapas and Oaxaca (Mexico), Uganda, Peru, Burundi, the United States, and other countries. Key principles of health justice have guided its work, especially the concept of liberation medicine, "the conscious, conscientious use of health to promote social justice and human dignity."[2] DGH has created transformative experiences for volunteers and communities by channeling idealism and social activism into concrete action and by serving as an alternative model to U.S. imperialism and the global political and economic status quo.

### Introduction

Let us first take you to a gathering of the twelfth annual DGH general assembly held in October 2007 in El Salvador.[3] Imagine people singing, teaching, conversing, and rejoicing in a retreat-center architecturally molded to the outer edge of a volcano. Many of us had first met decades prior in dire times when we were working to fight repression. We are health promoters and *campesinos* (a term that literally translates as "peasants" but carries a meaning of respect not expressed in the English word) from El Salvador, Nicaragua, Guatemala, and Chiapas; artists, students, health and education professionals, participants from the United States, and others, united in the quest for health and social justice. At this meeting, we discuss at length topics such as privatization of health care, transnational corporations and environmental threats, women's rights, and community empowerment. Lively theater, local musicians, and performances by small children remind the group of the *alta-alegremia* required to confront the violence that suppresses social, mental, and physical well-being around the globe. Alta-alegremia means "high blood-happiness"; that is, to be full of the joy of being human despite devastation or tremendous suffering.[4] It is an expression that was coined by Dr. Julio Monsalvo of Argentina, a DGH advisory council member.

After the meeting, we ride by bus through El Salvador's rural landscape to visit the project sites where DGH began. Visitors to these sites get and give counsel and inspiration, and experience how and where our legacy lives on. In Estancia, Morazán, in the northeast region of the country, there are now six child development centers; the community-built Jaime Solórzano bridge; and an enthusiastic, campesino-run, local NGO focused on primary health care. In Santa Marta, Cabañas—a highly organized community of former refugees who returned collectively midwar to repopulate their community in defiance of the violence—the dynamic youth group *Comité Contra el SIDA* (CoCoSI, Committee Against AIDS) inspires locals and visitors alike, as do myriad other projects. In El Mozote, we remember and honor the hundreds of people whose names are carved on the wooden memorial wall. El Mozote is a former pacifist community in Morazán where, in 1981, hundreds of mostly children and women were massacred by Atlacatl, a Salvadoran battalion trained by the U.S. Army's School of the Americas (SOA).[5] Forensic pathologists from Argentina, working with the United Nations Truth Commission after the signing of the 1992 peace accords,[6] gently unearthed from a mass grave in El Mozote more than one hundred infant and child skeletons, horrific evidence confirming the eyewitness account of lone survivor Rufina Amaya.[7] Such site visits as these, which form part of every DGH general assembly, are a way to become even more active with the local community organizing that year's meeting. In the case of the El Salvador gathering, the visits connected DGH with both its foundation and its future.

In the first part of this chapter, we look at the history and growth of DGH— how DGH went from working in a cluster of rural, isolated communities in postwar El Salvador to working with multiple communities around the world and becoming a key active member of the global People's Health Movement

(PHM), a broader social movement begun in the year 2000, to revive the principles of the 1978 *Declaration of Alma-Ata,* calling for "Health for All by the Year 2000" (see chapter 12).[8] We then examine how DGH has linked its global health efforts to local and national concerns in the United States, demonstrating the continuity and universality of health and human rights issues. We also review the principles of action, and in particular the concept of liberation medicine, upon which DGH as a volunteer-based, not-for-profit organization is built.

### The Sociopolitical Reality of El Salvador

DGH was born of international solidarity during the brutal conflict that plagued El Salvador from 1980 to the signing of the peace accords in 1992. During this time, Salvadoran armed forces funded by the United States government actively participated in human rights violations on a mass scale. They murdered seventy-five thousand people, disappeared innumerable others, and forced at least one million to flee as refugees. This had a devastating effect on the country of only six million inhabitants at the time. The Salvadoran government's massive bombardment and use of napalm caused severe deforestation, with accompanying deleterious effects on human settlements and health. Among the earliest murders was that of Catholic archbishop Oscar Arnulfo Romero (1917–1980), a liberation theology leader and advocate for the "voiceless." Inspired by the liberation theology premise that heaven should be created on earth, he was an indefatigable promoter of human rights and worked according to the principle of a preferential option for the poor.[9] The Salvadoran military response to Romero's message was to circulate the slogan: "Be a patriot: kill a priest." Romero's murder by an SOA-trained Salvadoran death-squad leader on March 24, 1980, marked the war's beginning.[10]

The war lasted for twelve years. During that time, El Salvador cut its health budget in half. The few health posts that existed in conflict areas were abandoned. The Salvadoran government, rather than respect human rights, encouraged their flagrant desecration, enabled by the massive financing and unwavering complicity of its northern sponsor—consecutive U.S. government administrations (see chapter 13).

### Community-Based Solidarity Leading to the Foundation of DGH

In 1992 DGH founder Lanny Smith, a physician from the United States, went to El Salvador as a volunteer with, and subsequent country coordinator and legal representative of, the French organization Médecins du Monde (MDM, Physicians of the World) at the direct invitation of several communities in Morazán, a department in northeastern El Salvador adjoining Honduras that saw some of the worst fighting during the civil war.[11] Community leaders, some of them ex-combatants of the Farabundo Martí National Liberation Front (FMLN), wanted to address health as a human right and to stop the fundamental causes of ill health plaguing their communities.[12] In consultation with Smith, they developed a project called "Building Health Where the Peace Is New," which focused on community-oriented primary care (see chapter 6),[13] centers for integral child development, medical student training, women's health and human rights, community-based rehabilitation, nutrition, and participatory evaluation.[14]

That same year MDM had considered leaving El Salvador, following the lead of the International Red Cross, Médecins Sans Frontières (Doctors Without Borders), and most international groups that had been there during the war years. Global solidarity movements were literally disappearing with the apparent resolution of conflict offered by the peace accords. But Building Health Where the Peace Is New, with its participatory process, inspired MDM to remain active in El Salvador for another decade and served as the foundation for DGH.

From the start, the project was fulfilling vital needs. Although the conflict in El Salvador was officially over, daily crises provoked by the structural violence characteristic of a war-ravaged nation—that is, poverty and lack of access to health care, education, and economic opportunities—had escalated. By 1994, twenty-two homicides were occurring daily, greater than the average during the civil conflict.

Communities in Morazán urgently needed outside witnesses to their travails as well as infrastructural aid, including financial support and other resources, from Salvadoran and international volunteers.[15] But no international solidarity group appeared ready or able to accompany the Morazán initiative, and MDM's support was at that point only a commitment from year to year. The people of Morazán urged MDM volunteers to create a participatory association (which in 1995 became DGH)—and through it broader social solidarity to support local needs. The aim was to demonstrate that collective work—inspired, directed, and implemented by community members with assistance from local, national, and international partners—could amplify the voices of those previously silenced and promote social justice.

In order to help build health infrastructure based on the principles of health as a fundamental human right, Building Health Where the Peace Is New encouraged political action and mobilization at several levels. Local communities chose candidates for health promoter training. Salvadoran medical students assisted in public health interventions as part of their community medicine course. The MDM team recruited Salvadorans and internationals living locally to promote the concept of health as reconciliation.[16] The civil conflict had caused deep divisions among the people. We highlighted the idea that health is a universal public good (and human right) and used it as a catalyst for both physical and mental healing. People formerly on opposite sides of the armed civil conflict, including other NGOs, the Ministry of Health, mayors, community leaders, and representatives from Catholic and Protestant churches, were brought together through a mega cluster-committee, in which representative leaders of groups based or working locally convened to shape and participate in rebuilding efforts.

Practicing health as reconciliation, sharing credit for achievements with the Ministry of Health in providing access to health care as a human right rather than as a political tool (to punish or reward backers or promote the ruling party), and inviting international solidarity[17] were important techniques that the local MDM team and local and international volunteers used to address death-squad threats and build health in Morazán and the greater El Salvador community. Salvadoran volunteer professionals and community leaders adopted this effort as their own and became active in seeking local and international resources. International students and fully trained volunteer professionals arrived to work under local leadership.

**Figure 16.1** Dr. Lanny Smith (*top center, in white t-shirt*), training Community Health Promoters using the Universal Declaration of Human Rights (the papers in hand) in 1994, Cantón El Tablón, Municipio Sociedad, Departamento de Morazán, El Salvador.

Copyleft. Courtesy of Doctors for Global Health.

The first long-term international volunteer in El Salvador accompaniment arrived in 1994.[18] On this volunteer's first day, he experienced a tragedy that would later be transformed into a catalyst for change. He was working with local Salvadoran medical and pharmacy students to deliver supplies to the communities in Morazán. At the time, the only way to get there was to swim across or travel around the Río Chiquito (Little River, a branch of the Torola River). While swimming against the strong current in an attempt to cross the river, a Salvadoran pharmacy student, Jaime Solórzano, drowned. His death struck a chord with local people and the international volunteers who would ultimately create DGH and marked an important turning point in their relationship. Together, they shared their sorrow and strengthened their common purpose.

For forty-two years the communities had been petitioning their government to build a bridge near the very site where Jaime drowned. He was one among many who died trying to ford the river. Twenty recorded deaths over the course of twenty years had been documented, five in 1994, including two children under ten who had to cross the river daily to attend school. In 1995 the MDM mission and the newly formed DGH group began working with the community to construct a bridge that would be named in Jaime's memory. In eighteen months, with $100,000 raised from many sources (including U.S. schoolchildren's bake sales), local community members and volunteers from fourteen communities, under the direction of a volunteer engineer from Spain, built a two-lane vehicular bridge. The bridge literally became a lifeline. No one else has drowned in the Río Chiquito since. Transport of critically ill patients to the nearest hospital has been greatly expedited. And the bridge connects previously isolated communities to each other and to the outside world and has facilitated construction of a health facility, six child development centers, and several government-run public schools.

In 1995, the Salvadoran MDM mission and associated volunteers became more organized. The group began fund-raising among its international solidarity contacts in order to continue its vital work while waiting for funds promised by the European Union. Former and current volunteers were invited to speak at conferences, universities, and other venues around the world, as part of an outreach effort to educate others about the health and human rights reality of El Salvador and the work being done in Morazán. An extensive global support network sprang from this fund-raising, education, and volunteer-recruitment effort. This set the stage for the formal incorporation in 1995 of DGH as a 501(c)3 not-for-profit organization in the United States. This status allows DGH to engage in fund-raising that is tax deductible for the donor but restricts DGH's direct participation in political processes in the United States.

DGH adopted a community-based, grassroots approach, initially staying relatively small in scope. It invested the first years in focused, comprehensive, holistic work in Estancia, Morazán, learning with the campesinos while collaboratively addressing acute and chronic health care needs identified through community participation. Issues and projects prioritized by the communities included the following: nutrition; soil conservation; cooking classes using local produce from community gardens; community-based rehabilitation; women's health and human rights; early child education; adolescent mentoring; and veterinary, medical, and dental care. DGH employed a praxis model, borrowed from liberation theology, which involves "observing, reflecting, acting, and then evaluating." DGH facilitated twice-yearly participatory evaluations to reflect on successes and failures and to plan future activities.

Since these formative days, the Salvadorans who inspired and gave birth to DGH continue to serve as advisors, members, and partners. In 2001, DGH helped to form *Asociación de Campesinos para el Desarrollo Humano* (CDH, Peasants for Human Development) through a partnership with members of the Estancia community. A testament to DGH's long-term capacity building, the Salvadoran government officially recognized CDH as a nonprofit organization in August 2004. Its mission is "to bring together, strengthen, and organize our communities in order to find solutions to the common problems we face, bringing about comprehensive human development."[19] DGH supports CDH with its operation of the Estancia community health center and six Centers for Integral Child Development (*Centros Infantiles de Desarrollo Integral,* CIDIs)—places where children aged two to six receive early childhood development instruction from community education promoters as well as Ministry of Education professionals (the latter were incorporated into the centers after a negotiated agreement with the Salvadoran government in 1998). Children are fed a hot meal daily, prepared by parent volunteers.[20] DGH also supports CDH through broader community health and development projects—microenterprises, high school scholarships, the building of another bridge (this one over the Torola River), as well as a campaign to stop the World Bank's plan to dam the Torola. Solidarity born from pragmatic action is the glue that binds us together.

## Guiding Principles

Continued solidarity with local partners has been among the goals of DGH since its inception. The mission of DGH is "to improve health and foster other human rights with those most in need by accompanying communities, while educating and inspiring others to action."[21] The key aspect of this statement is the notion of accompaniment. This means we do not do things *to* people or

**Figure 16.2** Jennifer Kasper (*right*) making a home visit to a mother and her children in Estancia, El Salvador, 1996. At the time, Kasper was serving as a volunteer pediatrician for Doctors for Global Health.

Copyleft. Courtesy of Doctors for Global Health.

*for* people but in solidarity with them, following their lead and guidance. This approach affirms people's right to control their own destiny, both at the community and the global level.

DGH's development and activities have been guided by the principle of a preferential option for the poor and the marginalized. That is, we choose to work together with, rather than ignore, these groups, while serving the entire community. It is a principle inspired by the Salvadoran people, including Archbishop Romero. Just as Romero's mandate was to be a "voice for those without voice," DGH works "to amplify the voices of the silenced."[22] DGH proactively avoids neo-imperialism (acting in the interest, economically or politically, consciously or unconsciously, of industrialized countries, rather than those of partner communities) by working with local partners only after they have extended a written invitation and by taking care to work at their rhythm and within their defined priorities. Local partners define their own criteria for cooperation and evaluate all potential international volunteers desiring to work with them. This means that DGH, in contrast to some other aid organizations, does not set the agenda or terms of its cooperative efforts but instead responds to locally defined needs and approaches based on DGH experience, resources, and principles of action.

The World Health Organization views health as "a state of complete physical, mental, and social well-being and not merely the absence of disease or infirmity."[23] DGH fully endorses this definition as well as the "Health for All" goal from the 1978 Alma-Ata Conference, which states "health is a fundamental human right, and attainment of the highest possible level of health is a most-important world-wide social goal whose realization requires the action of many other social and economic sectors in addition to the health sector."[24] A set of principles of action, described in Figure 16.3, guides the vision and everyday work of DGH.

Another defining aspect of DGH's work is the concept of liberation medicine, defined by Lanny Smith as "the conscious, conscientious use of health to promote social justice and human dignity."[25] Liberation medicine emphasizes using practical tools (notably *The Universal Declaration of Human Rights* and related documents, art such as street-theater, and community-oriented primary care) to plan and effect palpable action. Smith first used the term to describe DGH's work in El Salvador at the second Health and Human Rights Conference at Harvard University in 1996—organized by the late Dr. Jonathan Mann, one of the founders of the health and human rights field—and later that year at the American Public Health Association (APHA) annual meeting in New York City. Inspiration for this concept came from Ignacio Martín-Baró's *Writings for a Liberation Psychology,* which describes the community and international solidarity found in Morazán.[26] DGH members have given hundreds of presentations and workshops on liberation medicine around the world. Since 2001, a sixteen-hour seminar course on liberation medicine has been part of the core curriculum of the residency programs in social medicine at the Montefiore Medical Center, part of the Albert Einstein College of Medicine in New York.

DGH also recognizes the importance of celebrating the beauty of life through art and other means and of providing a "vaccination of hope"—against cynicism—to those engaged in the struggle against social injustice. DGH puts this spirit—this "alta-alegremia"—into practice during its assemblies, board meetings, and other fund-raising and educational activities. Volunteer musicians or other artists typically accompany each event. Besides being part of the meetings, they play music or exhibit their art in order to raise funds, raise consciousness, and celebrate the human spirit. Among the most important functions of DGH as a social movement is the creation of a space where observation about, reflection on, and action toward health and social justice can take place.

DGH affirms that every human being regardless of race, gender, class, religion, sexual orientation, physical or mental disability, culture, age, or other attribute has the right to a life of dignity, equal treatment, and social justice.

A. DGH works with those who are among the most poor, the most vulnerable, and the stigmatized of the world's population, amplifying their voices that they be heard.

B. DGH's approach is to accompany communities with small, community-oriented health initiatives that also promote human rights, encourage sustainability, and respect environmental concerns.

C. DGH sets an example for how medicine should be practiced by promoting liberation medicine: "The conscious, conscientious use of health to promote human dignity and social justice."[a]

D. DGH promotes health equity as more basic and fundamental than private, corporate interests. Its mandate is to strive for the optimal health and well-being of all members of the human race regardless of ethnicity, sex, sexual preference, or religion.

E. DGH is committed to advocacy and working for social justice both locally and globally. It encourages its members to take action in their own communities and participate in the accompaniment of communities around the world.

F. DGH pledges to be active in the struggle to expose and confront the pervasive and destructive nature of racism and classism (personal and institutionalized, conscious or unconscious) and all other forms of discrimination, both within DGH and in the world at large.

G. DGH is a volunteer organization that invites and encourages those with a desire to help humanity by providing them with a vehicle to use their unique talents and skills in support of the DGH mission. Special efforts are made to reach out to youth, students of all ages, and people with the wisdom of experience.

H. DGH respects and invites those of all backgrounds and beliefs who agree with its mission and principles to join; proselytizing is contrary to the mission and principles.

I. DGH integrates artistic expression that promotes healing and celebrates all life into its activities. These expressions include literature, music, drama, painting, drawing, sculpture, and other art forms.

J. DGH is vigilant to ensure that its projects, programs, affiliations, and fund-raising efforts don't involve even subtle compromise of its values.

K. DGH participates only in investigations, publications, and/or research initiatives that are important to the work of DGH, ethically sound, benefit the involved communities, and are compatible with DGH's mission. Both the involved local communities and the board must approve these efforts.

[a]"Liberation Medicine," www.dghonline.org/libmed.html (accessed January 28, 2009).

**Figure 16.3**   Doctors for Global Health Principles of Action.

## What Makes DGH Unique?

DGH membership includes not only health professionals but also people from diverse fields who are dedicated and willing to work for universal well-being and justice. DGH welcomes members from all walks of life and from any geographic location. Anyone who believes in DGH's mission and principles of action can join and make a difference; there is no membership fee. More than six thousand supporters have formally endorsed DGH and more than five hundred are members.

Participatory democracy is a major goal of DGH, which influences group processes at all levels of the organization, from leadership election to partnership interaction. A DGH member who actively works on health and social justice projects for at least one year, either individually or with any group, can become a voting member. At each general assembly, active voting members elect from their midst six persons to serve on an eighteen-member board of directors for a three-year term. Candidate presentations during elections provoke discussion and debate, which enhances the effectiveness of DGH as a social movement. Several members of communities that DGH accompanies have become voting members in the organization.

DGH has volunteers from the United States, Europe, New Zealand, Japan, Canada, Peru, Mexico, and many other places. It runs a virtual office using Internet, fax, phone, and mail communication. The DGH Web site maintains an archive of the semiannual newsletter, the *DGH Reporter* (which is mailed out to members), as well as the principles of action, official solidarity letters and statements, project descriptions, volunteer opportunities, and membership application forms.[27] Volunteers in the United States, some of them after having served in the field, manage all communication and bank accounts, provide space for DGH activities and files, plan fund-raisers, and make educational presentations about DGH, among other things. There is no paid staff within the United States. Local workers at the project sites, such as community health promoters, receive a living wage.

In addition to having necessary skills, DGH volunteers must understand the area's historical and sociopolitical background, speak the local language (or in the case of certain indigenous languages, at least the very basics to be respectful), and serve with humility and flexibility while respecting the local people, their work, and their culture. All applications must be approved by a DGH committee made up of former volunteers and by members of the community inviting the volunteer. The interview process—which usually includes a telephone interview following discussion of the written application with local partners and in committee—sparks participatory communication between DGH, partner site, and potential volunteer.

All volunteers pay their personal expenses. Industrialized country board members who earn a living wage pay their own transportation, lodging, food, and other fees to attend twice yearly board meetings. Other board meetings, usually held monthly, like the committee meetings, are conducted by telephone or through Internet communication. Frequent flyer miles donated by board members and friends help facilitate travel from global project sites to the United States and other meeting locations for those who otherwise cannot afford to attend.

Funds for community accompaniment and the *DGH Reporter* come from individual donors, institutions, and foundations compatible with DGH principles. To date DGH has not accepted funds from any government or the World Bank, or corporate grants from pharmaceutical company foundations or tobacco foundations. The principles of action that inform the group's work include clear directions on funding sources. It may seem odd that DGH chooses the source of its finances based on its principles rather than its needs, steering clear of special-interest donations, but that very quality has been cited by many local partners and donors as an important reason to work with DGH—because there is no perceived or actual ulterior influence or motivation. This differentiates DGH from countless international NGOs and aid agencies.

DGH's goals include promoting health and social justice in response to partner organization invitations, educating groups worldwide about the realities of social injustice, inspiring people toward constructive action, and implementing conscientious, process-oriented action as well as making concrete, measurable, positive differences at the community level. At the individual level, persons can participate in DGH in many ways, from assuming elected leadership positions to doing committee work, to volunteering globally or in their own community.

## Global to Local Accompaniment

Over the past decade, we have learned a tremendous amount from the campesinos of Morazán in El Salvador. They informed our work as we expanded our efforts to other countries. DGH has been particularly active throughout Latin America.

In 1996 leaders from communities in Chiapas, Mexico—who had been facing low-intensity armed conflict since the signing of the North American Free Trade Agreement (NAFTA) in 1994—asked DGH to assist them in implementing health and human rights projects. Their first request was to have an Internet connection installed and to receive e-mail training so that they could quickly broadcast human rights violations, invite international solidarity, and enhance fund-raising. DGH helped to staff a local referral hospital and since 1988 has been working with Dr. Juan Manuel Canales, winner of the 2006 Jonathan Mann Health and Human Rights Award, to facilitate community health worker training and community-oriented primary care, teach in the community-run high school, and assist with the women's rights and economic development project (women from the community run a sewing, artisan craft, and restaurant cooperative).

In 1997, DGH was invited to support community-based rehabilitation projects in Santa Marta, Cabañas, in northern El Salvador near the Honduran border. The people of Santa Marta, like those in Estancia, had been singled out for being sympathizers of the FMLN. At one point during the armed conflict they were attacked by both the Salvadoran and Honduran military as they were attempting to cross the Río Lempa and seek shelter in Honduras. Hundreds died in what became known as the Río Lempa massacre. Initially DGH was asked to focus its efforts on helping in the rehabilitation clinic, work that has come to include early childhood development and stimulation, elder health and well-being, attention to asthma, and massage. DGH now collaborates with CoCoSI, a dynamic youth group that produces radio programs on human rights, gender, self-esteem, HIV/AIDS, and pregnancy prevention. DGH members also contribute to a scholarship program that enables high school graduates to attend universities in San Salvador and Cuba.

From 2000 to 2004 DGH aided indigenous people near Iquitos, Peru, in legally establishing their land rights and cooperated with a German NGO in providing medical and dental services there. DGH members also helped identify health threats from pollutants being dumped into the Amazon River by transnational mining and oil corporations. Partnership with a parochial clinic in Cusco, Peru, from 2008 to 2012 addressed unmet health care needs for marginalized populations.

Since 2001, DGH has facilitated resource gathering for *Guatemala's Fundación Esfuerzo y Prosperidad* (Work and Prosperity Foundation), an organization of women working on community health and child development projects in poor, marginalized neighborhoods. And in 2009, DGH began working with *Primeros Pasos,* a local Guatemalan NGO promoting primary care in Quetzaltenango (more commonly known as Xela).

Starting in 2005, DGH has accompanied indigenous health promoters in Las Lomitas, Argentina, in projects focusing on women's rights and nutrition. Though not usually focused on disaster relief, DGH assisted in post–Hurricane Mitch relief in Honduras and Nicaragua in 1998, where we accompanied several community-based organizations in their reconstruction and development efforts, and in post-earthquake relief in El Salvador in 2001.[28]

In 2011 DGH expanded its work in Mexico by partnering with *El Centro Popular de Apoyo y Formación para La Salud* (CEPAFOS—The Community Center for Health Training and Support), an NGO in Oaxaca that serves marginalized communities through health promoter training and sharing of cultural knowledge, in part through promotion of traditional healing practices. One of the main goals of CEPAFOS is to strengthen community autonomy.

DGH has also expanded its work beyond Latin America. Invited to Uganda in 1999, DGH worked in coordination with other NGOs and Mbarara University of Science and Technology, along with New York's Montefiore Medical Center, to support local health professional education and hospital services. Through these efforts, the medical school and teaching hospital have improved health services and trained greater numbers of health professionals, most notably local Ugandans. In the more rural Kisoro District in southwestern Uganda, DGH has been promoting community health since 2006 through diverse projects that include village health worker training, malnutrition rehabilitation, and cervical screening.

As our work expanded, we recognized a need to work in solidarity with other people and organizations focused on a ground-up orientation to community development and advocating for reinvigorating the principles of the 1978 Alma-Ata Declaration, including "health for all." We learned of nascent plans for a People's Health Movement in 1999 and DGH members have been involved since its inception. Six DGH members joined the first People's Health Assembly held in Bangladesh in December 2000, attended by fifteen hundred people from seventy-five countries and leading to the official founding of PHM. Since then DGH has become a significant actor within PHM, with representation on its global steering group. DGH participated in the second assembly in Cuenca, Ecuador, in 2005, which had close to two thousand participants from more than ninety-two countries. In January 2007, a DGH contingent joined the PHM at the Nairobi World Social Forum (WSF), the sixth WSF that DGH members attended. DGH also helped PHM organize the first International People's Health University in the United States.[29] Designed as a series of short courses for health activists, to date IPHUs have been held in over fifteen countries, including Bangladesh, Brazil, Canada, Ecuador, Egypt, Greece, India, and the United States, and attended by over one thousand people from more than sixty countries. At the third People's Health Assembly held in Capetown in July 2012, DGH representatives helped coordinate workshops to unite the global justice fight against extractive industries around the world.

## DGH Activism in the United States

DGH has also brought many of the insights and lessons learned from international involvement to domestic activism. When we work with local initiatives and groups, for example, we do so at their own pace and according to their own agenda. We do not necessarily take credit for, or put the DGH name on, projects we help inspire. Since its inception, DGH has encouraged people to work at a local level, within a global perspective, which has helped to connect country struggles. People who act locally have been celebrated via DGH's Hal and Cherry Clements Award, named for two DGH founding board members who are now deceased.[30] Cherry was a teacher who also worked with homeless women. Hal was a school principal active in social justice.

Since 1995 DGH has inspired the creation of a community health center in Davidson, North Carolina; worked with Montefiore Medical Center in the formation of a South Bronx health promoter group; and joined in solidarity against U.S. Navy practice bombing in Vieques, Puerto Rico. DGH advocates against socially unjust policies supported, financed, or otherwise carried out by the U.S. government, such as the practices of the SOA and the Western Hemisphere Institute for Security Cooperation; U.S. torture practices and rendition policies; U.S. antidemocracy activities in El Salvador and Nicaragua; U.S. anti-women's rights policies such as the "Global Gag Rule"[31] and domestic discrimination against immigrants as a result of the 2001 U.S. Patriot Act and similar legislation. And since 2005, DGH has also recruited health professionals to the Common Ground Health Clinic in post-Katrina New Orleans, and cosponsored with Tulane University a conference on the health and human rights dimensions of the effects of the hurricane and its aftermath.

DGH and its members are active in professional and academic circles in Atlanta (as a founding member of the Atlanta Alliance for Health and Human Rights), North America, and beyond, regularly presenting work at APHA and other conferences, schools, and religious and civic organizations. DGH also helped found the U.S.-based Mexico Solidarity Network and was among the program leadership of the 2004 Boston Social Forum and the first U.S. Social Forum held in 2007 in Atlanta.

## Challenges

Some of the challenges faced by DGH are unique to its particular modus operandi, while others are similar to those encountered by any humanitarian organization. Because DGH works primarily through volunteers, its membership and especially its leadership are relatively exclusionary. DGH requires people to work without pay and to finance their own travel and other expenses, such that only people of substantial economic means—or those highly creative at achieving personal sponsorship—can volunteer. DGH tries to address this potential tendency toward elitism by helping secure support for persons from cultures underrepresented on the board to enable them to participate. DGH also created the Sandy Kemp Scholarships, which cover annual general assembly registration fees for people requesting assistance. One of our international challenges involves political obstacles to facilitating global participation at DGH events. United States embassies in El Salvador, Nicaragua, and some other countries have often treated local country DGH members who have applied for visas to travel to events in the United States as if they were inferior humans or would-be criminals, yelling at them for no reason, challenging their right to travel, and ignoring letters of invitation from universities and other legitimate sponsors. Since 2005, over 90 percent of visas applied for by DGH members have been denied, despite efforts by some U.S. congresspersons. This visa-rejection phenomenon—reflecting a clear racial and class bias—was one reason for locating the 2007 meeting in El Salvador, so that partners in Central America could readily attend.

Acquiring sufficient funds to address commitments to partner organizations is a difficulty not unique to DGH, but this is made perhaps more challenging given the group's self-restrictive and principled funding stipulations. DGH has many individual donors who give an astoundingly high portion of their limited income and a few others who are able to donate large sums. Sometimes private foundations have difficulty supporting ongoing projects even if the work is exemplary and they have been shown to make a positive difference in people's lives. At the same time, the commitment DGH has made to working at the rhythm, and according to the priorities, of local partners sometimes makes its goals and actions seem too flexible or open-ended for funding agencies that prefer to keep their recipients' work neatly packaged.

### Future Directions

DGH would like to work itself out of a job. But as long as there is social injustice, DGH and groups like it will need to persist and persevere. Even if health and social justice become the norm globally, some must remain vigilant in monitoring and safeguarding the well-being of people worldwide. As a social movement, DGH is motivated to become ever more effective at inspiring action and affecting change.

In the future, DGH accompaniment will continue to take on a broad scope, well beyond the provision of basic health care and fully addressing the social determinants of health.[32] We will continue our work in El Salvador, where the threat of a dam on the Torola River in Estancia has proven a focal point for recent community protest involving DGH and other international groups. Such a dam would destroy the economic and social lives of thousands. As a consequence of a Salvadoran version of the U.S. Patriot Act becoming law in 2007, Salvadorans can face years of incarceration simply for participating in peaceful protests, such that activism for health and related concerns means potential privation of liberty. In 2009 death-squad activity began again with the killing of Santa Marta community activist Marcelo Rivera on June 18 and subsequent death threats to DGH local partners. DGH publicized and condemned these acts.

In order to confront the current global climate of social injustice, DGH will continue to apply the tools of liberation medicine and celebrate the beauty of humanity through art and participatory democracy. DGH will continue to accompany communities and to grow our social movement toward health and social justice.

## Notes

The authors would like to thank DGH founding members Shirley Novak, Clyde Smith, and Renée Smith for their tireless editing of this manuscript, DGH volunteer extraordinaire Zenaida Izquierdo, and all members of DGH and its partner communities for their inspiration and accompaniment in the struggle for health and social justice.

1. The civil war took place from 1980 to 1992 between the Salvadoran government (which received up to five million USD a day from the U.S. government to prop it up) and the Frente Farabundo Martí para la Liberación Nacional (FMLN, Farabundo Martí National Salvadoran Liberation Front). Seventy-five thousand persons died during the war, most noncombatants.

2. Lanny Smith with Ken Hilsbos, "Liberation Medicine: Health and Justice," *DGH Reporter,* 3 (1999), www.dghonline.org (accessed September 23, 2009).

3. General assemblies are held every year, where all members and any others interested are invited to gather, discuss health and social justice issues, participate in the DGH election process, and talk with local partner representatives.

4. See "Alta Alegremia," www.altaalegremia.com.ar/ (accessed July 6, 2008).

5. In 2001 SOA was renamed the Western Hemisphere Institute for Security Cooperation. Located in Columbus, Georgia, it has been responsible for instructing thousands of Latin American military officers in torture techniques and other counterinsurgency training measures.

6. The peace accords, signed on January 16, 1992, were part of a negotiated ceasefire agreement between the Salvadoran Government and the FMLN.

7. Mark Danner, *The Massacre at El Mozote* (New York: Vintage, 1994); Mark Danner, "The Truth of El Mozote," *New Yorker,* December 6, 1993: 50–133; Leigh Binford, *The El Mozote Massacre* (Tucson: University of Arizona Press, 1996).

8. See PHM Web site for a more complete explanation of the group and a look at the PHM charter: www.phmovement.org. More information on Alma-Ata can be found in chapter 12.

9. Liberation theology is founded on the belief that human suffering and social justice are matters of concern to God, and that it is the duty of spiritual persons to fight for social justice for the marginalized, the silenced, and the stigmatized. Preferential option for the poor—sometimes called "O for the P"—is a concept from liberation theology that religions and social movements should preferentially work with the poor and stigmatized.

10. Michele Gierck, *700 Days in El Salvador: An Australian Woman's Unexpected Journey from Suburbia to a Guerilla War* (Melbourne, Australia: Coretext, 2006).

11. It currently possesses among the worst poverty indices in the country, while receiving among the least aid.

12. The concept of health as a human right was advanced by the late Jonathan Mann (1947–1998), a DGH founding advisory council member and first director of the World Health Organization's Global Program on AIDS (until 1990). He argued that health is indeed a human right, that all human rights in their aggregate are necessary

for good health, and that health and human rights, when operating together, produce a synergistic effect.

13. Community-oriented primary care was developed by Sidney and Emily Kark in Pholela, South Africa (see chapter 6), and subsequently implemented in many areas of the world as a way of working together with communities in a participatory, empowering, effective manner.

14. Lanny Smith, "Building Health Where the Peace Is New in Near-Postwar El Salvador," *Development* 50 (July 2007): 127–133.

15. The concept of witnessing implies not only accompanying persons and communities but also helping to amplify their voices in places and on occasions where those voices are silenced by oppression (or are not being heard).

16. Health as reconciliation means using health as a way to facilitate rapprochement between former enemies.

17. "Keeping the eyes of the world on El Salvador" as Ramiro Cortez and other health promoters termed this presence.

18. Accompaniment is a DGH term meaning to be with a community, both physically and in solidarity with their actions.

19. "History of DGH in the Community," http://www.dghonline.org/our-work/estancia-el-salvador (accessed September 15, 2011).

20. Centers are located in Estancia as well as Agua Blanca, Cacaopera. Cacaopera is a municipality in Morazán.

21. See DGH Web site, www.dghonline.org (accessed September 11, 2009).

22. See DGH Web site, www.dghonline.org (accessed September 11, 2009).

23. Preamble to the Constitution of the World Health Organization as Adopted by the International Health Conference, New York, June 19–July 22, 1946.

24. "The Declaration of Alma-Ata," www.righttohealthcare.org/Docs/DocumentsC.htm (accessed July 6, 2000).

25. Smith, "Liberation Medicine." See DGH Web site for more detailed information on liberation medicine: www.dghonline.org.

26. Ignacio Martín-Baró, *Writings for a Liberation Psychology*, ed. Adrianne Aron and Shawne Corne (Cambridge, MA: Harvard University Press, 1994).

27. See DGH Web site, www.dghonline.org (accessed September 11, 2009).

28. Hurricane Mitch brought terrible destruction to Honduras, and to a lesser extent Nicaragua and El Salvador.

29. Laura Turiano and Lanny Smith, "The Catalytic Synergy of Health and Human Rights: The People's Health Movement and the Right to Health and Health Care Campaign," *Health and Human Rights Journal* 10 (2008): 1–12.

30. Because DGH has members from around the world, acting locally means within one's own community in any country.

31. Also known as the "Mexico City Policy," a U.S. policy put into place by presidential mandate under Ronald Reagan in 1985, reinstated by President Bush in 2001, and repealed first by President Clinton in 1993, then by President Obama in 2009, that prohibited NGOs that received any U.S. funding from performing, advocating for, or simply discussing abortion under any circumstances, even if they used non-U.S. funds for these activities.

32. Commission on Social Determinants of Health, *Closing the Gap in a Generation: Health Equity through Action on the Social Determinants of Health. Final Report of the Commission on Social Determinants of Health* (Geneva: World Health Organization, 2008).

# Chapter 17

# Doctors Across Blockades

## American Medical Students in Cuba

**Razel Remen and Brea Bondi-Boyd**

Imagine a young generation of U.S. health progressives traveling to an "enemy state" to be trained in something that has eluded U.S. activists and policy-makers for a century: social justice in health. The *Escuela Latinoamericana de Medicina* (ELAM), the Latin American School of Medicine, was founded in 1999 as an inspired outreach program by then Cuban president Fidel Castro. Its mission is to use Cuban models and Cuban expertise to train primary care physicians for work in underserved communities outside of Cuba by offering full scholarships to low-income students from thirty different countries in the Caribbean, Latin America, Africa, and North America.[1] The first group of U.S. students was admitted in 2001, and now more than one hundred are in attendance. All U.S. students apply through the New York City–based Interreligious Foundation for Community Organization, whose mission is "to help forward the struggles of oppressed peoples for justice and self determination."[2]

At first, U.S. students did not have official permission to study in Cuba but could travel under the vague "fully hosted" clause of the Department of Treasury travel regulations for Cuba. But in June 2004, a week before ELAM's final exams, the administration of former U.S. president George W. Bush eliminated the fully hosted policy and sent out a bulletin stating that U.S. citizens in Cuba had one week to leave the island or face legal consequences.[3] A special notification was sent directly to the school for all seventy U.S. students, generating a lot of panic and concern about our future at ELAM. Thanks to the intervention of the Congressional Black Caucus, the program became classified as a "cultural exchange." Under State Department rules, the U.S. students were issued a two-year travel license, which has been renewed every two years since then, despite the U.S. embargo against Cuba.

Both of us were among the initial students from the United States and thus went to Cuba clandestinely and at personal risk. We both come from working-class families whose struggles taught us a different, critical view of the U.S. health experience. We come from opposite coasts, one of us (Razel) from New York City and the other (Brea) from Sacramento. Much of what we have learned from the ELAM experience has been the same, but it has affected our perspectives somewhat differently. We tell our stories in what follows.

## Razel Remen

My earliest memories are filled with images of my sick mother. I can remember the smell of illness, of her lying in bed calling for her own mother who had died long before I was born. Most distinctly I remember my fear during those times, the helplessness of being just four years old, and feeling the weight of being the only person around to help her. This was a time before my mother had health insurance or a regular job. It was a time when she did a lot of substitute teaching and had very little access to health care. More recently I am filled with memories of her last days being terminally ill in the Cabrini Hospice in New York City, a place that cared for her in a way I never would have been able to do at the time. I remember the day the hospice director came to tell us that my mother would have to leave the hospice because her health insurance plan only covered one week's stay. The news left me with a deep sense of despair, and yet at the time it seemed normal that the hospice had denied my mother the right to die with dignity because her insurance would only pay for a week. That experience has shaped one of my enduring impressions of the U.S. health care system—that it can be excellent, but only for those who can afford it. That memory was also one of the principal motivating forces behind my decision to study medicine in Cuba, where all citizens receive health care regardless of their economic situation.

I grew up in a single-parent household in Brooklyn. The eighties in NYC, as I remember it, was a time of survival. New York was a place of intense violence and poverty but also of social change and development. I remember the adults around me constantly debating the politics of the Vietnam War and conspiracies surrounding the deaths of socially conscious musicians like Bob Marley and John Lennon. We were members of the local food cooperative where we bought organic food and soy milk long before most people had even heard of such products. My house was always tuned to the independent, listener-supported Pacifica radio station, so I grew up to the voices of great independent journalists as well as other forward thinkers in the progressive political and arts communities. These influences instilled in me the belief that the creation of a better world was not only possible, but that it was an ongoing process in which I myself would one day have a role to play.

Ever since I was a child, I enjoyed helping others. I had a strong interest in health care, so I decided to become an emergency medical technician (EMT). I began to volunteer for the Bedford-Stuyvesant Volunteer Ambulance Corps (BSVAC) while I waited for my name to come up for the city EMT exams. BSVAC is a nonprofit organization that was founded in 1988 to address the lack of emergency medical services in "Bed-Stuy." When I was growing up, Bed-Stuy was one of the worst neighborhoods in Brooklyn. During my mother's childhood it had been filled with tree-lined streets and elegant brownstones. But times had changed, most of the trees had been cut down, and many of those once elegant brownstones had been burnt down, abandoned, and converted into crack houses or crash pads for the homeless. By 1998 Bedford-Stuyvesant had the highest infant mortality rate in the city, more than double the city average of 6.8 deaths per 1,000 births.[4] That was partly because 14 percent of Bedford-Stuyvesant residents did not receive needed health care, compared to 5 percent of those living in wealthier Brooklyn neighborhoods.[5]

These problems led to the creation of BSVAC. Before BSVAC, EMTs were often reluctant to take calls from the neighborhood due to the perceived and real risk to their personal safety. As a consequence, Bed-Stuy had one of the worst ambulance response times—thirty minutes, well below the five-minute average of the rest of the city. Within a year of its creation, BSVAC had lowered the ambulance response time for Bed-Stuy and the adjacent Brownsville neighborhood to four minutes, making this one of the few aspects of medical care that was comparable to the rest of the city.[6]

Through BSVAC we delivered emergency care for heart attacks, stabbings, and simple burns. It was there that I first began to understand the importance of community-based medicine. Most BSVAC volunteers had the same low-income, African American, African, and Latino backgrounds as the populations we were serving. The Bedford-Stuyvesant residents responded well to us not just because we fulfilled a basic need but also because they trusted us. We were from the same area, spoke the same lingo, shared the same culture, and understood the dynamics that affected their daily lives.

Over time, BSVAC grew into an informal community center. Aside from having a fully equipped ambulance always ready to take whatever 911 call that came in, it provided free EMT training for anyone interested in volunteering and formed the Youth Corps and Trauma Troopers to train neighborhood kids in CPR and other basic life-saving measures. BSVAC became a local fixture that helped to change and improve the overall morale of the neighborhood. By simultaneously caring for the community and offering life-saving, as opposed to life-damaging, options to local youth, BSVAC changed the current and future prospects of the neighborhood. It was my experience with BSVAC that instilled in me a desire to practice community-oriented medicine. I began to look into both medical and nursing programs; and nursing training seemed more community oriented. However, that year, 1999, New York State governor George E. Pataki cut the already drastically reduced budget for city and state universities. The cuts reduced the number of classes available, making it difficult to get into a City University of New York (NYC's public university system) nursing program. That same year, just ninety miles south of the Florida Keys, Cuba initiated one of the most creative approaches to addressing the global shortages in health care personnel among the poor by opening its doors to international medical students. I did not find out about ELAM until I graduated from the Evergreen State College (in Olympia, Washington) three years later.

One day, as I was conversing with a neighbor about my interest in medicine, she suddenly got very excited and told me about a new medical school in Cuba that she had heard about on the radio. I went home and immediately began researching Cuba's medical system and their new training program. I found out that ELAM was designed to be an international medical school whose primary mission was to train students from low-income backgrounds to become physicians who would serve as a permanent source of health care for communities in need. I also found out that in May 2000 members of the Congressional Black Caucus visited Cuba and were given a tour of the ELAM program. During this visit, Congressman Bennie Thompson from Mississippi met with Fidel Castro and expressed great admiration for the school. He also spoke of the Third World conditions that existed among his own constituents in the Mississippi Delta. At that point President Castro extended the scholarship program to U.S. students interested in returning to the United States to provide care to people in medically underserved communities. I figured that I qualified, so I applied through the Interreligious Foundation for Community Organization and was accepted.

My group was the third cohort of U.S. students accepted to ELAM. We were nine in total. I was both excited and intimidated. How would we be received as citizens of the country that was most responsible for the misery of the developing world? Would we be perceived as representatives of U.S. imperialism or as advocates for change? From the start we had a mixed welcome. On the whole, the Cubans we interacted with were happy to have us there. They viewed our presence as an important step toward improving relations between Cuba and the United States. The response we received from our Latin American peers varied greatly depending on the person's country and economic background. Oddly enough, it was Latin Americans from the poorer nations and poorer communities who were most receptive to us. Those from wealthier countries and more privileged backgrounds were more likely to believe that we had no right to be there. I struggled with my own conflicting feelings as to whether I, as an American, truly deserved to receive this wonderful gift of a free medical education.

As my medical training continued, my sense of responsibility deepened. These feelings only increased when I entered clinical training. It was one thing for me to be in the United States and read about the injustices of the U.S. economic blockade against Cuba and the hardships and shortages forced upon the island. It was quite another to actually be in Cuba for an extended period of time, witness the lives of my patients and the Cuban people generally, and have my daily life, work, and studies influenced by Washington's spite and whims.

These difficult conditions also helped build a sense of community. During my first two years of study, before Cuba had established strong political ties with Venezuela and stabilized energy supplies, there had been frequent blackouts, at least two or three times a day, which at times made preparing for exams difficult. We adjusted by studying by flashlight, or we would huddle around emergency rechargeable lights. Sometimes the blackouts would extend for several days, suspending the pumping of water into the dormitories. These difficulties fostered a comradeship among us. We would form bucket lines from the river to the dorms to fill up the tanks so that we could flush the dorm toilets. We did the same for the shower tanks when the water trucks came by. If it happened to rain during these times we would rush outside in our bathing suits with bars of soap in hand and laughingly shower in the rain. As Cuba's relations with Venezuela strengthened, the blackouts became less frequent and overall living conditions improved, yet shortages were still problematic in the clinics, and I struggled with my guilt regarding the passive role I had played in the United States in allowing the blockade to continue.

In my clinical years I had to use sterilized, recycled gloves to examine patients. Diagnostic tests frequently had to be postponed because there was no water to sterilize the equipment or the equipment was missing a part. During my orthopedic rotation I cared for a woman who suffered from a hip fracture and was forced to spend over a week in the hospital awaiting surgery because no materials were available to perform the operation. I tried to console her as best I could. Day after day I would explain to her that the prosthetic piece necessary to complete her surgery had still not arrived in the country and that she would have to spend another agonizing day in the hospital, barely able to eat or urinate because of the intense pain of her uncorrected hip fracture. Yet not once did I sense even the slightest hint that she or her family looked at me as if I were to blame. Nonetheless, it still made me feel guilty and angry that the U.S. blockade that caused so many of the general shortages in Cuba also affected the medical system and caused such enormous suffering.

What has set my education in Cuba apart from what I might have received in the United States has nothing to do with the actual medical content that was taught. Cuban and American medicine are fundamentally the same, and both use the same techniques and approaches to disease management and care. What separates Cuban medicine from American medicine is the former's strong primary care and community-based orientation. As a poor country, Cuba has been forced to rely on social cohesiveness and community building to maintain a functioning society. In terms of medicine this means that the family, the community, and health care are understood to be interdependent pieces of the overall system. This can be seen in several ways. Family practitioners live in the same neighborhoods in which they work, so they have the dual perspective of being both community members and caregivers. They fully understand the family and neighborhood dynamics that affect their patient population and are thus able to incorporate this knowledge into providing more integrative care. For example, when family members are needed and expected to stay in the hospital to care for loved ones, they are given paid time off to do so.

State social welfare policies underpin the community medicine approach. Pregnant women, underweight children, and people with certain chronic illnesses are furnished special diets to ensure that their health and well-being do not deteriorate. After giving birth, women are given a year of paid maternity leave to ensure that they will be able to breastfeed their children and provide them the nurturing needed for a healthy start in life. The elderly and the disabled also receive supportive services, and family members are paid a regular stipend to care for them. In cases where no family members can look after elderly and disabled individuals, the government pays community members to do so.

### Coming Back

The main problem with having been trained in Cuba is that we have been spoiled by being taught how to operate within an organized and integrated system of medical care. Health care in the United States is anything but organized. There is little continuity of care, and patients often jump from one practitioner to another or are treated by more than one type of specialist without any true dialogue among the various physicians. More often than not, the overall management of the patient is decided by the bottom line instead of what is best for the patient's well-being. In all honesty, I cannot imagine being happy working in such a system, though I do see myself participating in efforts to build a just health care system in the United States, similar to the one in which I worked in Cuba.

In my fifth year of medicine I spent nine weeks learning how to set up community-oriented models of medicine in settings that were lacking medical care. I can envision myself putting this knowledge to work in rural America, where there is typically very little or no health care available. At a recent health educators' conference in Cuba, I met a physician from rural Wisconsin who had been inspired to create a free health care system in his own small county for those without insurance. The more he did, the more others in his local health care community wanted to help. Soon, one local surgeon was performing free surgeries and two of the local pharmacists were providing free medications.

The actions of these physicians represent one of many examples of a reawakening social consciousness in the United States. As the debate over how to resolve the U.S. health care crisis raged in Washington in 2009–10, the main argument against providing a "public option" was that it would be too costly. If nothing else, Cuba, as a low-income country, continues to disprove the notion that universal health coverage is too expensive. Of course, the Cuban system's efficiency stems *both* from its public, universal design *and* the reality that the population has high general health due to more egalitarian social conditions than in most countries. A recent U.S. ELAM graduate, now doing her residency, told me that one of the most difficult aspects of her return to the United States is the absence of a cohesive public system of health care services. The patients admitted to a hospital are far sicker than those admitted in Cuba, something she directly attributes to the poor primary care system here. For the first time in her professional career, she has found herself having to decide how a patient will be managed based upon what they can afford to pay or what their insurance will (or will not) cover. The repercussions of these decisions are often the death of the patient.

After graduation, I joined this collective experience of U.S. ELAM graduates facing the deficiencies of the U.S. health care system in my work as coordinator for the Civilian Medical Resources Network. This nonprofit organization helps active duty soldiers obtain medical and mental health care services in the civilian sector when military services have failed to meet their needs. In my Family Medicine residency program, I am well aware that political activism is a prerequisite for medical practice. I participated in the 2010 Physicians for a National Health Program leadership conference and have also worked with the Network of Health Providers for a National Health Program (NHP2), a New Mexico–based organization that has co-proposed several amendments to the state constitution that would guarantee health care as a human right to all state residents.

## Brea Bondi-Boyd

At home in Sacramento, California, I volunteered during summer breaks from my studies in Cuba at a primary care clinic, around the corner from where I grew up, which served a mainly indigent population. Budget cuts had left the medical staff relying on fewer workers for an ever-growing number of patients. In the waiting area there were signs posted on the wall that said, "You are not guaranteed to see a doctor today." Every time I looked at those signs I asked myself, with hundreds of thousands of doctors working in the U.S. health care system, what are we doing to make the situation better for patients like these in Sacramento?

My interest in science and health began with animals. I took a special interest in the animals in my neighborhood and in the reptiles my dad found at his work sites as he was building bridges for the Union Pacific Railroad. To improve my chances of studying biology at university, my parents pleaded with principals of schools outside our district that had better educational programs to let me in. In the third grade, I was finally allowed to transfer to a school with a gifted educational program. Later, when I learned that there was no money for university, I resigned myself to the idea of going to community college, graduating early from my high school because it was becoming increasingly violent.

At the local community college, I started taking biology classes and found to my surprise that all my professors had their PhDs and loved their work. I was so inspired that for the first time in my life I felt hopeful about getting an education. I still remember the awe I felt when I held the heart of a cow in my hands during my first physiology class. After completing an associate's degree, I applied for financial aid and loans so that I could move to San Diego and complete a Bachelor of Science degree in physiology. I began volunteering in a high school outreach program in a marginalized neighborhood. I felt a bond with these students struggling with their personal and home lives, many of them wondering if it would be simpler just to enroll in the army. Like me, many of these students did not have role models in their families who had gone to college.

Before graduation, I went for an HIV test at my university's student clinic and experienced the scare of a false positive. The test was repeated and

**Figure 17.1** ELAM students participate in International Day of Workers national march, May 1, 2007. *From left to right:* Chilean ELAM student, Brea Bondi-Boyd, two Brazilian ELAM students, and Chilean ELAM student. Poster says: Union of Young Communists. Revolution: Independence Internationalism Patriotism Heroism Unity.

Courtesy of Brea Bondi-Boyd.

confirmed negative, but I began to think seriously about the implications of a positive result. I decided to volunteer as a counselor at a camp for children living with HIV/AIDS. There I met thirteen-year-old Erik, who was small for his age and had several developmental disabilities complicated by ADHD (Attention Deficit Hyperactivity Disorder). I spent eight days and nights as his counselor. This camp provided a safe haven for these kids, away from the struggles of their day-to-day lives. I was stunned by the volume of HIV medications they were administered, in some cases through a duodenal tube because their stomachs could not handle the toxicity of up to twenty pills at a time. As I learned more and more about the medical complications of HIV/AIDS from the doctors and nurses volunteering during their vacations, I began to consider going to medical school.

Shortly after my first year at camp, my closest friend from college, who was a member of the Socialist Workers Party, invited me on an educational trip to Cuba during which we toured schools and health facilities. I thought this would be a great opportunity to see how HIV was managed in Cuba and learn firsthand about their medical system. The reading material my friend loaned me complemented what was discussed in my household growing up and reminded me of the kinds of books my dad shared with me. My father had been a member of Students for a Democratic Society and my mother was a die-hard feminist. I was familiar with the history of workers' unions in the United States and how they had lost much momentum as the country began outsourcing and downsizing the means of production, not to mention the fact that McCarthyism had all but killed the word socialism. Though I had attended political meetings and protests with my parents, I felt disconnected from any sort of organized political movement. Nonetheless, I was eager to see how Cuba had not only achieved a revolution—implementing universal health care, education, housing, and other social rights—but also maintained it despite a fifty-year blockade by the most powerful country in the world.

That trip to Cuba in the summer of 2001 gave me my first real look at Cuba from the inside. All of the mainstream media images I had seen in the United States, about Cuba as a dictatorship and about its lack of freedoms, disappeared. I saw for the first time a country where social justice values, health, and medicine all worked together. Cuba's doctors were what I had always imagined physicians should be: humble, accessible, and knowledgeable. We visited ELAM, where I met with professors who explained their three-tiered medical system, anchored by primary care and preventive medicine. We also visited various research centers, where I was impressed by the fact that public health priorities were driving the vaccine and pharmaceutical research projects, based on population needs. I felt an immediate camaraderie with the Cuban health system's approach and with the Cuban people, and I knew that I wanted to be trained in this environment.

I arrived at ELAM in March 2003 to take accelerated Spanish language courses, six months before the school year began, and nearly two years after a long application and interview process. During my first two years at ELAM, while receiving basic science instruction, I realized that the U.S. delegation was afraid to associate with the word *socialism* even though ELAM's very existence was rooted in socialist ideas. While our delegation's attitude disappointed me, it was also a stimulus for me and a small group of fellow Americans to form a socialist student group as an act of solidarity with Cuba and the Latin American students. We wanted to show another face of the United States, one unfamiliar to these students. Our effort caught the attention of a group of students on campus who were planning a trip to Venezuela to help with the national literacy campaign started under President Hugo Chávez. They invited us to join them, but, unfortunately, after anti-Chávez groups began targeting Cuban physicians already working in Venezuela's poorest regions, the trip was deemed too risky for U.S. students.

The majority of the Latin American students arrived as proud representatives of left-wing political organizations in their home countries, such as MST (*Movimento Sem Terra*) from Brazil, the Sandinistas from Nicaragua, the Zapatistas from Mexico, MAS (*Movimiento al Socialismo*) from Bolivia, and MIR (*Movimiento de Izquierda Revolucionaria*) from Chile as well as respective Communist and Socialist parties from each country. I found that U.S. media reports on Latin America differed sharply from the perspectives and personal histories many students shared with me. The United States had portrayed Chávez's election in Venezuela as a military coup, but the students at ELAM illuminated its true nature as a democratic process. Chileans spoke with me about how Socialist president Salvador Allende's social transformations in the 1970s have all but disappeared from textbooks in today's Chile. These experiences made ELAM as much a political school as it was a medical school. In the same environment in which we studied medicine, we simultaneously learned new languages, customs, histories, tolerance, and internationalism.

Living those first two years at ELAM in one room with twenty other women from Nigeria, Cape Verde, and Mexico, I, together with the other U.S. students, discovered that no matter how different our own backgrounds and political commitments, there was indeed a U.S. "culture" that we shared and that affected our ways of interacting. Within the U.S. delegation, I found a sisterhood. One of my dearest friends was born in Ecuador and raised by her mother in New Mexico. Another close friend, originally from India, eventually brought her mother, who was Muslim and spoke Urdu, to live with her in Cuba so that she could receive better health care. A classmate of ours, who lost his home after Hurricane Katrina struck New Orleans in 2005, was welcomed in my hometown of Sacramento with a place to stay and a job after he was forced to relocate. We learned to put most of our political differences aside and found ways to integrate into ELAM by celebrating those U.S. health heroes and heroines who have supported social change. Particularly inspiring are those behind community clinics, like the Birthing Project in Sacramento. Its founder, Kathryn Hall-Trujillo,[7] motivates the U.S. students, as well as many other ELAM students who have collaborated with her abroad. Graduates from Honduras, for example, helped Hall-Trujillo to establish a Cuban-modeled clinic in the Garifuna community of Honduras, serving a population that previously had no medical care. In the San Francisco Bay area, La Clínica de la Raza and The Effort in Sacramento are further examples of well-established, family-focused community clinics. Physicians from these organizations visited us in Cuba and discussed the need for community doctors, affirming the purpose of our training.

Hall-Trujillo's Birthing Project is similar in principle to Cuba's model of integrated family medicine (*Medicina General Integral,* MGI), which grew out of the need to train doctors who came from the community they would serve. MGI teaches that the responsibility of doctors is to shorten the distance between themselves and their patients. I learned in Cuba that medicine should extend itself into the community and reach out to those who cannot come to the hospital because of poverty, sickness, or distance.

The first level of care in Cuba is the *consultorio,* a facility that serves two to three hundred families. During my clinical rotation through MGI, there was a dengue epidemic. As students, we were assigned to a *consultorio* team doing surveillance for cases of fever. I remember the Caribbean heat as I waded through the cramped corridors of housing structures, making sure to knock on every door. The community began to recognize my face and *gringa* accent, and on some days, even before I began knocking on doors, concerned neighbors would alert me to a new case of fever. This fieldwork became our class for five weeks, and our hospital was converted into Havana's center for dengue cases. The students rotated being on call with the other medical staff, twenty-four hours on, seventy-two hours off. We continued like this until the rainy season subsided and mosquito control measures began to counterbalance our surveillance efforts.

My experience during this epidemic instilled in me tremendous respect for the Cuban family physician and for the collaboration and cooperation that takes place among different branches of medicine and public health in Cuba. It also shed light on the community connection that goes into all consultorio tasks. Community members regularly come to the aid of their consultorio, either going out of their way to alert a doctor to a sick person or identifying an area that might need vector control. This extended approach to family medicine is what separates the Cuban model of family medicine from the model in the United States, where physicians typically do not live where they work, rarely make house calls, and almost never venture into the community in a public health capacity. The Cuban model has been so effective that thirty-five nations in the Americas, Africa, Asia, and Europe have adopted it.[8]

Working with family physicians in Cuba, I witnessed a large variety of programs, but I was most impressed by the HIV campaign, as a result of which Cuba can boast the lowest HIV incidence in the Americas. I observed HIV/AIDS care at the Pedro Kourí Institute of Tropical Medicine (IPK) where soft-spoken

**Figure 17.2**   ELAM students participate in International Day of Workers march, May 1, 2009. *From left to right:* Chilean ELAM student, Uruguayan ELAM student, Brea Bondi-Boyd, and Chilean ELAM student. Poster says: Our obligation is to succeed. Union of Young Communists.

Courtesy of Brea Bondi-Boyd.

doctors like Jorge Pérez have worked since the first cases arrived in the 1980s.[9] During my fifth year of training, I participated in an elective rotation at IPK. The doctors in the AIDS-oncology ward took time during rounds to explain the costs of manufacturing antiretroviral therapy (ART) medications. In 2001, Cuba began manufacturing generic ART medications so that it could afford to give them free to all AIDS patients requiring them.[10] In an effort to combat market domination by pharmaceutical companies, Cuba has tried to make AIDS treatment available and affordable by creating a submarket in which the commercialization and patent costs are eliminated. Since the introduction of the ART program in Cuba in 2001, deaths from AIDS have dramatically decreased.[11]

### Reflections on the Future

Because of my studies in Cuba, I realize that as a family physician I must educate myself not just medically but politically and socially. Upon graduation from ELAM in 2009, I was immediately greeted by media reports on the urgency of health care reform, the enormous need for primary care expansion, and the dearth of physicians willing to work in underserved areas. As I transition back to life in the United States, I am determined not to stand still. I have begun a Family Medicine residency program at Contra Costa Regional Medical Center, a county hospital in a very underserved community in Martinez, California. My aspiration is to adapt the Cuban delivery model to what Americans call full-spectrum family/community medicine. I'd like to create something similar to the *consultorio/policlínico* that takes into account public health conditions and family size and structure, focusing on incorporating the "patient" into the community, including enabling work and school attendance. I would also like to be able to use this information to determine medical need and the volume of house calls—anathema in the U.S. context. I think the biggest challenge being back in the United States is that communities don't really exist in the way they do in Cuba.

In Cuba, the purpose of education is to create a sustainable human resource. In his 1999 keynote address at the founding of ELAM, Fidel said, "We trust that [the students] will be better doctors than their predecessors and professors who are presently giving them the scientific knowledge and expertise acquired in forty years, both inside Cuba as well as in selfless and heroic services rendered to Third World countries in every continent. They will be doctors ready to work wherever they are needed, in the remotest corners of the world where others are not willing to go. Such are the doctors who will graduate from this School."[12] This training has made me part of an army of white coats, ready to fight inequalities in health in my home country.

### Notes

1. Razel Remen and Lillian Holloway, "A Student Perspective on ELAM and Its Educational Program," *Social Medicine* 3(2) (July 2008), www.socialmedicine.info.
2. Interreligious Foundation for Community Organization, www.ifconews.org (accessed September 21, 2009).
3. Mark P. Sullivan, "CRS Report for Congress, Cuba: Issues for the 109th Congress," Congressional Research Service. The Library of Congress. Updated January 13, 2005, http://fpc.state.gov/documents/organization/44012.pdf (accessed September 28, 2009).
4. Jennifer Steinhauer, "High Infant Mortality Rates in Brooklyn Mystify Experts," *New York Times*, February 29, 2000.
5. Adam Karpati et al., *Health Disparities in New York City* (New York: New York City Department of Health and Mental Hygiene, 2004).
6. Bedford-Stuyvesant Volunteer Ambulance Corps, "About Us," www.bsvac.org (accessed October 15, 2008).
7. Birthing Project USA, http://birthingprojectusa.com/kathrynhalltrujillo.htm (accessed September 15, 2009).

8. Ministerio de Salud Pública, "Programa Integral de Salud. Países que lo Integran Según Continentes. 2007," in *Anuario Estadístico de Salud 2007* (Havana: Ministerio de Salud Publica, 2008).

9. Jorge Pérez Ávila, *SIDA: Confesiones a un Médico* (Havana: Casa Editora Abril, 2008).

10. Programa Nacional de Prevención y Control de ITS/VIH/SIDA, "Fármacos y tratamiento," www.sld.cu (accessed October 12, 2008).

11. Jorge Pérez et al., *Approaches to the Management of HIV/AIDS in Cuba* (Geneva: WHO, 2004).

12. Keynote Address by Dr. Fidel Castro Ruz, President of the Republic of Cuba, at the Inauguration of the Latin American School of Medicine. Havana, November 15, 1999. http://www.cuba.cu/gobierno/discursos/1999/ing/i151199i.html (accessed September 15, 2009).

# Part VI

# Conclusion

# Chapter 18

# Across the Generations

## Lessons from Health Internationalism

**Anne-Emanuelle Birn and Theodore M. Brown**

For almost a century, U.S. health leftists have looked overseas for what they hoped to accomplish at home. They found sites of political struggle where they could join forces with those fighting for social medicine and social justice abroad and, as can be attested to by the narratives in this volume, they also used their international solidarity experiences as guides, exemplars, and inspiration in their attempts to transform conditions in the United States. In this chapter, we identify cross-cutting themes, patterns, and perspectives that emerge through the varied experiences of the mix of physicians, nurses, physician assistants, anthropologists, teachers, social workers, lawyers, health promoters, public health advocates, and academics described in the book. We also introduce the stories of certain other health internationalists who did not author chapters but whose work is likewise illustrative of important settings (including South Asia and the Middle East) and aspects of health internationalism.

### Intergenerational Learning

Although every generation makes its own era, the subjects and authors (including public health historians) of our book have also defied this dictum, eagerly learning from prior generations. The "heroes" of U.S. involvement in the Spanish Civil War, like Edward Barsky and Lini De Vries, motivated the next generation of activists, such as Milton Roemer and Jack Geiger, to face McCarthyism and racism with courage. Roemer and Geiger in turn mentored the subsequent generation, including Paula Braveman and Howard Waitzkin, who then taught and influenced the likes of Seiji Yamada and Timothy Holtz, Razel Remen, and so on. Many others mentioned throughout the book have served as important role models and mentors to later generations. Even within health-Left organizations such as Health Alliance International (HAI) intergenerational learning has clearly taken place. Domestic solidarity struggles also drew from such learning across the generations. The founders of the Medical Committee for Human Rights—the "medical arm of the civil rights movement," including health internationalists Geiger and Lear, together with African American founders James Anderson, Aaron Shirley, Robert Smith, Aaron Wells, and others in the 1960s—fashioned themselves after the American Medical Bureau (AMB) to Aid Spanish Democracy. To underscore that connection, they invited the AMB's former medical director Barsky to serve as an early advisor and executive board member.[1]

This transmission of experience, knowledge, and wisdom has inspired the passion and dedication of health internationalists through the last century and into the current one. It also highlights the role of intergenerational learning and collaboration and suggests a level of solidarity that has often escaped the U.S. Left more broadly.

This is not to presume that all health internationalists were or are alike or that the activists profiled in this book share any single political perspective, affiliation, or cause. Many internationalists continue to believe in accountable socialist government, some became disillusioned with the dream represented for a time by the Soviet Union yet have kept alive the spark that inspired their original health-Left engagement, and others have allied with social democratic approaches to bettering the world through reform rather than revolution. Regardless of where particular activists have fallen on the political spectrum, American health-Left efforts overseas have generated far more than the standard dose of international humanitarianism.

## The Personal Price of Health Internationalist Solidarity

For many of our health internationalists, engagement abroad not only provided formative experiences but also presented personal risks. As we saw in chapter 3, John Kingsbury's efforts to import what he learned in the Soviet Union as a legitimate basis for U.S. health policy discussions were quashed, and at the peril of his career. Likewise, those subject to medical McCarthyism often saw their careers go into eclipse. This was the fate that Bernard Lown faced, until his development of the cardiac defibrillator dramatically reversed his fortunes and circuitously ignited his subsequent internationalist activism against nuclear war.

In addition to the price paid by health internationalists during the lethal political climate of the Cold War, they also faced other forms of opprobrium. Max Pepper, a psychiatrist now at the University of Massachusetts at Amherst who figures in chapter 5 and who earlier in his career was a pioneer in medical education based on the social medicine work of Sidney and Emily Kark in South Africa (described in chapter 6), has been working in Israeli and Palestinian public health for over thirty years. He has served as a lecturer at Israeli medical schools and as a participant in the building of a graduate public health program at Bir Zeit University in the West Bank. Together with his wife, he has also been a longtime teacher, consultant, and clinician with the Ramallah-based Union of Palestinian Medical Relief Committees, which has built over thirty health centers at the international forefront of primary health care delivery and community-based assistance to women, under extremely difficult circumstances.

As a visiting American academic and a peace activist, he "came to know much about Israeli society" and has not hesitated to express his views about the "racist, increasingly belligerent and arrogant" stance of the Israeli Right. He has been ostracized by Israeli colleagues because of his associations with Arab academics but also recognized by a young Palestinian physician as "part of our history."[2] Back in the United States, Dr. Pepper has continued his activism after each trip to the Middle East by giving extensive interviews to the media—and facing angry phone calls from American Jews who accuse him of being a traitor or worse. Considering himself an activist-scholar who happens to be Jewish, rather than a Jewish activist, he has not allowed these challenges to deter his commitment, joining a Middle East peace group in his home region of western Massachusetts and remaining active in his advocacy for single-payer health care and other health-Left causes in the United States.

## Medicine, Politics, and Political Economy

One issue clearly present in these pages has to do with the tensions derived from a false dichotomy between medical and sociopolitical understandings of health. Mainstream international health and medicine—reflecting big business and private profit-making interests—have been uninterested in taking on anything remotely approaching an anticapitalist agenda. These fields typically sideline sociopolitical approaches as distractions from or beyond the boundaries of medicine and public health. Indeed, much global health work today addresses diseases that are a consequence of poverty yet, ironically, tries to do so without examining or questioning poverty's underlying structural determinants, particularly as they pertain to the accumulation of private wealth.

This is partly the result of long years spent in highly specialized technologically oriented medical training, which can blind health workers to the role of context—the societal determinants of health[3]—as well as serve as a rationale for practicing technically focused international health interventions as efficient, transportable, and adequate.

Even the work of Partners in Health (PIH), made well known by its cofounder Dr. Paul Farmer—an astute analyst of the structural determinants of health in *Pathologies of Power* and other works—privileges medical care over radical political and economic change. PIH's focused efforts to bring "First World" medicine and surgery to the "Third World" to deal with the pandemics of HIV/AIDS and drug-resistant tuberculosis, among other diseases, highlights the human right to the highest quality health care. Yet despite PIH's expressed commitment to building a movement to fight for health and social justice,[4] its involvement with local and international leftist movements that might address the structural determinants of health (including unbridled corporate power) is limited because, presumably, such alliances might detract from the pragmatic goals of fund-raising and saving lives.[5]

PIH's selective solidarity differs from the work of such health internationalist groups as the U.S.-based Health GAP (Global Access Project) founded in 1999 by the late U.S. activist physician Alan Berkman (who was declared an "enemy of the state" and imprisoned for providing medical care to a Marxist revolutionary in New York in the early 1980s).[6] Health GAP works to support the struggles of, among others, the Treatment Action Campaign (TAC) led by Zackie Achmat in South Africa.[7] Together with other professional and student groups in industrialized countries, Health GAP and TAC have challenged patent regimes and demanded the importation and government purchase of generic and reduced price antiretroviral medications for South African HIV/AIDS patients, as part of a battle against international corporate (pharmaceutical) power. Like HAI, the People's Health Movement, and Doctors for Global Health (see chapters 11, 13, and 16), these groups are guided by a principle of political and social solidarity with allies in the developing world and work hand-in-hand with working-class movements to redress the unequal distribution of political power and resources.

For these contemporary health internationalist groups, access to technically advanced medical care and political economy-inspired struggle against oppression and exploitation are two parts of the same agenda: it has been historically evident since at least the 1930s that the dichotomy between medical-technical and political-social approaches is a false one. Spanish Civil War hero Dr. Norman Bethune's organization of a mobile blood bank to help the survival of wounded forces supporting the Spanish Republican cause, and the Karks' defiant provision of antibiotics to "native" and "colored" tuberculosis and syphilis patients in viciously racist and segregated South Africa (and Americans' involvement in these efforts) made this abundantly clear, as have the accounts in this volume.

## Learning from the Source, and Bringing It Home

In contrast to many involved with global health today, whose humanitarian impulses often center on sharing their own technical expertise unidirectionally with populations living in conditions of extreme poverty or facing complex emergencies, the health internationalists covered in this book have engaged in ongoing multidirectional learning, recognizing that their privileges of training, relative wealth, and comfort demand that their work be carried out in solidarity, with humility, openness to new approaches, and a thirst for a deep understanding of context. They realize that their internationalist medical work cannot be separated from a willingness to learn from those they want to support, who themselves have even more important lessons to teach, which in turn are transported back home by U.S. health internationalists.

U.S. health internationalist learning abroad began in the 1920s and 1930s, with open-minded visits to the Soviet Union by the Quaker nurse Anna Haines as well as John Kingsbury, Henry Sigerist, and others like them. It continued in Spain, where the Republican (left-wing) government welcomed international volunteers and, in the 1950s, in South Africa, where Jack Geiger participated in local struggles to teach the principles of community-oriented primary care and implement community empowerment initiatives. All of our authors/subjects have been struck by the interrelationship of their work abroad and at home and have articulated with clarity the transferable lessons they learned in international settings, as well as the not-infrequent American resistance to learning from abroad. Vic and Ruth Sidel recount how they applied the barefoot doctor model they learned in China in creating a Community Health Participation Program in the Bronx (see chapter 7). Alicia Yamin describes how she brought an economic and social rights model for human rights advocacy back with her from Latin America and applied it to her health and human rights work in the United States (see chapter 14). Mary Bassett explains how her work as a deputy commissioner of the New York City Department of Health directly benefited from her many years of work in Zimbabwean public health (see chapter 12). Bernard Lown and Seiji Yamada, meanwhile, have both articulated the continuity between the global and local dimensions of their activist involvement to end nuclear weapons testing and forestall nuclear war (see chapters 8 and 15).

Some, such as Stephen Gloyd and Mary Bassett, have engaged in internationalist learning as health staff members or on-site consultants of revolutionary and postapartheid/postcolonial governments in Africa (see chapters 11 and 12); others learned as they worked as allies and supporters of socialist regimes in Central and South America (see chapters 9 and 10).

Americans have also interacted with the health internationalist teaching that has been employed consciously and proactively by socialist states, Cuba being a notable example. In this case, official government policy has supported left-wing health movements beyond its borders both for humanitarian reasons and to display—for purposes of solidarity and symbolic diplomacy—the medical and scientific achievements and generosity of the Cuban people.[8] Cuba has also welcomed many foreign medical students, including Razel Remen and Brea Bondi-Boyd from the United States, whose learning outside the classroom was as important as their formal training. Both have now returned to join the struggles to establish universal, community-based primary care at home (see chapter 17).

Cuba's health internationalist outreach via medical education had an earlier precedent in efforts by the Soviet Union. During the Cold War, a small number of Americans studied at Moscow People's Friendship University (later Patrice Lumumba University). Notably, Mary Louise Patterson, a pediatrician—and daughter of a prominent Communist Party leader and a labor and cultural organizer—was among the first African Americans to study medicine in Moscow in the 1960s. As an African American, she was deemed eligible because she "represented a neocolonized people." As she remembers:

> In the USSR I saw bureaucracy (. . . a vestige of czarist times), sloppiness, inefficiency, drunkenness, waste, and abuse of privilege and position. Those with authority, power, and prestige in the USSR lived much better than the general population. But I saw no unemployment, no hungry children's hollowed eyes, no open prostitution, a highly educated populace, and a wonderful culture available to and enjoyed by all. I also saw promise for a more equitable distribution of wealth . . . real assistance to national liberation struggles; free excellent education . . . [and] health care for all, real protection of children, the elderly, and the disabled. I . . . returned to the United States determined to dedicate my life to making a difference in the lives of those who are oppressed, dehumanized, discarded, undesired, and feared.[9]

## Dilemmas and Self-Criticism

While this book celebrates the accomplishments of committed and coura-geous people, the careers portrayed here may also be subject to a more criti-cal scrutiny. None of our subjects or authors is saintly—most had to confront, at times, contradictions between their values and their health internationalist work—and not one of them achieved all that she or he set out to do. At vari-ous moments in their health internationalist careers, they were naïve, arrogant, short-tempered, obtuse, dismissive, heavy-handed, impatient, or not attuned to the unintended consequences of their actions. They were also sometimes over-whelmed, depressed, burned out, and convinced that they had achieved little and that their work would come to naught. But what makes them exemplary and their lives admirable was that they found the motivation and marshaled the energy to work in solidarity with people engaged in health and social justice struggles. More often than not, they had the courage to act on deep convictions, even knowing that they could suffer serious consequences for their actions, yet they felt that personal sacrifice was a small price to pay for larger health internationalist goals.

Some of our authors have also grappled with the realization that the appli-cation of lessons learned abroad to challenges in the United States forced them to acknowledge just how much still needs to be done domestically for poor and oppressed populations who live in what is tantamount to Third World condi-tions. As Geiger puts it, "[In Mississippi I came to] the realization that I didn't have to go to Africa, Southeast Asia, or Latin America to do our work" (see chap-ter 6). Waitzkin is equally explicit: "Work with the United Farm Workers . . . taught me that one did not need to travel outside the United States to find 'the Third World.' Instead, conditions of underdevelopment and exploitation within the United States created or exacerbated the health conditions of farmworkers and their families" (see chapter 9). Geiger and Waitzkin thus faced a potential ethical dilemma: that a health internationalist focus abroad could detract atten-tion from problems at home. But they responded by recognizing that, properly understood, health internationalism actually better underscores our grim domes-tic realities and that one can act globally and locally at the same time.

New York–based public health and social justice lawyer Elisabeth Benja-min has articulated the tensions related to her work at home and abroad with particular clarity. Following international development training at Brown Uni-versity, she went to rural India in the mid-1980s to study what from the outside seemed to be the positive and relatively unproblematic application of radio communications to agricultural practices. Faced with severely malnourished children and entire villages lacking access to clean water, sanitation, and health services, however, Benjamin found it morally impossible to ignore such pressing human needs or reconcile these on-the-ground realities with naïve and overly optimistic technological-quick-fix development abstractions. She was further disheartened by discussions about health needs and politics with friends and colleagues overseas, when they repeatedly asked her, "But isn't it true you have poor people in America as well? Why not work on 'development' at home?"[10]

Before turning to that challenge directly, Benjamin retrained as an international human rights lawyer. After Iraq invaded Kuwait in 1990 and the United States was poised to invade Iraq, she joined law and public health colleagues to organize a health and human rights mission, the first independent humanitarian mission to Iraq immediately after the Gulf War. Publishing their findings in the *New England Journal of Medicine*,[11] Benjamin and her colleagues made the "novel at the time but in retrospect rather obvious discovery that systematically bombing a country's water, electrical and sewage infrastructure in a place with endemic infectious diseases like typhoid and cholera would result in excess infant mortality and widespread suffering."[12] Benjamin and her colleagues' work helped pave the way to the corroborative studies of public health professors Richard Garfield, Les Roberts, and others during both the first Gulf War and the Iraq war started in 2003, studies which are now considered definitive.[13]

As Benjamin reflects,

> The Iraq mission felt exactly right for the would-be health internationalist in me. I believe that citizens of powerful countries have an ethical obligation to document and publicize the abuses of our own country's power abroad. But I think my overseas colleagues were also right in directing me to work for health justice at home. I have been fortunate to be a legal services lawyer in the South Bronx and then launch the Health Law project at the New York Legal Aid Society, for the past fifteen years working to ensure that vulnerable low-income, working-class folks, immigrants, and people with disabilities have access to health care.

Currently, she is a highly acclaimed leader in New York's Health Care for All campaign, as vice president of health initiatives at the Community Service Society of New York, using the interdisciplinary advocacy skills learned from friends, colleagues, and experiences overseas as tools in the struggle for health reform and health justice in the United States.

## Solidarity and Counter-hegemony

Another important theme that runs through many of our chapters is the interrelationship among domestic solidarity movements to support struggles abroad, the recruitment of passionate health professionals to directly engage in these struggles, and the widespread awareness of how support for these struggles constitutes a loud counter-hegemonic statement of political opposition to official U.S. foreign policy. This interrelationship first became evident during the 1930s in internationalist support for the Republican side in the Spanish Civil War. As Walter Lear teaches us in chapter 4, recruitment to what became the American Medical Bureau to Aid Spanish Democracy was part of domestic solidarity struggles that crossed racial and class lines. This first effort of the American Left to engage thousands through outreach, coalitions, recruitment, and fund-raising in a people's struggle overseas was mobilized in the face of widespread hostility on the part of influential political, business, and media leaders, as well as official opposition from U.S. president Franklin D. Roosevelt's administration.

Some activists engaged in health internationalist solidarity and counter-hegemony even when the U.S. government impeded them from participating overseas. Dr. Lewis Fraad, a New York physician who worked for the Comintern in Vienna as a courier and printer (of political leaflets) from 1932 to 1936, was prepared to follow Bethune to join the revolutionary insurgency in China but was denied a passport by the U.S. Department of State.[14] Fraad's "retribution" was to enlist as a doctor in the U.S. Army during World War II, serving his country while simultaneously recruiting Communist Party members. Like many others, he struggled to survive in the 1950s. When the repressive climate of the McCarthy era finally began to change, he returned to past international solidarity models by raising funds to send medical supplies to revolutionary Cuba.

Howard Waitzkin (chapter 9), inspired by Bethune, followed a similarly counter-hegemonic path in the 1970s. Through the course of his work with the United Farm Workers Clinic in Salinas, California, Waitzkin became familiar with the contributions of Dr. Salvador Allende (president of Chile and head of the democratically elected socialist Unidad Popular government), hoping to contribute to social medicine advances there. But the 1973 coup that toppled Allende's government (widely and credibly suspected to have been engineered by the CIA) forced Waitzkin to change his plans. Instead of going to Chile, he became active and outspoken in an international solidarity movement that assisted Chilean health workers and others who were victimized by Chile's military dictatorship, which was supported by the U.S. government. This solidarity work led to Waitzkin's long-term support for Latin American social medicine and his leadership in efforts to counter and expose overt and covert U.S. government and corporate policies in Latin America.

Other examples of solidarity and counter-hegemony are much in evidence in these chapters. Michael Terry and Laura Turiano recount Michael's journey from the solidarity movement in Colorado supporting rebel groups in El Salvador against U.S.-backed government repression, to his acceptance as a *brigadista* in the combat zones of El Salvador (see chapter 13). Paula Braveman explains how her efforts in the early 1980s to serve directly the new socialist Sandinista government of Nicaragua were initially deflected but then converted into a ten-year commitment to provide U.S.-based support through the Committee for Health Rights in Central America (CHRICA). In solidarity with the Sandinistas, CHRICA mobilized material and professional support for the new government's efforts, facilitated information exchanges and short-term volunteer service, raised funds and donations, and worked hard to counter the silence of the mainstream press about how the U.S. government was destroying Nicaragua's revolutionary efforts to improve social conditions (see chapter 10).

Stephen Gloyd, James Pfeiffer, and Wendy Johnson have similarly drawn inspiration from Latin American solidarity and counter-hegemony movements, and the antiapartheid movement, to work across generations to build and sustain HAI in Mozambique (see chapter 11). Continuing to the present, among the many activities of Doctors for Global Health, as Lanny Smith, Jennifer Kasper, and Timothy Holtz discuss, exposure of (mostly) covert activities by the U.S. government against social justice movements in Latin America is high on the list (see chapter 16).

### The Future?: Liberation Technology

As evident in the numerouse health-focused NGOs now competing for resources and recognition in Mozambique and elsewhere, "global health" has become "hot" in recent decades and is an increasingly strong draw to large numbers of premedical and medical students. But students recruited to these newly fashionable international engagements may not fully understand what global health is or how the programs in which they participate usually focus on traditional and technical approaches, paying only minor attention to political, economic, and social perspectives, and typically ignoring the activist political work in which health internationalists continue to engage.[15] In recent years, large numbers of U.S. students have participated in health electives abroad,[16] American medical schools are building campuses overseas (for example, Cornell in Qatar; Harvard in Dubai), and countless medical relief trips are run every year by well-meaning nonprofit as well as for-profit organizations. Sadly, most of these initiatives amount to little more than "global health tourism" often wasting local time and resources and rarely, if ever, displaying the kind of long-term commitment and solidarity that characterizes health-Left internationalism.[17]

Of course, international/global health has long been politicized—through colonial control of epidemics, "goodwill" surgical training, and the competing Cold War–era hospital and health worker training programs in developing countries sponsored by both the Soviet and U.S. governments and aimed at forging strategic alliances and fending off the other's influence.[18] Perhaps the new wave of global health interest represents another stage, the neoliberalization—if not the corporatization—of international health, and part of its dynamic may well include the mainstream cooptation of successful progressive efforts that have been carried out by health internationalists. To be sure, those highlighted in this book represent a small, if influential, set of exceptions.

The exceptional nature of the health internationalist work described in this volume should in no way be confused with the celebrity philanthropy or philanthro-capitalism of Bono or the Bill and Melinda Gates Foundation.[19] These groups are major forces in contemporary global health and, with clever use of language around equity and human rights, purport on some level to emulate the moral legitimacy of health internationalism. But they do not challenge the tenets of capitalism—indeed they often view global health as a profit-making and corporate investment opportunity—and do not expose who is benefiting from the status quo (for instance, Big Pharma). Instead these groups seek to fix symptoms, typically through technologies divorced from an understanding of the social and political context, while disregarding who and what has created and sustains social inequality within and across societies. For example, the Gates Foundation, despite its stated goal of "increas[ing] opportunity and equity for those most in need,"[20] does not address the underlying causes of inequity and overwhelmingly addresses those "most in need" through narrow technobiological approaches and public-private partnerships that usurp the role of government agencies or international health institutions such as the World Health Organization.[21]

Another reason that global health has garnered so much attention in recent years is that it is tied in with the reach of the Internet and the explosion of digital communications. Digital media have been prominently used in global/international health by corporate interests, but they have also led to a new form of health-Left internationalism. In 2003 Ellen Shaffer and Joe Brenner founded the Center for Policy Analysis on Trade and Health (CPATH) as a virtual, online collaboration with a far-flung network of activists and advocates to bring, for the first time, a public health voice to the conversation about international trade agreements.

Shaffer and Brenner, whose previous backgrounds were, respectively, in progressive health policy and union training/organizing, started with a historic breakthrough in 2004 around the U.S.-Australia free trade agreement's attempts to inhibit access to affordable medicines in signatory countries by preventing the re-importation of pharmaceuticals below the initial export price.[22] Thanks to listserv and Internet links and alliances made with other experts in Australia's pharmaceutical purchasing system, CPATH was instrumental in removing the provision against re-importation from subsequent U.S. free trade agreements. CPATH's political activism has included visits to Guatemala in solidarity with local community organizations, and to South Korea at the invitation of the government and professional associations, and it has exerted ongoing pressure to ensure that trade agreements protect rather than undermine public health.[23]

**Figure 18.1**  Ellen Shaffer (*top center*) with a group of U.S. university students toward the end of their "Globalization and Health" study abroad semester, Cape Town, South Africa, 2006. Here they are reviewing their travels to India, China, and South Africa and discussing their firsthand knowledge of the impact of trade policy on health, including in terms of poverty and access to medicines.

Courtesy of Joe Brenner.

From the outset, Shaffer and Brenner have conducted their work as health internationalists from a U.S. base, directed primarily at a U.S. audience.[24] But they have refrained from drawing clear divisions between overseas engagement and domestic repercussions, hoping instead to involve the global and the local simultaneously. A hallmark of this approach was CPATH's "Globalization and Health" curriculum developed for a 2006 U.S. college semester abroad program. Unlike typical study abroad programs, which largely ignore activist solidarity, CPATH's students stayed with local families, including in Capetown, South Africa, townships, where they interviewed host families about their experiences during the struggle against apartheid. These students brought back with them not only a firsthand view of the impact of globalization on health in the global South, but an understanding of how health-Left international activism can take place virtually and from a distance.[25] This differs starkly from the far more widespread employment by mainstream international health of one-way knowledge/technology diffusion through e-health and tele-health, which overlook the political dimensions and uses of digital technologies.

**Reflecting Forward**

The glimpses of the complex and often-confusing world of contemporary international and global health that we have introduced in this concluding chapter make it all the more imperative to keep a sharp focus on the particular view of health internationalism to which this book is dedicated. Our authors and subjects stand out because of their consistent belief that the major factors determining health are embedded in the social and political order and that health justice and progress must therefore be intimately connected with social and political movements to improve the lives of the poor and oppressed. Our health internationalists have consistently understood that there is a difference between, on the one hand, attempting to address the health-damaging *effects* of poverty, worker exploitation, disempowerment, social inequalities, gender oppression, and racism, and, on the other, working to end the *causes* of poverty and unequal power and resource distribution in the first place.

Rather than focusing on the former alone, as do mainstream international/ global health actors, our authors and subjects have regularly engaged in left-wing political struggles and other forms of activism and solidarity across national borders. These expressions of resistance to inequity and brutality derive from both political and profoundly ethical commitments to social justice. In a sense, what the internationalists covered in *Comrades in Health* most deeply felt and feel comes into focus in nurse Lini De Vries's response to a question posed to her under FBI instructions during the 1940s. The question was, "What on earth has the fact that you were in Spain have to do with public health?" As the subjects and authors of this book can attest to, her implicit answer was, of course, "It has *everything* to do with it."[26]

Lini's perspective is a particularly important and compelling one. As we hope this volume has established, it is a perspective derived from and driven by passion for social justice, courage to act on that passion, and willingness to take risks by forming alliances with colleagues on the Left in other countries and with activist movements around the world. This perspective is about political commitment, not careerism, and it is about learning from those who are currently engaged, and who in the past have been engaged, in these efforts. And just as intergenerational learning has taken place among the subjects and authors of these chapters, so too do we hope that this book will contribute to the learning of present and future generations of U.S. health internationalists involved in local, national, and global contexts and struggles.

### Notes

1. John Dittmer, *The Good Doctors: The Medical Committee for Human Rights and the Struggle for Social Justice in Health Care* (New York: Bloomsbury Press, 2009).
2. Dr. Max Pepper, personal communication with Anne-Emanuelle Birn, 2010–2011.
3. Anne-Emanuelle Birn, Yogan Pillay, and Timothy H. Holtz, *Textbook of International Health: Global Health in a Dynamic World,* 3rd ed. (New York: Oxford University Press, 2009), 309–364.
4. Partners in Health, "Advocacy and Policy," http://www.pih.org/pages/advocacy/ (accessed June 1, 2012).
5. A highly critical perspective on Farmer, PIH, and its lack of political economy framing is Sam Dubal, "Renouncing Paul Farmer: A Desperate Plea for Radical Political Medicine," *Being Ethical in an Unethical World* (blog), May 27, 2012, http:// samdubal.blogspot.co.nz/2012/05/renouncing-paul-farmer-desperate-plea.html (accessed June 1, 2012). For more about PIH's viewpoint, see Rebecca Onie, Paul Farmer, and Heidi Behforouz, "Realigning Health with Care," *Stanford Social Innovation Review,* Summer 2012, http://www.ssireview.org/articles/entry/realigning _health_with_care (accessed June 1, 2012). The PIH model discussed here by Farmer and colleagues underscores its non "health leftist" stance in the context of U.S. health care reforms. The reforms proposed in the article, drawn from PIH efforts abroad and at home, are only likely to address poverty on the margins, perhaps by making people healthier so they are able to work/achieve more. There is no mention of an approach akin to the Geiger-Mound Bayou Community Health Center model, which included community organizing against discrimination and building a locally controlled cooperative economy, *or* of aligning with community organizing efforts that support patients to become protagonists in actually overcoming the structural causes of ill health. All of the article's proposed "solutions" to the structures that cause poverty and ill health are individualistic and charitable/humanitarian, never engaging in a political economy analysis of the health system to show what really drives costs and limits services. In fact, the article suggests that "private sector players

could likely sustain profits from scaling up cost-saving models of comprehensive, community-based care for the poorest."

6. Susan Reverby, "Enemy of the People/Enemy of the State: Two Great(ly Infamous) Doctors, Passions, and the Judgment of History," Fielding Garrison lecture, American Association for the History of Medicine, April 27, 2012.

7. Tony Karon, "South African AIDS Activist Zackie Achmat," *Time USA,* April 19, 2001, http://www.time.com/time/nation/article/0,8599,106995,00.html (accessed September 1, 2011); Health Gap [Global Access Project], http://www.healthgap.org/about.htm (accessed September 1, 2011).

8. Julie M. Feinsilver, *Healing the Masses: Cuban Health Politics at Home and Abroad* (Berkeley and Los Angeles: University of California Press, 1993); Enrique Beldarrain, "La salud pública en Cuba y su experiencia internacional, 1959–2005," *História, Ciências, Saúde-Manguinhos* (2006); Simon M. Reid-Henry, *The Cuban Cure: Reason and Resistance in Global Science* (Chicago: University of Chicago Press, 2010); Julie Feinsilver, "Fifty Years of Cuba's Medical Diplomacy: From Idealism to Pragmatism," *Cuban Studies* 41 (2010): 85–104.

9. Mary Louise Patterson, "Black and Red All Over," in *Red Diapers: Growing up in the Communist Left,* ed. Judy Kaplan and Linn Shapiro (Urbana: University of Illinois Press, 1998), 114–115.

10. Elisabeth Benjamin, personal communication with Anne-Emanuelle Birn, 2010–2011.

11. The Harvard Study Team, "The Effect of the Gulf Crisis on the Children of Iraq," *New England Journal of Medicine* 325 (1991): 977–980.

12. They made several return trips and out of this experience, her colleagues Roger Normand, Chris Jochnick, and Sarah Zaidi founded the Center for Economic and Social Rights—the first significant U.S. human rights organization to promote economic and social issues within a human rights framework.

13. Richard Garfield, Julia Devin, and Joy Fausy, "The Health Impact of Economic Sanctions," *Bulletin of the New York Academy of Medicine* 72 (1995): 454–469; Les Roberts et al., "Mortality Before and After the 2003 Invasion of Iraq: Cluster Sample Survey," *Lancet* 364 (2004): 1857–1864.

14. Rosalyn Fraad Baxandall and Harriet Fraad, "Red Sisters of the Bourgeoisie," in *Red Diapers,* 95–102; Rosalyn Baxandall, personal communication with Anne-Emanuelle Birn, February 2011.

15. Birn, Pillay, and Holtz, *Textbook of International Health,* 694–740.

16. Jessica Berthold, "U.S. Students Find Ways to Broaden Their Horizons," *ACP Observer* (October 2008).

17. Stephen A. Bezruchka, "Medical Tourism as Medical Harm to the Third World: Why? For Whom?" *Wilderness and Environmental Medicine Journal* 11 (2000): 77–78.

18. Marcos Cueto, "International Health, the Early Cold War and Latin America," *Canadian Bulletin of Medical History* 25(1) (2008): 17–41.

19. Ilan Kapoor, *Celebrity Humanitarianism: The Ideology of Global Charity* (New York: Routlege, 2012).

20. "Bill and Melinda Gates Foundation Guiding Principles," http://www.gatesfoundation.org/about/Pages/guiding-principles.aspx (accessed October 9, 2011).

21. Anne-Emanuelle Birn, "Philanthrocapitalism, Past and Present: The Rockefeller Foundation, the Gates Foundation, and the Setting(s) of the International/Global Health Agenda," *Hypothesis,* 10(1) (2013).

22. CPATH. The U.S.-Australia Free Trade Agreement Can Preempt Drug Reimportation Bills, http://www.cpath.org/sitebuildercontent/sitebuilderfiles/australia7–12–04.pdf (accessed July 12, 2004).

23. CPATH in South Korea: Public Health and KORUS FTA, http://www.cpath.org/sitebuildercontent/sitebuilderfiles/koreacpathonline6–07.pdf (accessed August 15, 2011).

24. Ellen R Shaffer et al., "Global Trade and Public Health," *American Journal of Public Health* 95(1) (2005): 23–34.

25. Ellen Shaffer, personal communication with Anne-Emanuelle Birn, 2009–2011.

26. Lini M. De Vries, *Please, God, Take Care of the Mule* (Mexico City: Editorial Minutiae Mexicana, 1969), 5.

# Notes on Contributors

Mary Travis Bassett, MD, MPH, is director for the African Health Initiative for the Doris Duke Charitable Foundation. From 2002 to 2009 she was deputy commissioner for health promotion and disease prevention in the New York City Health Department. Prior to that, beginning in 1985, she was a member of the Faculty of Medicine at the University of Zimbabwe in the Department of Community Medicine.

Anne-Emanuelle Birn, MA, ScD, is Canada Research Chair in International Health and professor of critical development studies, of social and behavioral health sciences, and of global health at the University of Toronto. Her research explores the history of public health in Latin America and the history and politics of international/global health. Her books include *Marriage of Convenience: Rockefeller International Health and Revolutionary Mexico* and *Textbook of International Health: Global Health in a Dynamic World,* with coauthors Yogan Pillay and Timothy Holtz. Her current projects examine the history of the international child health and child rights movement from the perspective of Uruguay, and Soviet-Latin American relations in public health and medicine.

Brea Bondi-Boyd, MD, was born in Juneau, Alaska, to working-class parents. In 2009 she graduated from the Latin American School of Medicine (ELAM) in Havana, Cuba. She is currently a resident in family medicine at Contra Costa Regional Medical Center. She is the resident leader in her residency's Global Health program where she is incorporating ELAM's model both locally and abroad. She has volunteered with *Compañeros En Salud* in Chiapas, Mexico, which works to bring primary care to rural, underserved populations.

Paula Braveman, MD, MPH, is professor of family and community medicine and director of the Center on Social Disparities in Health at the University of California, San Francisco. A member of the Institute of Medicine, she is nationally and internationally recognized for her research on social inequalities in health and her active leadership in bringing attention to this field.

Jane Pacht Brickman, PhD, is professor of history and until 2011 was head of the Department of Humanities at the United States Merchant Marine Academy,

Kings Point, New York. Her scholarship and publications are in medical history, with a focus on twentieth-century medical reformers. She also writes and speaks on issues involving the integration of women into predominantly and traditionally male environments, especially the federal service academies and the maritime industry.

Theodore M. Brown, PhD, is professor of history and of public health sciences at the University of Rochester, with expertise in the political, intellectual, and institutional history of medicine and public health. He is engaged in studies of the American health Left and its repression and of the history of international and global public health. He is a contributing editor (for history) of the *American Journal of Public Health* and editor of *Rochester Studies in Medical History*. He coedited and substantially coauthored *Making Medical History: The Life and Times of Henry E. Sigerist* and recently coauthored *The Quest for Health Reform: A Satirical History*. He is currently working with Marcos Cueto and Elizabeth Fee on a collaborative history of the World Health Organization.

H. Jack Geiger, MD, MSci, is Arthur C. Logan Professor Emeritus of Community Medicine at the City University of New York Medical School. He was a founding member of one of the first chapters of the Congress of Racial Equality in the United States and was civil liberties chairman of the Veterans Committee from 1947 to 1951. In the 1960s he was a founding member of the Medical Committee for Human Rights and its Mississippi field coordinator. From 1965 to 1972 he was codirector of the first health centers in the United States. Dr. Geiger was a founding member and later president of the Committee for Health in Southern Africa and in 1997 was a member of the consultative mission to South Africa's Truth and Reconciliation Commission to examine human rights violations in the health sector under apartheid and was one of the authors of the mission's report.

Stephen Gloyd, MD, MPH, is founder and executive director of Health Alliance International (HAI), and professor of global health and of health services and associate chair of the Department of Global Health at the University of Washington School of Public Health. He has worked for over thirty years in countries of Africa, Latin America, and Asia in clinical and public health practice. He began his work in Mozambique as a *cooperante* with the Ministry of Health in 1979.

Timothy H. Holtz, MD, MPH, FACP, is an adjunct assistant professor of global health at the Rollins School of Public Health at Emory University. He co-teaches courses on tuberculosis, health and human rights, and social medicine at the Emory School of Medicine. He is a founding member of Doctors for Global Health, and was a member of the board from 1995 to 2003. Since 2002 Dr. Holtz has worked in southern Africa, Eastern Europe, and South America on multidrug-resistant tuberculosis (MDR TB) control, TB/HIV program capacity building, and HIV prevention clinical trials in high-risk populations. Along with Drs. Anne-Emanuelle Birn and Yogan Pillay, Dr. Holtz is coauthor of *Textbook of International Health: Global Health in a Dynamic World.* His medical memoir of working in India with Tibetan refugees, entitled *A Doctor in Little Lhasa*, was published in 2009.

Wendy Johnson, MD, MPH, is a family practitioner and activist physician who has been involved domestically in the struggle for universal access to equitable health care, immigrant rights, and living wage laws. She has worked and volunteered internationally with Doctors for Global Health in Chiapas (Mexico), Guatemala, and El Salvador. She worked with Health Alliance International in Mozambique from 2004 to 2006 and is a clinical faculty member in the University of Washington's Department of Global Health. She is currently medical director of La Familia, a community health center in Santa Fe, New Mexico.

Jennifer Kasper, MD, MPH, is a pediatrician and the current vice president of Doctors for Global Health. She is a faculty member in the Division of Global Health at Massachusetts General Hospital, chair of the Harvard Medical School (HMS) Faculty Advisory Committee on Global Health, and tutor for the HMS courses "Introduction to Social Medicine and Global Health" and "Pursuing Inquiry in Medicine." She has worked and volunteered in El Salvador, Chiapas (Mexico), Nicaragua, Honduras, Haiti, India, Uganda, and Mozambique. Her interests include rural community and primary health care development; community health worker training; and mentoring students and trainees in global health.

Walter J. Lear, MD, MS (1923–2010), was, at the time of his death, director of historical research at the Institute of Social Medicine and Community Health in Philadelphia. Throughout his long career, he was a prominent medical and public health practitioner and administrator, a political organizer and activist, and a historian and archivist of the U.S. health Left. He served as associate medical director of the Health Insurance Plan of New York from 1952 to 1961 and as deputy commissioner of the Philadelphia Department of Health from 1964 to 1971. He also served from 1971 to 1979 as commissioner of health services for southeastern Pennsylvania and was responsible for the health service aspects of Pennsylvania's Medicaid program in metropolitan Philadelphia. He served on the national boards of the Physicians Forum and SANE, and helped found the Medical Committee for Human Rights, the Gay and Lesbian Center of Philadelphia, the Philadelphia AIDS Task Force, and the Lesbian, Gay, Bisexual, and Transgender Caucus of the American Public Health Association.

Bernard Lown, MD, is Professor Emeritus of Cardiology at the Harvard School of Public Health. Famous in cardiology for his invention of the defibrillator, Lown was also one of the founders of Physicians for Social Responsibility. With his Soviet counterpart, cardiologist Eugene Chazov, Lown in 1980 cofounded International Physicians for the Prevention of Nuclear War. This organization played a major international role in advocating for nuclear disarmament, and in 1985 was awarded the Nobel Peace Prize for its achievements. He is the author of over three hundred scientific papers and several books, has received more than twenty honorary degrees from universities in the United States and abroad, and has founded several outreach organizations to Africa and other parts of the developing world.

James Pfeiffer, MPH, PhD, is director of Mozambique Projects with Health Alliance International and is associate professor in the Departments of Global Health and of Anthropology at the University of Washington. He began his involvement with Mozambique as an antiapartheid solidarity worker in the 1980s with Los Angeles–based Friends of the ANC and the national Mozambique Support Network. He lived in Mozambique in the 1990s for about four years and has continued to support public sector health system development in the country for twenty years.

Razel Remen, MD, was born in Brooklyn, New York. She was raised by her mother, who often worked two jobs to make ends meet. Her experiences with both public and private institutions gave her an early sense of the inequities in American society and forged her desire to struggle for political justice. In 2009 Razel graduated from the Latin American School of Medicine in Cuba, and in 2012 she began a Family Medicine residency at The University of Alabama, Tuscaloosa. She plans on working with rural communities and vulnerable populations, paying special attention to women's health issues.

Ruth Sidel, MSW, PhD, is a professor of sociology at Hunter College of the City University of New York. She is the author of several books, including *Women and Child Care in China: A Firsthand Report, Keeping Women and Children Last: America's War on the Poor,* and most recently *Unsung Heroines: Single*

*Mothers and the American Dream*. Ruth and Victor Sidel have made several study visits to China—the first in 1971, the most recent in 2004.

Victor W. Sidel, MD, is distinguished university professor of social medicine at Montefiore Medical Center and Albert Einstein College of Medicine and adjunct professor of Public Health at Weill Cornell Medical College. He has been president of the American Public Health Association, of Physicians for Social Responsibility, and copresident of the International Physicians for the Prevention of Nuclear War. He is coeditor with Dr. Barry Levy of *War and Public Health, Terrorism and Public Health* and *Social Injustice and Public Health.*

Clyde Lanford (Lanny) Smith, MD, MPH, DTM&H, FACP, is Global Community Health Advisor in the Division of General Medicine and Primary Care, Department of Medicine, Beth Israel Deaconess Medical Center, Harvard Medical School, and adjunct associate professor of clinical medicine in the Departments of Internal Medicine and Family and Social Medicine at Montefiore Medical Center, Albert Einstein College of Medicine. He was the founder of Doctors for Global Health, a not-for-profit organization that promotes health, education, social justice, and human rights throughout the world. His main interests include liberation medicine and community-oriented primary care. He is cofounder and on the editorial board of the open-access, peer-review, dual-language journal *Social Medicine/Medicina Social* and coeditor of the textbook *Women's Global Health and Human Rights.*

Susan Gross Solomon, PhD, is professor of political science at the University of Toronto. Her research focuses on cross-national cooperation in medicine and public health in the 1920s and 1930s. She has edited the diaries of two German physicians who traveled to Russia in the 1920s to collaborate with their Soviet colleagues and written about the activity of the Rockefeller Foundation in Russia and Germany. Her most recent book is *Shifting Boundaries of Public Health: Europe in the Twentieth Century,* with coeditors Lion Murard and Patrick Zylberman. She is currently writing a biography of Alexander Roubakine, a Russian physician who worked as an intermediary between Soviet Russia and France in the first half of the twentieth century, about whom she has coproduced a documentary film entitled *In Search of Roubakine.*

Michael Terry is a physician assistant in the emergency department of a county hospital and part-time faculty member of a physician assistant program. He serves on the board of directors of Voices on the Border, an organization promoting sustainable and equitable development in El Salvador.

Laura Turiano is a physician assistant and activist who works with the international network People's Health Movement to promote the fulfillment of human rights and comprehensive primary health care as strategies to address the social determinants of health and achieve health for all.

Howard Waitzkin, MD, PhD, is Distinguished Professor Emeritus of Sociology and Clinical Professor of Internal Medicine at the University of New Mexico. He is the author of five books, including *The Second Sickness: Contradictions of Capitalist Health Care; At the Front Lines of Medicine: How the Health Care System Alienates Doctors and Mistreats Patients . . . And What We Can Do About It;* and, most recently, *Medicine and Public Health at the End of Empire*. He has received recognition as a Fulbright New Century Scholar, fellow of the John Simon Guggenheim Memorial Foundation, recipient of the Leo G. Reeder and Eliot Freidson Awards of the American Sociological Association for Distinguished Scholarship in Medical Sociology, and recipient of the Jonathan Mann Award for Lifetime Commitment to Public Health and Social Justice Issues from the New Mexico Public Health Association.

Seiji Yamada, MD, MPH, is a family practitioner teaching at the University of Hawai'i John A. Burns School of Medicine. He is actively involved in the movement for peace and demilitarization.

Alicia Ely Yamin, JD, MPH, is Lecturer on Global Health and director of the Program on the Health Rights of Women and Children at the Francois-Xavier Bagnoud Center for Health and Human Rights at Harvard University. She is also an associated senior researcher at the Christian Michelsen Institute (Norway). Yamin is a contributing author to and editor of *Millennium Development Goals and Human Rights: Past, Present and Future* (with Malcolm Langford and Andy Sumner); *Litigating Health Rights: Can Courts Bring More Justice to Health?* (with Siri Gloppen); and *Los derechos económicos, sociales y culturales en América Latina: Del invento a la herramienta* (*Economic, Social and Cultural Rights in Latin America: From Ideals to Tools*).

# Index

The letter *f* following a page number denotes a figure; the letter *n* denotes an endnote.

**Available titles in the Critical Issues in Health and Medicine series:**

Heather Munro Prescott, *The Morning After: A History of Emergency Contraception in the United States*

David G. Schuster, *Neurasthenic Nation: America's Search for Health, Happiness, and Comfort, 1869–1920*

Karen Seccombe and Kim A. Hoffman, *Just Don't Get Sick: Access to Health Care in the Aftermath of Welfare Reform*

Leo B. Slater, *War and Disease: Biomedical Research on Malaria in the Twentieth Century*

Paige Hall Smith, Bernice L. Hausman, and Miriam Labbok, *Beyond Health, Beyond Choice: Breastfeeding Constraints and Realities*

Matthew Smith, *An Alternative History of Hyperactivity: Food Additives and the Feingold Diet*

Rosemary A. Stevens, Charles E. Rosenberg, and Lawton R. Burns, eds., *History and Health Policy in the United States: Putting the Past Back In*

Barbra Mann Wall, *American Catholic Hospitals: A Century of Changing Markets and Missions*

Frances Ward, *The Door of Last Resort: Memoirs of a Nurse Practitioner*

CPSIA information can be obtained at www.ICGtesting.com
Printed in the USA
BVOW010209230513

321332BV00003B/11/P

9 780813 561202